EXPLAINING POST-SOVIET PATCHWORKS

Please also see

Explaining Post-Soviet Patchworks

Volume 2   Pathways from the past to the global

Volume 3   The political economy of regions, regimes and republics

Explaining Post-Soviet Patchworks
Volume 1

Actors and sectors in Russia between accommodation and resistance to globalization

Edited by
KLAUS SEGBERS
Free University, Berlin

LONDON AND NEW YORK

First published 2001 by Ashgate Publishing

Reissued 2018 by Routledge
2 Park Square, Milton Park, Abingdon, Oxon OX14 4RN
711 Third Avenue, New York, NY 10017, USA

Routledge is an imprint of the Taylor & Francis Group, an informa business

Copyright © Klaus Segbers 2001

All rights reserved. No part of this book may be reprinted or reproduced or utilised in any form or by any electronic, mechanical, or other means, now known or hereafter invented, including photocopying and recording, or in any information storage or retrieval system, without permission in writing from the publishers.

Notice:
Product or corporate names may be trademarks or registered trademarks, and are used only for identification and explanation without intent to infringe.

Publisher's Note
The publisher has gone to great lengths to ensure the quality of this reprint but points out that some imperfections in the original copies may be apparent.

Disclaimer
The publisher has made every effort to trace copyright holders and welcomes correspondence from those they have been unable to contact.

ISBN 13: 978-1-138-70253-0 (hbk)
ISBN 13: 978-1-138-62940-0 (pbk)
ISBN 13: 978-1-315-20973-9 (ebk)

Contents

List of Tables and Diagrams   *viii*
List of Contributors   *xiv*
Preface   *xvii*
List of Abbreviations   *xix*

1	Actors and Interests in a Changing Russia *Klaus Segbers*	1
2	International Financial Organizations and Globalization by Default *Ognian Hishow*	35
3	The Origins and Management of the Federal Debt to the World *Artos G. Sarkisiants*	55
4	Financial Supervision and Moral Hazard on an Emerging Market *Irina N. Iudina*	72
5	Large Corporations as National and Global Players: The Case of Gazprom *Andreas Heinrich*	97
6	Large Corporations as National and Global Players: The Case of Lukoil *Sergei P. Peregudov*	116

7	The Mining and Metals Industry and Globalization *Stephen Fortescue*	136
8	The Banking Sector and its International Involvement *Artos G. Sarkisiants*	164
9	Financial Groups and the Development of Market Institutions *Grigorii V. Krasnov*	177
10	The Mass Media between Political Instrumentalization, Economic Concentration and Global Assimilation *Ivan I. Zasurskii*	201
11	The Telecommunications Sector: Signs of Liberalization and Globalization *Elena K. Rytsareva*	228
12	High-Technology Defense Production: The Move into Foreign Markets *Ruslan N. Pukhov*	244
13	Defense Industry Managers and the Dynamics of Intra-Sectoral Divergence *Leonid I. Kosals, Rozalina V. Ryvkina*	268
14	Actors in Agro-Food Policy: Who Shapes Outcomes? *Evgeniia V. Serova*	292
15	Agrarian Actors in the Localities *Zemfira I. Kalugina*	310
16	Industrial Managers' Aspirations Towards Foreign Markets: Motives, Methods and the Consequences for Companies *Igor B. Gurkov*	331

17	Small Business in the Context of International Integration *Tat'iana A. Alimova*	351
18	The Self-Denying Middle Class in the Global Age *Harley D. Balzer*	366

Bibliography   385

Index   403

Reference to 'Explaining Post-Soviet Patchworks'   407
vol. 2 and vol. 3

List of Tables and Diagrams

Table 2.1	Government budget balance (as percentage of GDP)	37
Table 2.2	Dependence on international finance (in billion US$)	41
Table 2.3	Capital flight (calculation based on the balance of payments 1999, in billion US$)	43
Table 2.4	Quotas and votes, 1 April 2000 (in %)	45
Table 2.5	IMF-approved loans to selected members (in million US$ as of March 2000)	48
Table 2.6	Financial relief through restructuring and payment deferrals (in billion US$)	52
Table 4.1	Banking systems in countries hit by crisis (Ranking out of 73 countries)	78
Table 4.2	The budget policy of the Russian Government in 1992-98 (in % of GDP)	81
Table 4.3	Federal government debt (in billion rubles)	82
Table 5.1	Production and export of natural gas 1992-2000 (in bn cm)	99
Table 5.2	Gazprom's exports to Western Europe 1996-2000 (in bn cm)	106
Table 7.1	Russian and world steel exports (in mt)	140

Table 7.2	Production, consumption and exports of primary aluminum from the former Soviet Union (in mt)	141
Table 7.3	Technological structure of the Russian steel industry (in %)	149
Table 9.1	Market share of leading Russian auto producers, 1993-99	186
Table 9.2	Russian and Ukrainian automotive tire production trends, 1995-97 (in million units)	192
Table 12.1	Comparison of the volume of some AME purchased by the Ministry of Defense of Russia and exported by *Rosvooruzhenie* company in 1996 (in units)	247
Table 13.1	Roles of directors at their enterprises (in %)	270
Table 13.2	Roles of directors at enterprises with different ownership structures as of 1999 (in %)	271
Table 13.3	Distribution of directors' roles (in %)	272
Table 13.4	Differences in directors' attitude towards their work and in the position of enterprises run by directors with different social roles (in %)	274
Table 13.5	Why directors said they would not like to become official proprietors of their enterprises in 1996-1999 (directors' estimates, in %)	276
Table 13.6	State orders and exploitation of productive capacity (in %)	281
Table 13.7	Main drawbacks of government policy (in %)	284
Table 13.8	Impact of state bodies and natural monopolies on enterprises' operation (directors' estimate, in %)	287

Table 14.1	The balance of benefits and losses from accession to the WTO for Russia's major export and import commodities	307
Table 14.2	Foreign direct investments in the agriculture and food industry (annually, in million US$)	308
Table 15.1	Index of Russia's agricultural output by farm category, 1991-97 (comparable prices, percentage of previous year)	314
Table 15.2	Structure of agricultural production in Russia by categories of farms (at prices of that time, in %)	315
Table 15.3	Autonomous farms and land plots allotted to them in Russia in 1991-98	316
Table 15.4	Commissioning of social facilities in the Russian countryside	324
Table 15.5	Emerging types of economic agents (actors) in Russia's present agricultural sector	328
Table 16.1	Percentage of companies having expressed export orientation in various industries	335
Table 16.2	Correlation between the main goals of the top management	336
Table 16.3	Main goals of CEOs self-assessment (in %)	338
Table 16.4	The comparison of perceived competitiveness between export-oriented and domestically oriented companies in various industries (export-oriented/ domestically oriented)	338
Table 16.5	Assessment by CEOs of the qualifications of the key personnel	340

Table 16.6	'List of needed specialists' (percentages of CEOs bold-faced)	341
Table 16.7	Measures to improve business performance (percentage of companies implementing such measures in the past two years)	342
Table 16.8	Participation of company managers and key specialists in various retraining activities in the past two years (in %)	343
Table 16.9	An ideal CEO according to Russian CEOs (in %)	345
Table 16.10	Ideal qualities and qualities lacking in middle managers according to CEOs (in %)	346

Diagram 1.1	Post-Soviet patchworks	7
Diagram 1.2	Influence in 1999 (first round)	19
Diagram 1.3	Influence in 1999 (second round)	19
Diagram 1.4	Influence in 2004 (first round)	20
Diagram 1.5	Influence in 2004 (second round)	20
Diagram 1.6	The importance of political resources (first round)	21
Diagram 1.7	Pursuit of global strategies in 1999 (first round)	22
Diagram 1.8	Pursuit of global strategies in 1999 (second round)	23
Diagram 1.9	Pursuit of global strategies in 2004 (first round)	24
Diagram 1.10	Pursuit of global strategies in 2004 (second round)	24
Diagram 1.11	Protection from global competition, 1999 and 2004 (first round)	25
Diagram 1.12	Protection from global competition in 1999 (second round)	26
Diagram 1.13	Protection from global competition in 2004 (second round)	26
Diagram 1.14	Softening budget constraints (first round)	27
Diagram 1.15	Softening budget constraints (second round)	27
Diagram 1.16	Securing property rights, 1999 and 2004 (first and second round)	28
Diagram 1.17	Importance of public goods (first round)	29

Diagram 1.18	Interests in private goods (first round)	29
Diagram 1.19	Time horizons (aggregated) from expert poll 1999	30
Diagram 1.20	Time horizons (aggregated) from expert poll 2000	31
Diagram 2.1	Russia's money growth (left) and inflation (right) (in %)	38
Diagram 2.2	Real GDP index and external debt/GDP-ratio	39
Diagram 4.1	Russia: Credit Ratings (average of credit ratings by Moody's and Standard and Poor's)	79
Diagram 14.1	Share of the federal budget in financing the agro-food sector	296
Diagram 14.2	Federal and regional grain reserves (mt)	296
Diagram 14.3	Distribution of experts' responses to the question 'Do you believe the Agrarian party represents the economic and social interests of the rural and agricultural population?	300
Diagram 15.1	Percentage of different farm categories in the agricultural output of Russia in 1970-96 (in prices of that time)	314

List of Contributors

Alimova, Tat'iana A.
Born 1951, PhD (Economics), Leading Researcher at the Russian Independent Institute of Social and Nationalities Problems (RIISNP), Moscow, Russia

Balzer, Harley D.
Born 1948, Associate Professor of Government and Director of the Center for Eurasian, Russian and East European Studies, Georgetown University, Washington D.C., USA

Fortescue, Stephen
Born 1952, Associate Professor, School of Politics and International Relations, University of New South Wales, Sydney, Australia

Gurkov, Igor B.
Born 1965, PhD (Economics), Professor, Head of the Laboratory for Organizational Development at the Higher School of Economics, Moscow, Russia

Heinrich, Andreas
Born 1970, PhD Candidate, Research Fellow at the Institute for East European Studies, Free University of Berlin, Germany

Hishow, Ognian
Born 1951, PhD, Researcher, Foundation Science and Politics (SWP), Berlin, Germany

Iudina, Irina N.
Born 1960, PhD Candidate, Senior Lecturer, Chair of World History and International Relations, Altai State University, Barnaul, Russia

Kalugina, Zemfira I.
Born 1938, Professor of Sociology, Head of Department of Social Problems, Institute of Economics and Industrial Engineering, Russian Academy of Science, Siberian Branch, Novosibirsk, Russia

Kosals, Leonid I.
Born 1956, PhD, Leading Researcher at the Institute for Socio-Economic Problems of the Population, Russian Academy of Sciences, Moscow, Russia

Krasnov, Grigorii V.
Born 1973, Senior Associate - Private Equity, Bank of America Equity Partners - Europe, London, UK

Peregudov, Sergei P.
Born 1925, Professor, Senior Researcher of the Institute of World Economy and International Relations of the Russian Academy of Sciences, Moscow, Russia

Pukhov, Ruslan N.
Born 1976, Aspirant of the State Institute for International Relations (MGIMO), Director of the Center for Analysis of Strategies and Technologies (CAST), Moscow, Russia

Rytsareva, Elena K.
Born 1969, special correspondent, Ekspert magazine, Moscow, Russia

Ryvkina, Rozalina V.
Born 1926, Professor for Political Economy, Head of Department at the Institute for Socio-Economic Problems of the Population, Russian Academy of Sciences, Moscow, Russia

Sarkisiants, Artos G.
Born 1958, PhD (economics), Deputy Head of the Department of International Financial Institutions, Ministry of Finance of the Russian Federation, Moscow, Russia

Segbers, Klaus
Born 1954, Director of the Institute for East European Studies and Professor for Political Sciences at the Institute for East European Studies and the Department for Political and Social Sciences, Free University, Berlin, Germany

Serova, Evgeniia V.
Born 1956, Professor, Head of the Centre of Agri-Food Economics (Institute for Economy in Transition), Head of Department on Applied Microeconomics at the Higher School of Economics, Moscow, Russia

Zasurskii, Ivan I.
Born 1974, PhD Candidate, Senior Researcher, Faculty of Journalism, Moscow State University, Moscow, Russia

Preface

This book presents the basic results of the research project 'Transformation and Globalization'. It was implemented 1998-2000.

The Volkswagen Foundation generously funded this project. I am especially grateful for the cooperation from the program director, Dr. Alfred Schmidt, and for recommendations provided by anonymous referees. The Institute for East European Studies of the Free University Berlin agreed to host this project and to offer space and technical facilities.

The question of transliteration was resolved in favor of the Library of Congress rules. Exceptions are Moscow, Petersburg and some 'trademark names' (like Leontief Center). Composite names of enterprises and government organizations have been translated into American English (indicating the Russian abbreviation, where appropriate), while brief and well-known Russian designations (like *Sviaz'invest, Lukoil, Gazprom*) have been preserved - in italics.

The realization of such a project with about 70 partners in many, not only post-Soviet, countries is not possible without a committed, creative coordinator who communicates with the participants and who functions, in a way, as the virtual social center of the project. Gesa Walcher did an excellent job - cooperating courteously with all the authors, meticulously organizing and recording expenses, keeping the time schedule on track and doing many more indispensable things. Thank you, Gesa - this was the most difficult job, and you did it superbly. Thanks, too, for sending out so many optimistic signals when, sometimes, it seemed difficult to hold everything together.

Two research fellows were responsible for the two main subject axes of this project. Andreas Heinrich's special task were the actor-related studies, while Graham Stack focused primarily on institutions. They also handled the different stages of the papers - from proposals on drafts to the semi-finals and, finally, to the final-finals, and they prepared the book technically for the publisher. Both did much more than was formally required, and their spirit was invaluable for the product that you, the reader, are holding in your hands now.

Other people were important in realizing this undertaking. Oskar Niedermayer, my colleague from the Otto-Suhr-Institut of the Free University, was kind enough to help in designing the expert polls. Two postgraduate students, Markus Soldner and Jürgen Bruchhaus, volunteered for testing the poll questionnaires. Lars Jochimsen designed the project's homepage (http://userpage.fu-berlin.de/~oeiabpol/psp2). Galina Kozlova, as many times before, kindly helped us in organizing project meetings in Moscow. Stefanie Harter and Tatiana Dolgopiatova joined the project meeting in Nida (September 1999); they provided valuable observations and comments regarding the project's structure.

During the difficult process of making the texts readable in proper American English, six language editors assisted us: Olaf Grobel in Berlin, Rebecca Kilhefner (US Institute of Peace, Washington, D.C.), Matthew Rendall, Roger Schoenmann and Sondra Venable (all at Columbia University in New York). Björn Warkalla was diligent in doing the final proof reading.

Thanks to all of you. Even under serious time constraints - were there any? - I always had the feeling that I could rely on you.

Klaus Segbers
Positano/ Berlin, September 2000

List of Abbreviations

ADR	American Depository Receipts
AME	Armaments and Military Equipment
AO	*Aktsionernoe Obshchestvo/* Joint Stock Company
APR	*Agrarnaia Partia Rossii/* Agrarian Party of Russia
ARKO	*Agentstvo po Restrukturizatsii Kreditnykh Organizatsii/* Agency for the Restructuring of Credit Organizations
ATD	Administrative-Territorial Division
BIS	Bank for International Settlements
bn cm	billion cubic meters
bp	basis point
CEO	Chief Executive Officer
CIS	Commonwealth of Independent States
COMECON	Council for Mutual Economic Assistance
CPSU	Communist Party of the Soviet Union
EBRD	European Bank for Reconstruction and Development
EES	*Edinaia Energeticheskaia Sistema/* United Energy System
EU	European Union

FDI	Foreign Direct Investment
FEC	Fuel and Energy Complex
FIG	Financial Industrial Group
FSU	Former Soviet Union
GDP	Gross Domestic Product
GKO	*Gosudarstvennye kratkosrochnye obligatsii*/ Short-term treasury bills
GNP	Gross National Product
GNS	*Gosudarstvennaia Nalogovaia Sluzhba*/ State Tax Service
Goskomstat	*Gosudarstvennyi Komitet Rossiiskoi Federatsii po Statistike*/ State Committee of the Russian Federation on Statistics
IANS	Interest Arrears Notes, interests from PRINS
IBRD	International Bank for Reconstruction and Development
ICEM	International Federation of Unions of Employees in the Chemical, Mining, Energy Industries and General Workers
IEPP/ IET	*Institut Ekonomiki Perechodnogo Perioda*/ Institute for the Economy in Transition
IMF	International Monetary Fund
JSC	Joint Stock Company
JV	Joint Venture
LPKh	*Lichnoe podsobnoe khoziaistvo*/ Part-time Farming

MAPO	Moscow Aviation Production Organization	
MIC	Military-Industrial Complex	
MinFin	Ministry of Finance	
MinFins	internal foreign currency bonds emitted by the MinFin	
MPS	*Ministerstvo Putei Soobchsheniia/* Ministry of Railways	
mt	million tons	
MTCR	Missile Technology Control Regime	
MTE	*Ministerstvo Topliva i Energetiki/* Ministry of Fuel and Energy	
MVD	*Ministerstvo Vnutrennykh del/* Ministry of Internal Affairs	
NATO	North Atlantic Treaty Organization	
NGO	Non-governmental Organization	
OAO	*Otkrytoe Aktsionernoe Obshchestvo/* Open Joint Stock Company	
OECD	Organization for Economic Cooperation and Development	
OFZ	*Otkrytye federal'nye zaimy/* Long-Term Treasury Bonds	
PRINS	Principals, restructured Soviet-era loans	
R&D	Research and Development	
RAO	*Rossiiskoe Aktsionernoe Obshchestvo/* Russian Joint Stock Company	
RF	Russian Federation	

SBS	*Stolichnyi Bank Sberezhenii*/ Capital Savings Bank
SOE	State-Owned Enterprises
TNCs	Transnational Corporations
TWG	TransWorld Group
VAT	Value Added Tax
VE	Virtual Economy
WB	World Bank
WP	Warsaw Pact
WTO	World Trade Organization

1 Actors and Interests in a Changing Russia

KLAUS SEGBERS

This book addresses actors - the causal agents of change in the Former Soviet Union (FSU), and specifically in Russia. The studies presented here are part of the research project 'Transformation and Globalization'. The aim of this undertaking is to address the ongoing transformations in the post-Soviet spaces (predominantly in Russia) as processes shaped primarily by two groups of factors: institutions and structures from Soviet times, on the one hand, and the impacts related to globalization, on the other hand.

These two sources have a decisive impact on actors and institutions[1] in the post-Soviet world. They both offer incentives and constraints, opportunities and risks. Actors - individuals and groups - respond differently to the legacies of the past and the stimuli of the present in local and global contexts. Accordingly, the transformation processes are uneven and heterogeneous, even contradictory. The different reactions of various actors to these challenges are the central dependent variables of these studies.[2]

Shaping Contexts: The Independent Variables

There are two independent variables of this project: the Soviet past, and the global context. In both cases, there are significant debates going on. Transformations in Eastern Europe, especially their causes, their forms, and

---

[1] For the studies on institutional change, see vol. 2 of this trilogy: Segbers 2001a.
[2] The work presented here has three axes: actors, institutions, and space. Accordingly, the findings are presented in three volumes. The introduction to the volume related to institutions presents the general ideas of the project design. In this volume, we are interested in actors, their interests, their preferences and their strategies.

their directions are the subject of many public and scholarly discussions.[3] The same can be said about debates related to globalization.[4] Certainly, there is a significant and growing body of literature in both fields.[5]

FSU Legacies

When analyzing post-Soviet changes, it is useful to look for continuities.[6] The supposedly great ruptures are popular because they were visible and easily presentable by the media. But these events do not necessarily indicate rapid change. In the non-political realm - social relations, forms of interaction, cultural codes, the behavior of economic agents - there seems to be a coexistence of Soviet and post-Soviet rules. The result cannot but resemble a patchwork, a complex web of actions and relations, a texture which is resistant to easy access. Making sense of all this requires decipherable endeavors - inspired and organized by social sciences.[7]

The current changes were not comprehensible without specific mechanisms of integration - the Soviet-type institutions, which were shaping and constraining actors' behavior. The most important of them[8] were:

- soft budget constraints;
- economics of shortage;
- the administrative market;
- the diversified way of life;
- the system of administrative-territorial division (ATD);
- the institutionalization of ethnicity;
- the difference between official discourses and private niches.

---

[3] For a first overview, see the literature in the OEI ASP Politik Working Paper No. 1, electronic version at <http://userpage.fu-berlin.de/~segbers/index4.html>; see also the discussion in Johnson's Russia List <http://www.cdi.org/russia/johnson>; the publications of the PONARS project at <http://www.fas.harvard.edu/~ponars>; and the journals Europe-Asia Studies, Post-Soviet Affairs, Post-Communist Studies, Russian Review, Slavic Review.
[4] For an overview, see the literature on my homepage at <http://userpage.fu-berlin.de/~segbers/>, go for courses/ss2000/millennium.
[5] For more details on both independent factors, see my introduction to Segbers 2001a. The following paragraphs are only a brief summary.
[6] It goes without saying that we do not have in mind mythical constructs like 'the Russians always want to be dominated' or 'the return of totalitarianism must be expected, even more so with a former spy as president'.
[7] Cultural competence and understanding - 'Verstehen' - may enhance and, to some extent, work as a filter to check research designs and results.
[8] For the meaning of these concepts, see Segbers 2001a.

Without any doubt, the final crisis of the Soviet system was generated endogenously. The burden of an inorganic, overstretched world power could not but lead to disaster; the questions were 'only' when, in what form and how manageable the breakdown would be.[9]

The consistency and stability of Soviet political regulation rested on the ability of the political center to distribute and redistribute resources. Those interest groups and lobbies which were strategically better positioned or tactically more effective succeeded basically in getting subsidies and preferential treatment from the Soviet government or the party leadership. This leadership formally administered the final days of the USSR. In reality, it was caught in endless bargaining processes for which it was increasingly ill equipped because of ever scarcer resources. The inevitable result was the break-up of this model. The structural defects could not be resolved within the USSR framework. The playing field was too big, the structural contradictions too significant. On this level of action, no new equilibrium was conceivable.

In order to gain majorities for some economic 'reforms', the political leadership had to let go of central political power monopolies, which even before were rather more symbolic than real. For tactical reasons, the political center was weakened, but without the much expected economic and social tradeoffs. On balance, the principals legalized defections, and they tried to build coalitions with some of the defectors, thereby finally emasculating the political center, i.e. themselves. While this may seem paradoxical, it describes adequately what happened. Also, it demonstrates once more that most political actions have unintended side effects, and that many political moves designed with tactical and short-term aims result in strategic and long-term outcomes rather different from the intentions of the actors.

The loss of the ability to maneuver and balance between principals and actors led to collapse. The regional and sectoral elites, the members of clans and networks in the web of the all-encompassing Soviet pyramid of administrative, social, political and economic markets realized that the center was weakened. The old mechanisms of integration became ineffective.

It would be strange if the old, Soviet-type institutions and the experience of the dissolution of the USSR did not continue to have significant effects in shaping post-Soviet rules and post-Soviet actors' expectations and strategies.

---

[9] Segbers 1989, chapter 4.

The Global Context

Globalization is a concept with many connotations and meanings. For our purposes, we understand it as a world-wide interplay of capital and communications flows enabled by new technologies, which - in one way or another - connect countries, societies, firms and individuals. While perceptions of these trends and abilities to cope with them differ, it becomes ever more difficult, if not impossible to 'opt out' and to pursue auto-centric, de-coupled paths of development.

Relevant indicators for globalization[10] are:

- the increasingly uncontrolled and apparently uncontrollable movement of capital;
- new possibilities for transporting and transmitting goods, services, people and information;
- digitalization of information and communications;
- diverse forms of reaction to the permanent influx of multiple stimuli related to work, leisure and information;
- the creation of new centralities - mega-cities, headquarters, internet providers, transnational institutions;
- changing contents of space and place.[11]

In any case, we have to accept that the relative decline of the regulatory capabilities of nation states and states in general is a given. The tools, concepts and approaches with which they interpret national and international politics are no longer sufficient. They may even become obsolete. Traditional terms and concepts of politics and political science like sovereignty, territoriality, borders, domestic/ foreign, and the state itself are losing their traditional interpretative powers. They are insufficient for covering and explaining today's political phenomena and interactions.

While we will not and cannot discuss the merits and problems of the globalization debate, we make some reasonable assumptions regarding what lessons can be drawn for the purposes of our project.

While states play a role in setting frameworks and shaping institutions for regulating these flows, there are many other groups of actors who are influential and who form parts of an increasingly complex configuration of players on different levels of action. To be effective, these new forms of regulation must also be felt, and should work, in the FSU. They at least must have anchors there.

---

[10] For more details, see my introduction into Segbers 2001a.
[11] See Segbers 2001b.

Individuals, social and interest groups exposed to these flows do have options - at least in principle - regarding how to react: they can accommodate themselves to these impacts, accepting them as creating new opportunities and trying actively to participate. But they also can try to opt out or to resist these impacts. Finally, they may attempt to ignore them - at least for some time. In any case, there are winners and losers.[12]

Globalization in this sense is the second decisive independent variable for shaping institutional change in post-Soviet spaces.

From Common Assumptions to Explaining Patchworks

The significant changes that have taken place - and are continuing to evolve - in post-Soviet spaces since 1989 cannot productively be explained by the usual, traditional and most common assumptions which are still predominant. Especially the role of states and governments is usually over-emphasized. This leads to assumptions suggesting that wide-scale and multi-layered changes can be introduced and executed by design. But in a certain way, expectations of effective social engineering resemble the spirit of the makers and fellow-travelers of the 1917 revolution, and of other grand design concepts and deeds of the 20th century. Those were romantic concepts, far from reality.

What is needed is a more sober approach, enabling analysts to make sense of the historic developments in Eastern Europe which became visible in the mid-1980s but started much earlier. Required are new tools for new ways of political and social mapping. The world can be better understood if we replace - or at least supplement - the old way of mapping according to states with borders as core units with a new way representing relevant political entities and actors.

The concept of the state must be relaxed and made more flexible. Relevant concepts should be able to handle a multitude of actors, located at different levels of analysis. Instead of one place where power may be organized, we should look for the places where new centralities are located. Instead of a central (federal) government, we would do better to focus upon institutions and governance.

At least for some decades, we already do have a multitude of actors on different levels of action who bypass, erode, contest and transform the traditional concept of the state. The process of European integration and the

---

[12] As a matter of fact, one may classify reactions differently, or try to offer subgroups of positive and negative attitudes and behavior. Still, for political purposes, it matters most if a given group tries to block or, on the contrary, tries to further the integration of a given region, city, sector, enterprise, bureaucracy, and so forth into global contexts.

accompanying forms of regulation demonstrate this. The modern forms of political regulation that were developed in the 1960s and 1970s of the 20th century are more similar to bargaining and negotiating systems (*Aushandlungssysteme*) than to classical unitary actor concepts. So the reduction of political and analytical expectations toward the traditional state is not new at all.[13]

Still, with globalization gaining speed and acceptance, additional modifications of our state views are required. Actors and institutions are organizing - and are being influenced by - flows. The image resembling this process may most appropriately be defined as a 'patchwork'. In this kind of residual state framework, subnational groups like regions, economic sectors and huge enterprises, social and societal interest groups, and also bureaucracies, compete with each other and build coalitions. The predominant forms of interaction are bargaining processes, networks and clans and, accordingly, weak institutional frameworks (see diagram 1.1).[14]

Without any doubt, this scheme is powerful, and it is realistic (in the real meaning of this word). But it is not what theorists require from good theories: parsimony. I plead guilty on this count.

Still, by focusing not on each and everything but on the most relevant (influential) actors and groups and by reconstructing their interests and preferences, we can make this scheme useful and even operational. If we - as scientists, decision-makers and civilians - ignore who really acts, and if we once again replace this heterogeneous picture, the patchwork Russia, by assumptions about master plans and unitary actors, we will fail - and to a greater extent than by misreading the intentions of some of those particularistic interest groups.

Yes, the situation is complex. And this project is intended to contribute to understanding this complexity - not by reducing it to fake unitary actors or to traditional assumptions.

Does this scheme allow for power? Well, it does. But not necessarily or primarily the power of the Kremlin, but rather the power of those players who control resources enabling them to execute power.

To be sure, the patchwork model is not handy. It is not easy to swallow and to run. It is difficult to operationalize. But that is the very reason why, under the given conditions, it is adequate.

---

[13] See Grande and Risse 2000, 245, 253-254.
[14] There is an extensive discussion about dividing sovereignty. Quoting Perry Anderson, Katherine Verdery writes about the 'parcellization of sovereignty' (Verdery 1996, 208). Steven Solnick discusses the concepts of oligarchy and feudalism for the El'tsin- and Putin-Russia (Solnick 1999).

Segbers, Actors and Interests in a Changing Russia 7

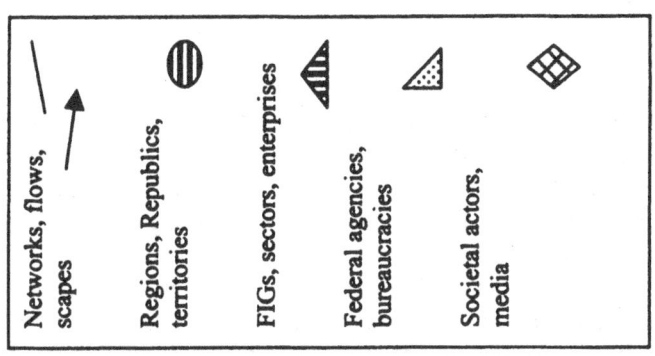

Diagram 1.1 Post-Soviet patchworks

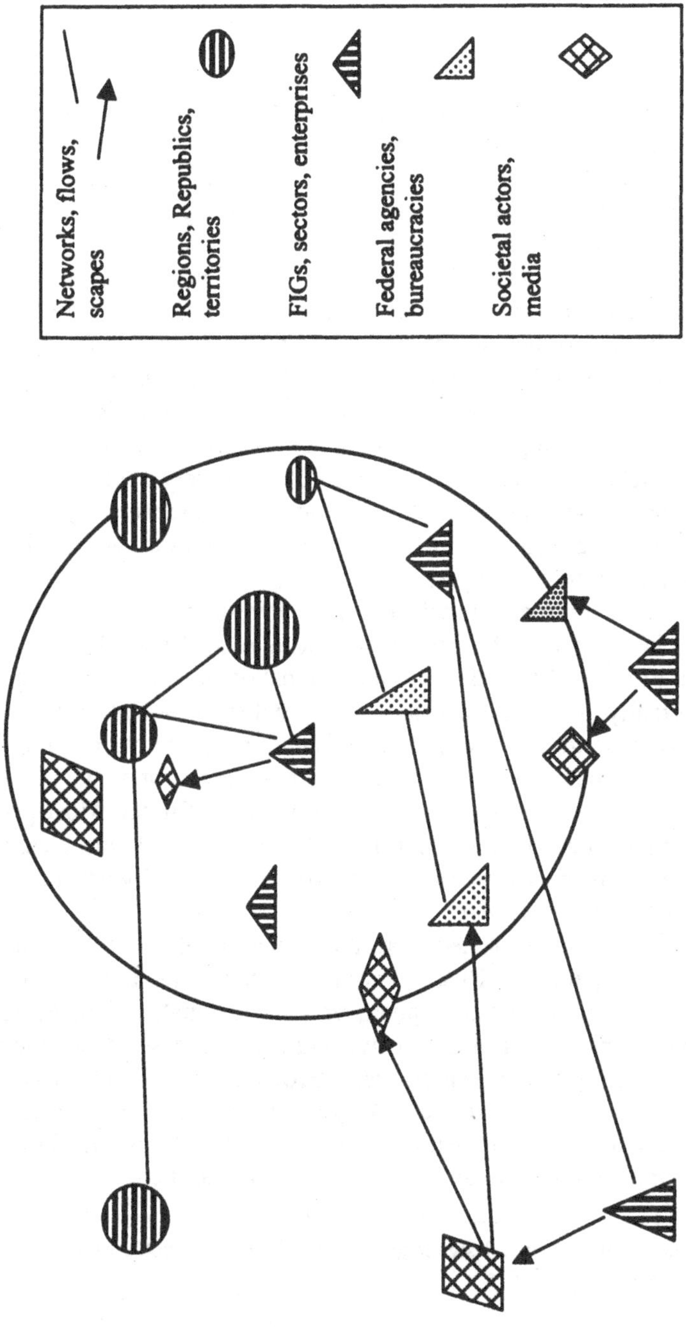

Research Design

As outlined above, the guiding question of this project is about actors and institutions in post-Soviet spaces, and on how they cope with the double impact of national legacies on the one hand, and globalization on the other.[15] That these two factors are decisive in shaping transformation profiles is also the first hypothesis for our project. Logically, this assumption also shapes this volume on actors' orientations.

The analytical tasks resulting from this are promising and difficult at the same time. Actors and their interests are certainly in many ways still affected by the former Soviet model - as there are visible traces of Soviet institutions in post-Soviet spaces. But the FSU is also increasingly exposed to tendencies and mechanisms of worldwide integration of production, circulation, consumption, and communication. The impact of these processes and flows is, in most cases, not effectively mediated by existing state structures and administrations. In at least some way, the strategies of most actors take into account the global configuration, while still bearing the imprints of the Soviet past.

The attraction of capital flows, of investment, of information and services is needed for further development. Also, Russia has to become a member of most of the relevant international organizations and regimes - at least formally. The impact of the global context on social groups seems to be significant: global life styles, consumption patterns, communications and entertainment habits are everywhere - they cannot be blocked and redirected so as to be unperceived and unfelt in Russia. Most people are increasingly aware of their transnational context, and this changes their points of reference when they make comparisons, and when they develop strategies for their own lives.

So it can be expected that the global context will have various immediate impacts on Russia - while, at the same time, never simply leading to homogenization. Rather, various regional, social, generational, functional and other groups perceive and convert these impacts in specific ways, according to their experience, interests and the resources available to them. Global impacts are, as everywhere, refined and perceived in a specific context - the indigenization of external patterns and flows is what really and meaningfully can be observed and researched.

---

[15] For details of the research design in general and for project hypotheses, see my introduction to Segbers 2001a.

These two factors: the internal background and legacies of the Soviet model, and the external, inter- and trans-national environments help us properly to understand the demise of the USSR. And they can and will also explain the specific character of post-Soviet changes.

A second hypothesis (more relevant to volume 2) matches the first one: It is characteristic of post-Soviet transformations that significant changes do take place. But they are only partly organized and directed from above. Consequently, transformations and their progress are compatible with weak institutions, and with weak or even failing states.

Because of the specific forms of post-Soviet changes, it is not too promising to focus analyses on the national state as the core level of explanation. In Soviet times,[16] the state was formally dominant and hegemonic, but it did not effectively control all the important economic and social processes. There were many informal mechanisms and rules that, in reality, compensated for the functional deficiencies of the official model.

The post-Soviet state resembles a rather imaginary, fictitious entity. It is and remains an open question if there ever will be a 'normal' state structure. This question is not answered positively by recent administrative moves in President Putin's Kremlin. The basic point here is not the lack of sufficient concepts, but rather the difficulty of imagining that Russia could become a laboratory for the resurrection of a strong statehood in global times. The tools for central administration disappeared with the USSR. There are ever fewer classical states in the world, anywhere. This tendency started some decades ago, and it has produced new forms of governance on supra- and sub-state levels. This is a strong additional indicator that the recent mechanisms of world economics and politics do not allow for the return of the classical nation state, notwithstanding the continuing attempts of various elites to engage in nation-building.[17] So we are simply forced to look for relevant, real, units and levels of analysis.[18]

For the reasons briefly described above - the ongoing processes of transformation, difficult and complex tendencies in nation and state building, the general weakness of institutions (especially formal ones), continuing shadows of former legacies and (sometimes conflicting) signals from the external environments - the formally ruling elites in the successor

---

[16] Chervyakov 1995.

[17] These attempts of elites 'in search of states' (Ernest Gellner) will continue as long as there are premiums and incentives to do so, even when the 'international community' and its most influential components are highly selective regarding when, and to whom, such premiums are offered.

[18] This was the task of 'Post-Soviet Puzzles', which in a way was the predecessor of 'Explaining Post-Soviet Patchworks' (Segbers and De Spiegeleire 1995).

states of the FSU are in reality not in a position to organize and to control the current processes of change. There is no 'transformation by design'.[19]

Here, of course, is the core of the widely perceived impression of anomy, lawlessness, arbitrary decision-making and other phenomena of low-intensity or failing governance. In this sense, the recently intensified debates on governance in political sciences may be productive for post-Soviet constellations.[20]

For purposes of this book, we defined two strategies to make clear why and how actors' preferences and interests are being shaped by the legacies of the past and by local, regional and national contexts, on the one hand, and by transnational and international configurations, on the other.

Firstly, we asked some 25 experts[21] to write in-depth studies of post-Soviet actors and the development of their interests. The authors received rather detailed guiding questions and were asked to develop their studies along the lines of these reference points. The most interesting texts (17) are presented in this volume. Unavoidably, and probably fortunately, it is not possible to make the studies structurally identical. Still, they are for the most part sufficiently similar in their architecture as to offer many opportunities for comparison. Similarities and differences in the actors' groups' positions between the past and globalization, and in their resulting strategies, are made obvious.

The second instrument we used for determining the interests, preferences and strategies of actors were expert polls.[22] The questionnaire as well as a list of the experts and their regional locations can be found on the project's homepage.[23] While this tool certainly is not an exact technique of measurement, it offers important hints for our purposes. Also, it avoids

---

[19] See Stark and Bruszt 1998, 80-83.
[20] Still, the overwhelming impression of chaos, often combined with apocalyptic expectations and highly stereotyped Western discourses about Russia, is rather misleading. Again, as in Soviet times, the weakness of formal institutions is at least partly being compensated for by informal regimes and rules on a regional or sectoral level, and by informal or private forms of governance replacing the less effective state administration. For details, see Segbers 2001a.
[21] 13 authors are Russians (one with two contributions), one of them actually working in London (Krasnov). Two writers are German, and two others live in Australia and the USA, respectively.
[22] In two rounds, we asked 48/ 60 experts to give us their assessments on 32/ 22 Russian interest groups. In the first round, which lasted from 1 July to 19 August 1999, we received 33 responses; in the second round, which took place between 6 April and 1 May 2000, we got 25 responses. We included persons professionally related to the groups under research, but not employed by these structures. We are aware of the limitations of this tool. Yet the possible alternatives - doing opinion polls or conducting interviews with representatives of the groups we were interested in - were for methodological and practical reasons no real alternatives.
[23] See <http://userpage.fu-berlin.de/~oeiabpol/psp2/poll.html>.

problems associated with opinion polls and interviews with individuals related to the organizations and groups of interest. The respondents of opinion polls do not have the required knowledge to produce more than their perceptions of other groups - a possibly interesting question, but beyond the framework of this project. The second tool may be useful as an additional research technique, but the results are likely to be biased toward the views of the groups the professionals approached represent.

So we selected up to 60 experts who are not related to the groups of interest, but who are professionally qualified to evaluate the interest of these actors' groups. In two rounds, we asked them to give us their assessments on a scale from 0 to 5 for four reference years: 1990, 1994, 1999 and 2004. Each of these years represents an assumed divide: 1990 was the last full year of the Soviet Union and five years after *perestroika* began; 1994 stands for the peak of post-Soviet, new Russian anomy, right after the fall crisis of 1993; 1999 represents the last year of the El'tsin regime and the possible beginning of a new consolidation after the 1998 crisis; finally, 2004 was intended to encourage the experts to offer some prospective views for a not too distant future. The questions themselves reflected the project organizers' interest in three main dimensions:

- Russian actors' groups' positions regarding the global context;
- Russian groups' interests in public and private goods;
- Russian groups' time horizons.

Before the expert poll started, we drafted a list of the potentially most relevant interest and influence groups.

State structures

1. President and his inner circle (family, presidential administration, Kremlin security)
2. Power ministries: Ministry of Internal Affairs, Ministry of Defense, Ministry for Civil Defense, Federal Security Service (*FSB*)
3. Federal financial actors: Ministry of Finance, Ministry of Economics, Tax Service (*GosNalogSl*), Pension Fund
4. Central Bank group, regional branches of Central Bank, *Sberbank*, *Vneshtorgbank*
5. Ministries with (potential) control functions over economically-important sectors: Ministry of Fuel and Energy, Ministry of Rail (MPS), Ministry of Atomic Energy, Ministry for State Property, Ministry of Telecommunications
6. Duma deputies
7. Federation Council members (regional leaders)
8. Elite-groups of previous and present donor regions: Moscow city,

Moskovskaia oblast, St. Petersburg, Iakutiia (Sakha), Khanty-Mansiiskii autonomous okrug, Iamalo-Nenetskii autonomous okrug, Krasnoiarskii krai, Tatarstan, Samarskaia oblast, Primorskii krai, Nizhnegorodskaia oblast, Sverdlovskaia oblast

9* Mayors (except federal cities)
10* Procurators, Constitutional Court, Arbitrage Court, other high courts
11 Armed state structures or senior military personnel

Domestic economic actors with international interest

12 Gasprom (gas companies, pipeline companies)
13 Oil companies, *Transneft'*
14 Electricity companies (*EES*)
15 Commercial banks on federal level who are linked with industrial holdings
16 Other mineral, raw material and partly-processed goods companies with export potential like metals, diamonds
17 Aviation, Aerospace, other high-technology defence industry branches with export potential, Rosvooruzhenie

Foreign organizations

18* CIS-based state actors
19 International state-linked organizations: IMF, G7, Paris Club, World Bank, EBRD
20 International business and finance interests: transnational corporations, London Club, credit rating agencies, investment banks

Domestic economic actors with orientation to domestic market

21 Mass media companies (television and radio, newspapers)
22 Telecommunication companies
23* Private service and retail sector companies: financial services, wholesale importers, food and textile producers
24* Automobile companies
25* Defense industry companies with no export potential
26* Agricultural-industrial complex components
27* Coal industry companies

Social groups

28* Political parties
29* Trade unions
30 Church hierarchies
31 Criminal groups
32 Oligarchs (top businessmen and bankers as social elite)

* actors' groups which were included only in the first round in 1999

The original list was discussed in the first project seminars with external experts, and it was then reworked and modified. The final list for the first expert poll consisted of 32 groups.

For the second tour, we shortened this list and took out those ten groups which were, according to the first round, the least influential.[24]

Setting clear criteria for determining which groups are relevant, and which are less important or do not matter at all, is notoriously difficult - probably in many countries of the world. The definition we put forward was that 'influence' should be assessed according to the groups' ability to significantly influence or change the rule of the - political - games in post-Soviet Russia: i.e. to shape (formal or informal) institutions. According to this criterion, some favorites for Western attention were dropped - especially political parties, and the State Duma, the Federation Council and other formal bodies as organizations (though in some cases their individual members as a corporate or status group have been included).

Another assumption had to be made regarding the basic interests of those groups: i.e. are the common classifications along the lines of reformers/ anti-reformers, hard-liners/ liberals, Westerners/ Slavophiles, etc., of any use, or do we have to look for better and rather non-ideological criteria for dividing those groups. We decided that the traditional typologies are too unclear and confusing. Instead, we made the basic assumption that the basic preferences of all groups are survival, and utility maximization in terms of resources and positions. Under post-Soviet conditions and in environments characterized by weak formal institutions, the primary form of maximizing their utilities was strategies:

- to gain access to the distribution and mobilization of resources of all kinds;
- to gain control of production and distribution potentials and channels;
- to legalize accumulated resources and positions already gained by re-defining property rights; and
- to stabilize, and possibly strengthen and enhance, those positions that were inherited from the administrative market texture of the USSR.

Most of these strategies were embedded in networks that had their roots in Soviet times. For most of the 1990s, the resource-directed strategies were implemented in an environment without strong third party arbitration - the Russian state was, in the form of its bureaucratic

---

[24] The following groups have *not* been included in the second round: Mayors, procurators, CIS-based state actors, private service and retail sector companies, Automobile companies, non-export armaments, companies of the agricultural sector, the coal industry, political parties and the trade unions.

components, rather dissolved and took part in the quarrels. Logically, this behavior reproduced the weakness of central administrations. Only toward the late 1990s are there indications that a new equilibrium[25] has been reached, characterized by increasing interest in consolidation and stabilization and in establishing and observing new rules. But catch-as-catch-can, rent-seeking and violent forms of conflict were all too common.

There are problems with such an approach. We do, for this purpose, assume that the general assumption of goal-orientation of actors as suggested by rational choice approaches is useful and productive. But on a more concrete level, in highly fluid times, as the 1990s in Russia certainly were, the question of shifting interests may be appropriate. Yet when we accept this point, the only useful research strategy would be the commissioning of case studies. Generalizations would on the whole be problematic.

We decided to go ahead with our research design. In our view, it proved to be successful. It is up to the readers to draw their own conclusions. The basic results will be presented at the end of this introduction.

Organization and Structure of this Volume

The actor groups covered in this volume are exposed in different ways to globalization. Some are rather affected by this context and active in accommodating to it. Others are skeptical or non-competitive. So both questions are interesting: who is effectively linked to global contexts and who is not, but rather determined by the past.

The structure of the book is as follows. Ognian Hishow (Berlin) describes the role of international financial organizations. Especially the IMF is of overwhelming importance because it provides macroeconomic assistance, whereas other institutions work on the microeconomic level. Unlike the private capital markets, the fund's lending to Russia will continue to play a decisive role in solving the country's balance of payment problems.

Artos Sarkisiants (Moscow) discusses the effects of Russia's debt restructuring on emerging market economies' access to global financial markets. The serious change in Russian funding policy was the result of several factors, affecting both the revenue side of the equation and the relative cost of domestic as opposed to international financing. The Russian Federation has become one of the key borrowers in the international

---

[25] For the requirements of equilibria in post-Soviet conditions, see Solnick 1999.

markets. But the financial crisis of 1998 actually ruined all the positive results that Russia had gained within the framework of a comprehensive restructuring of the former USSR debt owed to the Paris and London Clubs of creditors, and Russia has yet to regain the creditors' confidence.

The important aspect of the quality of financial supervision and the related problem of moral hazard in the Russian emerging market is addressed by Irina Iudina (Moscow). Her article examines key aspects of financial globalization (the 'external challenge') and the reaction of emerging markets. According to this analysis, the key factor resulting in destructive financial crises in the developing markets is not capital flows, but the incompleteness and the slowness of the adaptation of banking systems and budget policy to the new external economic situation. Taking the financial crisis in Russia of 1998 as an example, the author demonstrates that it was the uncoordinated and uncertain measures of the monetary authorities and the deficiencies of institutional reforms which produced the collapse of the financial system.

The next group of texts covers important economic actors with a high export potential. Andreas Heinrich (Berlin) and Sergei Peregudov (Moscow) analyze the interests and the role of large corporations - in this case, of the firms *Gazprom* and *Lukoil*, respectively. Heinrich deals with *Gazprom*'s role as a global actor, concentrating on the question how *Gazprom* tries to realize its interests abroad, which instruments are employed, and which factors limit the company's international strategy. The main activities of *Gazprom* outside Russia include the expansion of export capacities and the effort to secure access to international financial markets in order to obtain the necessary finance. Strategic partnerships with foreign companies, the struggle for control over transit pipelines in Eastern Europe, and the rivalry with Central Asian gas producers are also part of his paper.

On the basis of his case study of *Lukoil*, Peregudov demonstrates a clear tendency among the most successful, export-oriented Russian corporations towards closer integration into the world economy. To achieve this in the context of the strong regulatory role of the state, they have to increase their political and especially lobbying activities. At the same time, the paternalistic tradition of the Soviet past and the social situation in the country stimulate them to develop their internal relations along the lines of the participatory model.

Finally, Steven Fortescue (Melbourne) takes up the Russian mining and metal sector. He shows that four aspects of globalization are relevant to the Russian mining and metals industry: international sourcing of inputs, a large proportion of outputs entering international trade, cross-border capital integration, and cross-border technology transfer. Although shifts in the direction of globalization are found in all four cases, those shifts are still partial and idiosyncratic.

The next two papers address the Russian national financial sector. Artos Sarkisiants (Moscow) explores in his second contribution the Russian banking sector and its international involvement. The Russian banks were formed over a three-year period, during which more than 2,500 commercial credit institutions were born. Most of these organizations were not banks by any recognizable Western standards, doing little lending or deposit-taking. Russian financial ethics are still different from those of the West, and so is its system. It is therefore difficult to base financial decisions on financial reports only.

Grigorii Krasnov (London) discusses Russian financial groups in connection with the development of market institutions. His paper argues that the ongoing process of industrial restructuring in Russia is closely intertwined with the development of market institutions, and that the Financial-Industrial Groups (FIGs) are at the center of this process: firstly, by having pre-empted and internalized the development of market institutions, and secondly, by virtue of their economic dominance. The FIGs have become one of the main conduits of values associated with the effective integration of the Russian economy into the global marketplace.

The next two texts, produced by two Moscow-based journalists, take up important sectors with a 'natural' exposure toward the global arena - mass media and telecommunications. Ivan Zasurskii highlights in his article the influence of global information culture on the new Russian media, the importation of political technologies (scriptwriting political spectacles) and their further development, the concentration of media and the rise of the internet. The author also covers the influence of foreign investors in Russian media. He shows how global corporations attempted to enter the media sector in the 1990s but generally failed to do so, and how the situation is changing now. Elena Rytsareva's paper describes the ownership structure and the telecommunications infrastructure and puts forward the question of this sector's strengths and weaknesses in the 'information age'. The author focuses especially on the actors and their differing references, aims, capacities and conflicts, but she also demonstrates cases of cooperation. The relationships among state actors, foreign actors, the Russian monopoly corporations *Rostelecom*, *Sviaz'invest* and others, and private Russian actors, etc., is interpreted. How are their interests shaped by the twin challenges of the Soviet heritage and global integration?

Four contributions address two key sectors of the Russian economy - defense production and agriculture. Both sectors are notoriously crisis-ridden, and both are quite heterogeneous. Ruslan Pukhov (Moscow) describes the interests of the Russian high defense sector and its moves into foreign markets. The change from the etatist paradigm of development of the Russian defense industries to the adoption of a more commercial paradigm is a major reflection of globalization trends. The Russian defense industries exist basically in the absence of internal military procurement. The substantial decrease in financing research and development encourages a more active export orientation of defense enterprises.

Leonid Kosals and Rozalina Ryvkina (Moscow) are interested in the same sector, but focus rather on the directors of armaments enterprises. Their article deals with the economic stratification of defense enterprises and analyses the socio-economic factors and consequences of variations in the economic position of defense enterprises. They also show the new status and attitude of their directors to the state. This stratification is one of the main indicators of adaptation to the economic market system and of the reaction to globalization.

Evgeniia Serova (Moscow) and Zemfira Kalugina (Novosibirsk) research the agricultural sector's relations with the past and with the global environment. Serova is interested in the role of interest groups in Russian agriculture. She maintains that countries in transition have their specific features in this respect. Agro-food policy in Russia, as in the rest of the world, is formed under the influence of the various interest groups that were actively institutionalized during the recent period. Globalization is still hardly reflected in domestic agriculture policy. Kalugina's paper analyses institutional transformations in the Russian agrarian sector between 1991-99, specifically in the three segments of the agrarian economy: collective and private farms and household plots. This analysis explores the main results of the agrarian reform in Russia and suggests the causes of its failures. Attention is drawn to the expansion of small commodity production, the destruction of work motivation, the failure of agrarian economy 'capitalization' and the degradation of the rural social sphere.

Three groups of actors are, allegedly, especially important for Russia's further integration into world structures: managers, small and medium enterprises, and the middle strata (classes). These groups are portrayed in the last three texts of this volume. Igor' Gurkov (Moscow) shows when and how Russian industries received unique impulses for both import substitution and export expansion. This process of 'forced accelerated globalization' has had, and continues to have, profound effects on the behavior of Russian companies, as they are now more strongly subjected to international business standards. Export-oriented companies are generally more attuned to foreign management practices. Yet export-orientation does not automatically lead to superior financial performance or eliminate common business problems.

Tat'iana Alimova (Moscow) devotes her analysis to the impact of world-wide changes on Russia's small business. Objects of her analysis are the small business sector as a whole and its separate groups. Alimova reviews the preconditions, mechanisms and perspectives for Russia's small firms' participation in globalization. Special attention is given to the identification of globalizing agents in this sector, and to the effect of economic integration as a mechanism for strengthening the influence of such firms.

Harley Balzer (Washington D.C.) pursues three related questions regarding the Russian post-communist middle class. The first aspect is its self-denying nature. The second topic is the general lack of institutional representation of those social groups that potentially make up the new middle class. And the third theme is the relationship of these groups toward globalization. On the one hand, the Russian middle class should be the social group most affected by global impacts. On the other, some portions of the middle class seem to be the *avant-garde* of anti-modern sentiments in Russia.

Unfortunately, but unavoidably, the readers will detect that some important categories of actors in Russia and in post-Soviet spaces are missing in this volume, at least in the form of separate papers. This is regrettable, but as often in life, there are limits even to good concepts. Mostly for practical reasons, we were unable within our time constraints to find high-quality analyses of the Russian Internet, the nuclear complex, importers for the automobile industry, and others.

Still, the importance of the information, communications and entertainment sectors is repeatedly mentioned, even when it is not analyzed separately - with the exception of the development of the mass media. As for the Russian Internet, there is an increasing literature available.[26]

Conclusions

Now let us draw some necessarily preliminary conclusions from our findings.

Let us look at the results of the expert polls. As indicated above, the first question was how influential the actor groups were (at the time the poll was taken) in terms of their ability to shape and to change the rules of political games. Between the first round in the summer of 1999 and the second in the spring of 2000, there was some variation.

---

[26] Harter 1999.

Diagram 1.2 Influence in 1999 (first round)

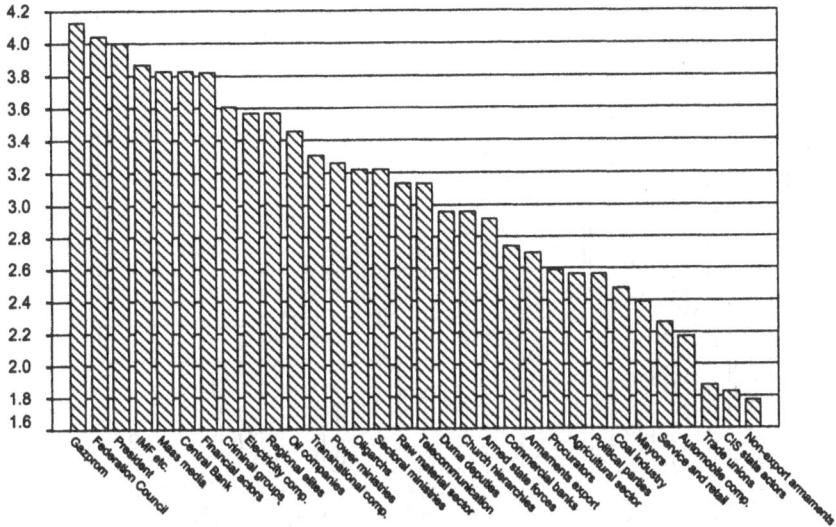

Diagram 1.3 Influence in 1999 (second round)

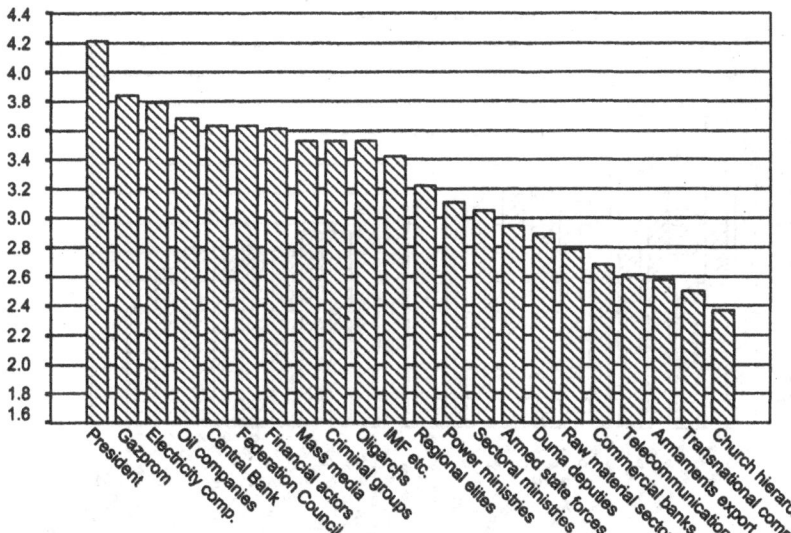

Diagram 1.4 Influence in 2004 (first round)

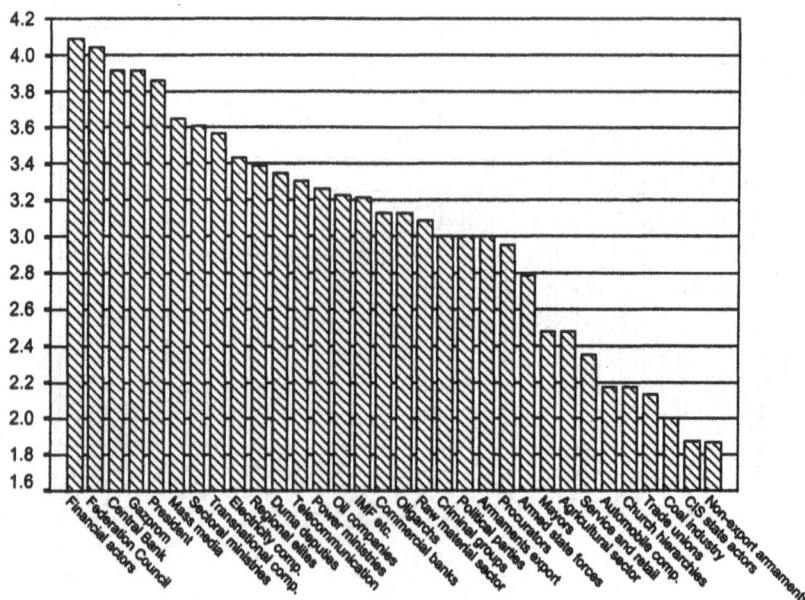

Diagram 1.5 Influence in 2004 (second round)

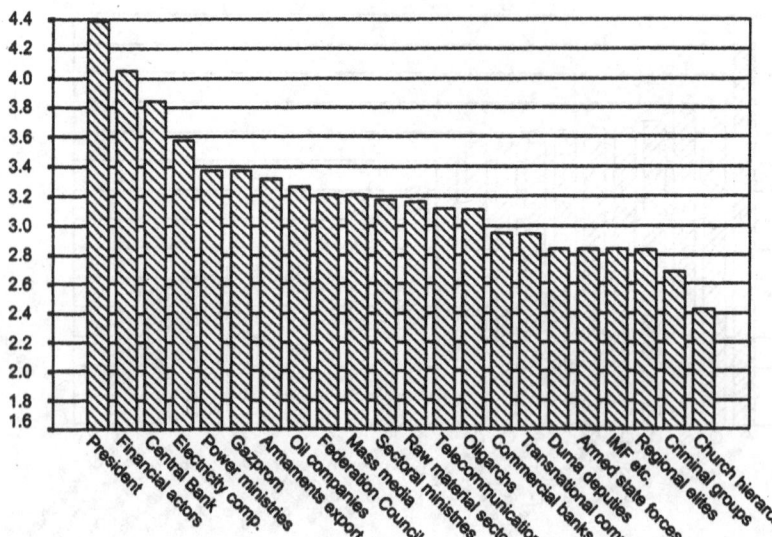

In both years, *Gazprom*, the President (and his entourage), the Central Bank and the members of the Federation Council are represented among the six leading groups, with some shifts of position back and forth. The promotion of the president to the number 1 spot certainly reflects the new person of Vladimir Putin. *Gazprom*, the leader in 1999, in 2000 leads the rest of the field after Putin. The structure-building and resource-generating sectors (oil, electricity) have been elevated from 1999 to numbers 3 and 4, respectively, in 2000.

The assessment of who will be influential in 2004 obviously reflects the expectation of the experts that state structures (the president, the Finance Ministry, the Central Bank, and the power ministries in position 5) will become more influential over the next few years - they occupy four out of the first five positions. In general, according to the second poll, only the first four positions (the groups mentioned above plus the United Energy System, *EES*) are evaluated as more influential than the rest of the field, in which the lower-ranking groups earned relatively similar marks for their influence.

A second, related question[27] was what resources are important for the actors' groups. The experts' assessment is difficult to interpret because we do not have comparable data for other countries. Still, it is obvious that that the Soviet-specific resources like ideology and charisma are expected to decline significantly in importance, while Western-type resources like hard currency earnings (which also explain the high increase for the 'natural monopolies' like *Gazprom*) are on the rise.

Diagram 1.6 The importance of political resources (first round)

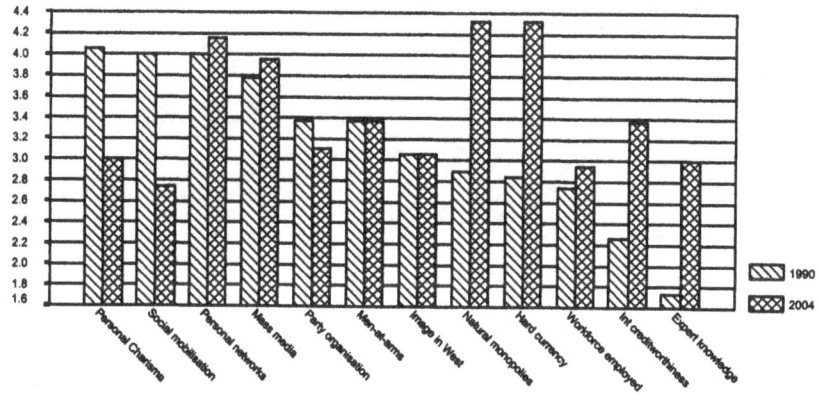

---

[27] This question was included only in the first round - 1999.

The second group of questions is related to the Russian actor groups' reactions to the opportunities and constraints provided by the global context. Here we were interested in the actors' position regarding globalization: do they pursue an active, accommodating strategy, or are they reluctant, preferring protectionist options?

The leaders in terms of a positive attitude toward the global environment in 1999 were, in the first round, the gas and oil companies, the 'oligarchs', the exporters of weapons and mineral resources, followed by the regional elites. The second round confirms these results - only the 'oligarchs' have lost some ground.

Diagram 1.7 Pursuit of global strategies in 1999 (first round)

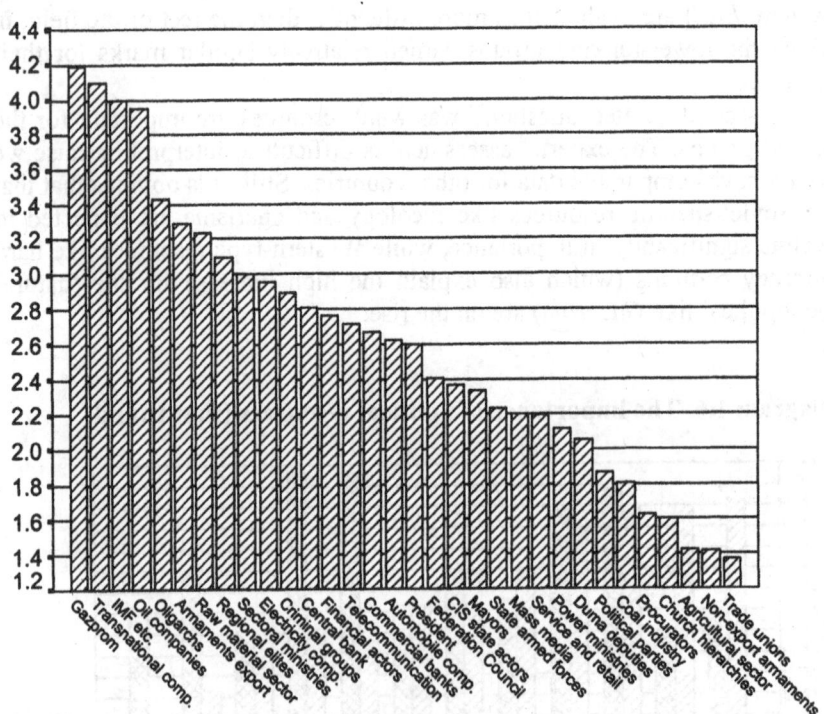

Diagram 1.8 Pursuit of global strategies in 1999 (second round)

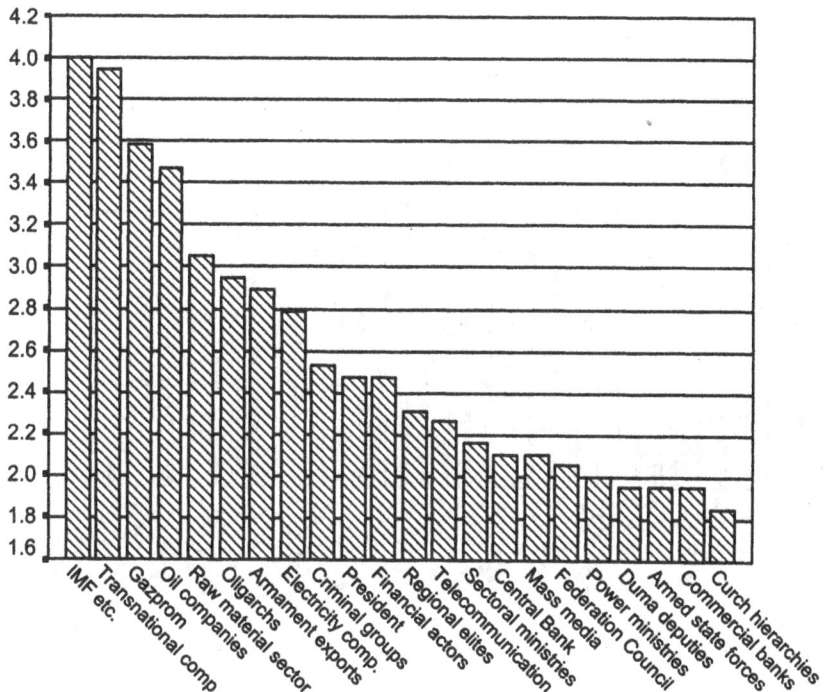

This tendency, again, is reconfirmed by the prospective assessments of the groups' positive attitudes toward globalization in 2004. *Gazprom* and the oil companies lead the field, followed by the exporters of mining and mineral products, arms exporters and the electricity giant *EES*. During the first round, it was expected that the financial and economic bloc of the government and the media would catch up dramatically in their openness toward the global environment - an assessment not confirmed by the results of the second round.

Diagram 1.9 Pursuit of global strategies in 2004 (first round)

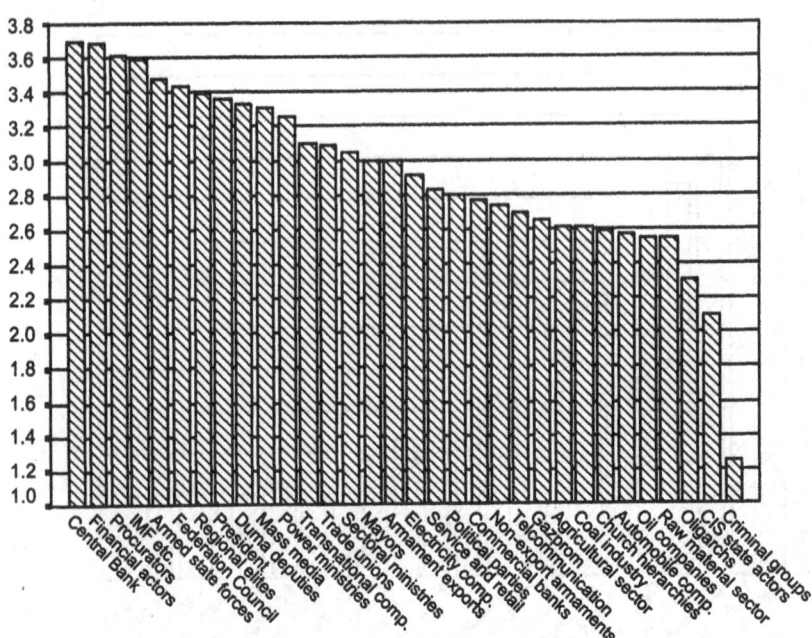

Diagram 1.10 Pursuit of global strategies in 2004 (second round)

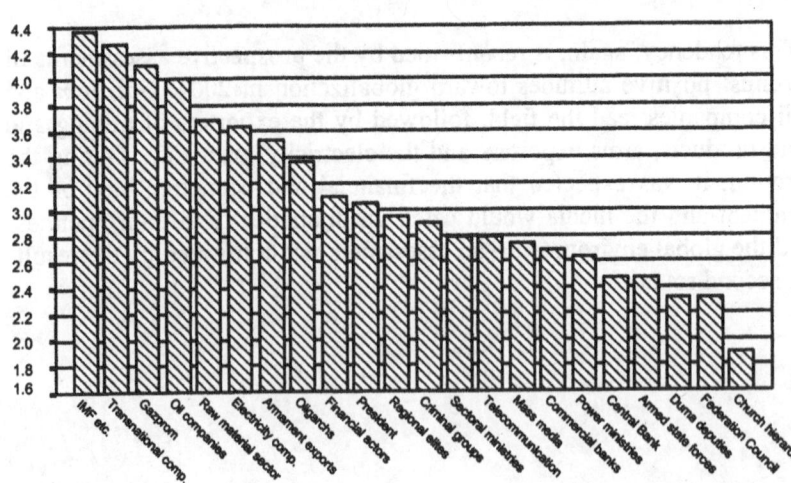

Now, what does the picture look like when we ask which groups are the most hesitant regarding the global context? In the first round, these were (for 1999) the producers of cars, the agro-industrial complex, the 'oligarchs', the mineral exporters and the commercial banks. The second round basically confirms this picture, with only two groups who are more skeptical than the broad middle field: the commercial banks and the 'oligarchs'. The results for 2004 are not significant enough to be interpreted.

Diagram 1.11 Protection from global competition, 1999 and 2004 (first round)

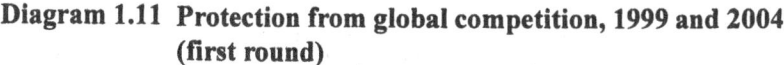

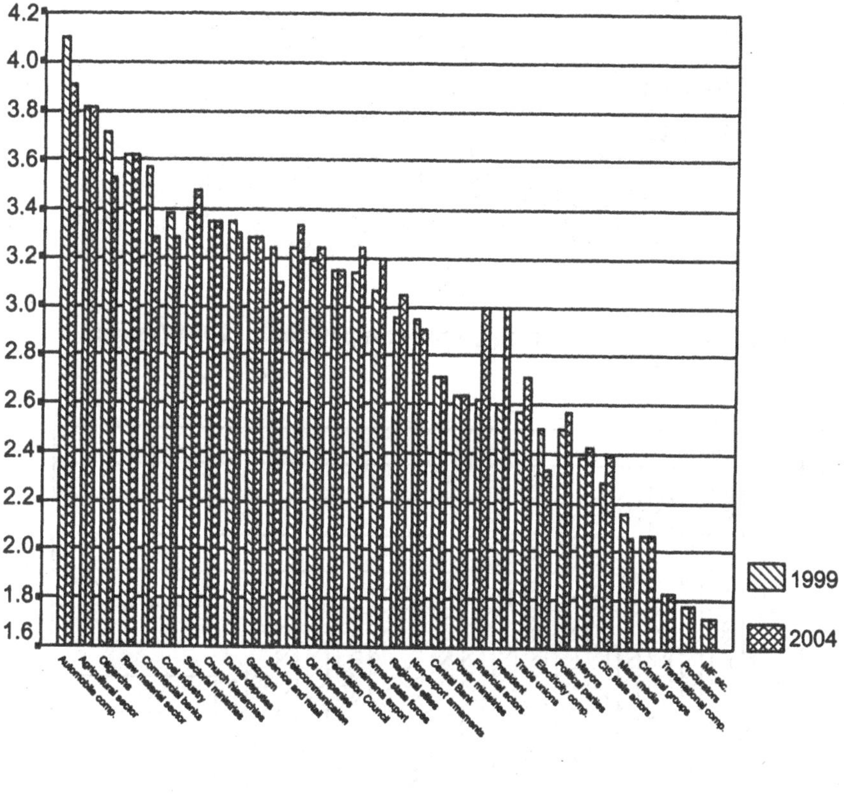

Diagram 1.12 Protection from global competition in 1999 (second round)

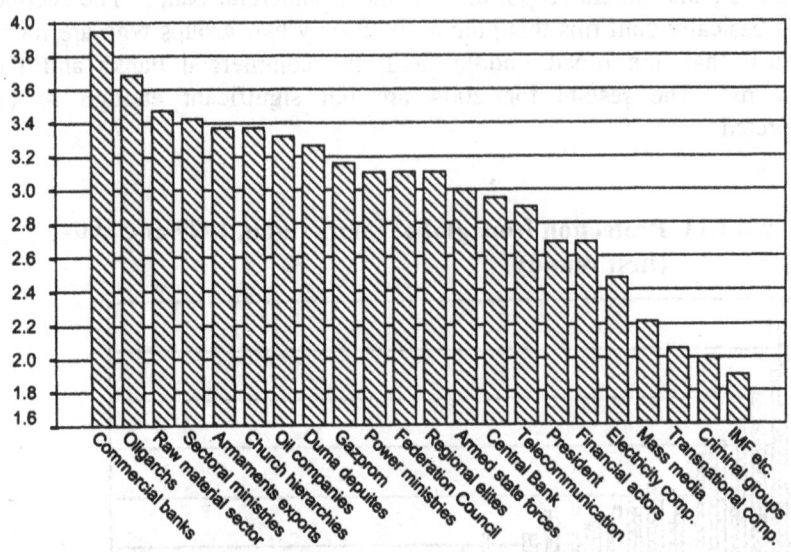

Diagram 1.13 Protection from global competition in 2004 (second round)

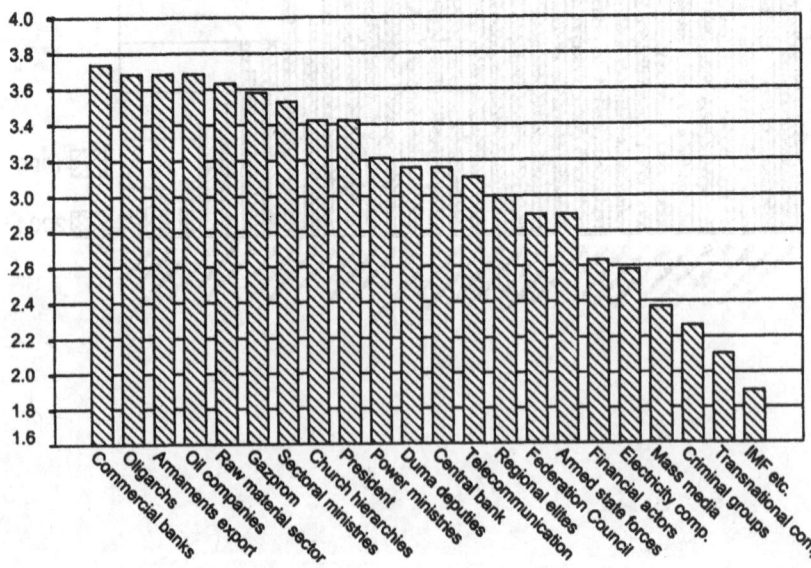

The third group of questions addresses the problem of the actors' groups' attitudes toward public and private goods. It was common knowledge that the reliability of public goods like hard budget constraints, protection of property rights, personal and general security, and, in general, the effective functioning of the state was, during the 1990s, rather low.

Consequently, we included questions on these public goods in the questionnaire. In terms of historical development, the readiness to accept the enforcement of hard budget constraints (and, thereby, to accept that inefficient firms would go bankrupt) was very low in 1990 and 1994. It was increasing in 1999 and was expected to increase further by 2004. The second round of the poll confirms this tendency with even slightly higher grades.

Diagram 1.14 Softening budget constraints (first round)

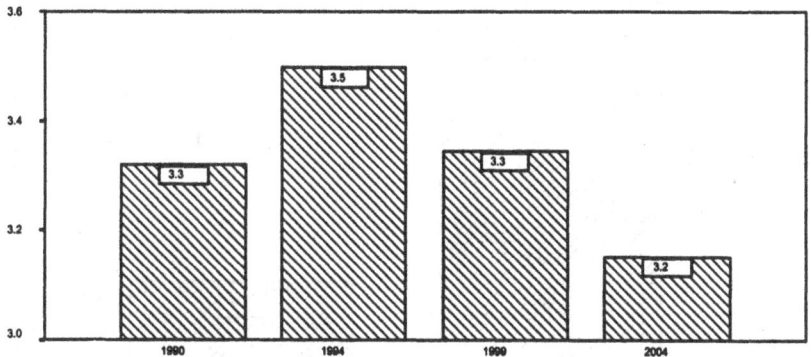

Diagram 1.15 Softening budget constraints (second round)

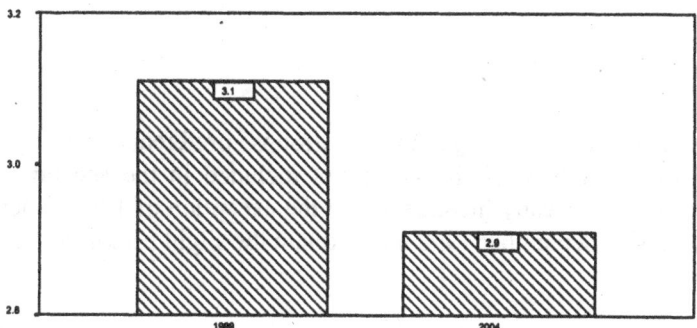

Another question related to public goods concerns the protection of property rights. Here, the general tendency is the same as for budget constraints - a steady increase in the groups' interest (on average) in living with clearly delineated property rights has been established. According to the second round, the increase between 1999 and 2004 for fixed property rights is higher (+ 0.7) than for hard budget constraints (+0.3).

Diagram 1.16 Securing property rights, 1999 and 2004 (first and second round)

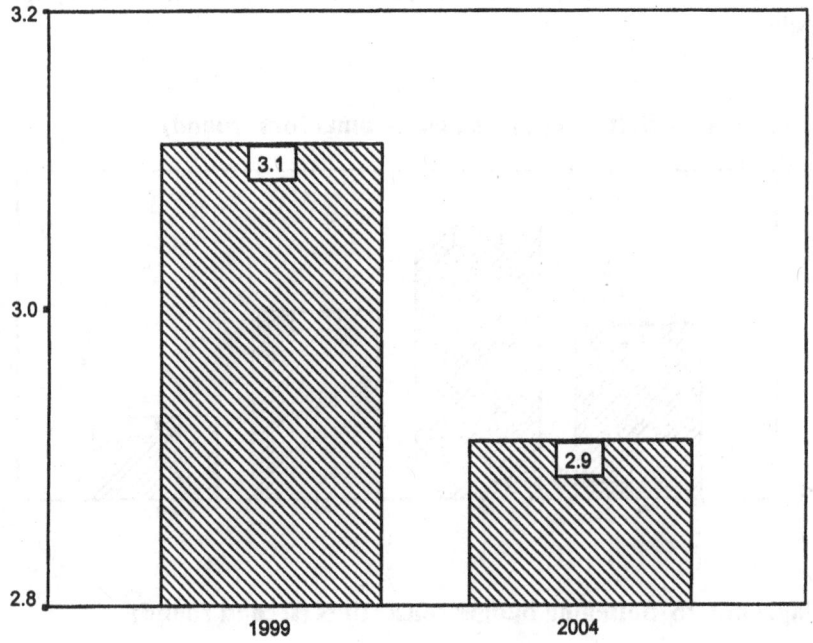

The general question regarding the groups' preferences for 'securing effective state functions' (which was not included in the second round) displayed, again, a steady increase - with the exception of 1994, where the violent events of September 1993 may explain the slight backlash.

Diagram 1.17 Importance of public goods (first round)

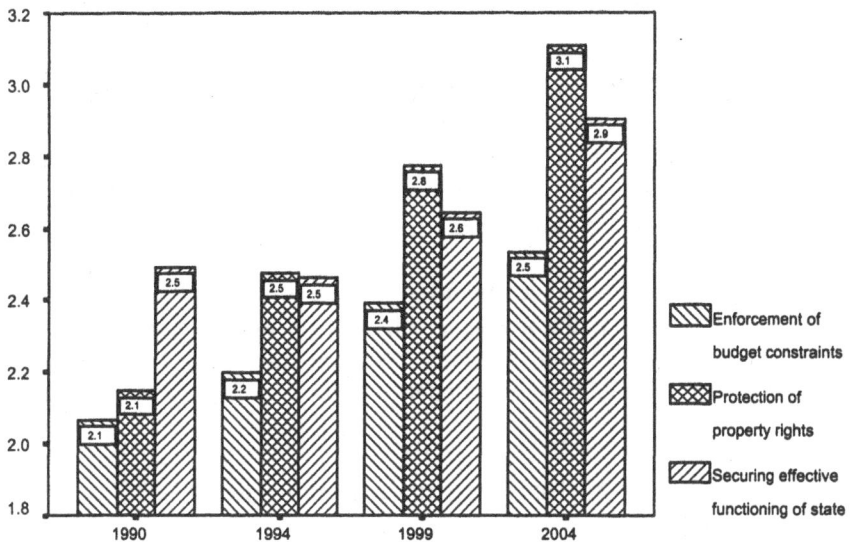

Diagram 1.18 Interests in private goods (first round)

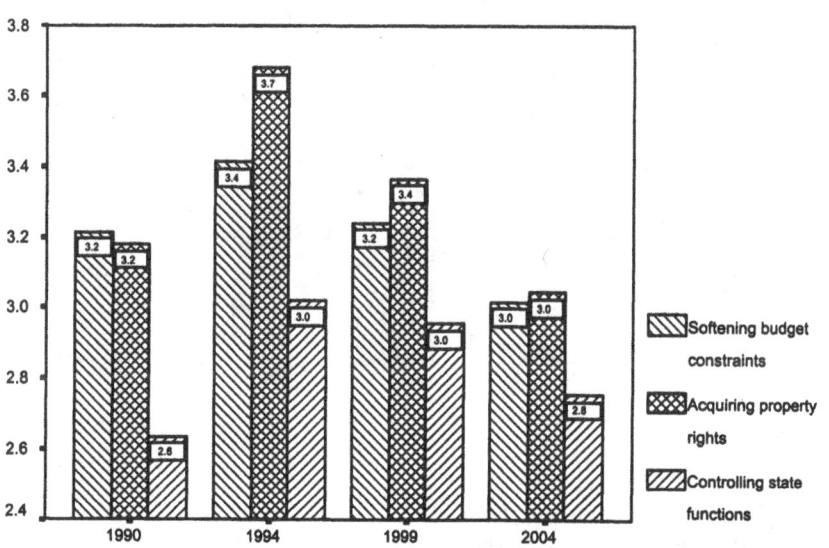

30 *Actors and Sectors between Accommodation and Resistance*

Fourth, there is a question related to the time horizons of the relevant actors. The results have been presented in the volume on institutions.[28] As explained there, the time horizons of the actors involved are very important for their strategies, and for the prospects for institutional change.[29]

So it seems appropriate to discuss the assessments of time horizons of crucial groups of actors in the context of institutions: Time horizons are decisive for elite groups and their strategic behavior. As a rule, there is a strong positive correlation between short time horizons and the behavior of a roving bandit, and vice versa: the longer the time horizons of relevant actors, the more we can expect them to cooperate and to pursue stability in a given context.[30]

Now, the expert polls we organized show a strong tendency to assume that time horizons, on the average, will become longer. The two expert polls in summer 1999 and in spring 2000 are interesting in this regard because the results are strikingly similar:

Diagram 1.19 Time horizons (aggregated) from expert poll 1999

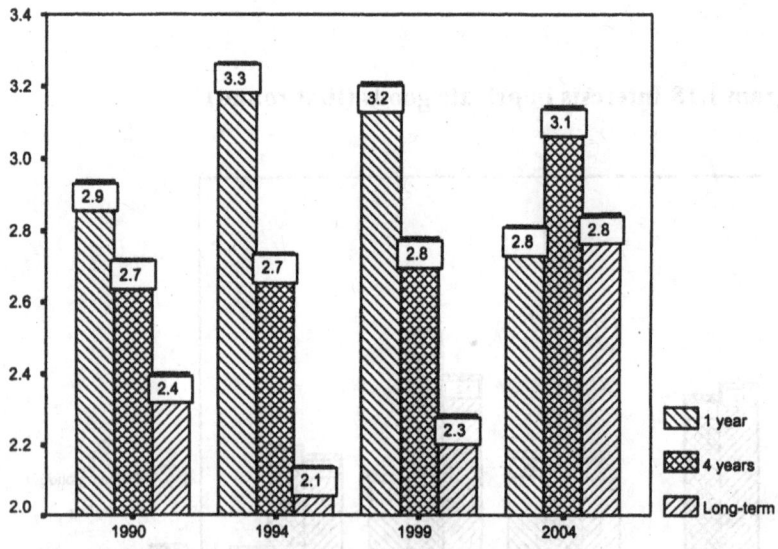

---

[28] See my introduction in Segbers 2001a.
[29] We decided to present most of the results of the expert polls we did in this frist volume.
[30] See, for example, Olson 2000, chapter 2.

Diagram 1.20 Time horizons (aggregated) from expert poll 2000

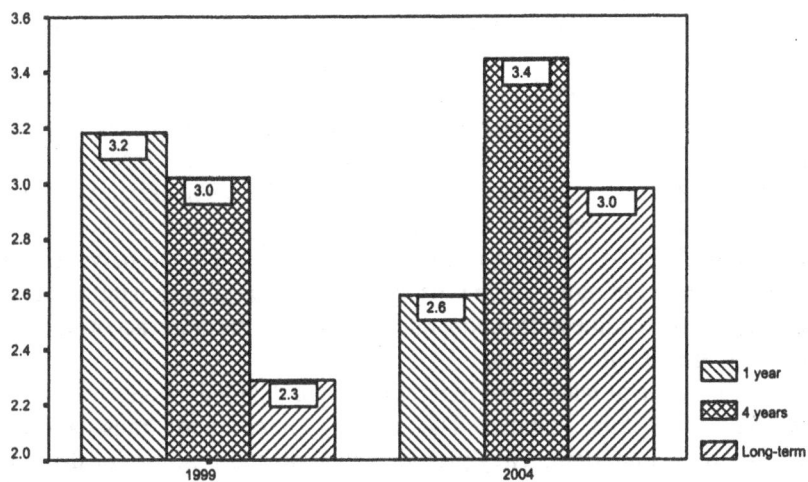

Short time horizons of up to one year became even more common in the early 1990s, reflecting the highly volatile nature of the first years of post-Soviet changes. The violent events of October 1994 probably contributed to shortening expectations of stability. Only in 1999 do we see a slight reduction in very short-term horizons; this decline is expected to continue in the next few years. Consequently, medium-term horizons (one to four years), assumed to be more or less stable in the period 1990 to 1999, are likely to grow and are expected to become the dominant form of time calculation by 2004. This medium perspective corresponds to the usual election cycles that basically shape politicians' and decision-makers' dominant time horizons for making their calculations. Long-term time spans, not very popular among decision-makers who depend on elections, are, according to our experts, dramatically increasing among Russian economic and political actors. They are expected to become more important than short-term calculations in 2004. If these assessments are correct, there will be much more grounds for building viable institutions in Russia in the future. The rationality of the actors' groups would then work in favor of reliable institutions and their enforcement.

In general, the results from the two expert polls show two things:

First, the actor groups' attitudes toward their potential to shape the rules of the game, toward globalization and toward public goods differ - sometimes significantly. This was to be expected. It reflects a social patchwork of different adaptation potentials and different levels of access to resources.

Second, there are important common trends across the groups and the two polls. In general, the imprint of Soviet attitudes and legacies is decreasing, in part quite dramatically. According to the experts, this tendency will continue until 2004.

The disappearance of expectations that soft budget controls are the rule and can be relied upon, and that property rights are insecure and permanently in flux, correlates with the increasing openness toward the global context (though this differs among actors), and it correlates especially with the lengthening of time horizons. This is good news for all who are interested in more stable prospects for Russia. It goes hand in hand with increasing readiness to cooperate with other partners according to established and monitored rules.

Now, here are at least some highlights of the detailed studies on actors as presented in this volume. The role of inter- and trans-national organizations is important. They provide expertise and funding for driving the institutional changes ahead, and for keeping the government afloat. And it is easily forgotten that much worse scenarios were in the cards in the mid-1990s. The trendy opinions which started to dominate some Western media in 2000 that the so-called Washington consensus was all ill-intended, that meaningful structural reforms should have been given priority, that the Clinton administration and the IMF 'lost Russia', that Harvard-Moscow 'transactorships' misused US taxpayers money and, in general, that Russia was not up to Western intentions and expectations tells a lot - about Western intentions and expectations.[31]

I do not deny for a moment that mistakes, indeed serious mistakes, have been made by Western governments in their Russia policy, and that Western perceptions have been derailed. But, if we discount political warmongering in Western contexts and problems related to the weakness of Russian institutions, the basic problem, again, is the idea that changes of such magnitude can be designed and implemented from top to bottom according to pre-arranged plans. As long as this thinking prevails, we will not move ahead conceptually.

It is unfortunately true that changes in formal institutions are slow, and that, consequently, some prerequisites for economic and social developments may be missing. This is the case in the banking and the whole financial sector, as demonstrated by Sarkisiants. At the same time, the ongoing transformations are dependent also on the export potential of a few sectors - namely of the gas, oil, mining and arms production

---

[31] For clues on the debate, see Lloyd 1999; Wedel 1998; Stiglitz 2000; and most convincingly Mau 2000.

enterprises. This shows the high dependency of Russia's performance on world trends, but it also betrays the uneven development of some important sectors.

The role of the Financial-Industrial Groups and of the 'oligarchs' was, and remains, ambivalent. While these conglomerats are modernizers in some respects, they are powerful rent-seekers in others. They also dominate the development of two key sectors of globalization - the media and telecommunications. At the same time, these sectors work as transponders of global influences into Russia.

The military and the agro-industrial sectors were the most powerful components of the Soviet economy, next to the energy sector. Both are allegedly depressed under the macro-economic consolidation course of the last couple of years. On closer inspection, though, there are important differences. Both sectors are highly fragmented. Successful enterprises (and the related cities and regions) coexist with depressed and idle production colossi and former *kolkhoses*. Yet while the agro-sector is almost exclusively dependent on domestic markets, the weapons producers are - partly- competitive in world markets.

Some of the true globalizers, according to Sklair, are managers, the owners of small and medium enterprises, and the middle 'class'. On all three counts, Russian globalizers are making progress.

On balance, now, it is even more important to ask what we have learned about Russian actors and their relation to the globalizing, though not homogenizing, world. Are Russian actors integrated in trans-national activities, or do they stay apart?

Some years ago, Leslie Sklair proposed a typology of those actors who represent the real globalizers. According to his model there are four groups composing a transnational capitalist class': TNC executives as the corporate fraction; globalizing bureaucrats and politicians (the state fraction); globalizing professionals (the technical fraction); and merchants and the media (the consumerist fraction).[32] One does not have to subscribe to the term 'class', but this typology is useful. It is not all-encompassing: students are missing, as are migrant artists and groups related to the service sector. Still, the question looms how these groups are represented in Russia.

The project whose results are presented here cannot answer the question with quantitative data. But what we can establish is a) that all these groups do exist in Russia, and b) that they are on the rise. At the same time, there are other groups which do not - and probably never will - belong to one of these globalizing agents. Both strata are not neatly

---

[32] Sklair 2001, 17, 22, passim.

separated. They coexist - and closely - in most parts of early 21st century Russia.

Since the crisis of 1998, there are many indicators of an economic take-off. Surely, there are external reasons - the rising prices for oil and gas have flooded billions of dollars into Russia. Certainly, there are the effects of import substitution after the 1998 crisis. And yes, data are still not totally reliable. Also, urgently needed structural reforms in the institutional realm of economic activities are lagging behind.[33] But all these caveats do not amount to denying that Russian actors and institutions are integrated, for good or ill, into the global flows of the world economy.

The riddle is gone. Time has become precious. Time and space of this vast country are becoming commoditized. The Russia patchwork has been re-integrated into the bigger patchwork of the world. Who would dare to determine what this means for Russia's people? Let history judge.

Klaus Segbers
Berlin, January 2001

---

[33] See Segbers 2001a and current press reports.

2 International Financial Organizations and Globalization by Default

OGNIAN HISHOW

Economists see globalization as affecting the location of manufacturing and gains from trade. Nations have had extensive manufacturing and trade relations in the past, but when advances in technology cause the costs of manufacturing and transport to fall below a critical value, a core-periphery relationship forms spontaneously, and nations that find themselves on the periphery suffer a decline in real income.[1] Globalization also affects the world labor market, increasing the demand for skilled labor. Research shows that, in addition, there is a rise in income inequality in the West and a widening of the North-South gap. But trade has always existed; what is new is that economies that were once separated by artificial barriers are now linked, as a result of changes in technology, in an increasingly dense network of financial interactions. This has come about so suddenly over the last few years that its complex effects are only dimly understood.[2]

The demise of the old communist system in Russia entailed a phenomenon almost unthinkable in the past - openness and a decentralized interaction with the rest of the world. In the early 1990s, imports flooded a domestic market which was greedy for goods; foreign investors looked for valuable assets to acquire; a take-over of the deposit-rich gas and oil sectors was considered, and Western banks planned to establish subsidiaries. But the performance of the Russian economy soon fell short of hopes because the core sector of the economy remained unreformed and market entry

---

[1] Krugman and Venables 1995, 857. Modern expectations concerning international economic relations are based on the old discussion over the costs and benefits of trade. Though David Ricardo argued in favor of specialization and the division of labor almost two hundred years ago, skepticism continues.
[2] Sachs 1998, 97.

barriers were left high. At the same time, there was a deepening economic crisis in which both the state and business ran out of cash. The authorities quickly identified the West as a reliable source of money necessary to overcome budget constraints and keep firms alive. As a result, Russia, because of her desperate and persistent need for cash, turned to outsourcing (that is, the export of intermediate inputs to Western firms), unlike other emerging markets tied to the rest of the world, and especially to the West.

Accordingly, this paper identifies Russia's shackled finances as the crucial link to the global economy, making cooperation with the West of paramount importance - at least until the crisis has been overcome. One might thus conclude that the Russian economy is in this way already involved in the overall process of globalization, but only partially. This, in turn, would allow one to draw the conclusion that, at least on a macro level, globalization per se is not the main issue in Russia, let alone the reason for the failure so far of reform.

The first section of this paper explains the financial dead end of the 1990s. In discussing the reasons for the country's ongoing dependence on the West for the coming period, the paper puts forward the hypothesis that, due to the financial crisis, Russian opportunities to control the pace and style of integration into the world economy have more or less disappeared. Conversely, in the long term the West will be the active actor, defining the role Russia is to play. In the second and third sections, the paper focuses on the most important partners who either cooperated with the Russians in designing their reform policy (the International Monetary Fund), or provided financial aid partially to offset the harshness of the transition (the Paris and London Clubs of Western creditors). A brief history of the Russia-IMF relationship, as well as a comment concerning the impact of IMF involvement on the economic transition, is included.

Financial Dependence on the West

As the former Soviet Union broke up, many observers believed that Russia would make a rapid transition from a command economy to a market-based economy. The country sought to join the process of globalization, claiming to be a global player, less now because of its vast military establishment than because of its ongoing integration into the world's economy and finances. Hopes arose, based on macro economic facts: namely, a large domestic market, a skilled labor force, abundant natural resources, and - last but not least - a significant relief in public expenditure stemming from the reduction of the nation's defense burden. However, some years later, Russia's main economic indicators had come to resemble those of a third-world country, and none of Russia's special advantages appeared to have contributed to a successful transition. Some remaining features of the former great power are its large area (Russia still has the biggest territory of any country in the world) and its nuclear missile capability, though the equipment is poorly maintained and in poor overall condition. In terms of economics, contemporary Russia has shrunk from being allegedly the world's second largest economy (the former USSR) to the status of a small country with a gross domestic product (GDP) as small in nominal terms as Belgium's or Poland's.

This dramatic decrease in the size of the economy placed a heavy burden on the population, since the newly independent Russian Federation inherited the Soviet structures and needed to rush to transform them. The rush to do this was unsuccessful, so that Russia did not share the situation of other post-communist countries such as Poland, Hungary, or the Baltic states, who were well advanced in their transitions. In the midst of a deepening crisis, the Moscow government had little choice but to approach the West for financial aid, and the West did not hesitate to respond. Western aid was intended to mitigate the problems, both with the budget and the balance of payments.

Budget, Inflation and External Debt

Already the former Soviet Union had begun to face increasing difficulties in balancing her budget, and the situation became unbearable in 1992, when the Gaidar government struggled with a federal deficit of up to 22% of nominal GDP. This was a clear signal that a new tax collecting system urgently needed to be set up. The tax legislation failed, however, and despite some improvements in the following period, the budgetary situation remained unsatisfactory, leading finally to the collapse of the ruble in 1998.

Table 2.1 Government budget balance (as percentage of GDP)

	1992	1993	1994	1995	1996	1997	1998	1999*
Revenues	44.2	33.6	34.6	30.2	28.3	26.2	26.0	24.1
Expenditures	65.8	41.7	45.1	35.7	36.0	33.3	28.6	22.4
Balance	-21.6	-8.1	-10.5	-5.5	-7.7	-7.1	-2.6	1.7

Note: * Estimate.

Sources: World Bank 1996, 5; *Russian Economic Trends* (1997), No. 1, 10; *Russian Economic Trends*, Monthly Updates, tables 11, 12.

Especially in 1992 and 1993, the Treasury could rely only on Central Bank loans. The Bank also poured money into the business sector and into the republics of the Commonwealth of Independent States (CIS) as well, thus fuelling inflation. There is strong evidence that the link between a loose monetary policy in the early 1990s and the exorbitant rate of inflation contributed heavily to the decay of the economy (see diagram 2.1). This is why the authorities sought to avoid further monetary expansion and looked for credits other than Central Bank loans.

Diagram 2.1 Russia's money growth (left) and inflation (right) (in %)

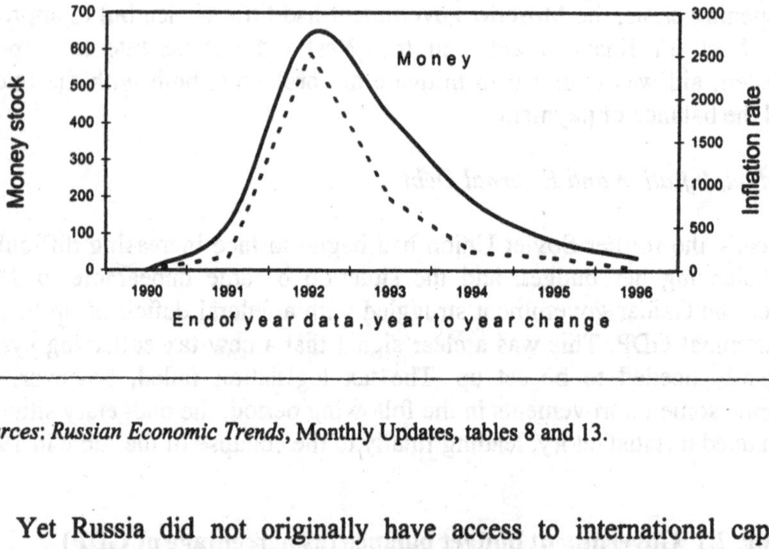

Sources: *Russian Economic Trends*, Monthly Updates, tables 8 and 13.

Yet Russia did not originally have access to international capital markets; she received external financing mostly as a result of bilateral official agreements. As of mid-1995, it seemed that the stabilization policy was increasingly successful. This improved the creditworthiness of the Russian Federation, and by the end of 1996 the first Russian Eurobonds were issued. In 1996-98, there were nine Eurobond issues with a total par value of approximately US$15.9bn. In 1992, Russia started to draw IMF and World Bank loans, intended to ease the transition bottlenecks. While the IMF ceased or slowed its disbursement programs after the ruble crisis of 1998, the World Bank continued to extend loans. Deducting repayments already made, the net debt to the Fund and other multilateral creditors currently reaches US$25bn. Total foreign debt is approximately US$50bn.

But these hard currency liabilities constitute only a fraction of the total outstanding debt of the Russian Federation. Against the background of the thaw in international relations which began in the mid-1970s, and with the stagnation in output suffered under Brezhnev, the former Soviet Union started to draw credits in the West - from governments as well from private banks. After the breakdown of the planned economy and of the Soviet Union itself, Russia decided in 1993 to assume all assets and liabilities of the former USSR, worth US$107bn. The impetus behind this crucial decision was partly a miscalculation of Russia's economic strength and growth potential, partly the ambition to continue playing a decisive international role as a great power and the heir of the Soviet state.

Diagram 2.2 Real GDP index and external debt/GDP-ratio

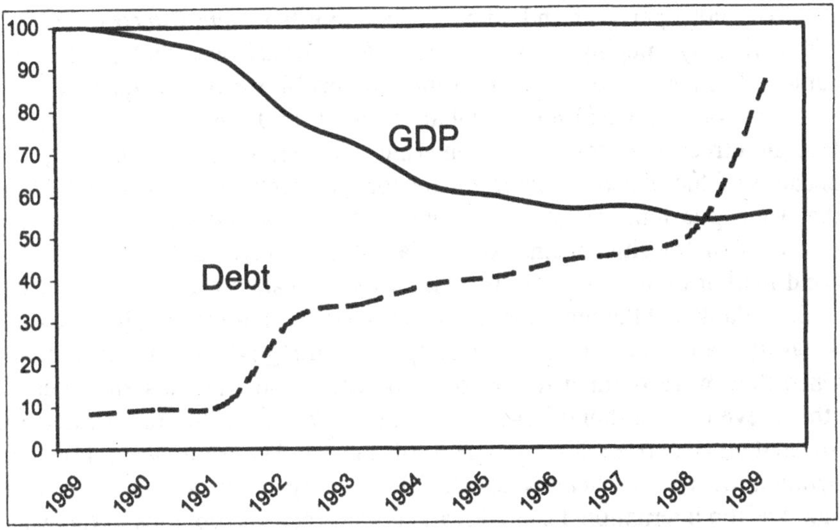

Sources: Russian Economic Trends, Monthly Updates, table 1; IMF 1999b, table 33.

Unfortunately, the evolution of Russia's economic transition was disappointing: while overall output shrank to half the 1990 level, dollar-denominated governmental debt alone soared to almost 90% of GDP (see diagram 2.2). Adding in the liabilities of local authorities and of the banking and industrial sectors, the overall amount even exceeded the nominal GDP.

Global Finances and the Second Collapse

After an awkward response to the challenges of transition in the early 1990s, Russian stabilization policy became more coherent in 1995, and was aimed at reducing the rate of inflation and building up confidence in the financial markets. By introducing a special tool - a nominal exchange rate anchor - the Central Bank struggled to break expectations of price increases, to attract more foreign investment, and to launch a growth in output. Foreign money was desperately needed to loosen budgetary constraints and build up depleted exchange reserves. Though the Treasury started issuing ruble-denominated bonds already in fall of 1993, it was three more years before foreigners were allowed to enter the domestic bond market in the fall of 1996. The reason was a rather pragmatic one: interest rates on short-term government bonds (*GKO*) had reached the astronomical level of 200% per year and above. The authorities were forced to enlarge the market by opening it to foreigners. A drawback was that outstanding ruble liabilities of the Treasury to foreign portfolio investors quickly rose, reaching roughly US$19bn in dollar terms by mid-1998. Simultaneously, foreign direct investment was entering the real economy as well, but because of the uncertain environment for entrepreneurs, less than 10% of the per capita amount going to some of the advanced Central European countries in transition came to Russia. Western investors considered the bond market more attractive because of the exchange rate guaranty of the Central Bank and the high nominal returns. Up to one-third of claims on the Treasury came into foreign hands (partly through Russian straw men). Once they were obliged to roll over the debt,[3] the Russians struggled to attract even more bond-buyers, and in 1997 and 1998 the authorities lowered entry barriers for foreigners still further. The result was a financial pyramid which was heavily exposed to the expectations and the overall mood of the international capital markets. This became obvious in the wake of the Asian financial crisis, as players in the Russian market suddenly withdrew considerable amounts in the fall of 1997 - up to US$8bn. Many of these players tried to avoid their own financial collapse, for instance Korean banks engaged in the Russian securities market. Because the Asian crisis rendered them short of cash in Korea, they reshuffled money from Russia and endangered the ruble-dollar exchange rate. To avoid speculation with the exchange rate, the Central Bank was forced to make massive raises in the prime rates, thus damping down overall prospects for growth.[4]

---

[3] Roll over: to repay current bonds by issuing new ones, resulting in a permanent growth of debt.

[4] Prohibitive interest rates discourage speculators, because they usually draw a ruble credit to buy foreign exchange (say, dollars). Following devaluation they buy rubles back to repay

Table 2.2 Dependence on international finance (in billion US$)

	1995	1996	1997	1998	1999
Capital flows to government	2.5	5.5	8.8	9.5	4.5
Repayment, net	-12.6	-10.9	-4.6	-4.1	-3.0
Foreigner's *GKO* claims	0.0	5.9	16.8	19.6	Debt rescheduled
Bond rates (%)*	162.0	85.1	26.0	45.0	20.2
Roll-over demand	0.0	5.0	4.4	8.8	0.2
Net *GKO* inflow	0.0	5.9	10.9	2.8	N/A
Demand coverage	0.0	0.9	6.5	-6.0	0.0
CBR reserve	17.2	15.3	17.8	12.2	13.2
FDI, net	1.7	1.7	3.6	1.2	0.7

Note: *Average year's data.

Sources: World Bank 1996, 5-8; Central Bank of Russia; Moscow Times, here quoted from: *Russian Economic Trends*, Monthly Updates, tables 10 and 15.

Soon markets, while continuing to mistrust the emerging Asian economies, regained their confidence in Russia, and the inflow of hot money rebounded in the spring of 1998. One reason may have been the lack of alternative investment opportunities, as returns in Europe and the USA remained low. Another explanation may have been the 1997 Russian output data, pointing to real growth - good news after six consecutive years of GDP decline. Nevertheless, nervousness grew, boosting GKO yields to historically high levels of about 100%. Capital inflows were insufficient to cover the demand, and the foreign exchange reserves of the Central Bank were depleted. In summer of 1998, they lay far below the short-term dollar-denominated liabilities of the Treasury, and it became clear that without international support, the ruble, and thus the whole economy, would collapse (table 2.2, 1998 column).

At the same time, concerns among Western governments about Russia's future forced the IMF to put together a rescue package of US$22.6bn. The attempt fell apart because it rather convinced market players that this was an opportunity to bail out, and indeed they rushed to pull out of Russia. As dollar demand soared, the ruble depreciated, and the economy collapsed for the second time since 1991. The Russian Federal

---

the credit. Their profit results from the increased ruble amount after devaluation, minus the initial credit sum. High interest rates imposed by the Central Bank discourage such transactions.

Government defaulted on its domestic debt, while the Fund faced increasing criticism.

The Balance of Payments Constraint

As a result of the financial debacle, the opportunities for Russian access to the international capital markets deteriorated, while a debt burden bigger than the nominal output threatens to suffocate the economy. Actually, it is not necessarily worrisome when a country's debt to GDP ratio exceeds 100%. There are a lot of examples of industrialized nations bearing such a load without being plunged into economic collapse, or even into recession. In the mid-1990s, Belgium, Italy, Greece and Sweden maintained debt/output ratios of 134%, 126%, 120% and 115%, respectively.[5] Yet Russia is perceived as deeply indebted because her state and overall external debts exceed the World Bank benchmark of 50%. It is worth noting that the European Monetary Union criteria place a limit on the overall government debt of member countries at 60% of GDP. There is no theoretical justification for such a limit. A thumbnail calculation can, however, be indicative: consider an average interest rate of, say, 5%; then the debt service would not exceed 3% of the GDP, or 15% of the Central government budget.[6] The historical experience of developing countries, as well as of countries in transition, shows that exceeding this level has caused such countries to run into debt problems. Thus, the question is how, if at all, Russia can sustain its debt burden.

For an answer, one should investigate the country's balance of payments more closely. The balance of payments reflects a country's financial relations with the rest of the world and also gives an idea of how national savings are being used. In an open economy, private sector savings are usually channeled into investment, but they often have to meet the financial demands of the state and of foreigners, as well. In the case of Russia, a considerable trade surplus in 1999 was been accompanied by a federal government deficit of almost zero; this is expected to be repeated in 2000. This implies a gap between savings and investment equal to the current account surplus, and gives an idea why output growth in Russia has been so disappointing. To prevent disturbances in the exchange rate, large surpluses on current account have to be offset by the same level of capital exports. What is happening in Russia is that regular capital export plus illegal capital flight are causing the country to be unable to service its international debt. Because of capital flight, the required amounts of money

---

[5] Institute of World Economics, Kiel, here quoted from Willms 1995, 247.
[6] If Central government expenditures are, for instance, one-fifth of the nominal GDP.

cannot be raised, and the authorities are forced to apply for aid. For example, the total (governmental and non-governmental) debt service due in 1999 was US$22.5bn.[7] Of that amount, Russia serviced only US$11bn. Thus, a question arises as to where the rest of the roughly US$11.5bn might have gone. Another question regarding the huge Russian trade balance is linked to Russia's permanent demand for more financial support.

In 1999, the country's trade and service balance ended up at US$22bn: US$24bn trade balance and US$2bn service balance. Interest payments amounting to US$8bn and US$3bn in repayment of principal were transmitted abroad, while nearly US$1bn in interest, as well as US$4bn in capital imports, were received (of which US$0.65bn was extended by the IMF, with the remaining US$3.35bn being foreign direct investment). Taking into account an increase of US$1.5bn in Central Bank reserves (but excluding changes in the stock of gold) and the fairly high amount of US$3.0bn in errors and omissions, the undefined amount of US$11.5bn remains. This corresponds to the money Russia refused to pay to her creditors (US$11.5bn) and may be regarded as capital flight (table 2.3).

Table 2.3 Capital flight (calculation based on the balance of payments 1999, in billion US$)

Trade balance	24.00
Service balance	-2.00
Interest paid	-8.00
Interest received	1.00
Current account	15.00
Net international reserves	-1.50
Capital balance	-13.50
Principal service	-3.00
IMF loans	0.65
Foreign direct investment	3.35
Errors and omissions	-3.00
Capital flight	-11.00

Sources: *Russian Economic Trends*, Monthly Update February 2000, table 10; IMF 1999b, table 26.

---

[7] On the difference of US$35bn US$3bn of interest and US$2bn of principal, payments per year are calculated.

Unless the economy catches up, such a balance of payments situation leaves Russia's finances dependent on Western aid for many years and severely restricts any independent reform policies.

The Role of the IMF

The IMF Rationale and Working Mechanism

When an economy runs a trade balance deficit it has certain opportunities for restoring the equilibrium: if the country's exchange rate is pegged, the government may try to boost exports and reduce imports by imposing tariffs, or it may try to impede the supply of nontradables (services) by taxing them at higher rates and thus switching domestic demand towards more imports. The latter course would mean a real devaluation of the domestic currency with a positive effect on the trade balance. If the domestic currency is free-floating, the exchange rate would immediately respond to the higher demand for imported goods, making them more expensive and thus reducing demand.

In both cases, another solution may also apply: since trade imbalances entail a shortage of foreign currency, the country can import capital (i.e. receive a credit) to pay the net import bill. Policy makers prefer this solution because of the lower social costs, at least in the short run. But markets are imperfect, and Western governments are sometimes reluctant to extend loans to emerging or developing economies. Thus, a specialized institution set up as an emergency lender and advisor on macroeconomic adjustment would be welcome.

The IMF was created (along with the World Bank) in 1944[8] to adjust current-account imbalances and manage the exchange-rate system. While playing only a marginal role in the early years after its creation, the Fund became more active in the mid-1950s. Membership increased, more countries drew on the Fund's resources, and the amounts drawn rose. In the 1970s and 1980s, the Fund played an important role in capital-account lending to recycle the revenues of oil-producing countries after the rise in oil prices.[9] In the early 1990s, countries of the former Soviet block became new members, and conditional lending procedures were further extended.[10]

---

[8] The IMF came into official existence on 27 December 1945 when 29 countries had signed the Charter agreed at a conference held in Bretton Woods, New Hampshire, USA, from 1-22 July 1944. The IMF commenced financial operations on 1 March 1947.
[9] Meltzer 1999.
[10] Conditional lending, unlike lending upon collateral, presumes that the borrowing country will fulfil certain conditions for macroeconomic adjustment.

On 1 April 2000 the IMF boasted 182 members. On joining the IMF, each member country contributes a certain sum of money, called a quota subscription, as a sort of credit union deposit. Member countries contribute 25% of their quota in gold or convertible currency, while the remaining 75% is paid in domestic currency. There are incentives, not only for developing countries, but for industrialized nations as well, to join the Fund. They are in a position to influence the Fund's policies and also benefit from use of their (convertible) currencies, as members earn interest on their quota contributions when other members borrow currency from the pool.

From the very start, quotas have been set according to economic criteria, such as national incomes and the values of external trade and payments,[11] and are reviewed every five years. In 1946, the then 35 members of the IMF paid in US$7.6bn; by 2000, IMF members had paid in US$293bn, although only half of this amount is available to the IMF for loans to members. The reason for this is that member countries pay 75% of their quotas in domestic currency, and most national currencies are not in demand outside the countries issuing them. Quotas also determine the voting strength of members. A few major industrialized countries subscribe the bulk of the quotas, and therefore hold the bulk of the votes (table 2.4).

Table 2.4 Quotas and votes, 1 April 2000 (in %)

Country	Quota	Votes
United States	17.68	17.35
Japan	6.33	6.23
Germany	6.19	6.08
France	5.11	5.02
United Kingdom	5.11	5.02
Total	40.42	39.70

Source: World Bank, 'About the IMF', <http://www.imf.org>.

A member country with a payments problem can immediately withdraw from the IMF the 25% of its quota that it paid in gold or a

---

[11] A formula known as the Bretton Woods formula was defined as follows: $Quota = (0.02Y + 0.05R + 0.10M + 0.10V) \times (1 + X/Y)$, where Y was national income in 1940; R was gold and dollar balances on 1 July 1943; M was average imports during 1934-38; V was the maximum variation in exports during 1934-38; and X was average exports during 1934-38. A multi-formula approach was adopted later, and formulas were last modified in 1982-83, although their basic structure was retained.

convertible currency. If this is insufficient for its needs, a member may borrow up to three times, and under certain circumstances even more, of what it paid in as its quota subscription. Sometimes, instead of being paid in convertible currency, a country is paid in an asset called the SDR (special drawing right, introduced in 1969). A value based on the average value of the world's five major currencies is assigned to the SDR. Today, SDRs in existence account for about 10% of the total quota.

The highest authority of the IMF resides in its Board of Governors, which consists of one Governor and one Alternate Governor, usually drawn from the ministers of finance or heads of central banks of the member countries. As it normally meets only once a year, the Board of Governors has delegated many of its powers to the IMF's Executive Board. This Board generally meets three times a week at IMF headquarters in Washington, and consists of 24 Executive Directors that are appointed by member countries.

The Executive Board is chaired by the IMF's Managing Director, currently Germany's Horst Köhler, who is elected by the Executive Board He serves a five-year term (renewable for successive terms) and is also the head of the organization's approximately 2,200 staff members, representing 123 nationalities.

The Funds's Policy towards Russia

Russia became an IMF member on 1 June 1992, with a quota of ca. US$6bn, or ca. 2.5% of the total. It started immediately to draw loans for balance of payments support and to finance the fiscal deficit of the federal government (indirectly real sector modernization, structural adjustment programs, etc). While the Russians invested great hopes in the Fund for providing them with cash, its policy toward Moscow was from the very beginning somewhat ambiguous. On the one hand, it announced generous aid; on the other hand, the aid was been partially withheld, thus fueling patriotic and nationalistic criticism of 'foreign dictates'. The Fund managed to provide only 11% of the assistance it was called upon to deliver in 1992: that is, US$1bn instead of US$9bn. Even the figure of US$1bn overstates the aid, since the US$1bn was granted on condition that it not be spent, but rather held as a bank reserve. In 1993, the IMF repeatedly delivered only a fraction of the assistance that was expected - a total of US$1.5bn out of US$13bn. The fund rejected additional transfers with the argument that the Russian authorities had not implemented appropriate stabilization and structural reform policies. Critics argued, however, that the IMF was also responsible for the shortfall - by failing to devise a working framework to match Russian stabilization efforts with external financing.[12]

During the early 1990s, the subject of discussion was not whether the IMF should insist on proper handling of budget deficits, which were widely seen as the main source of inflation, and thus as an obstacle to investment and growth. A debate arose on the question of how to handle the problem: while the Fund advocated cuts in expenditures, analysts called on it to extend more money to the Russian authorities in order to finance the deficits in a non-inflationary way. The debate with the IMF was, therefore, not about goals, but about means to achieve those goals. The IMF was criticized for pressing for greater budget expenditure cuts when such cuts were economically and politically unjustified. While many budgetary subsidies could have been cut, it was also true that many areas of social spending should have been kept in line with a more sensitive approach to Russia's domestic realities. The IMF's obsessive focus on budget cuts rather than deficit financing deflected Russian attention from social spending, creating the impression that a market economy causes poverty. The IMF's argument that financing a budget deficit only postpones the difficulties while accumulating public debt for the future was questionable also on the grounds that a trade-off between rapid stabilization and indebtedness was possible at the time. Later, the economy shrank while foreign debt increased, and this opportunity had passed.

The uncertain relationship between the Fund and Moscow continued in the following years. Stand-by and Extended Facilities (EFF) were approved in 1995 and 1996. The EFF, projected for a three-year period, illustrated the typically shaky approach of the Fund toward Russia's transition policies: only about 40% of the contracted amount was disbursed. Again, the Fund argued that the economic reform process had been too protracted. Yet, amazingly enough, when the stability of Russia was perceived to be at stake in mid-1998, the Fund endorsed even bigger aid - the infamous rescue package of US$22.6bn. As pointed out earlier, the aid did not work, partly because the Fund failed to make clear how the money was to be used. A small sum, US$1bn, was sent to the Treasury for inclusion in the country's budget. The Russian Finance minister at the time, Mikhail Zadornov, asked the IMF to give more money to his ministry, in order to keep Russia's debt service on track. Instead, the Fund added US$3.8bn to the dollar reserves of the Central Bank, where they would be available to private Russian banks trading rubles for dollars.[13] As a result, market players believed the Federation's short-term liabilities to be larger than the assets available, and

---

[12] Sachs 1994b, 6.
[13] Powell and Hosenball 1999.

pressed for their money, triggering a ruble collapse. In the following period, the Fund abstained from further financing, until - roughly one year after the August 1998 crisis - it announced a new US$4.5bn credit line. This was an accounting transaction which ensured that the proceeds could be used only to repay the Fund. The IMF had no choice but to extend the credit; otherwise, the country's ability to service its debt to the IMF would have been at risk. A default by Russia would have dealt a hard blow to the Fund's credibility: since 1993, the IMF has lent Russia more than US$20bn, making the country its largest debtor (table 2.5). The loan allowed the Russians a respite to continue market reforms; it offered other benefits as well, such as the additional funds being provided by the World Bank, and the possibility of reaching agreements with the London and Paris Clubs on restructuring the Soviet debt.[14]

Table 2.5 IMF-approved loans to selected members (in million US$ as of March 2000)

Russia	Mexico	Indonesia	Korea	Brazil
27,664	25,137	23,142	21,679	17,270

Source: IMF, Country Info 'Member's Position in the Fund', <http://www.imf.org>.

The IMF Money-laundering Scandal

After the ruble crisis of August 1998, the world started to take a closer look at the financial affairs of the Russians. Doubts arose as to whether some portion of the IMF loans had been misused, since Russia's banks moved billions of dollars abroad in the months after the crash. Benex, a company that specializes in funneling Russian money abroad, may have redirected IMF dollars to the Bank of New York. President Boris El'tsin and his family were dragged deeply into the unfolding financial scandal. In the end, probes in the United States and Switzerland indicated that money laundering through the Bank of New York and other American and European banks had indeed taken place. The US Customs Service monitored the activities of Russian immigrants based in Philadelphia who, over the past two years, may have moved an estimated US$500mn through accounts in 15 to 20 banks in the Northeast of the USA. The money came from Russia, spent a day or two in American banks, and was then

---

[14] Westin 1999, 6.

transferred to tax havens offshore. Some of the funds may have been diverted via the Kremlin from IMF transfers to the Russian Federal budget.

Actually, these suspicions remain hardly proven. There is no clear sign that any laws were broken in the disposition of the vast sums received from the IMF. The purpose of the July 1998 loan was to increase the amount of dollars on hand in Russia's Central Bank, in order to support the ruble and repay creditors. A review by the accounting firm Price Waterhouse Cooper showed that the US$3.8bn went, as planned, to the Central Bank, which later sold US$4.1bn of hard currency to about 20 of Russia's major private banks, most of which were, however, virtually insolvent by then. Even if sums were siphoned off, they could have been stolen from the budget, since the IMF transfers were added to the budget revenues. This, however, should be no concern of the IMF. No evidence has been presented that the money laundering scandal involved the diversion of Fund loans.[15]

An overwhelming percentage of the IMF transfers has left Russia legally, via transactions by commercial banks. Ironically, the Fund encourages free capital flows, according to article VIII of its charter.

The Western Involvement Assessed

Did the IMF Fail?

For roughly 20 years, the IMF has been engaged in a remarkable expansion of its activities. Public criticism has grown concomitantly. While economists have been relatively reserved, politicians, lawyers, and academics have dominated the discussion. For instance, in a recent book and article the anthropologist Wedel, barely acquainted with economics, questions Western aid to Russia, asking whether billions of IMF dollars would have been necessary in 1998 if previous aid had been effective.[16] But if aid is ineffective, why does Russia, like other emerging markets, apply for it? The answer is that there are not many sources right now for emergency financing of current account deficits, and Russia desperately needs the cash which its unreformed economy cannot deliver. Without aid, more strains on the balance of payments, a fall in government demand, exchange rate depreciation and inflation would have resulted, harming the economy. Most analysts agree that the Fund's leverage for encouraging reform ideas containing critical elements, such as tax or legal reform, is not strong enough. Rather, the IMF needs to respect the sensitive Russian

---

[15] Fisher 1999a.
[16] Wedel 1999, 7.

public and the sovereignty of the country: i.e. to rely on officials, especially in Russia, where problems arise from the Byzantine interaction of business and political interests, and where the forces of reform have often been defeated by those seeking control over natural resources and the nascent market economy. The Fund's dilemma results from its commitment to continue supporting reforms in Russia, and to avoid errors. So it has moved ahead, learning by doing. The Russian authorities lied about the level of Central Bank reserves in 1996, and the IMF extended money. It subsequently came to light in an audit that the level of reserves had been artificially lowered through the transfer of sums off-shore, and the IMF belatedly tightened controls over the use of its funds.

Much criticism results from a misunderstanding of how IMF money transfers work. The Fund provides general balance of payments assistance. When the Russian government purchases foreign exchange from the IMF with rubles, it deposits the ruble amount in an account maintained by the IMF in the Central Bank of Russia. The foreign exchange provided by the IMF is deposited in an account maintained by Moscow in the country whose currency is being used (say, the USA or Germany) and becomes part of the international reserves of the Central Bank of Russia, freely available for use in the same manner as all other international reserves. Therefore, there is no meaningful way in which the use of IMF resources can be tracked, as lending by a commercial bank for a specific project might be.

Thus, the conclusion to be drawn is that IMF policy towards Russia does not show a very different pattern from that towards other big debtors. The IMF has shown little interest in encouraging appropriate institutional reforms. This assessment is linked to the general question whether the IMF-mechanism is flawed or not, and it goes beyond the particular Russian case. While IMF emergency loans to cover current account deficits may seem like the best solution, analyses show the Fund's programs moving a country's balance of payments toward equilibrium by raising interest rates, reducing spending, and increasing taxes.[17] This fuels criticism from the left about austerity recipes from Washington, while outraging the right because of the waste of money.

At issue is whether IMF lending increases the risks in the international financial system by playing down the moral-hazard problem. It results in too much short-term lending by private banks and too few losses on risky loans for 'gamblers'. Another problem is the ambiguity of the effects of conditional lending. Lending may encourage reform, for example, by reducing transition costs and strengthening the position of reformers. But lending may also delay reform by permitting governments to continue

---

[17] Krugman 1999, 112.

inappropriate policies. Critics of the Western approach to reforms in Russia argue that the pace has been too fast for a society not accustomed to managing the problems resulting from private, as opposed to centralized, decision-making. As to the speed of reform, there were two episodes of shock therapy in Russia - price liberalization in 1992, and privatization in 1992-95.[18] In both cases, the decision to move fast was made by the Russian authorities. In a different political environment, a more gradual process of privatization, following the creation of the legal and institutional framework for a market economy, could have made sense. But this was not the view of Russian policymakers. There are other respects in which reform has been too slow, rather than too fast.[19] The Russian economy remains rather closed by some standards. Only about 2% of business assets are in foreigners' hands, and foreign banks' share of capital in banks working in Russia stands at 12.6%, against 50% and more in some advanced post-communist countries in transition.[20] If Russia had implemented reforms in 1996, its economy would now be stronger, incomes would be higher, and it would have avoided the 1998 collapse. This, admittedly, makes the IMF partly, but not mainly, responsible for the failure of reform.

The Importance of the Paris and London Clubs

The former Soviet Union realized already during Perestroika that it was incapable of servicing its hard currency-denominated debt; this problem became acute after the economic collapse of the early 1990s. The only way out of the difficulty was to reschedule, and this is what Moscow did. Between 1993 and 1996, it signed four rescheduling agreements with the Paris Club. While the first three provided only temporary relief, the agreement of April 1996 covered US$38.5bn to be repaid within 25 years, with a long grace period of six years. Following this success, roughly one hundred London Club member banks signed a similar agreement on 6 October 1997, allowing Russia to stretch out service of its US$32bn debt over 25 years, after a six-year grace period as well. As a result, the real payments amounted to only 40% of the payments due (table 1.6). The reduced debt service expenditures amounted to a total saving of US$75bn - the considerable amount of roughly half the 1999 nominal GDP.

---

[18] Åslund 1999b.
[19] Fisher 1999a.
[20] 'Foreigners own 12.6% of Russian bank capital', in *Financial Times* (1999), 25 October.

Table 2.6 Financial relief through restructuring and payment deferrals (in billion US$)

	Debt service		Saving	Debt-service ratio (in %)		Saving (in %)
	due	real	due - real	due	real	due - real
1993	20.7	3.6	17.1	31.8	5.5	26.3
1994	20.2	4.6	15.6	29.8	6.8	23.0
1995	20.2	7.1	13.1	24.4	8.6	15.8
1996	18.1	7.1	11.0	20.0	7.8	12.1
1997	13.7	7.4	6.3	15.4	8.3	7.1
1998	13.1	7.8	5.3	17.5	10.4	7.1
1999*	17.5	11.0	6.5	25.0	15.7	9.3
Total	123.5	48.6	74.9	-	-	-

Note: * Estimate.

Sources: IMF 1999b, tables 33, 34.

Nevertheless, Russia's financial woes generated additional demands for money, and the government pressed for even more debt relief. The West responded again, and with even greater generosity: the London Club in February 2000, agreed to a debt forgiveness for Russia equal to about US$10.6bn. Moreover, not only was about one-third of the some US$32bn in loans written off, but debtor and creditors agreed that Russia would repay the remaining US$21.2bn in stages, staggered over a 30-year period.

The burden of scheduled repayments over the next several years is relatively low. For the year 2000, Russia's debt to London Club institutions is to be cut from US$1.45bn to US$480mn. The extra US$1bn saved represents a hefty favor, given that Russia's entire federal budget in 2000 is equal to only about US$25bn.[21] The deal goes at the expense of Western banks and taxpayers, since banks will write off these assets and deduct the losses from the tax amount due.

Nevertheless, the Paris Club is expected to help too, as the London Club deal will provide only slight debt service relief. The Russian authorities have unambiguously indicated that Russia will work for rescheduling terms comparable to the terms negotiated with the London Club. Despite the concerns of Germany, Moscow's largest creditor by far, the West will have to move to respond.[22] This seems inevitable, because

---

[21] Semenenko 2000.
[22] 'Germans hold out against Russian debt forgiveness', in *Financial Times* (2000), 15 February.

Russia's ability to service even a rescheduled debt will depend on the pace of recovery of the economy. Output contracted by one-half in the 1990s, and it will be decades before the backlog is offset. Consequently, the West will be bound to Russia's finance troubles for decades to come.

Conclusion

In summary, the Western financial contribution to Russian reforms has been significant and is expected to continue. Unfortunately, results have been small because the Western approach was too hesitant. Only weak links between lending and structural transformation were established, and reform efforts were often torpedoed by moral hazard effects. Admittedly, there was no previous experience on which to base transformation policies in Russia. For security reasons, the EU and the US hoped to transform Russia into a more democratic society with a market economy. But the G-7 governments were either unwilling or believed themselves unable to obtain more funding from their parliaments. The amounts provided were lower than the sums demanded; thus, the West's ability to enforce Russian commitments was restricted. Like most borrowers, the Russians quickly realized that the West had a stake in democratic change and the development of a market economy. The IMF sometimes delayed or withheld payments. As in previous cases, however, the Fund, the US, and the Europeans did not want the program to fail. The Russians understood that the Fund's 'commitment to success' weakened its ability to enforce threats. Regression analyses have suggested that the IMF may have tended to overstate the macroeconomic data to justify lending.[23] Moscow's Western partners have also been prepared to swallow such striking facts as widespread corruption, failure to pursue privatization of land, and maneuvers to reduce reported budget deficits through refusal to pay civil servants, coal miners, soldiers, and others.[24] Further, the IMF has tolerated the combination of large trade surpluses and massive capital flight, while extending credits to relieve the balance of payments. Worst of all, the West was aware that private banks siphoned off money abroad on behalf of government officials and their political supporters.

A critical question is whether IMF policies have actually delayed reform, both directly by lending, and indirectly by encouraging large inflows of 'hot money'. Analysts point out that there is no single answer for all countries. As a rule of thumb, the more committed a country is to

---

[23] Beach, Shavey and Isidro 1999, 1-21.
[24] Meltzer 1999.

making a fast transition, the less will be the country's reliance on official lending. In the case of transition 'laggards', however, it seems clear that IMF lending, and the private capital flows that follow, permit unbalanced budgets, fragile financial systems, government subsidies through the banking system to specific programs, and corruption to continue longer and at higher levels. The IMF loans to the Russian government obviously affected the commitment of the Russian authorities to improve tax collection or cut subsidies. But once again, it is first and foremost the national government that bears the responsibility for successful reforms, while international lending and advice can only support transition and mitigate its overall pain.

3 The Origins and Management of the Federal Debt to the World

ARTOS G. SARKISIANTS

The cardinal question raised by the recent world financial market turmoil is why the announcement of Russia's forced debt restructuring in August 1998 had such a dramatic effect on emerging market economies' access to global financial markets. The internal post-Soviet changes as well as the external context heavily influence current developments in the country. The serious shift in Russian funding policy was the result of several factors (including an IMF package) that affected both the revenue side of the equation and the relative cost of domestic as opposed to international financing. The Russian Federation has become one of the key borrowers on international markets. And the financial crisis almost ruined temporarily all the progress Russia had made within the framework of a comprehensive restructuring of Soviet-era debt. Although not especially high by the standards of most developing countries, the current level of total debt in Russia (state and private) is nevertheless remarkable. In comparison with 1998, by 2000 it had increased by 6%, to US$215bn. This article considers the causes, structure and system of the management of Russia's sovereign debt. At the same time, the question of the influence of globalization and, especially, the effect of the last international debt crisis on Russia and the effect of the Russian crisis on global financial markets is taken up in the present analysis.

The Causes of the Russian Debt Crisis

The dramatic change in funding policy was the result of several factors affecting both the revenue side of the equation and the relative cost of domestic as opposed to international financing. The essential cause of the crisis of August 1998 lies in the enduring problem of tax collection. Russia's outdated fiscal system has actively discouraged corporate tax declaration. As a result, the tax burden has fallen heavily on the small business sector of the economy, and the poor record in this area has had a serious effect on federal revenues. The collection of personal taxation is also a problem: more than half the Russian population simply does not pay tax. There have been attempts to improve this record, but the culture of non-payment now seems firmly entrenched. Taxation receipts in Russia (taking all levels of government together) are currently about 13% of GDP, compared with a range of 30-35% in most developed countries.[1] This shortfall was the major reason behind the build-up of domestic and then foreign debt that ultimately led to the August crisis.

While the government was failing to make progress on the taxation issue, it also suffered from a shortfall in the sort of extraordinary revenues that might have tided it over a short-term crisis. It was the government's misfortune to attempt to sell its majority holding in the oil company *Rosneft'* when world oil prices were at their lowest level this decade. The decline in the world price of oil has also been a problem for the country's balance of payments. The devaluation of the ruble ought to help the current account, although since many of Russia's commodity exports are denominated in hard currency, export performance may not improve that much.

In 1997-98, as federal revenues continued to fall short of requirements at the beginning of 1998, it became increasingly expensive for the government to make up the difference through recourse to the domestic debt market. The key problem here was the position of the currency, with its implications for domestic interest rates. Before the effective devaluation of the ruble in August, Russia had suffered three waves of speculation against its currency in the past twelve months. In each case the source of the attack was in Asia, where devaluation in Thailand and Indonesia encouraged waves of speculation against perceived candidates for devaluation in other regions. Currencies tied to the dollar or trading in a fixed range, such as Brazil's real and the Russian ruble, were obvious targets. Until the August devaluation, the ruble had been trading inside a range that extended 15% on either side of a central rate of Rbl6.2/US$.[2] This allowed more flexibility than did practices in much of Asia before the

---

[1] 'Federalnyi budget 2000', in *Vedomosti* (2000), 17 January; 'A bear with a sore head', in *International Financial Review, Review of the Year 1998* (1999), 48-51, here 49.

[2] Tsentral'nyi Bank Rossiiskoi Federatsii (1999), *Biulleten' bankovskoi statistiki No. 1*, 15.

crisis - where currencies were pegged to the US dollar or traded within a narrow band - and it was thought that the government could resist the pressure to sell.

Given this room for maneuver, the Central Bank declared itself determined to protect the ruble, and thereby safeguard the main (indeed only) economic achievement of the Russian government. The Central Bank reacted to the pressure against the ruble with sharply higher interest rates, accompanied by intervention in the currency markets. Rates were raised to a high of 150%, which pushed the yields on *GKOs*[3] towards an annualized rate of 200-250%.[4] At this level of yield, the Russian government could clearly not continue financing itself on the domestic market. By contrast, it seemed relatively easy to raise money abroad. Russia was not a highly indebted country, judging by its ratio of gross external debt to GDP of less than 50%,[5] so this switch was not unsustainable in itself. Although emerging market bond spreads had widened since the beginning of the Asian crisis, the cost of dollar funding still represented a big saving for the government.

First, the Federation raised DM1.25bn of seven-year money in a deal lead-managed by Deutsche Bank and Warburg Dillon Read. This was followed by a L750bn five-year issue via JP Morgan and Credito Italiano. After that, Russia made larger and more frequent forays into the markets. Goldman Sachs lead-managed a US$1.25bn five-year deal at a spread of 650bp over US Treasuries.[6] JP Morgan and Deutsche brought a US$2.5bn 30-year issue with a 10-year put. The spread on that occasion was 753bp over Treasuries.[7] At the beginning of August, when the Russian Federation had already raised US$11.3bn, the external funding ceiling was raised again, this time to US$14bn.[8] Although the Finance Ministry promised to stay away from the Euromarkets for a couple of months, there was a clear intention to issue a new international bond in the last two months of the year.

Despite these foreign currency issues, the government was increasingly caught up in the spiraling cost of servicing its short-term ruble debt. In mid-

---

[3] *GKO* (*Gosudarstvennye Kratkosročhnye Obligatsii*) - short-term government bonds.
[4] Tsentral'nyi Bank Rossiiskoi Federatsii (1999), *Biulleten' bankovskoi statistiki No. 1*, 17.
[5] Calculations of author, based on World Bank 1998b and Tsentral'nyi Bank Rossiiskoi Federatsii (2000), *Biulleten' bankovskoi statistiki No. 1*.
[6] The abbreviation bp stands for basis points - 1/100 of 1%, i.e. 0.01%. Used to express yield spread or differential.
[7] Farrow 1998a, 40.
[8] Farrow 1998b, 148.

summer 1998, foreshadowing what was to come, Russia employed Eurobonds for a *GKO* swap to restructure existing domestic debt. The *GKO* swap was arranged by Goldman Sachs as a US$5.9bn transaction, which completely surprised the markets.[9] Holders of *GKO*s were able to exchange them for seven- and twenty-year Eurobonds. As confidence in the Russian management team ebbed away, the spread on this and other sovereign papers continued to increase.

For more than a year *GKO* was almost a swear word for foreign and local investors in the Russian domestic debt. In February 2000, Russia revived its domestic Treasury bill market by placing two new issues at very low prices, and the government promised the paper would not be the first brick of another ill-fated debt pyramid. The Finance Ministry sold Rbl4.46bn worth of 98- and 196-day T-bills, both of which were heavily oversubscribed. The 196-day paper, proceeds from which can be used to buy dollars for repatriation under a restructuring scheme for previous *GKO*s, was sold at a premium and its average yield was an unprecedented minus 0.54%.[10]

The new *GKO*s were meant as an aid to the market, in need of tools to regulate liquidity, rather than to raise budget cash. The *GKO* pyramid will not repeat itself, if the government implements a correct policy without getting carried away borrowing on the domestic market to plug gaps caused by low revenues. However, the high price of 100.29% for the 196-day paper meant that foreign investors were still unwilling to operate on the market.[11]

While Russia was looking abroad to tide it over the crisis in the domestic markets, it was also seeking to establish a more solid base for the future with the backing of a new IMF package, upon which agreement was finally reached, including contributions from the World Bank and the Bank of Japan, and totaling US$22.6bn.[12] This parcel, being much larger than the US$10-15bn originally expected, was a calculated risk,[13] and showed the commitment of the G7 countries[14] (expressed via the IMF) to supporting Russia. Yet although in terms of covering short-term debt, it was larger than that of Korea or Thailand, it was too small to be effective.[15] That the

---

[9] 'Emerging Market Debt', in *International Financing Review* (1998), No. 1243, 68.
[10] *Reuters* (2000), 23 February.
[11] Ibid.
[12] Tsentral'nyi Bank Rossiiskoi Federatsii (1999), *Biulleten' bankovskoi statistiki No. 1*, 19.
[13] Fisher 1999b.
[14] The G7 consists of France, Germany, Japan, Great Britain, the USA, Canada and Italy.
[15] See also Hale 1998.

default and devaluation package was announced so soon after this vote of support was evidence of the depth of the country's problems. It also served to show the limitations of IMF support, with worrying implications for those Asian economies also under the Fund's tutelage.

In essence the IMF program resembled the private confidence-building strategy implied in the Mexican rescue package of 1995. But the difference from the Mexican package was that in the case of Russia, no currency devaluation preceded the exercise. When the ruble position finally proved unsustainable, the support that was intended to come from the IMF's mere presence proved illusory. Nonetheless, initially the IMF agreement did offer the embattled government a definite lifeline. The fund released the first tranche of US$4.8bn, which was swiftly used to defend the currency, and as part of the package the World Bank approved a US$1.5bn structural adjustment loan.[16] The World Bank facility had a grace period of three years and a tenure of seven years, compared with the usual seventeen years. The loan was to be released in stages over 1998-99, but only as long as Moscow stuck to the agreed reform program. This included specific measures, such as *Gazprom* setting a standard contract for carrying gas through its network. But the moratorium package and Kirienko's replacement by Viktor Chernomyrdin reopened the whole question of G7 support.

If any money is forthcoming, it could still provide a useful breathing space for the new administration. But in the medium term, Russia will have to put its own house in order. There could be a role for some external funding, if any is on offer, but it is essential for the government to seek to fund itself. This can only be done through improved domestic revenues and with the recreation of the domestic debt market from the wreckage of the enforced restructuring of *GKOs* and *OFZs* (T-bonds).[17]

On the assumption that foreign financial investors will probably give Russia a wide berth for the foreseeable future, foreign direct investment will be the most important source of external private sector support for the economy. The weaker ruble should offer new opportunities in this area, but any investment will depend principally on increased confidence in key areas of economic life. The government must succeed in passing a workable budget. The 1998/1999 budget, as passed, was largely a work of fiction - a luxury that Russia can no longer afford. There is also the still pending reform of the tax code. Another area that needs strengthening is

---

[16] Farrow 1998b, 148.
[17] *OFZ (Obligatsii Federal'nogo Zaima)* - federal bonds.

the field of bankruptcy legislation. Traditionally, Russian legislation has preferred reorganization of bankrupt companies to their liquidation. The correct legislation would help to protect the interests of bank lenders, domestic and foreign, and so encourage lending to the private sector. The fate of the banks will be critical in this area, especially as foreign investors stand to lose billions of dollars from local banks defaulting on forward contracts linked to *GKO* investments.

A genuine recovery in investor confidence would be reflected in a virtuous cycle of successful privatization, less costly domestic financing, and, ultimately, easier access to external funding, although that must now be seen as a distant prospect. The government originally aimed to raise US$5-6bn a year from privatization.[18] Falling oil prices and pre-devaluation concerns about the ruble made investors hold off in the earlier auctions.

As international and domestic banks count the cost of the devaluation, the foreign moratorium and the *GKO* default, the effects are beginning to penetrate to the broader economy, which had already begun to suffer from the high domestic interest rates that were imposed to try to defend the ruble. One positive effect of a slow economy should be on inflation. However, the huge devaluation has already pushed its level much higher, as the cost of imported goods rose.

In short, after years of market reforms, Russia is back on the rack. Future progress will depend on the achievement of support across the political spectrum for genuine change in the issues mentioned.

The Last International Debt Crisis and Russia

The last financial market confusion, first evident in Asia in the summer of 1997, intensified sharply following Russia's decision on 17 August 1998 to devalue the ruble and impose a forced restructuring of domestic government debt. These events, and, to a lesser extent, Malaysia's decision to impose capital controls, which followed shortly thereafter, were decisive in leading not only to a dramatic reassessment of different risks associated with holding emerging market financial instruments, but also to a general decline in risk tolerance among mature market investors. Some highly leveraged institutions that have been important investors in emerging market securities suffered large losses or were even dissolved as a result of the Russian debt restructuring, and faced higher margin calls. A relatively

---

[18] Farrow 1998b, 150.

indiscriminate sell-off in emerging market securities ensued, which led to a sharp widening of secondary market interest rate spreads and the virtual cessation of financial flows to many emerging markets. Following the extreme financial market turbulence and collapse of new issuance activity during the post-crisis period, secondary bond and equity markets rebounded. Private capital flows showed a tentative recovery following an easing of monetary policies in several mature markets and the announcement of a support package for Brazil. The financial market disorder that followed the Russian debt restructuring led to a sharp deterioration in the terms and conditions under which many emerging market economies could obtain access to world financial markets. As a result, issuance of new emerging market debt and equity instruments virtually collapsed in 1998-99.

The main question raised by the recent financial market turmoil is why the announcement of Russia's forced debt restructuring had such a dramatic effect on emerging market economies' access to global financial markets. It is hard to impute the extent of the financial market turbulence either to the scale of Russia's activities in global financial markets or to the relative size of Russia's domestic financial markets. For example, Russia's external debt just before the forced debt restructuring amounted to about US$150bn.[19] Yet this was equivalent to only one-third of the combined external debts at the end of 1996 of the five Asian countries (Indonesia, Korea, Malaysia, the Philippines, Thailand) most affected in the early stages of the current crisis, and just 8% of emerging markets' total external debts. Similarly, the exposure of the Bank for International Settlements (BIS) reporting-area banks to Russia at the end of 1997 was 28% of their exposure to the five relevant Asian countries. Moreover, Russia accounted for just over 3% of the total international loan commitments and issuance of international bonds and equities by emerging markets in the period from 1992 to the end of June 1998.[20] And as for the domestic ruble-denominated market, it was worth at most a paltry US$50bn in 1998, whereas bad bank debt in Japan was at the same time closer to US$530bn, and the derivative notional outstanding alone of Japan's Long Term Credit Bank was US$350bn.[21]

Another serious consideration is that the events in Russia (and, to a lesser extent, in Malaysia) highlighted the perceived vulnerability of even hedged local currency positions to counter party default and convertibility

---

[19] World Bank 1999, 29.
[20] Ibid.
[21] 'Japan, not Russia', in *International Financing Review* (1998), No. 1248, 1.

risk, and led to a fundamental reassessment by many investors of the attractiveness of holding emerging market instruments. Furthermore, a reassessment of the risks associated with holding high-yield instruments in mature markets was evident even prior to the Russian debt restructuring. This was reflected in both a decline in equity prices and a widening of the interest rate spreads between high-yield corporate bonds and US treasury bonds. Nevertheless, this overestimation of risks and adjustment of portfolio positions accelerated as a result of both the losses incurred by some highly leveraged investors on their holdings of Russian securities and the portfolio adjustments required by the risk management systems employed in many commercial and investment banks when asset price volatility increases sharply.[22]

The extent and scale of the recent financial market turbulence certainly cannot be explained by the potential direct impact of the unilateral debt restructuring in Russia. First, the value that could be lost from an outright default was relatively small, and only one third of it was held by non-resident investors. Second, interest rates on Russian GKOs in the period leading up to the unilateral restructuring were high relative to the cost of borrowing by other emerging market sovereign credits. In the end, Russia was perceived as unique among emerging markets in one significant regard: long-standing political and foreign policy considerations implied to many investors that Russia might continue to receive the funds it required from the international community to finance the required adjustments. In effect, Russia was perceived as 'too big to fail'.

Unlike the Tequila crisis of 1995,[23] the Russian crisis meant huge losses for bondholders as well as equity investors. Unlike the Asian crises, the Russian debt problems triggered mature market turbulence because of differences in the nature of the shock. The Russian crisis was a unilateral restructuring of sovereign debt - a traded financial market instrument - that in a market-to-market environment would immediately trigger the unwinding of leveraged positions by large, internationally active financial institutions. In the Asian crisis, by contrast, the bulk of the financial contracts that were immediately at risk consisted of (non-tradable) inter-

---

[22] A new trend since 1997 has been the correlation between movements in the Russian and US markets. The correlation is hard to explain, since the two markets have few value drivers in common. It is true that movements in US interest rates lead to changes in Russian sovereign debt prices. However, in many cases movements in the US markets cause movements in Russian equity prices simply because traders put too much trust in the existence of the linkage and try to ride the trend.
[23] The debt crisis in Mexico in 1995.

bank loans. In addition, Russia's unilateral restructuring was a sudden and defining event, whereas the Asian crises developed more slowly in several stages. One more difference is that the Russian crisis occurred amid greater concerns about the health of the US economy and the sustainability of the valuation of US equity markets and other mature ones elsewhere.

Finally, the Russian unilateral debt restructuring triggered an abrupt, post-Asian-crisis flight from a wide range of emerging financial markets, a sharp widening of emerging market interest rate spreads to 1,700bp (secondary market spreads on Russian benchmark sovereign bonds increased by more than 6,000bp),[24] and a drying up of liquidity in international capital markets. The related flights to quality and liquidity in international capital markets set off a process of deleveraging of financial transactions and virulent turbulence in mature financial markets that rapidly and sharply affected many investors and a wide range of mature financial markets.

In any case, some of the immediate impact on mature markets of the unilateral debt restructuring in Russia reflected the fact that a significant share of financing for Russian and other emerging market investments had been arranged and leveraged in the mature markets, in particular US financial markets. For example, some investors had purchased Russian *GKOs*, on margin, through investment banks that had funded the purchases with short-term repurchase agreements and commercial paper in US markets. Other Russian and emerging market securities purchases had been funded in Japan and swapped into local currencies or dollars. Accordingly, the initial unwinding of financing for emerging market positions, hedges, and leverage meant that mature market positions related to these investments also had to be unwound or hedged, because the Russian restructuring triggered margin calls and led to a widespread increase in margin requirements. Because many of the investments that needed to be unwound were highly leveraged, the downward price adjustments were unusually sharp in a wide range of markets. The leveraging of investments magnifies returns when asset prices are appreciating, but it also magnifies losses, and requires the expenditure of scarce capital to meet margin calls, when adverse price movements occur, thereby forcing market participants to liquidate positions as rapidly as possible. Thus, the simultaneous presence of a high degree of leverage in a wide range of interconnected markets forced a large number of investors simultaneously to sell assets into declining markets.

---

[24] World Bank 1999, 30.

The widening of spreads and liquidity pressures that immediately followed the Russian crisis and the flight from emerging markets destroyed value in fixed-income positions that had been predicated on the perception that 'credit risk' spreads between low-quality and high-quality (sovereign) borrowers in the advanced countries had widened beyond sustainable levels because of the 'Asian virus'. These so-called credit-risk 'convergence plays' were widely engaged in. They were made up of financial positions in advanced country fixed-income markets in which the investor would simultaneously be 'long' in relatively high-risk debt securities (such as US, German, and Danish asset-backed and corporate securities) - expecting their value to appreciate - and 'short' in sovereign debt instruments of similar currency denomination and maturity (such as US, German, and Danish government bonds) - expecting their value to depreciate. Instead of narrowing credit risk, spreads widened further. Depending on how the transactions were financed, these adverse price movements were associated with further margin calls, liquidations, and hedging, leading to further significant demands on the shrinking pool of liquidity. This led to even wider spreads in some markets as more positions were liquidated to make margin calls in other markets.

The debt crisis in Russia has significantly affected developments and prospects in many other transition countries, especially those that are dependent on external private financing or have maintained strong trade and financial ties with Russia. Trade-finance and payments systems arrangements in the Commonwealth of Independent States were interrupted and trade declined sharply as Russian demand collapsed. The exports and balances of payments of Central and Eastern European countries deteriorated as well, as sluggish growth in Western Europe translated into weak external demand for the more diversified regional exporters, slowing the internal dynamics of the region.

The System of Sovereign Debt Management

The share of state debt in the total Russian debt is 78%; the share of local governments is about 1%. The external debt of the private sector (corporations and banks) accounts for 21% - a very small figure compared with that in the East Asian crisis countries (in the Republic of Korea, 90%; in Thailand, 69%; in Indonesia, 60%).[25] The Russian Federation has

---

[25] Ibid., 84.

become one of the key borrowers on the international markets. This development is in part a function of the amounts the Russian sovereign was seeking to raise externally - at least US$5bn a year.[26] But it is also because Russia's keenness to borrow externally has contributed to widening spreads across the emerging markets.

Judged by some ratios, Russia is heavily indebted. Gross external debt stood at 85% of GDP at the end of 1999. That figure is even higher than the ratio for the troubled Asian economies of Indonesia (67%), or Thailand (59%).[27] Russia's increasing demands on the international financial markets are the result of a situation in which it was far cheaper for the sovereign to borrow abroad than at home. We can single out the issue of foreign debt settlement among three major 'threats' that might greatly harm the country's economy, the other two being an ever-worsening banking system crisis and soaring inflation. The financial and banking crisis wiped out all tangible advantages the government had gained by completing in 1997 a comprehensive restructuring of the Soviet-era debt. The immediate implication was that the country no longer had access to resources in international financial markets that could be channeled into foreign debt servicing and redemption. These pressures were merged with that of a chronic federal budget deficit aggravated by payment delays and, in some cases, by inter-bank clearing system failures. And a situation developed which in 1997 would have seemed simply incredible: in August 1998, Russia stopped payments on the Soviet-era debt. Largely as a consequence, in November 1998, the Russian government and its agent *Vneshekonombank* were forced to appeal to the Paris and London Clubs to negotiate a new restructuring of the already rescheduled financial obligations.[28] The aim of these negotiations should be to agree upon a schedule and volume of payments that would allow the Russian government to service its foreign debt effectively. These appeals opened up a new page in the debt record of the Russian Federation.

This does not mean that the government gave up its main principles of honoring external financial obligations. As was agreed with creditors at the very outset of the procedure for rescheduling the Soviet-era debt, all indebtedness under loans and credits obtained after 1 January 1992 is to be

---

[26] Ibid., 30.
[27] Farrow 1998a, 40.
[28] The Paris Club is an informal forum where negotiations between debtor and creditor governments take place regarding the rescheduling of public debt. The London Club is the name for ad hoc committees of bank creditors established to consider debt rescheduling by sovereign debtors.

serviced in strict compliance with the existing credit agreements. As of 31 December 1999, the sum of 'new' Russian debt amounted to US$52.0bn.[29] The bulk of the increase (US$11.5bn) in recent years arose from placing different bond issues. About 30% of these bond issues were the result of exchanging *GKOs-OFZs*. The sum owed to the IMF and World Bank, totaling US$26.0 billion, including US$19.4 billion owed to the IMF, is a major portion of this debt.[30] Russia accords a high priority to its relations with the IMF and the World Bank. As a matter of fact, in 1998-99 Russia fully honored its obligations to these creditors. A considerable proportion of the 'new' Russian debt is the indebtedness owed under bond issues (totaling approximately US$16.0bn)[31] that were placed with private investors from some industrialized nations throughout the period of 1996 to mid-1998. Just as with the IMF and World Bank, Russia fully met its liabilities under these bond issues. It should be noted that the Russian government rules out even the slightest possibility of having this category of debt restructured. Still another category of the 'new' Russian debt comprises liabilities under 'tied' loans obtained by the Ministry of Finance and *Vneshekonombank* from industrialized nations under sovereign guarantees of the Russian government. The overall volume of these liabilities arising from 368 credit agreements amounts to US$10.0bn.[32]

The financial crisis ruined all the positive results that Russia had reached within the framework of a comprehensive restructuring of the Soviet-era debt owed to the Paris and London Clubs of creditors. A direct consequence of payments suspension was that the aggregate value of that debt resumed growing. In recent years, Russia had continued to regularize its relations with the banks and other financial institutions known as the London Club of Soviet-era creditors. Russia managed to avoid arbitration proceedings stipulated by the underlying London Club agreements in case a dispute and/or a conflict should arise. The efforts undertaken by Russia in that area encouraged the emergence and development of secondary market for London Club instruments. Actually, Principals (PRINS) - restructured Soviet-era loans - and Interest Arrears Notes (IANS) - interests from PRINS - proved a very popular segment of the international financial market. In total, the year of 1998 recorded 7,191 PRINS assignments for the sum of US$3.5bn.[33] According to some estimates, the overall volume of

---

[29] Vneshekonombank 1999, 9.
[30] Ibid.
[31] Ibid., 11.
[32] Ibid.
[33] Ibid.

trading in these instruments (PRINS plus IANS) exceeded tens of billions of US dollars. In fact, they came second after Brazilian debt trading. It has always been a strategic policy of *Vneshekonombank* to maintain these instruments' quotations at the highest level possible.

By February 2000, Russia and the London Club of creditor banks had reached a deal offering Moscow considerable relief on US$32bn of debt.[34] The deal cut the debt by an average of around 36.5%, and stretched repayments of most of the debt over 30 years. The overall debt relief is over 50% in present value terms. The London Club banks wrote off $10.6bn of principal, and offered a grace period of seven years. Soviet-era long-term bonds, known as PRINS (US$22.2bn), are to be exchanged for new 30-year Russian Federation Eurobonds at a discount of 37.5%. IANS (US$6.8bn) are to be exchanged for new bonds at a discount of 33%. The new paper is to pay an interest rate of 2.25% for the first six months, 2.5% for the next six months and 5% in years two through seven. Years eight to maturity are to carry a rate of 7.5%. In addition, US$2.8bn in interest due on these debts is to be exchanged for a new Russian Federation Eurobond with a final maturity of 10 years and an interest rate of 8.25% per annum.[35] The agreement appeared to be broadly in line with market expectations. It looks like the deal that the markets had been pricing in.[36]

Russia's deal with private bankers closes the chapter on a cataclysmic default that rocked financial markets worldwide and paved the way for its return to capital markets. This deal gives Russia the ability to normalize relations with investors and eventually to test the market by bringing a new bond issue at some stage. The debt deal with private bankers has widely been viewed as the first step necessary for Russia to recover the ability to borrow from international investors. But Russia has to establish a history of performing debt. This is the beginning of the healing process. Having won a deal with foreign investors, Russia will now need to win the confidence of its own citizens to rebuild its economy, because the country still has low foreign exchange reserves, despite rising exports, that point to ongoing capital flight. But Russia is optimistic that the breakthrough with the London Club could improve chances for an agreement on similar terms regarding Russia's US$42bn debt to the Paris Club, which negotiates on sovereign debt.[37] This could cause a split between Western governments in the Paris Club of official creditors, where the German government (which

---

[34] *Reuters* (2000), 14 February.
[35] *Reuters* (2000), 15 February.
[36] Ibid.
[37] Ibid.

owns about half of the Soviet sovereign debt) has been strongly opposed to any debt forgiveness.

The question is whether official creditors are prepared to take the same kind of hit as have private creditors. It was highly unusual for the London Club to agree on a restructuring deal in advance of sovereign creditors. Under the principle of comparability of treatment, the Paris Club should not be treated worse than the private sector, but neither should it be treated better. Despite months of tortuous talks, bondholders will still have to take sizable losses on their investments, though these are broadly in line with previous debt restructuring. Debt forgiveness has never been calibrated to anyone's ability to pay. The roughly 35% debt forgiveness that Russia obtained is within spitting distance of the generic Brady forgiveness level, referring to the restructuring of the debt of many Latin American countries in the past decade. Mexico, Brazil, Argentina and other Latin American countries have restructured defaulted debt into new bonds linked to US Treasuries and named after the architect of the program, former US Treasury Secretary Nicholas Brady.

US$35.3bn of the Soviet-era debt owed to the Paris Club creditors has already been restructured. The governments of industrialized nations are thus holding about one third of the foreign liabilities of the Russian government. These and the debt owed to the IMF and International Bank for Reconstruction and Development (IBRD) total about 50%. And since Paris Club membership provides these creditors with a powerful and efficient debt policy coordinating mechanism, their negotiating position is, obviously, of critical importance in working out settlement terms on Soviet-era debt that Russia would find acceptable.

The crisis also affected the settlement of debt to other official creditors that did not join the Paris Club (Bulgaria, Hungary, China, Poland, Slovakia, Oman, Thailand, Turkey, Uruguay, the United Arab Emirates, the Republic of Korea). Agreements with these countries stipulate the terms and procedures for handling settlements and payments of Soviet-era liabilities. With other creditor countries (Kuwait, Romania, the successor states to Yugoslavia), negotiations designed to arrive at adequate debt settlement schemes are coming to an end. One proposed scheme provides for delivery of Russian high-tech goods to creditor countries as a form of debt repayment. That would ensure and facilitate both the fulfillment of foreign obligations and support of domestic producers, since federal funds would be channeled into production of goods to be delivered in repayment of debt.

Besides authorized banks, many other authorized exporters and importers, as well as manufacturers, exchange control and tax authorities are involved in operations for the repayment of sovereign debt. Should the Paris Club creditor countries accept the goods scheme of debt repayment offered by the Russian Ministry of Finance, it would obviously help Russia to overcome the debt crisis.

Some progress was made in implementing the strategy of settling trade debt owed to foreign suppliers. Reconciliation documents were signed with representatives of the national clubs of commercial creditors from Austria, Great Britain, Italy, and Japan, as well as with a number of individual creditor firms. A package of reconciliation documents to be signed later covers debt claims amounting to US$840.0mn, out of US$2.2bn of commercial debt.[38] The financial crisis and debt crisis suspended the process of finalizing documentation that would set out terms and procedures of a settlement of Soviet-era commercial debt. But it is quite obvious that once the Russian government agrees on an economic program with the IMF, and once new parameters for settlement of Russia's foreign debt are accepted by the creditors of the Paris and London Clubs, the process will gain further momentum.

In compliance with federal law, indebtedness under the internal foreign currency bonds (Minfins) was assigned to the category of sovereign foreign debt. This decision only legalized the facts that, first, payments on these obligations should be made in foreign currency rather than in rubles, and, second, a considerable proportion of the Minfins was held by foreign legal entities. In the last two years, acting in its capacity as agent, the *Vneshekonombank* made an additional bond issue for the sum of US$180.0mn and thus settled the currency and special accounts 'frozen' earlier. Within a year, Russia redeemed bonds for the sum of US$7.2mn and paid coupon for the sum of US$316.0mn, getting equal receivables from the Ministry of Finance.[39] It should be noted that after the default by a number of authorized banks on the Minfins servicing and their failure to maintain relevant trading records, the scope of functions and responsibilities of *Vneshekonombank* was accordingly expanded.

A substantial worsening of macroeconomic indicators of the sovereign foreign debt was a direct consequence of the financial crisis. Debt/GDP, debt/export, debt servicing/export (on schedule) calculated at year-end, rose to 85%, 203% and 23%, respectively, approximating the ratios considered

---

[38] Vneshekonombank 1999, 14.
[39] Ibid.

by the IMF 'critically dangerous' for the country's ability duly to service its outstanding debt.[40] But much more threatening is the situation when, in order to make payments scheduled for the following year, the country is expected to transfer almost 90% of its budget receipts to foreign creditors. Full redemption and servicing of sovereign foreign debt on schedule would require Russia in the coming 8-10 years to maintain a surplus of budget receipts over budget expenditures of 6-8% of GDP per annum, which is at the moment an impossible burden for its economy. The Russian government has therefore no alternative but to seek ways to drastically restructure the Soviet-era debt, to consistently promote market-oriented reforms, to make domestic products much more competitive, and, finally, to create and effectively implement a system of active sovereign debt management.

Acting as an agent for the Russian government, *Vneshekonombank* is actively engaged in the management of Russia's external financial assets. Its role is not altogether reduced to maintaining records of claims on the debtor countries, although bookkeeping and accounting in this matter remain a major function of the Bank. Moreover, in 1998 a number of actions were undertaken to evaluate the solvency of the debtor countries, primarily of those without agreements with the Paris Club and whose outstanding debt tends to grow. Another initiative is aimed at conducting a detailed study and analysis of specific schemes of foreign debt repayment. It implies the use of conventional market instruments and/or innovative ones such as swap operations (debt/export, debt/equity, debt/debt), securitization of debt claims, buy-back operations, etc. Taking into account the permanent pressures and challenges of financial hardships that most debtor countries are going through, these instruments and schemes might facilitate the debt restructuring procedure under agreements to be approved by the Russian government.

As of 31 December 1999, the total sum of debt claims registered on *Vneshekonombank*'s books and owed to Russia by foreign states under credits granted earlier (prior to a front discount stipulated by Russia's full-fledged membership in the Paris Club) was estimated to exceed US$131.1bn, with arrears of US$93.2bn.[41] The debt was recorded by tens of thousands of relevant documents, some of them twenty or even thirty years old. It is all the more disappointing that, having reconciled the claims,

---

[40] Ibid.
[41] Ibid., 17.

some of the states would not make payments to Russia though they continued repaying debt owed to other creditors.

Conclusion

The external debt of many countries of the former Soviet Union has been growing rapidly in recent years, and has played an important part in the transition process. Though Russia's current level of debt is not especially high next to that of most developing countries, it is nevertheless remarkable. On the one hand, it clearly makes sense to borrow abroad to help finance the difficult transition period. On the other, there is a risk that the option of borrowing abroad will weaken efforts to transform the economy and its institutions. A balance must therefore be struck between taking advantage of growing external borrowing opportunities and not allowing such borrowing to finance wasteful expenditures or delay the transition process.

The main causes of the unsatisfactory situation with the Russian debt are: first, a bad system of tax collection; second, lack of development of the domestic debt market; third, orientation to the raising of money abroad. But all of these can be traced to one overarching problem: bad management of the economy in terms of transformation in times of globalization.

4 Financial Supervision and Moral Hazard on an Emerging Market

IRINA N. IUDINA

This article examines key aspects of financial globalization (the 'external challenge') and the reaction of emerging markets (transformation as 'internal reply'). According to our analysis, the key factor resulting in destructive financial crises in the developing markets is not capital flows, but, for the most part, the incompleteness and the slowness of the adaptation of banking systems and budget policy to the new external economic situation. Taking as an example the financial crisis in Russia, we believe that it was the uncoordinated and uncertain measures of the monetary authorities - the Ministry of Finance (Minfin) and the Central Bank of Russia (CBR) - and also the incompleteness of institutional reforms (the banking, budget and tax policies of the Russian government) which resulted in the collapse of the financial system. Within the framework of the project 'Globalization and Transformation' we try to show that the institutional changes in Russia were insufficient to allow the anti-crisis measures of policymakers during the financial crisis to be effective.

The new direction in the study of global financial flows and the ability of national governments to adapt to them is connected with research into geo-finance. This new field of research has arisen as a result of financial globalization and the emergence of global actors who can subsequently influence domestic markets. It is also understood as a means of influencing policy: to make money and financial movements more compatible with the common political aims of a nation-state. The national authorities need to strengthen their ability to use international financial resources in their own interests, to evaluate the negative and positive sides of cross-border movements of money, and to deal with the influence which speculative streams can exert on monetary stability, interest rates, and the balance of payments (in which capital movements are the most important item). There is also the problem of the monetary sovereignty of governments.

The purpose of my research is to show how, as this process has emerged, Russia is involved (as an emerging market), with all the positive and negative consequences flowing from this involvement. During the recent past, the new situation has confronted the state both with the objective possibility that external factors will influence its internal and financial stability, as well as with the subjective attempts to reduce its absolute sovereignty - not by other states but rather by slippery global actors, working internationally. How to build policy under these conditions? The so-called 'triangle of incompatibility' is made up of the stability of the exchange rate, the independence of monetary policy, and freedom of capital movement. Lessons concerning the international monetary system are probably best understood in the context of the important insight that a pegged exchange rate, independent national monetary policy, and unrestricted international capital mobility cannot be achieved simultaneously. Much of the international financial system's experience in the twentieth century deals with changing government priorities regarding these objectives.

A closed financial market is an anachronism in our conditions. But in conditions of an open market, the responsibility of government to its citizens, institutions, and to the international community for its behavior in the field of internal finance (budget) has grown. Analysis must deal with the opposition between the operating area of the state (at the national level) and the operating area of finance (at the global level) and determine the boundaries of state activity in each of them. The economic problem is resisted with a political problem, and the economy sometimes becomes the 'hostage' of internal and external politics.

We must hereinafter consider what changes have occurred in the external environment, which - given improper internal government policy - can cause a financial crisis and even the resignation of the government.

Changes in the Global Financial Environment

Many experts pay attention to changes in the world financial environment, which, on the one hand, work positively, meeting the appetite of international investors for high yields and portfolio diversification. On the other hand, financial crises in different regions of the world are becoming more frequent.

A striking development of the 1990s is the rapid international integration of financial markets, following the general trend toward liberalization of financial markets in the industrial countries in the 1970s and 1980s, and the reduction in capital and exchange controls in emerging market countries more recently. As a result, the 1990s have witnessed private capital flows to emerging market countries unprecedented in scale (relative to economic activity), at least since the First World War. However, the large flows into emerging market countries during the build-up to the recent crises in such countries also reflected, in part, unsustainable developments in gross and, more particularly, in net terms in the recipient countries (including explicit and implicit exchange rate guarantees), together with a low demand for capital in Japan and Western Europe associated with the weakness of activity in those economies through much of the 1990s.

The trend worldwide since the breakdown of the Bretton-Woods system has been toward exchange rate flexibility. In the 1990s, short-term exchange rate volatility has remained high with no clear trend, which is somewhat surprising in view of the decline in worldwide inflation. As a result, exchange rates have been allowed to reflect more clearly differences in policies and investment opportunities. Is there any link between these developments and the pervasive macroeconomic instability experienced in the 1990s? It is clear that the achievement of broad price stability throughout most of the world economy has not been sufficient to eliminate macroeconomic instability. But the factors that have contributed to continued instability are complex. Some observers have argued that market forces ('capitalism') are prone to generate excess and instability. Others have suggested that, although low inflation may be necessary for maximum sustainable growth, it may also provide fertile soil for market instability since it may induce investors to take excessive risks in their search for high yields: 'As recent experience attests, a prolonged period of price stability does help to foster economic stability. But, as we have also observed over several years, as have others in times past, such a benign economic environment can induce investors to take on more risk and drive asset prices to unsustainable levels'.[1]

---

[1] IMF 1999a, 10.

The deepening of financial crises is due to the interaction of the following set of factors: First, the globalization of financial markets, allowing the simultaneous carrying out of operations in various segments of the market, and also the deregulation and liberalization of capital movements. The mobility of capital puts great pressure on the choice of measures and the directions in economic policy of this or that country or enterprise. Second, modern financial innovations, i.e. new procedures and operations, developed by the operators of the financial market with the aim of covering risks more reliably. Such mechanisms for covering risks have achieved a certain independence in relation to the initial (primary) financial documents. For the past 20 years, the daily volume of transactions in the global currency markets has increased up to US$1,200bn, while the volume of world trade in goods has increased by only 50%. Third, the expansion of the operations of banks in the financial markets (financing of speculative operations or investments in real estate), resulting in the growth of losses.

Globalization and the New Political Paradigm

A main challenge is to strengthen and expand the open world trading and financial system and reduce its potential for disruption. Twentieth-century experience has shown that international trade and capital movements are essential in order to realize the vast potential benefits of the global division of labor and to accelerate the diffusion of technology. But it has also shown that the resulting interdependence of national economies can lead to the rapid propagation of adverse shocks that may seriously set back even well-managed economies. And large amounts of internationally mobile capital, combined with domestic policy imbalances and the expectation of volatile exchange rates, can generate serious international financial crises.

However, a retreat from globalization is no solution, as shown by the inter-war experience, which led to a prolonged disruption in international trade, capital movements and diffusion of technology, with detrimental effects for the growth of output in rich and poor countries alike. Strengthening the network of international trade and capital flows and making this network less vulnerable to sudden disruptions requires both skilled economic management at home and economic cooperation on the international level, including a useful and constructive role by the various international financial institutions. Finally, it requires political leadership that is willing and able to explain the advantages of the system to the electorate at large and to prevent special interest groups from gaining exceptional treatment, undermining the principles of free trade.

The answer to the challenges of globalization involves national authorities' attempting to adjust monetary and fiscal policy in such a way as to minimize the negative influence of the forces of globalization. Establishing a new monetary policy operating framework to replace the earlier exchange rate-centered policy regime and designing and implementing efficient banking regulation have occupied the international community for the better part of the last quarter century, but progress has so far been very gradual, with no universally applicable optimal solution to the problem being developed. There is a failure of vision: the failure of policymakers to articulate a clear and coherent alternative monetary strategy before a crisis strikes.

This dismal experience led to a search for a new policy paradigm in the 1980s and 1990s. An important aspect of the new paradigm was the willingness to concede increasing autonomy to the monetary authorities in an attempt to reduce the political pressure for 'easy money' and to strengthen the objective of medium-term price stability. Equally fundamentally, the new paradigm placed much greater weight on market forces while attempting to narrow the scope and change the nature of government intervention in the economy.

The Russian government must adjust its policies in due course, which means it must also adhere to an open and market-oriented policy, but on the condition that it strengthens internal structures and carries out a more responsible policy, creating a strong institutional base.

Growth of Risk Perception in the Developing Markets after the Russian Crisis

The spillover effects associated with the recent emerging market crises are larger and more complex than those seen in earlier periods of turmoil. In part, this contagion was the result of common external shocks, wake-up calls about common domestic weaknesses, and macroeconomic linkages. But financial linkages have proven stronger and more complex than in earlier periods, and they have increased the rapidity with which shocks are reflected in asset prices. Moreover, the portfolio decisions of market makers and large global players, including those that operate with a high degree of leverage, have often played a key role in determining short-term movements in asset prices. By contrast, the role of traditional 'fundamentals' in short-term price movements sometimes appears quite modest.

The Russian episode marked a new phase in the financial crisis. The decline of participation of developing countries in international capital markets since the Russian debt moratorium reflects several factors. The huge losses investors incurred (largely through the use of Russian treasury securities as collateral for highly leveraged derivatives transactions, rather than actual investments in the Russian stock and bond markets) have increased perceptions of the riskiness of emerging market investments. The lack of a rescue package heightened investors' fears over the potential for loss on other emerging market investments. The losses suffered in Russia led to a sell-off of other emerging market debt instruments because highly leveraged speculators sold emerging market bonds to meet collateral requirements. Investors' reactions to the Russian crisis were more severe than during the 1997 East Asian crisis because the events in Russia coincided with increased concerns over the slowing of the global economy. Investors deserted emerging market instruments for safer and more liquid assets, and they liquidated holdings to rebuild balance sheets damaged by the large write-down of Russian obligations. The situation in the stock markets remained complex, caused by their being undeveloped ('emerging') and the significant expansion of foreign portfolio investments. With the collapse of the ruble in August, nervousness concerning the emerging markets has developed into loss of confidence and a 'flight into quality'. The unilateral debt moratorium and the unwillingness of the international community to provide a rescue package without progress in reforms made creditors conscious that they cannot always rely on international guarantees, thus sharply increasing the potential costs of risky private credits.

The crisis has underscored the risks associated with investing in emerging markets, including the possibility of large losses of principal, as happened in Russia. It may also encourage some countries to delay capital account liberalization measures, or it may restrict capital outflows.

The crisis has underlined the risks to the sustainability of flows posed by fragile financial systems in recipient countries, including high levels of short-term debt, unhedged foreign exchange liabilities, and highly leveraged corporate sectors. There is now a better understanding of the contribution of implicit guarantees, a lack of transparency, and an inadequate legal framework to poor lending and investment decisions.

Accordingly, the capital markets have become more suspicious of large current account deficits associated with surges of capital inflow.

Given the time required to clean up the bad loans of the crisis countries' banking systems, to improve regulation and supervision of the financial sector, and to strengthen legal frameworks, enhanced perception of these risks is likely to have a deterrent effect on capital flows. The process of financial sector reform in the countries hit by the crisis has only begun. The banking systems of the crisis countries were fragile before the crisis, and the deep recessions of 1997-98 have exacerbated their difficulties. Of the 73 national banking systems rated by Moody's in June 1998, the five countries hardest hit by the financial crisis are close to the bottom of the list (table 4.1).

Table 4.1 Banking systems in countries hit by crisis (Ranking out of 73 countries)

Russian Federation	64	Thailand	71
Republic of Korea	70	Indonesia	73

Source: World Bank 1999, 35.

Risk Perceptions and International Financial Support

Massive growth in nonresidents' holdings of Russian assets occurred in the face of downgrades in Russia's credit rating and in sharp increases in yields that indicated a substantial probability of default. The actions announced by the Russian government on 17 August 1998 came as a major surprise to the financial markets, even though Russia had been downgraded by one rating agency (Moody's) in March 1998 and then by all three major agencies in May or early June, and despite the fact that yields on Russian securities clearly reflected a substantial default risk (Figure 4.1).

Investors' willingness to assume Russian risk in the face of the large budget deficit and increasing debt burden has been attributed by many to the belief that the G-7 countries would not allow Russia to default on its government debt. If the high level of capital flows in the mid-1990s was even modestly supported by expectations of rescue packages, the lack of assistance to Russia in the summer of 1998 should help discourage the notion. In this sense, moral hazard clearly played a role in the buildup of claims on Russia in a way that cannot realistically be said for any of the other crisis countries. But in addition to (or in combination with) this moral hazard, there is also clear evidence that Russia represents a case where many investors bought securities that they did not fully understand, and where they did so in the face of developments that should have raised concerns.

Diagram 4.1 Russia: Credit Ratings (average of credit ratings by Moody's and Standard and Poor's)

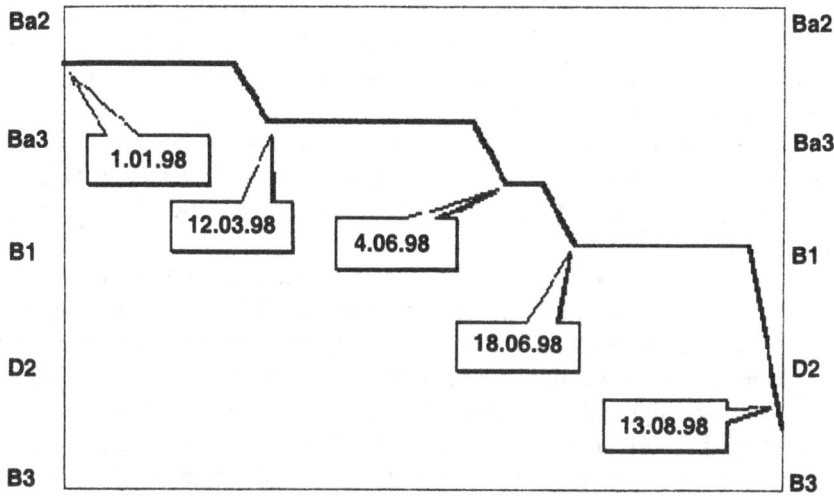

Source: IMF 1999c, 71.

Investors were particularly surprised by the decision to restructure domestic debt - on terms that were viewed as extremely harsh. The Russian measures appeared to make it more likely that other countries might also adopt similar policy actions and led to a major reassessment of risk in other emerging markets.

The refusal to provide funds to Russia without adequate policy reform should encourage investors to differentiate more accurately among countries. One explanation of the general retreat from emerging markets after the Russian debt moratorium is that the failure of the Russian package led to dramatic increases in market perception of the risk of lending to emerging markets.

The Ministry of Finance and the Central Bank: The Contradictions of Financial Stabilization

Inclusion of Russia in the global economic and financial community, liberalization of access by foreign capital to the internal financial market, and the almost unlimited access to foreign financial markets granted to Russian banks, enterprises, and regional administrations was not accompanied by an effective control mechanism. As a result, the vulnerability of the internal financial market to adverse external factors, such as crises in the world markets or the migration of international speculative capital, has increased.

The progress made in institutional transformations is insignificant, and sooner or later Russia was bound to be confronted with very big, hitherto neglected, problems. External shocks have played the role of 'triggering' the internal difficulties.

The general conclusion to be drawn from the analysis of events preceding the crisis (in other regions of the world) and the consequent flight of capital is that countries allowing major deviations in the exchange rate from its long-term equilibrium position usually attract short-term funds and maintain high interest rates to support the currency. When clouds appear on the horizon and investors evaluate this policy as unstable, then capital outflows become a serious problem (as in the case of the Mexican crisis of 1994).

The root of Russia's high level of vulnerability during the world financial crisis was an imbalance in public finances. In fact, the budget and monetary policies of the Russian Government and the Central Bank of Russia (CBR) were mainly responsible for the development of the financial crisis. Let us consider the budget performance of the federal government since 1992 (table 4.2):

Table 4.2 The budget policy of the Russian Government in 1992-98 (in % of GDP)

	1992	1993	1994	1995	1996	1997	1998 (January to July)
Federal budget							
Revenue	15.6	13.7	11.8	12.2	13.0	11.6	10.6
Taxes	13.0	12.4	9.2	10.8	9.9	9.4	8.9
Expenditure	38.0	24.3	23.2	17.6	22.1	18.4	15.5
Transfers	1.7	2.8	4.2	2.1	3.1	3.8	1.5
Balance	-22.4	-10.1	-11.4	-5.4	-9.1	-6.8	-4.3
Budget of extended government							
Revenue	38.3	36.2	34.7	31.9	32.1	33.0	32.8
Taxes	35.8	34.5	32.6	30.3	29.2	31.1	29.7
Expenditure	56.7	45.6	45.1	37.6	41.5	40.5	38.1
Balance	-18.4	-9.4	-10.4	-5.7	-9.4	-7.5	-5.3

Source: Illarionov 1998, 26.

The financial burden of the state is too heavy for the Russian economy. Taxes amount to 42-50% of real GDP. Therefore, the real volume of taxes actually will be lower, as the maintenance of an excessive tax burden leads inevitably to the reduction of real GDP and tax receipts. The tax liabilities of economic agents in budgets at all levels have been growing. The financing of budget deficits in non-inflationary ways (by internal and external credits) has resulted in a fast growth in government debt and in the costs of debt service, simultaneously reducing the size of national savings and adversely affecting the current balance of payments. Since 1995, the internal government debt has grown rapidly due to the drawings on stock market (table 4.3).

Table 4.3 Federal government debt (in billion rubles)

	1992	1993	1994	1995	1996	1997	1998 July	1998 September
Total	43.0	134.0	490.6	749.9	1059.9	1238.2	1360.9	2749.6
including								
in foreign currency	34.7	118.5	402.2	558.7	694.3	737.2	854.9	2279.6
in rubles	8.3	15.5	88.4	191.2	365.6	501.0	506.0	470.0
in *GKO-OFZ*	–	0.2	10.3	73.7	237.1	384.9	436.0	387.1
Percentage of GDP	226.0	78.1	80.3	47.3	48.2	47.6	49.5	100.0
including								
in foreign currency	182.3	69.1	65.9	35.2	31.6	28.3	31.1	82.9
in rubles	43.7	9.0	14.5	12.1	16.6	19.3	18.4	17.1
in *GKO-OFZ*	–	0.1	1.7	4.7	10.8	14.8	15.9	14.9

Source: Illarionov 1998, 26.

There was a lack of internal liquid savings, and the solution of admitting nonresidents to the internal government debt market was accepted. Investments by foreigners in *GKO-OFZ* snowballed: in the first three quarters of 1996, there was a net inflow through type 'S' accounts of US$1.7bn, and in the last quarter as much as US$4.2bn. In 1997, this figure reached US$10.9bn, and in the first quarter of 1998 another US$3.1bn.[2] According to Ministry of Finance data, by the beginning of August 1998, nonresidents accounted for 32% of the market.[3] This policy was a serious mistake and predetermined the further development of the crisis. The fully liberalized internal debt market was not accessible to nonresidents after 1 January 1998 (in particular, a guaranteed level of yield and the regulation of terms of profit repatriation were cancelled).

The government external debt service was approximately equal to the level of government revenues projected in the budget. Balancing of public finances by further reduction of non-percentage expenditures was not only necessary, but also possible. The authorities did not do so, and the default became inevitable.

After the depreciation of the ruble, government debt in foreign exchange terms increased more than three times, and total government debt doubled. The quality of government debt management was unusually low. For a short period, Russia was included in the group of severely indebted middle-income economies (debt equaled about 156% of GDP).

Despite the progress made in reforming the tax system and reducing inflation during 1996-97, by 1998 the situation was critical: the budget deficit had reached almost 7% of GDP, with revenues covering just half of expenditures. In addition, falling oil and commodity prices reduced foreign exchange earnings, and the government was rolling over US$1bn per week in short-term ruble-denominated debt.

Budget and currency resources were completely insufficient for debt retirement, and the pyramid of *GKO-OFZ* had failed. The situation worsened following the devaluation and unilateral domestic debt restructuring in Russia. Confidence in the authorities was undermined on the part of participants in the financial market and the public, and it

---

[2] 'Platezhnyi balans Rossii za 1996 god', in *Vestnik Banka Rossii* (1997), No. 29, 1-77, here 6; 'Platezhnyi balans Rossii za 1997 god', in *Vestnik Banka Rossii* (1998), No. 43, 1-55, here 6; 'Platezhnyi balans Rossii za I kvartal 1998 god', in *Vestnik Banka Rossii* (1998), No. 56, 1-55, here 5.

[3] 'Osnovnye napravleniia edinoi gosudarstvennoi kreditno-denezhnoi politiki na 1999 god. Otchet CBR', in *Den'gi i kredit* (1998), No. 12, 3-35, here 24.

provoked a crisis in the banking and worsened the reputation of Russia in international financial circles. The combination of debt restructuring, devaluation, and a moratorium on private principal repayments announced by Russia on 17 August came as a major shock to emerging market investors.

Error Committed by the Central Bank

In the end, the epicenter of the crisis was concentrated on gold reserves, intended to be spent on ruble conversion for nonresidents, and on support of the ruble/dollar exchange rate through interventions on the internal exchange market, which was under high pressure. By the middle of 1998, there were only US$13bn, compared to US$25bn one year earlier.[4]

Beginning with the second quarter of 1997, the current balance of payments was a mainly negative indicator; but the balance of capital account (including transactions with financial instruments) remained positive in 1997 (19.5 billion rubles or 4.2% of GDP) with an inflow of foreign portfolio investments.

By the end of October 1997, the confidence of foreign investors in the continuation of a stable financial and macroeconomic situation in Russia had decreased, accompanied by a fall in prices of Russian financial instruments and a growth in demand for foreign exchange. In November, the RTS-1 index fell to 328.5, i.e. quotations had fallen by 32%.[5] The annual average weighted yield in the liability market had grown from 22% to 28%.

The trade-off was between bad and very bad solutions. In November, the CBR tried to maintain the interest rate by means of *GKO* package increases, and only on 11 November (i.e. with a two week delay) did it increase the rate of refunding from 21% to 28% - insufficient for achieving equilibrium in the government obligations market. But the increased demand for foreign currency by nonresidents, who sold-off their own *GKO* packages, resulted in a rapid decrease in gold reserves, and the stability of the exchange rate policy came under pressure.

In the last week of November, the CBR lost one-fourth of its international reserves, rejected a policy of low interest rates and left the *GKO-OFZ* market. The annual average weighted yield of *GKO* had

---

[4] 'Krizis finansovoi sistemy Rossii: osnovnye faktory i ekonomicheskaia politika', in *Voprosy ekonomiki* (1998), No. 11, 36-65, here 53-54.
[5] Entov 1998, 235-240.

increased up to 40%. The catastrophic growth of an external payments deficit, financed from the reserves of the Central Bank, had already begun by the end of 1997 and the first half of 1998. To attract further foreign investments was impossible.

The broad participation of foreign investors in financing the government budget sharply strengthened the dependence of the Russian economy on world financial markets. Under such conditions, any attempt to change the exchange rate would be bound to cause a massive withdrawal of financial assets, an increase in interest rates, increased pressure on the currency, a reduction in international reserves, and a growth in the risk of default and depreciation. By announcing the extension of a currency corridor, the Central Bank had given a negative signal about the foreign exchange risk, but at the same time continued to support the low rates of ruble depreciation.

Default Risk

Pressure on the Russian ruble formed in 1998. Internal political disagreements interrupted progress on the reduction of the budget deficit, which was partially being financed by short-term external borrowing through the banking system. The drop in world oil prices, caused in part by the recession in East Asia, reduced export income and government receipts. Negotiations over the Russian government debt were protracted and difficult, owing to the huge discounts necessary to resolve the problem and the difficulties the Russian authorities faced in formulating an effective adjustment program. The rescue package for Russia was a calculated risk, and the results were disappointing.[6]

After long negotiations, Russia and IMF declared on 13 July 1998 that agreement had been achieved, and a week later the Board of Directors of the IMF reached a decision on the allocation of a first tranche of US$4.8bn. The basic requirement - to pursue the former monetary policy - was an error. After obtaining the tranche, the Central Bank attached the Minfin accounts. The Minfin then tried in one day to raise in the home market a sum exceeding the tax receipts of the federal government for an entire month. This was a technical error which served as a negative signal for the markets. And, finally, the refusal by *Sberbank* to carry out the traditional rollover resulted in the financial crash (i.e. default) of the government. The spectacular financial crash through the fault of the government and central

---

[6] Fischer 1998, 24.

bank has become a classic demonstration that, without serious internal institutional reform, with a heavy financial burden on the government, and with the extremely ineffective use of available resources, participants in the market and the public have to pay a large price.

Given the unsustainable debt situation, in August 1998 the government announced a 90-day moratorium on about US$40bn of its ruble-denominated debt to private creditors, of which foreigners held about US$17bn at the exchange rate prevailing before the moratorium. In November 1998, the government announced that Russia and foreign banks had reached an agreement in principle on restructuring more than US$10bn of frozen treasury debt. Under the agreement, the foreign banks would get 10% cash payment in rubles, 20% in securities tradable for tax debts or stakes in Russian banks, and the remaining 70% in interest-bearing, ruble-dominated securities.[7] It has not been decided when the ruble payments could be repatriated. In addition, Russia has experienced considerable difficulties in servicing the already restructured debt to commercial banks and the Paris Club inherited from the former Soviet Union.

Crisis of the Banking Sector

The liberalization of the banking sector in the 1990s and the deregulation of the whole financial sector took effect in conditions where there was not enough supervision and control over the activities of banks and other credit institutes. These measures simply opened the way to large-scale speculation and fraud, accompanied by bank practices involving high credit risks. They also strengthened the instability and vulnerability of banking institutions, and national supervisors lost control over financial markets, preparing the way to a crisis.

A significant part of short-term financial means and banking profits were used to finance speculative operations in the stock market, the currency markets, and real estate. The growth of commercial banks' portfolio liabilities in foreign currency deprived the central bank of opportunities to act as a lender of last resort, thus refunding their liabilities to support liquidity.

The central bank tried to delay the collapse of the banking system as long as possible, though the necessity of devaluation should have been realized as early as in the spring of 1998. By continuing the former

---

[7] World Bank 1999, 84.

exchange rate policy, the central bank tried to subsidize Russian commercial banks on the verge of bankruptcy. However, there were not enough currency reserves for this purpose; therefore, an unprecedented campaign was launched in June-July 1998 to attract external loans.

The expansion of credit in the real economy sector is restrained by the large-scale redistribution of bank assets in favor of government lending. In the structure of the banks' requirements, the government's share quickly grew (from 39.9% at the beginning of 1997 to 42.6% in the middle of 1998[8]) and, as is well known, this had a great effect on bank liquidity in conditions of financial crisis. As an example, while the fall in asset prices in the turmoil of August and September 1998 certainly reflected a reassessment of credit and other risks, this initial impact was magnified substantially by the subsequent drying up of market liquidity.

Liquidity Crisis and Losses of Investors

Besides credit activity (balance sheet), banks are involved in off-balance sheet transactions (futures, options, forwards, credit lines, etc.), which are constantly being reassessed; the difference between initial and market cost is covered with the help of remittances to remove the risk of default. Recently, the most popular off-balance activity has been the sale of liabilities, restructured into securities, and also forward contracts on currency delivery. Some institutions incurred losses when Russian banks were unable to deliver on forward contracts on the ruble, or when Western banks refused to deliver, claiming that the policy actions of the Russian government constituted a form of *force majeure*. As losses on holdings of Russian securities were revealed and market volatility increased, many leveraged investors began to face much higher margin calls from their creditor banks. This combination of external and internal margin calls contributed to contagion, a sell-off in a broad range of debt securities, and a sharp spike in yield spreads causing a liquidity crisis.

The availability of derivatives instruments, coupled with weak institutional and legal frameworks, increased opportunities for speculation that resulted in significant losses with the downturn in markets during the financial crisis. The use of forwards, futures, swaps, and other derivatives instruments enabled investors to take on greater exposure relative to their capital, and to greatly increase the potential for loss. For example, the

---

[8] Tsentral'nyi Bank Rossiiskoi Federatsii (1997), *Biulleten' bankovskoi statistiki No. 12*; Tsentral'nyi Bank Rossiiskoi Federatsii (1998), *Biulleten' bankovskoi statistiki No. 2*.

investor who is short in the foreign exchange futures market can lose many multiples of his investment, compared to spot transactions in which the downside is limited to the currency held. The Russian debt moratorium imposed huge losses on both foreign and domestic creditors trading in over-the-counter derivative instruments, perhaps as much as US$90bn.[9]

Exposure by foreign investors to risk from ruble-denominated debt (*GKO*) was magnified by techniques to increase leverage, such as investing borrowed funds from commercial banks. Some banks accepted *GKO*s as collateral supporting total-return swaps based on *GKO*s. The collapse of the *GKO* market meant that the banks were due substantial sums from the swaps, but collecting the amount due was problematic because the value of collateral that could be seized to enforce payment had plummeted. Similarly, investors were willing to invest in *GKO*s in part because they were able to use forward contracts to hedge their ruble exposure. However, foreign currency hedges could not protect investors from the sudden drying up of liquidity in the market because of the debt moratorium and Russian government prohibitions against servicing debt. It is unlikely that investors would have assumed the same level of exposure to *GKO*s if derivatives had not been available.

Actual refusal of the government to pay under its obligations has brought about the freezing of almost 7% of bank assets (*GKO-OFZ*). The obligations to nonresidents were collateralized by these securities, which made up 12.7% of the bank passives.

Following the collapse of a large number of banks in the aftermath of the 1998 crisis (figure 4.2), the authorities made little use of the authority granted within the existing legal framework to place ailing banks under administration. By the time these banks were subjected to bankruptcy procedures, they had become mostly empty shells. One result is that bank restructuring will be more expensive than it otherwise would have been.

The crash of the banking system, the moratorium on international payments, panic among depositors - all this testifies to the failure of the official economic policy pursued up to now. Financial stability in Russia was constructed on a completely inappropriate base in conditions of a deep decline in national output, disarray in the tax collection system and public finances, degradation of the money system (non-payments, barter), and, mainly, the construction of the government (internal and external) debt pyramid.

---

[9] World Bank 1999, 39.

The main problem, common to all banks, is that the financial market has changed fundamentally: state bonds were not present, the stock market was barely alive, and the interbank credit market was in poor condition because of the pervasive mutual mistrust among banks. The lesson is that banks should learn to earn their profits on classical banking operations instead of financial speculation. The heaviest consequence of the crisis has not been the drop in manufacturing or the depreciation of the ruble, but a general crisis of confidence. To restore confidence, so that the money will return to the banks, and through the banks to the economy, is extremely difficult.

Russia after the Crisis

In the wake of the August 1998 crisis, the Russian authorities faced a range of major challenges. They had to address the consequences of the crisis for domestic financial markets and the banking sector, and for the country's relations with international creditors. Moreover, they were confronted with the need to tackle the fiscal and structural problems that were at the root of the crisis. The subsequent record has been mixed. Monetary, and subsequently fiscal, policies were relaxed in the aftermath of the crisis, but were tightened again in the first half of 1999. Also, steps have been taken to revitalize domestic financial markets and to normalize relations with key international creditors. On the other hand, only limited progress has been made in restructuring the banking sector and in addressing the pervasive fiscal and structural problems, with backtracking in some areas.

Restoration of the Financial Sector (Budget, Financial Markets)

Long-standing fiscal problems were at the root of the August 1998 crisis, including the federal government's poor revenue performance and tax and expenditure arrears. Much remains to be done to address these problems; nevertheless, some signs of progress are apparent in the revenue and expenditure measures introduced to reach the 2% primary surplus target included in the new stand-by arrangement. Moreover, the fiscal situation at the federal level has improved since the beginning of the year, with a strong recovery in revenues reflecting both the improvement in the macroeconomic environment, including higher oil prices, and reinforced tax collection efforts. Federal government revenue in the second quarter of

1999 was around 14% of GDP compared with less than 11% in the same quarter of the previous year, and revenue collection has further improved since then, exceeding nominal budget targets. In particular, cash revenues relative to GDP have risen from the very low levels recorded in the second half of 1998. Non-interest expenditures have been restrained further, and the primary balance has swung into surplus, in part due to tight financing constraints since the government lost access to new financing in domestic and international financial markets. Furthermore, the current account surplus of US$18bn was largely offset by continuing high outflows of private capital, reflecting an ongoing lack of confidence in economic policies and prospects. Thus, gross reserves increased by only US$1.6bn in 1999.

The authorities have also taken steps to restart the operation of the domestic fixed income markets and to avoid a further deterioration in relations with international creditors. A final conversion scheme for the domestic treasury bills that were frozen in the August 1998 debt restructuring was adopted in March 1999, and a reorganization of the treasury bill market was completed in June. As a result of these steps, by the end of June the face value of outstanding treasury bills had been reduced by more than one third (more than two thirds when adjusted for inflation) and their average maturity extended to around 33 months from less than 12 months just prior to the 1998 restructuring. However, the domestic treasury bill market remains highly illiquid and secondary market yields, at more than 60% in early September, very high; reflecting these unfavorable conditions, the government has not returned to the market to raise new financing. In the context of the treasury bill conversion scheme, incentives were provided to major companies to issue domestic currency corporate debt instruments, opening the perspective of a revival of the corresponding market. But overall, among the domestic financial markets, only the equity market has as yet resumed activities on a substantial scale, with broad investor interest, including among banks, contributing to the sharp rally in Russian equity prices during 1999.

Some progress was also made on the external debt front. The authorities continued their dialogue with major international creditors, following the announcement in late 1998 that the country would be unable to make payments on Soviet era debt but would fully honor debts incurred by the Russian sovereign. The dialogue has been successful in avoiding a formal default toward Paris or London Club creditors, although Russia has effectively failed in recent months to make a series of scheduled payments to both groups of creditors. In the middle of June, in the context of the Cologne summit, the major industrial country members of the Paris Club announced their support for a restructuring (but not partial write-off) of the Soviet debt owed to official creditors, and an agreement to reschedule around US$8bn of this debt was reached at end of July. The June announcement was interpreted by investors as also an improvement in the payment prospects for London Club debt and eurobonds, and secondary market prices for these instruments subsequently staged a significant recovery. The government has continued to meet its obligations on eurobonds, and also on the US$-denominated domestic debt instruments issued in 1996.

On 16 April 2000, the Chairman of the Central Bank of Russia, Viktor Gerashchenko, declared:

> In order to achieve sustainable growth, however, a number of structural reforms need to be carried out in the economy. We must complete as quickly as possible the restructuring of the banking system, which was hit hard by the financial crisis. Strengthening payment discipline continues to be an important objective, along with preventing mutual nonpayment among enterprises and reducing the degree of barterization of the economy. The implementation of tax reform is an ongoing objective, which should serve as a basis for improving the investment climate in the country. A comprehensive program of structural reforms is currently being devised, and the new Russian government will have the implementation of this program high on its list of priorities.[10]

Without a reinvigorated effort to move ahead with banking sector rehabilitation and fiscal and other structural reforms, the recent macroeconomic stabilization and turnaround in industrial output are unlikely to last. Robust fiscal progress would also reduce pressures for central bank financing of the deficit and would thereby contribute to further disinflation and stronger confidence in the ruble. Determined progress is also needed with banking sector reforms, supported by the implementation of a stronger legal framework to facilitate public intervention in troubled banks and, if necessary, their closure. Particular attention needs to be given to determining the future role and structure of state-owned banks. More generally, much remains to be done to develop the institutional and legal

---

[10] Statement by Mr. Viktor V. Gerashchenko, Governor for the Russian Federation, to the International Monetary and Financial Committee, 16 April 2000, in <http://www.imf.org/external/spring/2000/imfc/rus.htm>.

underpinnings of a market economy and hence to provide a reliable framework for improving governance, strengthening the rule of law, reducing corruption, and attracting the long-term capital needed for deep restructuring and sustained growth.

The failure to strengthen the rule of law and improve governance both in the public and corporate sectors is at the heart of weak investment, the failure of enterprises to restructure, and capital flight. It helps account for the extremely low level of foreign direct investment. FDI in Russia has run below 1% of GDP, compared with around 3% of GDP in the Central European transition economies. An improvement in the investment climate could reap big rewards for the economy in this regard. It could also help reverse capital flight, which has averaged US$10-20bn per year since the early 1990s. Russia's economy, and Russia's financial needs, will look very different when Russian savings, instead of fleeing abroad, are used to finance productive investments in the domestic economy.

Supervision by the Central Bank

The measures undertaken by the Bank of Russia to enhance financial stability include the granting of special credits for reorganization, multilateral clearing of mutual bank liabilities, and adjustment of the level of reserve requirements (raised to 5% on ruble and foreign currency deposits after 1 December 1998).This has marginally improved bank liquidity.

The new conditions of banking activity and the level of the Bank of Russia's own means predetermined the decision to cancel the minimum requirements for the size of banks' own capital. First of all, the Bank of Russia was guided by the assumption that the right to function as a bank is determined not by the size of the bank's own capital, but by its willingness to limit the scale of its activities and not to exceed an acceptable level of risk.

Support of the financial stability of the banking sector requires strengthening the system of prudential oversight. An important role in this sense is played by the Interdepartmental Coordinating Committee for Assisting the Development of Banking in Russia. The restructuring of the banking system should be the responsibility of the government.

The main vehicle for bank restructuring is the Agency for the Restructuring of Credit Organizations (ARCO; *Agentstvo po Restrukturizatsii Kreditnykh Organizatsii - ARKO*), created in October

1998 and slated to acquire controlling stakes in banks in distress, manage bad assets, and initiate bank liquidations.[11] However, the agency's resources are modest compared with the restructuring and re-capitalization needs, and significant deficiencies in the legal framework governing banking sector reform remain. The central bank has been reluctant to withdraw licenses from ailing banks and place them under administration, although there has recently been some progress in this regard as part of the new IMF program. The central bank has also failed to act decisively against extensive asset stripping of insolvent institutions.

The lack of progress in bank restructuring has further eroded commercial banks' willingness to extend new lending to households and firms, and new credit to the private sector has continued to decline in real terms since the crisis, from already very low levels. In the absence of investment opportunities other than equities, many commercial banks have built up large liquidity positions in their correspondent accounts at the central bank.

Conclusion

Organized Movement toward Liberalization

The most obvious lesson from the recent financial shocks is that the liberalization of capital movements should proceed in an organized way. The main problems are the speed and the sequence of steps to be taken in liberalizing capital flows. The usual conclusion is that for emerging market economies improper management of the opening financial markets can easily bring about periodic booms and bankruptcies during the transitional period. Some successfully developing countries with transitional economies give priority to placing sensible controls over the banking system rather than over capital flows. Governments which do not tighten market discipline and/or conduct unreasonable fixed exchange rate policies are at fault. The recovery of the financial sector, political stability, and a balanced economic policy are extremely important for improvement of the situation in the capital market.

Prudential oversight and other elements of official involvement constitute preventive and corrective mechanisms, which - like market discipline - provide a degree of insurance and stability to national financial

---

[11] Turbanov 1999, 4. The author is general director of *ARKO*.

systems and, more broadly, to the international financial system. This presumes that the degree of official involvement remains within reasonable boundaries and does not unduly influence market participants into thinking they can engage in imprudent risk-taking without suffering the consequences of bad outcomes. The presumption should be that official involvement occurs only so far - up to the point where it encourages normal and prudent risk-taking. The challenge is for banking supervision, market surveillance, and financial policymaking more generally to balance efforts to manage systemic risks with efforts to ensure that market participants - in particular, the systemically important institutions - will bear the costs of imprudent risk-taking and, accordingly, will have the right incentives to avoid imprudence. Accountability also needs to be in place, and perhaps bolstered in some cases, to foster and promote discipline in the exercise of official supervision and surveillance.

In addition, there is an element of dynamic competition - a race - between the regulated and the regulator. Because of the combination of technological advances and private incentive structures, private financial practices may be changing more quickly and dynamically than it is possible for supervisory and regulatory frameworks to adapt to monitor them. Likewise, because of differences in resources and incentives, the ability of the private sector to capture the gains from technological advances may have exceeded the ability of officials to learn how these technologies can be applied to the measurement, calibration, and management of systemic risk. As noted by one former senior regulator, the relationship of supervisors and financial institutions is like that of a 'bloodhound chasing after a greyhound': regulators have trouble keeping pace with the ability of internationally active financial institutions, and the gap between them may be widening.

System Risk and Moral Hazard Problem

The transformation of the modern financial system is changing the nature of systemic risk. As noted recently by former President Tietmeyer of the Deutsche Bundesbank,

> ... systemic risk is not a given quantity. To a large extent, it is an endogenous variable which depends on the structures of the financial markets, on the

supervisory framework at the national and international levels, and on the decisions taken by the political and monetary authorities.[12]

A fundamental concern is that private incentives are not strong enough to prevent excesses and that the existing lines of defense inadequately address at present some aspects of the transformed, more market-oriented systemic risk. A desirable approach is to consider reforming existing private and public mechanisms (including crisis prevention and management mechanisms) for dealing adequately with all of these evolving elements of the international financial system.

The appropriate balance between market discipline and official intervention involves difficult trade-offs between different objectives. On the one hand, financial safety nets appear to have significantly lessened the deadweight losses and collateral damage associated with financial crises earlier in the twentieth century. On the other hand, the safety nets themselves may be contributing to excessively risky behavior and may involve potentially large costs to taxpayers. A complicating factor in seeking to rely more on supervision and regulation is that the large globally active financial institutions are able to circumvent regulation through gaps between the information sets of supervisors and the institutions themselves. Banking supervision, official market surveillance, and systemic risk management are the tools for monitoring. The buildup of financial vulnerabilities that only became evident once the turbulence occurred in 1997-98, was a wake-up call: existing frameworks for banking supervision, official markets surveillance, and managing systemic risk may not be sufficient for the modern financial system.

Ultimately, the part of the insurance provided by the public sector that may create the most obvious moral hazard is that the public sector has in the past intervened to save institutions, either directly or indirectly through markets. One possibility for limiting moral hazard is to take more frequent decisions that reduce the perception that interventions are the rule and failures the exception, for example, by gradually but deliberately reducing the size and scope of the safety net. The more general objective would be to have greater involvement by the private sector in preventing systemic problems, not just through improved private risk management to protect themselves, but also through greater awareness that their actions have systemic implications and are affected by systemic problems created by others. Given that the scope of official financial safety nets is unlikely to be

---

[12] IMF 1999c, 83.

reduced quickly or entirely, the ability to monitor, supervise, and exercise surveillance over modern financial systems remains critical.

5 Large Corporations as National and Global Players: The Case of Gazprom

ANDREAS HEINRICH

Russia is confronted with a double challenge: after the collapse of the USSR, the political, economic, social and cultural forms of regulation are changing significantly and dynamically.[1] But at the same time, actors and institutions also are objects of global integration processes and world-wide changes in the context of globalization. Globalization means - among other things - the active dissemination of practices, common rules, values and technologies throughout the globe.[2] Among the main agents who determine the form and pace of globalization in a given country, large corporations, i.e. their managements, play a leading role. These corporations can change the relations between nation states and the world economy.[3]

Additionally, the authority of national governments of all countries has been weakened as a result of globalization.[4] The transformation of the Russian state structures and society fostered the weakening of state authority to a high degree. That is why the large corporations influence not only the economic, but also the political development in Russia to a growing extent. Accordingly, these actors play an important role in Russia's institution-building process.

This contribution tries to answer the following questions: is *Gazprom* a globalizer disseminating international standards and business behavior in

---

[1] The author would like to thank Heiko Pleines for his support and his comments.
[2] Albrow 1996, 88.
[3] Sklair 1996. *Gazprom* portrays itself as an important global player. 'Industrial technologies and business environment are rapidly changing, international trade and business rules are evolving as well as the intergovernmental relations profile is getting drastic changes. ... Our Company, being a world market player, is facing global issues.' *Gazprom* 2000, <http://www.gazprom.ru/eng/report99/3htm>.
[4] Strange 1996, 13-14.

the Russian economy? Does the company try to foster the development of a market economy?

It will also elaborate on the following questions: is *Gazprom* developing encompassing interests in spite of a weak state authority in Russia, or is it continuing the rent seeking behavior of Soviet times? Has the company developed a long-term perspective, giving it a vested interest in the Russian economic and political future, or is *Gazprom* only trying to maximize short-term profits, making it behave as irresponsibly towards the country's fate as Olson's roving bandits.[5]

The natural gas company *Gazprom* plays an exceptional role in the Russian economy but also on the international level. The text begins with a brief portrait of the company, including organization and ownership structure. In the second part of this paper, *Gazprom*'s domestic activities on the economic and political level will be analyzed. This includes a discussion of the company's role in the so-called 'virtual economy'. The third part deals with *Gazprom*'s role as a global actor, concentrating on the question how *Gazprom* tries to realize its interests abroad, what means are employed, and what factors limit the company's international strategy. Outside Russia, *Gazprom* is of considerable economic relevance. The company is the most important energy supplier for many countries of the Former Soviet Union (FSU) and the biggest single supplier in the West European natural gas market.

Gazprom: A Portrait

Organizational Structure

In 1989, the Ministries of the Oil Industry, of the Gas Industry and of Petroleum Refining were reorganized and amalgamated to create a single Ministry of the Oil and Gas Industry. Plans were developed to establish one state company for the oil industry, *Lukoil*, and another one for the gas industry - *Gazprom*.[6] The plan for the gas industry was realized within a few weeks, and nearly the whole staff of the ministry transferred into the management of the new company. This meant that the gas industry was virtually removed from the jurisdiction and control of the new ministry.

---

[5] See Olson 1995 and 1996.
[6] *Gazprom* is the abbreviation for *Gazovaia promyshlennost'*.

Gazprom became responsible for all enterprises directly involved in production, refining, transportation and storage of natural gas. Thus, Gazprom holds the monopoly on production, transport and export of natural gas. In addition, Gazprom incorporated construction and machine building companies, agricultural units and consumer goods producers which all had been set up to supply the gas industry and its employees. Finally, the Soviet export company for natural gas was incorporated into Gazprom, making the company responsible for all Soviet supply contracts with foreign customers.[7]

With the transformation of the Soviet natural gas industry into a single enterprise, Russia created the world's largest producer and exporter of natural gas. With 545.6 billion cubic meters (bn cm) in 1999, the company accounted for around 25% of the world's total natural gas production. With its exports the company controls about 30% of the West European and more than 50% of the Central and East European natural gas market.[8]

Table 5.1 Production and export of natural gas 1992-2000 (in bn cm)

	1993	1994	1995	1996	1997	1998	1999	2000
Russia	617.7	606.8	594.7	600.2	569.3	591.0	590.7	584.2
Of which Gazprom	577.7	570.7	559.5	564.7	533.8	553.7	545.6	523.1
Total exports of Gazprom[9]	179.4	184.3	190.6	195.8	188.9	172.9	174.0	129.1*

Note: * Exports outside the FSU only.

Sources: Gazprom 1998, 15, 29; Gazprom 2000, <http://www.Gazprom.ru/eng/report99/2.htm>; *Petroleum Economist* (1997): Gas in the CIS and Eastern Europe. Special Issue, September, 72; ZGG Zarubezhgaz Erdgashandel GmbH, 'Förderung von Erdgas, Erdöl und Kondensat', <http://www.zgg.de/d53.htm>; *FSU Oil and Gas Monitor* (2001), No. 2, 16 January; *Reuters* (2001) 9 January.

---

[7] Kryukov and Moe 1996, 7-9; Kryukov 1998, 217-227.
[8] Heinrich 1999b, 537.
[9] Until the end of 1997, *Gazprom* managed the transit through Russia of natural gas supplied by the ITERA corporation from Central Asia to Armenia. (*Gazprom* 1997, 25) Some statistics add these supplies from ITERA to the exports of *Gazprom*. For 1998 and 1999, Zarubezhgaz gives a total export amount of 204bn cm for each year (ZGG Zarubezhgaz Erdgashandel GmbH, 'Förderung von Erdgas, Erdöl und Kondensat', <http://www.zgg.de/d53.htm>).

In Russia, *Gazprom* also plays an important role as an employer. *Gazprom* has set up whole towns near its production units like Urengoi or Nadym. In the remote regions of northern Siberia, the company is the only organization able to ensure supplies for households and a normal social life. But in 1997, *Gazprom* restructured subsidiaries not related to its core business - like construction companies and agricultural units - into independent enterprises or handed them over to the local government.

Instead, *Gazprom* has tried during recent years to establish a holding company comprising enterprises from some key branches of the Russian economy - chemical industry, metallurgy, electricity, banks, mass media and communication. Often, *Gazprom* gets its stake in a company in exchange for unpaid gas debts. *Gazprom*'s attempts to create an industrial holding company are the main reason why the company is regularly considered to be one of Russia's major informal Financial-Industrial Groups (FIGs). Additionally, the company has heavily invested in foreign, and especially West European, natural gas industries.[10]

Ownership Structure

After the collapse of the Soviet Union, the natural gas industry became the property of the Russian Federation. In February 1993, the state company *Gazprom* was transformed into the Russian Joint-Stock Company (RAO) *Gazprom*.[11] The government held a stake of 40%; 35% was reserved for the people in the gas producing regions, 15% for the company's employees, and 10% for the company itself. The possible stake of foreign investors was restricted to 9%.[12]

Since October 1996, foreign investors can buy ADRs,[13] which represent around 2% of the company's capital stock. The largest foreign investor is the German Ruhrgas AG, which holds 5% of *Gazprom*'s shares. The largest single shareholder is the Russian state with a 38.4% interest in *Gazprom*.[14] According to a law enacted in April 1999, the state is obliged to

---

[10] Pleines and Westphal 1999, 7-9.
[11] Since 1998, Open Joint-Stock Company OAO *Gazprom*.
[12] Kryukov and Moe 1996, 13-17; Pleines and Westphal 1999, 10-12.
[13] ADRs (American Depository Receipts) are negotiable US securities that generally represent a non-US company's publicly traded equity held by a US bank.
[14] Shareholder base as of 30 December 1999: 38.37% Russian Federation, 31.53% Russian legal entities, 19.79% Russian individual shareholders, 10.31% foreign investors. The share of foreign investors increased from 4.48% in 1998 to more than 10% in 1999. (*Gazprom*

keep at least 35% of *Gazprom*. At the same time, the share available in principle to foreign investors was extended to 20%.[15]

Gazprom as National Player

Gazprom and the Russian Government on the National Level

Gazprom belongs - like some other raw material producers - to the few Russian companies which are in principle able to work profitably. Such companies are interested in working independently from the Russian state because state regulations and taxation reduce their profitability. Since cash-backed demand on the Russian domestic market is very low, and since domestic prices for many important raw materials are considerably below world market prices as a result of state regulations, export activities are very attractive for Russian raw material producers. However, most raw material producers are dependent on the state's export infrastructure-like railways and oil pipelines, which are run by the state monopolies *MPS* (Ministry of Railways) and *Transneft'*. The only relevant exception is *Gazprom*, which owns the natural gas grid. This gives *Gazprom* an especially strong position vis-à-vis the government.[16]

The Russian government, in turn, depends on *Gazprom*, as the largest single taxpayer and the largest source of foreign currency for the state budget. To push through state interests against *Gazprom*, various governments have used different issues to put pressure on the company.[17] Political conflict surrounding the company focuses on its monopoly position, on the amount of taxes to be paid by *Gazprom*, and on the government's influence as the largest shareholder. Up to now, reform forces in the Russian government have attacked the position of *Gazprom* five times.[18]

2000, <http://www.gazprom.ru/eng/report99/7.htm>; *Financial Times* (1999), 25 May; Osetinskaia 1998).
[15] *FSU Oil and Gas Monitor* (1999), No. 6, 9 February and No. 12, 23 March; *Russia Morning Comment* (1999), 19 May; 'O gazosnabzhenii v Rossiiskoi Federatsii' (1999), in *Sobranie zakonodatel'stva Rossiiskoi Federatsii*, No. 14, 1667.
[16] Slay and Capelik 1997, 410; Pleines and Westphal 1999, 11.
[17] For an overview see Pleines and Westphal 1999, 12-19.
[18] By Egor Gaidar as prime minister in 1992 and as first deputy prime minister in 1993, then by Boris Nemtsov (as energy minister in 1997) and by Sergei Kirienko as prime minister in 1998 and finally by the government of Mikhail Kazianov in 2000.

Within the framework of competition policy, the government has tried to put an end to the gas company's monopoly position. The intention was to create competition, at least in parts of the natural gas industry.[19] This attempt was fostered by the IMF, which called for a break-up of *Gazprom* into several single enterprises. The IMF made this demand a condition for a several billion-dollar credit to Russia.[20] After the monopoly position of *Gazprom* was guaranteed by a Russian law in the spring of 1999, the IMF gave up its demand.[21]

As the largest stakeholder, the government also made efforts to gain influence over decision-making processes within the company by questioning the agreement which had handed over in trust most of the state's stake in the company to the *Gazprom* management.[22] After conflicts in 1997-98, a new agreement was reached in which the position of the Russian government was strengthened. The management was no longer allowed to make structural decisions and to issue new shares without the government's consent.[23] In summer 2000, the management lost for the first time its control of the company's board of directors. Government representatives, though one vote short of an absolute majority, now form the largest group.[24]

The government has also used taxation as a means to put pressure on the company. The state is able to change *Gazprom*'s tax burden. Especially in 1997 and 1998, probably pressured by the growing budget deficit, the government concentrated its efforts on making *Gazprom* pay outstanding taxes. Quarrels over the new trust agreement were merely used to put the *Gazprom* management under pressure. The company was forced to pay most of its taxes. However, with the financial crisis in August 1998, the

---

[19] Slay and Capelik 1997, 412-414; Genkel' 1997, 11-21; Kravets 1997, 20-23; Kriukov 1997, 89-106; Sagers 1995, 523-524; Troschke 1998, 174-178, 251-255.
[20] Krotova 1997, 28-31; 'Gazprom – at the eye of the storm', in *Petroleum Economist* (1998), No. 9, 7-8.
[21] 'O gazosnabzhenii v Rossiiskoi Federatsii' (1999), in *Sobranie zakonodatel'stva Rossiiskoi Federatsii*, No. 14, 1667; *Segodnia* (1999), 31 March. For a discussion of the issue of company restructuring see Troika Dialog 2000.
[22] Slay and Capelik 1997, 411-412; Kuznetsova and Kuznetsov 1999, 433-445; Troika Dialog 1999, 65-66.
[23] *RFE/RL Newsline* (1997), 15 September, 19 December and 23 December; *Segodnia* (1997), 23 December.
[24] Out of the 11 seats, 5 are held by government representatives, 4 by the company management, and 2 by representatives of minority shareholders (*FSU Oil and Gas Monitor* (2000), No. 26, 4 July).

pressure on *Gazprom* collapsed.[25] Only in July 2000, when the tax police raided *Gazprom*'s offices, did the state again use open pressure against the company.

Gazprom and the 'Virtual Economy'

The most important argument of the *Gazprom* lobby, in trying to defend the company's monopoly position and arguing for a lower tax burden, is the role the company plays in the domestic economy. It is claimed that by making cheap gas deliveries to industry, households, and social institutions, *Gazprom* is subsidizing the Russian economy and at the same time fulfilling some of the state's obligations in the social sphere. In other words, due to low gas prices and the non-payment crisis, *Gazprom* is working at a loss on the domestic market, and the fact that it is still selling gas to Russian consumers is not the result of economic calculation but of a 'feeling of responsibility', as *Gazprom* head Rem Viakhirev has put it.[26] This argument, however, is questionable.

To analyze economic transactions on the Russian market - especially barter deals - Gaddy and Ickes developed the concept of the 'virtual economy' (VE).[27] They suggest that the bulk of the country's Soviet-era enterprises is still subtracting value from inputs rather than adding it. In Russia, companies disguise their destruction of value by charging arbitrarily high prices for their products, the argument goes. Artificial pricing of this kind is first of all based on barter and other forms of non-cash payments. The enterprises can procure inputs, hire workers and produce lots of worthless output almost without the use of cash.

Companies could pay their suppliers and, until recently, even their taxes with barter goods 'priced' far above their true market value. It is only the workers who do not accept this pretence and want hard cash: hence the problem of wage arrears. Given that bankruptcies are rare, companies are able to stagger on, accumulating massive inter-enterprise debts.

The reason they can operate like this is that value is being transferred to them from other sectors of the economy that actually do produce value.

---

[25] Gray 1998, 47-48, 55, 66-68; Preuss-Neudorf 1996, 76-77, 232-234; Troschke 1998, 96-97, 100-102; Kriukov 1998, 247-248; Sagers 1995, 528; Sagers, Kryukov and Shmat 1995, 410; *Pipeline News* (1996), 5 July; Slay and Capelik 1997, 399.
[26] *Nezavisimaia gazeta* (1997), 25 March.
[27] Gaddy and Ickes 1998a; Gaddy and Ickes 1999. They call it a 'virtual economy', because it is 'based on illusion or pretence about almost every important parameter of the economy- prices, sales, wages, taxes and budgets'.

Demonstrating the relevance they attach to *Gazprom* in this context, Gaddy and Ickes have labeled this value-adding sector 'G' for *Gazprom*.

But in return for supplying the entire domestic economy with natural gas nearly free of charge, *Gazprom* is allowed to continue to export gas for hard currency. According to Gaddy and Ickes, *Gazproms*'s support of the domestic economy is the price it has to pay in order to remain an independent management-dominated company.[28]

The VE is robust, well-organized, and broadly popular. To break it would be very costly, socially and therefore politically. That is why Russia's government cannot reform in a true sense. But while the VE provides stability in the shorter term, in the long term it is a dead end.[29]

The concept of the VE is criticized for many reasons. Many critics concentrate on the point that Gaddy and Ickes suppose that the behavior of the actors involved in the VE differs from behavior assumed in classical economic theory. This aspect should be discussed in regard to the case of *Gazprom*,[30] where the counter argument was formulated by Woodruff.[31] Woodruff claims that *Gazprom*'s activities on the Russian domestic market are also guided by the aim of profit maximization. Because of limited transport capacities, the company is not able to increase its exports in the short term. In the long run, too, *Gazprom* will have to sell most of its production on the domestic market, due to the limited demand in countries that can be reached with the current gas grid. So for *Gazprom* there is no alternative to the domestic market, apart from a sharp reduction in output. From the economic point of view, to sell natural gas on the domestic market is viable as long as the price is higher than the variable production costs. Woodruff simply assumes that this condition is fulfilled for *Gazprom*. It takes part in the VE not because of pressure from the state or because of 'social consciousness', but for purely economic reasons. In his argumentation, the gas company is less a victim of the VE than a driving force in it.

But Woodruff's analysis is not able to explain why *Gazprom* continues to supply insolvent customers. This can be explained by the role of the state mentioned by Gaddy and Ickes. In the past the government has repeatedly enforced the supply of insolvent customers in 'strategic branches' of the

---

[28] Gaddy and Ickes 1999, 89-91; Gaddy and Ickes 1998b.
[29] Gaddy 1998.
[30] For a summary of different critical assessments of the model in general, see the special issue of *Post-Soviet Geography and Economics* (1999), No. 2.
[31] Woodruff 1999, 130-148.

Russian economy.[32] Accordingly, some energy experts believe that there was a 'gentlemen's agreement' reached in 1992-93 between the Russian government and *Gazprom* which 'offered *Gazprom* control over gas exports in return for the guaranteed supply to the domestic market'.[33]

This means that, apart from the aim of profit maximization, there are other factors influencing the behavior of *Gazprom* on the domestic gas market. The most important ones are, first, pressure from the government to make deliveries to insolvent customers and, second, *Gazprom*'s desire to get state support for business activities in the FSU.

Gazprom as Global Player

Expansion of Export Capacities

The main activities of *Gazprom* outside Russia include the expansion of export capacities and at the same time access to international financial markets in order to obtain the necessary finance, the conclusion of strategic partnerships with foreign companies, the struggle for control over transit pipelines in Eastern Europe, and rivalry with Central Asian gas producers.

Gazprom has to increase exports in order to receive foreign currency payments to compensate for non-payments and barter deals on the domestic market. Accordingly, *Gazprom* has developed plans to expand natural gas exports in all possible directions.[34] Especially in Western Europe,[35] *Gazprom* is trying to diversify the structure of its consumer base and to increase participation in deliveries to end-users. Moreover, the company has initiated an attempt to gain direct access to large industrial and gas-fired power generation markets in Western and Central Europe.[36] *Gazprom* hopes to profit from the European Union's (EU) gas market liberalization attempts by getting access to the downstream business in Western Europe. At the same time, the expansion of export capacities requires an increase in

---

[32] See, for example, *FSU Oil and Gas Monitor* (1999), No. 3, 19 January.

[33] Kryukov 2000, 115.

[34] This paper focuses on Western Europe, the company's main export market. On the other export activities of *Gazprom* - Southeast Europe, Turkey and China - see Heinrich 1999a, 8-10.

[35] For the history of Soviet, respectively Russian, gas deliveries to Western Europe see Stern 1989, 31, 33, 59.

[36] Pryce and Twomey 1997, 63. On the development of the natural gas sector in Central and Eastern Europe see Berenyi 1998, 22-24 and Shkuta 1999.

gas production, therefore the development of new gas deposits, and in addition provision of the necessary investment capital.

Table 5.2 Gazprom's exports to Western Europe 1996-2000 (in bn cm)

	1996	1997	1998	1999	2000*
Germany	32.9	32.5	32.5	34.9	34.1
Italy	14.0	14.2	17.3	19.8	21.8
France	12.4	10.9	10.9	13.4	12.9
Austria	6.0	5.6	5.7	5.4	4.6
Finland	3.7	3.6	4.2	4.2	3.8
Greece	–	0.2	0.9	1.5	1.4
Switzerland	0.4	0.4	0.4	0.4	0.3
Total	69.4	67.4	71.9	79.6	78.9

Note: * Preliminary figures.

Sources: Sergeev 1998, 115; *Gazprom* 1998, 25; *Gazprom* 1999, 29; *Gazprom* 2000, <http://www.Gazprom.ru/engreport9/14.htm>, *Reuters* (2000) 23 December; *Interfaks* (2001) 15 March.

The expansion of export capacities, however, meets with both external and internal problems. Production costs will rise, problems with transit countries will continue, and prognoses of future demand on the West European gas market are over-optimistic.[37]

Internal Problems

Apart from the fact that *Gazprom* uses outdated technology, the development of new gas fields under the difficult climatic conditions of Russia's Far North will increase production costs. However, the current dimensions of domestic consumption and projected export demand make the need to exploit these new gas fields - most notably the *Iamal* field - very questionable. Even if domestic and foreign demand increase significantly, there are cheaper gas sources in Russia.[38]

---

[37] See Heinrich 1999b.
[38] From the economic point of view, the import of natural gas from Turkmenistan and Kazakhstan would be an alternative (Stern 1997, 110, 112).

To sum up, difficult climatic conditions, outdated technology, and the extremely long transport routes to the customers will lead to increased costs in the next few years. For these reasons, *Gazprom* is losing its price advantages over competitors on the European natural gas market.[39]

These problems are reflected in the company's difficulties in attracting the financial means necessary for investment in modern technology. Estimates put the infrastructure requirements for *Gazprom*'s existing operations at US$3.5-6bn.[40] After the Russian financial crisis in August 1998, *Gazprom* has found it even harder to get foreign loans.[41]

Problems with Transit Countries

Until now, Russian natural gas - for Western Europe as well as for Southeast Europe and Turkey - is being exported via Belarus and Ukraine.[42] After the collapse of the Soviet Union, conditions for the transport of natural gas from Russia to Western Europe changed radically. The newly independent states, Belarus and Ukraine, introduced transit fees which made gas deliveries more expensive. Because of long-lasting quarrels with Ukraine about transit fees, and because of accusations that gas was being siphoned off during transit, *Gazprom* developed plans for an alternative transit route to break the transport monopoly of Ukraine and to reduce transit across FSU countries as much as possible.[43]

The *Iamal* pipeline from the Western Siberian gas fields on the *Iamal* peninsula will bypass Ukraine, going instead directly through Belarus and Poland and further on to Germany over a distance of 4,105km. The pipeline is being constructed step by step from west to east, partly via existing pipeline capacities. Capital spending on the *Iamal* project will total approximately US$40bn.[44] *Gazprom*'s payment problems, causing delays in the delivery of pipes and the withdrawal of an international credit after the financial crisis in 1998, have delayed the construction works.[45]

---

[39] Quinlan 1997, 66.
[40] Moors 1999, 10.
[41] See below for details.
[42] More than 80% of *Gazprom*'s gas exports to Europe cross Ukraine (O'Sullivan and Avdeev 2000, 26).
[43] An overview is given by Pleines 1998. On the quarrels with Ukraine see also Heinrich 1999a.
[44] Wingas (1999), 'Iamal-Europe project. Wingas integration into the European grid', <http://www.wingas.de/Wingas.nsf/vwByID/6F37CA0015E5BBFB41256841003CACF7>.
[45] *Petroleum Economist* (1998), No. 10, 36.

The transit of gas to the West European market is one of *Gazprom*'s main problems. Long-lasting quarrels with East European transit countries have not yet been solved. The transit countries have often forced *Gazprom* to accept a compromise on their debts for natural gas deliveries. Especially Ukraine has tried to use its near monopoly position on Russian gas transit to Western Europe to offset its weak position as a customer for Russian gas and as a debtor to *Gazprom*. However, a solution to these conflicts can not be reached through the construction of the *Iamal* pipeline.

At best, the construction of the pipeline can moderate the problems with Ukraine because Ukraine will be bypassed and Belarus can more easily be persuaded to cooperate with *Gazprom*. A real solution of the transport problem could perhaps be reached through a pipeline via Finland, Sweden and Denmark to Western Europe.[46]

To secure control over the transit pipelines will be a major task for *Gazprom* in the next few years. This control can not be reached through transit countries' debts. That is why *Gazprom* has been trying for years to swap these debts for stakes in the gas transit infrastructure in these countries. However, this strategy has been successful only in Moldavia. Ukraine and Belarus have ignored all related demands.[47]

Future Demand in Western Europe

Most prognoses for Western Europe's natural gas demand are overoptimistic. A tendency towards a growing discrepancy between general economic development and energy demand in Western Europe can be observed: economic growth no longer leads to an equivalent rise in energy consumption. Also, in the main national markets the residential and commercial sector are already integrated into a country-wide gas supply system. The quantitative increase in natural gas consumption will only be slow, so that there is not much room for dynamic growth. Additionally, new suppliers will make the European gas market more competitive.[48]

---

[46] *Gazprom* plans to deliver natural gas to Sweden through a pipeline from Finland across the Baltic Sea. Ivanov 1998; *FSU Oil and Gas Monitor* (1999), No. 26, 29 June.
[47] Heinrich 1999a, 24.
[48] Thackery 1998, 16, 18; Heinrich 1999b, especially 530-537.

The Financial Situation of Gazprom

The proportion of cash payments for gas deliveries on the domestic market has crept up from 16.1% of payments in 1998 to 18.5% in 1999. However, receivables, too, have continued to rise. The overall debt of Russian consumers to *Gazprom* for 1999 supplies has grown to Rbl120bn.[49] *Gazprom* has reorganized payment mechanisms in a way which it believes will help it improve collection rates and reduce the level of receivables. The main measures are: first, the 1999 agreement with the electricity monopoly *EES* (one of the largest debtors); second, strengthening the role of *Mezhregiongaz* (a company which enforces payments on the regional level); third, reducing or suspending deliveries to recalcitrant consumers within Russia and the CIS (Commonwealth of Independent States).[50]

Because the Russian capital market is underdeveloped, *Gazprom* has used the international financial markets to get loans and to issue ADRs for financing its expansion plans. In 1999, *Gazprom* paid about US$1.75bn on a total international bank syndication debt believed to amount to about US$25bn.[51] In its behavior in international financial markets, *Gazprom* differs less and less from the main Western companies. It works with international auditing companies and investment banks to attract loans, service its debts, issue ADRs, and publish company reports according to international accounting standards.

After the August 1998 crisis, and international gas prices being very low, it became harder for *Gazprom* to get foreign loans. The company lost its privileged position as the preferred Russian company. In 1999, *Gazprom* received no large foreign loan but only small ones for specific upgrading projects. As a result, the company had to reduce its investment program by two thirds. In order to finance its main long-term projects, *Gazprom* has had to draw on the assistance of its Western strategic partners.[52] These long-term projects include development of the domestic gas grid, the *Iamal*-Europe pipeline, the building of storage facilities, the acquisition of new gas deposits, and the 'Blue Stream' pipeline (*Goluboi potok*) across the Black Sea to Turkey.[53]

---

[49] *Analytica Newsletter* (2000), Profili kompanii, 19 February.
[50] O'Sullivan and Avdeev 2000, 26-27.
[51] Moors 1999, 11.
[52] See the following section on *Gazprom*'s strategic partnerships.
[53] Vlasov 1998, 6.

The attempts of *Gazprom* and its strategic partner Eni from Italy to get loans to finance the Blue Stream project dragged on for nearly two years. In June 2000, the relevant deals were finally made. Altogether, finance for the Blue Stream project will come from: a US$1.133bn loan provided by a consortium of German and Italian banks; an additional US$627mn loan provided by a Japanese consortium of Mitsui, Sumitomo and Itochu; and loans variously guaranteed by export credit agencies.[54]

Strategic Partnerships

Gazprom is engaging in strategic partnerships with leading Western natural gas companies in order to gain access to new markets and new sources of finance. It is a means of bringing in foreign companies that have their own access to loans at more affordable rates.[55] In long-term cooperation, the Russian company has proven that it is a reliable partner. In Germany, *Gazprom* is cooperating with Ruhrgas and BASF/ Wintershall,[56] in Italy with Eni. The company is also cooperating with the international Royal Dutch/ Shell Group.

At the end of 1997, Shell and *Gazprom* signed an agreement on a strategic partnership including cooperation in the exploitation of oil, gas and liquid gas. The partners are also planning projects in the energy transportation sector. Through this alliance, *Gazprom* hopes to open up markets in Asia, the Far East and South East Asia.[57] Despite this alliance, both companies were competitors in the Turkish natural gas market. While *Gazprom* is planning a pipeline across the Black Sea ('Blue Stream'), Shell was until June 2000 involved in a project which would have delivered Turkmen gas to Turkey via a pipeline across the Caspian Sea.[58]

The cooperation with Ruhrgas - which has a market share of more than 60% in Germany - helps *Gazprom* to increase its access to the West European gas market and to prepare for the partial liberalization of the EU gas market. The partnership with Ruhrgas started in 1970, when the first

---

[54] O'Sullivan and Avdeev 2000, 28.
[55] Moors 1999, 11.
[56] BASF is the abbreviation for Badische Anilin und Soda Fabrik.
[57] Koshkareva and Narzikulov 1997; Shell (1997), 'Creation of a Strategic Alliance between RAO Gazprom and the Royal Dutch/ Shell Group', press release 17 November, <http://www.shell.com/library/press/>.
[58] *Kommersant"* (2000), 29 June; Shell (1999), 'Shell Exploration B. V. signs a Strategic Alliance Agreement with the Government of Turkmenistan', press release 6 August, <http//www.shell.com/library/press/>.

supply contract between the Soviet Union and Ruhrgas was signed. Soviet, respectively Russian, natural gas sales to Ruhrgas in the period 1973-97 amounted to a total of 355bn cm, worth around US$32.5bn (at current prices). By 2020 an additional 370bn cm, worth US$35.5bn, are to be delivered according to present contracts.

Beginning in 1989, *Gazprom* began to look for new business opportunities in the West European downstream sector. However, Ruhrgas seemed to be unwilling to grant its Russian partner access to that profitable part of the gas market. As a result, *Gazprom* signed a cooperation agreement with Wintershall - a subsidiary of BASF and one of the main competitors of Ruhrgas in the German natural gas market - in order to participate in the German downstream market. The agreement includes the joint marketing of Russian natural gas, as well as the joint planning and construction of gas pipelines and storage facilities in Germany and in the neighboring countries. The resulting tensions with Ruhrgas disappeared only very slowly. The cooperation with Wintershall offers *Gazprom* lasting access to the West European gas supply system in the downstream sector.[59] In March 1999, *Gazprom* formed a strategic alliance with BASF for exploiting oil and gas in Russia.[60]

Gazprom's cooperation with Eni, which can be traced back to the end of the 1960s, follows similar patterns. At the beginning of 1998, a strategic alliance was formed for the development, exploitation, transport, and sale of oil, gas, and gas condensate in different countries. Most importantly, Eni is involved in the 'Blue Stream' project. The agreement also includes the development of natural gas fields in the Russian Astrakhanskaia oblast. In addition, *Gazprom* is trying to use its partnership with Eni in order to enter the de-monopolized Italian gas market and to strengthen its position on the Southern European gas market.[61]

Weakening the Central Asian Competitors

Gazprom is trying to weaken the position of Central Asian gas producers, which are trying to reach the world market. Since all producers in the former Soviet republics of Central Asia need the Russian pipeline system for gas exports beyond the region, *Gazprom* has so far been successful. But

---

[59] Heinrich 1999a, 16-18; Heinrich 1999b, 538.
[60] Koksharov 1999, 44; Osetinskaia 1999.
[61] Heinrich 1999a, 18-19. On the liberalization of the European natural gas market see also Feigin 1998, 139-144.

Central Asian producers are now planning alternative export pipelines avoiding Russian territory. Most of these ambitious plans are unlikely to be realized. Accordingly, Central Asian gas producers will continue to depend on *Gazprom*, at least for some years to come.[62]

In order to solve the transit problem and eliminate Central Asian competitors, *Gazprom* aims at the establishment of a unified energy sector within the FSU. This project is promoted by the Russian government. The main instrument for its realization is the acquisition of controlling stakes in energy companies in the relevant states.[63]

In 1999, *Gazprom* signed a deal with the Dutch gas trader Gasunie for delivery of 80bn cm over a 20-year period starting in October 2001. To fulfill this contract, Russia resumed imports from Turkmenistan for the first time since 1997, signing an import deal for a one-year import of 20bn cm. *Gazprom* needs Turkmen gas in the medium-term for the 'Blue Stream' pipeline to Turkey, as well as for the Gasunie deal, because the company's recent cash crunch forced it to cut upstream investment.[64]

Gazprom and the Russian Government on the International Level

Gazprom has not succeeded in using the payment arrears of the transit countries in order to gain control over the transit pipelines. However, these countries' debts to *Gazprom* give the Russian government an instrument for putting pressure on the relevant governments and thus promoting its foreign policy aims. In the case of Ukraine, negotiations concerning the payment of energy bills were held by the Russian government, and not the company management, for a long time. The Russian government used the negotiations as a lever in the quarrels over the future of the Black Sea fleet.

It can be assumed that *Gazprom* and the conservative faction in the Russian government had identical interests in the case of the proposed union between Belarus and Russia. The problem of payment arrears would not be solved through such a union, but it would be easier for *Gazprom* to control the export pipelines going through Belarus. However, the Russian

---

[62] For an overview of the pipeline plans see Heinrich 1998 and Lubin 2000.
[63] For details see Heinrich 1999a, 25-31.
[64] EIA 2000; Gasunie (1999), Key developments in 1999, <http://www.gasunie.nl/eng/p_ga_fi_99.htm>.

government has tried to foster this union by urging *Gazprom* to make cheap gas supplies available to Belarus.[65]

In Central Asia, *Gazprom* has succeeded in getting property rights to gas companies and in enforcing the establishment of joint ventures. Through pressure related to its monopoly on transit pipelines, *Gazprom* was able to become a member of the consortium which exploits the *Karakhaganak* natural gas field in Kazakhstan. In the same way, *Gazprom* entered the gas business in Turkmenistan. In 1995, *Gazprom* enforced the establishment of the joint venture *Turkmenrosgaz*, with a monopoly on Turkmen natural gas exports.

In Central Asia, personal networks between *Gazprom* and the Russian government ensure a conformity of interests regarding the transit policy of *Gazprom*. However, in the case of the joint venture *Turkmenrosgaz*, *Gazprom*'s short-term aim of profit maximization has damaged the long-term interests of Russia in the conflict over the regulation of the legal status of the Caspian Sea. As a result of *Gazprom*'s conflict with Turkmenistan in 1997-98, Russia lost an important ally.[66]

Conclusion

In order to answer the questions whether *Gazprom* is a globalizer and whether the company has developed encompassing interests, one has to distinguish between three levels of action: the national level, the FSU level (the so-called near abroad), and the international level beyond the FSU (the so-called far abroad).

On the international level beyond the FSU, *Gazprom* already developed encompassing interests a long time ago. Since the end of the 1960s, Soviet, respectively Russian, natural gas has been exported to Western Europe. To make these exports possible, the Soviet gas industry, and since 1989 *Gazprom*, has had to establish itself as a reliable partner of the West. The company is looking for cooperation with customers in the West. *Gazprom* pursues a reliable and fair company policy based on the rules of international business behavior. This is the only way for the company to get international loans, to issue ADRs, and to engage in

---

[65] *FSU Oil and Gas Monitor* (1999), No. 29, 20 July; *Itar-TASS* (1999), 15 November and 14 December.
[66] Christophé 1998, 232-235; Götz 1998, 1205. On the quarrels over the legal status of the Caspian Sea see Heinrich 1999c.

strategic partnerships with leading Western natural gas companies. As a result, the Russian gas giant differs less and less from other big national or multinational oil and gas companies.

While *Gazprom* behaves like a global player on the international level, the company does not really function as a globalizer within the FSU. Here, solvency, payment behavior and loyalty to the terms of a contract differ from Western standards. The Russian gas monopoly sees control over the energy sector of the former Soviet Union as an opportunity to maximize profits under these unfavorable conditions. The company tries to externalize costs and to weaken its competitors from Central Asia. A good example was the purchase of Turkmen natural gas through the joint venture *Turkmenrosgaz* at a very low price. *Gazprom* sold this gas at a much higher price in Ukraine and other successor states. At the same time, *Gazprom* was able to sell its own gas production in Western Europe at world market prices.

Gazprom's strategy, though, has so far had only limited success. Neither the restrictions on transit of Central Asian gas through Russia nor the gas debts of Western FSU countries have helped *Gazprom* to gain control over the natural gas sector of the former Soviet Union. Instead, the Central Asian gas producers have been looking for alternative export routes. Western countries - especially the USA - are interested in supporting these attempts as a way to roll back Russian influence in the region. *Gazprom* has also failed to bend the transit countries to its will. On the contrary, the transit countries, and most notably Ukraine, have often forced *Gazprom* to accept a compromise on their debts for natural gas deliveries because of their importance for gas exports. It can be expected that *Gazprom*, together with Russia as a whole, will continue to lose influence in the FSU.

As a result of economic and political conditions similar to those in the other FSU countries, *Gazprom* does not really function as a globalizer in Russia's domestic economy, either. In Russia, too, *Gazprom* is forced to accept rules of the game which differ sharply from internationally accepted modes of behavior.

In addition, the acquisition of Russian companies is increasingly becoming a burden for *Gazprom* because of the losses they produce. Therefore, instead of converting these companies to international accounting standards and promoting their access to international financial markets, which would be an important step towards the globalization of the

Russian economy, *Gazprom* is likely to reverse its engagement in branches of the economy not related to its core business.[67]

It remains unclear how far *Gazprom* will be able to realize its goals. Its success on the international level depends on the further development of Western Europe's and Turkey's demand for gas, which is highly likely to remain below earlier expectations. *Gazprom*'s success in the FSU economies is increasingly being questioned by independent-minded national economic policy makers. The company's role in Russia is likely to be redefined under President Putin. The efforts of the present government under Mikhail Kazianov seem to indicate that state control over the company will increase, limiting the ability of the management to continue its rent-seeking strategy.

In summary, it can be said that *Gazprom* pursues two completely different strategies on its different levels of action. On the international level, the company aims at further integration into a globalizing world economy. On the FSU and national level, however, it tries to preserve regulated and hierarchical markets as a pre-condition for successful rent-seeking behavior based on the externalization of costs. This means that the company has globalized that part of its business which is related to operations with foreign partners and customers. In the FSU, including Russia, however, this globalization does not really have an impact on the company's behavior. In short, *Gazprom* itself is globalized, but it does not function as a globalizer in Russia.

---

[67] See for example Moors 1999, 13.

6 Large Corporations as National and Global Players: The Case of Lukoil

SERGEI P. PEREGUDOV

Among the main agents who determine the nature and the pace of the process of integration of Russia into the global economy, the big Russian corporations and the corporate sector of the economy in general are especially important.

Like most of the other actors in this process, the corporations are not a homogeneous group or entity, and they act in a broad economic and political context. Hence the need to explore the role they play in the Russian economy and in political decision-making, an exploration which would certainly contribute to the assessment of this sector's chances for constructive participation in the process of globalization. Closely related to this problem is the question of the effect of globalization on the actor himself, as well as on the institutional changes connected with it (including property relations). One more aspect of this particular research are the differences within the corporate sector itself. These differences not only influence the pace of its integration into the world economy, but the character of this integration as well.

There are two main factors which make the analysis of the role of the corporate sector in this process in some degree specific. First, the development of the corporate sector itself is still in its formative stage. Second is the transitional character of the Russian economy, which has not yet acquired the qualities of a genuine market economy. In this situation, it is the author's opinion that one of the most fruitful avenues of research are case studies either of individual corporations or of groups of corporations.

This paper is based on a case study of the biggest Russian oil corporation - the *Lukoil* company. Its economic and political activity, as well as the system of social relationships within its enterprises, are in certain ways characteristic of other big Russian corporations, especially of those acquiring global dimensions. The well-known limitations of such studies have stimulated the author to place this particular piece of research into a wider context of observations so as to examine the major tendencies in the development of the corporate sector as a whole.

The Growth of the Corporate Sector in Russia

Russian corporations have a very short history as predominantly market-oriented units. At the same time, they have an important prehistory which is not only a thing of the past. In fact, the 'backbone' of most modern Russian corporations was created in the years of Soviet industrialization, when hundreds of big plants and factories (or enterprises - *predpriiatiia*) as they are usually called in Russia) were built. They composed the very heart of the Soviet economy. But despite their size, the big industrial enterprises were not autonomous bodies, and their management was only one link in a complex hierarchical bureaucratic machine. Nevertheless, from the very beginning there was a clear tendency by management to maintain a certain freedom of maneuver for the biggest enterprises and to develop cooperation among them. As a result, *kontserny* (concerns), *trasty* (trusts) and other similar structures emerged virtually from the very beginning of industrialization.

But the real breakthrough was made, first, during Khrushchev's experiment with the so-called *sovnarkhozy* (regional economic zones) at the beginning of 1960s, and then during the Brezhnev years. In addition to the above, two new kinds of structures were created: the state industrial and the intersectoral state units or groups. Both of them were called *ob"edinenie* (plural: *ob"edineniia*), i.e. a combination of enterprises, the biggest being the 'head' of the group. In the oil industry, the *ob"edineniia* emerged even before the experiment with the *sovnarkhosy*. Sometimes they were called *kombinaty*.[1] By decree of the Council of Ministers of the USSR dating 23 September 1973, the managements of the *ob"edineniia* were given a large degree of autonomy, and they were organized on the principle of vertical integration.[2] A typical example of these was the *Noril'skii Nikel' kombinat*, which united 76 pits, plants and other enterprises of various

---

[1] Kriukov 1998, 75.
[2] Petukhov 1999, 21.

kinds. At the beginning of *perestroika*, the number of such groups reached 500.[3]

Despite the strict hierarchy in the planned Soviet economy and ministerial control, the *ob''edineniia* became important actors in regional, republican and central economic decision-making. They were the main participants in the so-called bureaucratic or administrative market,[4] which functioned alongside the planned economy and was the predecessor of the market economy of today's Russia. In a more general political context, they acted as the key participants in bureaucratic corporatism.[5] This double bureaucracy was not the best system of management, and it quite logically led to economic stagnation.

One of the most important economic decisions during *perestroika* was the decree 'On the state enterprise (*ob''edinenie*)' approved by the Supreme Soviet of the USSR in November 1987. The result was a serious change in the position and role of such economic units and of their management. They and their subdivisions were given much more autonomy in economic decision-making and in the formation of management (from 'top' to 'bottom'). But contrary to the expectations of the reformers, the result of this measure was not to strengthen the *ob''edineniia* but rather to seriously weaken them. The management of single enterprises (even small ones) began to behave as virtually separate units. At the same time the industrial ministries, seeking to preserve their authority, tried to accentuate their direct links with the single enterprises, avoiding 'intermediate' links, i.e. the *ob''edineniia*, which had begun to endanger their positions. However, this 'strategy' met with strong resistance from the management of enterprises, who tried to free themselves completely from any supervision and 'command'. As a result, the existing hierarchy of decision-making broke down, and lobbying emerged as the predominant form of state-business relations. So, I prefer to characterize the economic order of that time as 'chaotic pluralism'.

The liberal reforms carried out under the Gaidar government and the privatization fathered by Chubais changed the political context and the ownership structure of Russian enterprises still further. As a result of these economic policies, not only private and semi-private companies emerged, but the state-owned ones became legally more autonomous. One of the

---

[3] Ibid., 18.
[4] For a description of the term and the substance of the reality behind it see: Naishul 1992, 69-81; Aven and Shironin 1987, 32-41.
[5] See, for example, Peregudov (2000), 128-130.

important aspects of this new development was the arrival of foreign companies in Russia and the establishment of partnerships with their Russian counterparts. A most serious 'penetration' by foreign capital was especially characteristic of the development of the fuel and energy sector and of metallurgy. Despite the narrow base of this cooperation (limited mainly to the raw material and export-oriented industries), it was a serious step in the direction of a more organic integration of the Russian economy into the global context.

But there was another serious consequence of the liberal reforms for Russian industry. The dogmatic neoliberal approach of the Gaidar-Chubais team of reformers led to even more dramatic disorder in the industrial structure and to the factual dissolution of many potentially effective *ob"edineniia* and *konzerny*. It was quite logical that in the federal law 'About enterprises and enterprising activity' of 1992, the term *ob"edinenie* was not mentioned at all. As one of the well-known Russian economists of the new generation, Mikhail Deliagin, recently wrote, during privatization the 'severing of technological production chains was taking place'.[6]

Only in the mid-1990s, when the advocates of the neoliberal approach had moderated their liberalism and the negative consequences of their policy had became widely evident, did a new, more favorable, situation for the development of the corporate sector emerge. However, this development was accompanied by some serious anomalies. The first stemmed from the abnormal expansion of the new banking oligarchy. Using their close relations with the state bureaucracy involved in the privatization process, they acquired through the so-called loan-for-share auctions many of the enterprises and companies with the greatest potential and built up huge financial-industrial conglomerates.[7] The main deficiency of these structures was the lack of constructive relationships between their financial and industrial sections and, as a result, the continuing stagnation of the latter.[8] Despite definite obligations in the agreements between the state and the banks, hardly any investments in these companies were made, and in many cases the reverse process of sucking out resources and money took place.

---

[6] Deliagin 2000, 4.
[7] The most accurate description of them has been given in the book: Pappe 1997.
[8] As head of the biggest conglomerate based on *Onexim* bank, Vladimir Potanin said in one of his interviews later that 'financial-industry groups like *Onexim* were no more than collections of assets', *Izvestiia* (1999), 14 March.

The second anomaly originated from the state strategy of creating so-called financial-industrial groups (FIGs). This was considered by many influential intellectuals and politicians as the most appropriate and up-to-date way to modernize the industrial economy of the country. As a rule, such groups were created by presidential decrees, and in reality their financial and economic base was often either very weak or almost non-existent. The weaknesses of both kinds of corporation came to the surface immediately following the financial crash of 17 August 1998. Many conglomerates and financial industrial groups either disintegrated or were decimated.[9]

But it would be wrong to underestimate the process of corporate formation which was under way despite the activities of the oligarchy and the bureaucracy. Even the underdeveloped market and the 'imperfect competition' which emerged in Russia after *perestroika* encouraged a substantial part of management, including old management, to apply new, more or less up-to-date, methods of management and organization and to make their companies and enterprises efficient enough to survive in critical situations. Even serious critics of 'official' FIGs admit that, despite their failure, a number of them continue to play a 'noticeably constructive role', especially in cases where they are evolving into genuinely integrated business groups.[10]

The impact of the August crash on the corporate sector was on the whole more positive than negative. By destroying weak structures and connections, it put an end to the artificial, bureaucratic approach to corporate 'construction' and freed the space for real, 'natural' processes. According to data published in the *Ekspert* journal, during the year following the default of 1998, the list of the 200 biggest Russian industrial companies was renewed by about 20%.[11] It is also worth noting that the most dynamic corporations, the so-called growth leaders, could now be clearly identified in the manufacturing industry (including aircraft and other companies in the defense industry), the chemical and construction industries, and industries producing food, clothing and other consumer goods. Nevertheless, the companies of the fuel and energy complex and

---

[9] As a well-known expert of the Association of Russian Banks, Lev Makarevich, writes, 'the August crisis shook the financial-industrial groups to their roots'. Many of them freed themselves from the grip of banks, deprived them from their most valuable assets, threw out their managers and personnel. (Makarevich 1999, 136).
[10] Pappe 2000, 37.
[11] 'Ezhegodnii reiting krupneyshikh kompanii Rossii', in *Ekspert* (1999), 27 September, 54-56.

metallurgy remain the largest among the 'big 200'. Together with other companies producing raw materials, they account for about half of the list (96 companies) and more than four-fifths of the largest 20 of that list (17).[12]

One of the main factors influencing the changes in the corporate sector of the economy at the end of 1990 and the beginning of the new millennium is the continuing process of redistribution of ownership. The slow-down in privatization of state and semi-state property after 1996 was compensated for by the growing number of changes of ownership control through bankruptcies of privately owned companies. According to specialists of the Institute for Systemic Analysis of the Russian Academy of Sciences, about one-third of ownership control in the economy as a whole shifts from one person or group to another every year (with a great deal of corruption and criminal pressure accompanying these changes).[13] All these changes accelerate the process of consolidation of corporate control and the expansion of the most successful and aggressive companies, a process which has intensified from 1998 on. One of the consequences has been the emergence of some big new 'stars' in the corporate sector.[14]

Side by side with the spontaneous process of corporate formation, the state authorities (mainly the Ministry of Economics) have taken some new initiatives. According to the Deputy Minister of Economics, Sergei Mitin, the main reason for such initiatives is the fact that the share of goods and services produced by the FIGs in Russia is three times lower than the share such units produce in the world economy.[15]

As is evident from a large number of reliable sources, and despite the many irregularities (to put it mildly) of various kinds accompanying the present stage of corporate sector formation, the process of building up a more or less genuine corporate sector is gaining momentum. This sector will seriously influence the space and the forms of its integration into the new global economic and political order.

---

[12] Ibid., 46-47.
[13] Dubrovskii 2000.
[14] Pappe 2000, 110.
[15] *Nezavisinaia gazeta* (2000), 12 January.

The Case Study

The Lukoil Company as an Economic Actor

The history of *Lukoil* as a homogeneous entity began in 1991, when it was organized as a *kontsern* uniting a number of big enterprises of various kinds in the oil industry. In November 1992, it was given the status of a shareholding company by presidential decree, and after reorganization in April 1993, it functioned as a holding company with many affiliated autonomous 'daughter' companies. In 1994, the process of privatization began. In 1996, the shareholdings of the 'daughter companies' were concentrated in the central company. But from the very beginning, *Lukoil* operated as a vertically-integrated corporation. As the leadership of the company has stressed, this structure was formed in the course of a bitter struggle with the neoliberal privatizers, who tried to split the oil industry into hundreds of independently functioning units.

As was mentioned earlier, *Lukoil* is the biggest among Russian oil companies. In 1998, its wells extracted about 65 million tons (mt) of crude oil, or about 20% of the total amount of national oil production. The oil processing enterprises of the company produce about 12% of the national total of petrol and other oil products. The company owns about 1,000 petrol filling stations, more than 800 of them in Russia. For some years, it has been building its own fleet of tankers and possesses a large number of railway tank cars and trucks. At the end of 1998, the company controlled over 13% of the Russian tanker fleet (66 ships altogether),[16] and there were several more tankers under construction, including ten icebreakers. In 1999, construction of seven of them was completed (five in the shipyards of Germany and two in St. Petersburg).[17] It is worth noting that the whole of the nuclear-powered, ice-breaker tanker fleet of Russia is owned by the company.[18]

The activity of the company embraces more than 30 regions and republics of Russia and more than 14 foreign countries, among them Azerbaijan, Kazakhstan, the Baltic states, Ukraine, Romania and Iraq. It has about 40 daughter and ten dependent companies which act as operationally independent bodies. The company is in a state of permanent expansion. In 1999, it bought a controlling packet of shares in the company

---

[16] Lukoil 1999a, 5.
[17] *Neft Rossii* (2000), No. 2, 19.
[18] Pappe 2000, 188-194.

which owns the port of Murmansk and its tanker fleet. Its most recent acquisition is the *Komitek* company, which possesses the rich oilfields in the Timano-Pechora basin in the north of European Russia. This is the biggest merger in the Russian oil industry since the beginning of privatization. As a result, the productive capacity of the enlarged company has risen to 75mt of crude oil, and the share of *Lukoil* in Russian oil production has risen to 24%.[19] In 1998, the company bought 51% of the shares of the largest oil refinery plant in Romania. It also keeps a controlling packet of shares in the biggest oil refinery plants in Ukraine and Bulgaria. In 1999, it entered into negotiations over the purchase of the biggest oil refinery in the Czech Republic.

Lukoil now ranks fourth among the oil-producing companies of the world, and by the quantity of confirmed oil reserves in its oilfields, it holds first place.[20] According to an interview by the vice-president of the company, Leonid Fedun, in 1999 the amount of oil and gas stocks controlled by *Lukoil* rose to 17bn barrels, and the company intends to increase them still further in 2000 to 20bn barrels (7bn of them abroad).[21]

Besides the CIS countries, the company is striving to establish and strengthen its cooperation with major Western oil companies. Its closest partners include the American oil corporation Arco, together with which the joint company LukArco has been established. 54% of LukArco's assets belong to *Lukoil*, 46% to Arco.[22] The main sphere of its activity is the exploration and extraction of oil in the Caspian region.[23] Besides cooperation with Arco, *Lukoil* is participating in a joint project '*Severnie territorii*' with the American company Conco for the exploration of oil fields in northern European Russia. The legal basis for such cooperation is the law on production sharing, for which *Lukoil* was one of the most influential lobbyists. There are many other projects, including construction of several hundred filling stations in the USA and in Western Europe. In December 1998, *Lukoil* and the Indian oil company ONYC signed an agreement on the mutual development of oil fields in Kazakhstan, Turkmenistan and Iraq. In cooperation with the Italian oil company Agip, *Lukoil* is exploring oil fields in Egypt. The company currently sells about

---

[19] *Neft' Rossii* (2000), No. 2, 16.
[20] Lukoil 1999a, 17.
[21] *Vedomosti* (2000), 16 February.
[22] Lukoil 1999a, 34.
[23] After the proposed merger between BP-Amoco and Arco some changes in *Lukoil*-Arco cooperation may be possible.

40% of its oil production in the world market. One of the most ambitious international projects in which *Lukoil* participates (with a 10%-share) is the Caspian pipeline consortium. There are eleven oil companies, most of them are transnational, taking part in it. The pipeline will connect the Tengiz oil field in Kazakhstan with the Russian port of Novorossiisk, and its capacity will be 1.3 million barrels a day. The opening date is set for the middle of 2001.[24]

Lukoil is the first (and up to now the only) Russian oil company selling (since 1996) its shares (in ADR form) in the international financial market.

In fact, *Lukoil* is one of the first Russian transnational corporations. But as its leaders constantly stress, the company has not yet acquired some of the important features of genuine TNCs. Its technological base and the skill of its personnel and staff do not allow it to act on equal terms with its main competitors. It intends to reach this stage only in several years, after a serious modernization of its production base and other facilities.

As underlined in official documents of the company, most of the projects in countries and regions outside of Russia are in an 'initial state of realization'.[25] Striving to proceed as quickly as possible, the company is rapidly increasing its oil exploration and production in foreign countries. In 1996, it produced 0.3mt of crude oil abroad; in the following year, 0.6mt; in 1998, 1.2mt, and in 1999 about 2mt.[26] The potentially most fruitful region for oil production abroad is the Western Kurna II in Iraq, where the share of *Lukoil* in proven oil stocks is about 380mt (plus 300-400mt of potential stocks).[27] There are about 80 projects for oil exploration and production in Kazakhstan, Azerbaijan, Turkmenistan, Iran, Syria, Libya, Algeria, Sudan and some other countries.[28]

The company has close ties with some Russian and foreign banks, but in contrast to corporations based on banks, *Lukoil* belongs to the industry-based type of corporation. This was one of the major factors helping the company to pull through the 1998 August crisis without serious setbacks and to use the more favorable opportunities in the domestic market to strengthen its internal and external positions.

---

[24] *Neft' Rossii* (2000), No. 1, 5.
[25] Lukoil 1999a, 27.
[26] Ibid., 12.
[27] Ibid., 11.
[28] Ibid., 11-12.

The Lukoil Company as a Political Actor

From the very beginning of its existence, the leadership of the company stressed the importance of constructive cooperation with the state.[29] Among the many factors accounting for such an orientation is the composition of its top management, which originated mainly from the former industry's *nomenklatura*. Its president is Vagit Alekperov, the former first deputy minister of the oil and gas industry of the USSR. Eight of the 11 members of the board of directors elected at the annual shareholders meeting in June 1999 belong to the former managerial elite of the oil industry. Their managerial careers began mostly in the 1970s and 1980s, and they are as a rule between 40 and 50 years old. The president of the company was born in 1950.[30] Approximately of the same age and level of professional qualifications is the top management of the 'branch' companies and enterprises. But there is a continuous process of change in the composition of the management, and a growing number of lawyers, economists, and public relations officers is stepping in.

The effectiveness of the industrial and commercial activities of the company is to a great extent dependent on the regulatory functions of the federal authorities, and this is another major factor influencing its general attitude to the state. The most important forms of state regulation are control of access to the state-owned oil-transportation system (through the pipelines of the *Transneft'* company), the system of price and export regulation, financial and distributional control, and taxation. The existing weak juridical base and (consequently) the 'freedom of action' for the state authorities in all these spheres of regulation compel the leadership of the company to be as close to the state as possible.

One more factor influencing the company's relations with the state is the latter's financial stake in the company. At the end of 1995, the state owned 80.4% of company shares; by the end of 1999, this had dropped to 26%. Following the sale of 9% of company shares in 1999, and 1% in March 2000, state ownership dropped to about 15%. The on-going privatization of state holdings of *Lukoil* is definitely in the interests of its management and private shareholders. The obvious reason for this is the desire to be sovereign master of the company, and not the 'half-master' (*polukhoziain*) as they feel themselves to be when the state shareholdings are proportionately large.

---

[29] Alekperov 1996, 94.
[30] Lukoil 1999b.

Despite the presence on the *Lukoil* board of directors of three representatives of the state, the company is now virtually privately-owned (in contrast to *Gazprom,* United Energy System *(EES)* and some other big semi-state corporations). The biggest shareholders are the so-called nominal keepers closely associated with the corporation (the investment company *Nikoil*, the pension fund *Lukoil-Garant*, and the depositary company *Nikoil*).[31] The proportion belonging to individual shareholders is only about 4% of the total. Among foreign shareholders of *Lukoil*, the biggest one is its American partner Arco, which purchased 8% of the company's shares in 1995-96. There are some other foreign shareholders, but their shares are mostly dispersed and held by nominal keepers. Such a disposition of shareholdings makes the top management of the company its real master. It is quite logical that seven of the eleven seats on the board of directors belong to the leading figures of the corporation, its 'daughters', and dependent companies. It is worth noting that the 9% packet sold at the end of 1999 was purchased by a company closely associated with *Lukoil*.

Despite ongoing privatization and the strengthening of management's position in the company, the state authorities' 'freedom of action' vis-à-vis the company is not diminishing. The tendency of the state to strengthen its economic regulatory and redistributive activities makes even wholly private companies more and more dependent on the state. As mentioned earlier, the top management of the company tries to be as close to the state as possible. But to be close to the state does not mean to identify with it or to be its servant; quite the contrary, in this case. The very fact of its enormous dependence on the state motivates the leadership of the company to use its close relations with the state authorities to take an active part in decision making having to do with its own interests.

Such influence is exercised in two main ways. First is the direct participation of the company's top personalities in the decision-making process, mainly on the level of the executive branch of the state. Crucial to this participation are formal and informal meetings by the Russian president and premier with the so-called oligarchs. The president of *Lukoil* is one of the most important participants in such meetings, and this is a factor accounting for his significant political influence in the country.

---

[31] Investment and depositarian *Nikoil* companies belong to the Investment banking group *Nokoil*. They are keepers and managers of the 'Checks investment funds' (CIF's) formed during the first stage of *Lukoil*'s privatization. Altogether they keep about 1/6 of the company's shareholdings. The pension fund of *Lukoil* company *Lukoil-Garant* keeps about 7% of its shares (Lukoil 1999a, 44; Zatsepilov 2000).

According to the average rating for 1999, Vagit Alekperov is one of the 100 most influential Russian politicians, and he occupied 26th place on the list.[32] In contrast to some other major Russian corporations, none of the senior managers of *Lukoil* are, or were, government officials. Instead, the company maintains close relations with ministers and other senior officials of the government, especially in the Ministry of Fuel and Energy, Ministries of Finance, Economy, Foreign Economic Relations, Foreign Affairs, Natural Resources and the Federal Energy Commission. This means, in particular, that the main channel of the company's relations with the government is 'outside' lobbying. In fact, there is a very thin distinction between political intervention at the highest level and 'outside' lobbying, and it is sometimes difficult to distinguish one from the other.

There are two main ways of lobbying in today's Russia: the 'shadow' approach and the open or 'transparent' approaches. *Lukoil* uses both of them. There are some indications that the company is acquiring valuable experience in the latter, and the author considers this tendency as a very positive one. Its importance will be more evident if we take into consideration the number of 'dirty' techniques used in Russian lobbying today. One of the factors enhancing the political influence of the company is its stake in the mass media. Following the example of some other big political players among Russian business 'oligarchs', it acquired almost 50% of the shares in the newspaper *Izvestiia* and participates in the shareholdings of some magazines and TV companies, especially in regions where it is industrially active. *Lukoil* has control over several regional and local TV channels and other PR facilities. The growing network of various PR structures at the regional level has helped it to enter the next stage in its electoral activity. Previously, the company used money mainly to support candidates, parties and 'blocks'. During the last general election, held on 19 December 1999, it was able successfully to use not only its money, but its own central and regional PR services. In some cases, it acted as a 'mini-party'. The company supported some electoral blocks and parties in many ways, as well as several candidates in 'one member' electoral constituencies in regions. Together with the candidates supported by *Gazprom* and some other oil companies, there is a numerous group of deputies in today's Duma with more or less close relations to the oil and gas sector of Russian industry. According to reliable sources, this group is more numerous now than in the previous Duma. Thus, in contrast to 'outside' lobbying in the executive branch of the state, the lobby of *Lukoil*

---

[32] '100 vedushchikh politikov Rossii v 1999 godu', in *NG-Stsenarii* (2000), No. 1.

and other units of the fuel and energy complex (FEC) in the legislative assembly of the country is mainly 'inside'.

All that has been said above about the economic and political potential of the company and its activities enhances its political position in dealing with various partners outside Russia. According to statements by the president and other officials of the company, priority in the company's external activities is given to the Commonwealth of Independent States (CIS). The loose legal framework of relations between Russia and the other CIS countries gives the company in many cases a virtually free hand in dealing with the companies and officials of these countries. It is also an influential participant in official negotiations between Russia and the CIS and other countries in the area of 'oil diplomacy'. The statute of the company authorizes its top management 'to take part in negotiations between states and governments about agreements regulating the trading activities of the company'.[33] The diplomatic activity of the company often goes beyond the scope of cooperation with the state authorities and acquires some features of an 'oil diplomacy' of its own, replacing the state's activity in this field. Such activities have increasingly led to protests, especially from the Ministry of Fuel and Energy, which seeks to normalize the situation by means of official directives and other, similar measures.[34] The author suggests that such conflicts are not accidental, but indicate the growing political potential (and ambitions) of companies like *Lukoil* and their increased capacity for performing as influential global actors. Of course, the focal point of these activities is economic. But at the same time, they have a significant political dimension and are an organic part of the political economy of the Russian corporate sector.

The Lukoil Company as a Social Institution

Three main areas of social relations determine the role of *Lukoil* as a social institution and influence its position in the global market: first, management-employee relations; second, interaction between the company and local communities; and third, the positions and influence of individual shareholders. Most important are the first and the second levels, and both of them are developing in the context of strong Soviet paternalistic traditions and the growing pressures of the international or global market. The Soviet paternalistic tradition is reinforced by the functioning of the company's

---

[33] Lukoil 1996, 3.
[34] Kalyzhniy 2000.

strong trade union, which inherited from old times a 100% employee membership (including not only middle, but top management as well). The president and the other senior managers consider the company as a 'family'. This is not merely an empty slogan: behind it are effective policies in such areas as housing, health, pensions, professional education, food supplies at the work place, rest and leisure facilities, and so on. Three-fourths of the 85,000 individual shareholders are company employees. An active social policy is considered by the owners and managers of the company to be not only a necessary means against social unrest, but also an effective incentive for maintaining productivity and a positive work ethic.

Like almost every other big oil company, *Lukoil* has its 'own' towns and areas in big cities where its employees and their families live in compact communities. Despite some changes in recent years, the company retains close 'family' relations with these communities and their authorities. In the company's 'capital', Kogalim, a Siberian town of 40,000 inhabitants, for example, it has built not only houses for employees and buildings for recreation, sport, shopping, and health services, but also a very impressive Russian orthodox church and a big Muslim mosque.[35] Under pressure from global market competition, and in line with the general strategy of Russian business, the company makes serious efforts to free itself from the 'outside' social infrastructure. But this does not mean that it intends to free itself from the 'obligations' towards its employees mentioned above. These obligations are undergoing a significant change. In previous times, they were mainly (though not only) territorial ones; now they are becoming mainly functional ones.

In accordance with the facts given above, social relations within the *Lukoil* company are developing in the direction of a social partnership model. So it is quite natural that the general secretary of the International Federation of Unions of Employees in the Chemical, Mining, Energy Industries and General Workers (ICEM) has said that *Lukoil*'s union has been able to realize many of the principles of its strategy in TNCs which are only in the preparatory stage in the ICEM.[36]

---

[35] Gareev 1999.
[36] Iashchenko 1999, 108.

Typical or Atypical Russian Corporation?

As an economic, political and social actor, *Lukoil* is closely related to the big export-oriented companies. Most of these belong to the oil and gas complex which accounts for about 65% of the budget revenue of the country.[37] But within this sector, there are not only similarities, but also significant differences. *Lukoil* is not only the biggest, it is also the most effective oil company. One of the reasons for this is that - like *Surgutneftegaz*, another effective oil corporation - *Lukoil* has no financial superstructure above it. Many other big oil corporations (*Iukos*, *Sidanko*, *Sibneft'*) were 'occupied' in 1995-96 by the 'oligarchs' and were used by them mainly as a source for enriching themselves. All of these companies have experienced serious problems, especially following the crisis of August 1998. But the crisis resulted in weakening the grip of the oligarchs (as in the case of *Sidanko*) and in changing their behavior in a more constructive direction (*Sibneft'*, *Iukos*). Another new development in almost all these companies was a change in their organizational structure towards a vertically integrated model (i.e. like *Lukoil*).

As political actors, most of them are far behind *Lukoil*, thus giving the latter the opportunity in many cases to act as a representative of the oil industry as a whole, especially in situations where the 'Oil and Gas Producer's Union' is not effective enough. The weakness of this association is not accidental, of course. Like the inadequacy of most other sectoral and main central business associations, this weakness reflects the very low level of corporate solidarity among big business actors and of the entire business elite in Russia. The formation of a more effective group of deputies representing the FEC in the Duma is an indication of new trends towards strengthening this solidarity. But it is too early to say how far and how quickly this process will develop. The acquisition of real political strength by the major oil and gas producers' organization just mentioned would represent a real breakthrough, but there are no serious signs of this.

Alongside the evolution of a more homogeneous organizational structure, there are also clear signs of normalization in the social relations of oil-gas corporations. In fact, almost all of them have taken the path of the modernized paternalism which has so far been successfully followed by *Lukoil*'s managerial elite.

---

[37] *Neft' Rossii* (2000), No. 1, 3; *Sovershenno sekretno* (2000), No. 1, 6.

The Russian Corporation between National Peculiarity and Global Universality

One of the most important political problems arising from the case study of the *Lukoil* company is the problem of corporate-state relations. Three main models may be identified here on the basis of this study. One is the strong statist model, preferred by many of the 'problematic' business corporations. What these corporations want is state assistance of various kinds, and in many cases, their managers are even ready for the re-nationalization of their enterprises and companies. At the opposite pole is the liberal-market model, which is favored by the more economically successful corporate managers with a neoliberal mentality. They prefer minimal state regulation, limited only to setting the 'rules of the game'. Between these two polar models, there is a third which may be called 'neostatist'. The businessmen behind it are in fact also in favor of minimal state regulation, but at the same time they prefer close and constructive interaction with the state.

As is clear from the case study, *Lukoil* top management at *Lukoil* strives to work within this intermediate model. But it is not a model without variations, and individual actors accentuate its different aspects. The top management of *Lukoil*, for example, is definitely moving from a modern statist position to a more liberal-statist one.[38] Some tendencies in state policy, especially in taxation, prices, currency, customs and distributive regulation, and oil and gas transportation, often go against the interests of the company and its development as an effective competitor in the world market. But as we have seen, a paradox emerges at this point: the weaker the state regulation preferred by the company, the stronger are its efforts to enhance its political potential and its political role in order to be able to withstand state intervention.

The factors making for the politicization of *Lukoil* are valid for many, or even most, other big corporations, and not only the export-oriented ones. The processes of on-going politicization are aimed, among other things, at strengthening their positions and their influence in the world market. The

---

[38] In his book published in 1996, the president of *Lukoil* wrote about 'necessity of it (state) participation in the reproduction process' (Alekperov 1996, 94). Three years later, the head of the PR service of the company, Aleksandr Vasilenko, said in an interview that if the state wants to have an efficient economic management in the oil industry, it should give its ownership rights to the competent owners and free itself from a direct managerial role. *Vedomosti* (2000), 18 January.

general effect of this will favor the deeper involvement of the Russian economy in the process of globalization.

The economic and political interests of *Lukoil* and other export-oriented companies and their owners and chief executive officers make them especially good candidates for complex integration into the global economy. Striving to achieve such integration, they play the role of 'key globalizers' in Russian economic and political circles. In contrast to the other real or potential globalizers among the representatives of federal and local administrations, politicians, professional and media elites, they are not divided into 'pro-global' and nationalistic factions. Their economic and political influence in general, and their lobbying in particular, have strengthened the position of the 'pro-western' faction of Russian ruling circles, in this way enhancing tendencies toward Russia's integration into the world economy, and the process of globalization in general.

However, we have to keep in mind that companies like *Lukoil* and other 'outward-looking' corporations are only a part of the corporate sector, and that the political influence of other statist-oriented and 'inward-looking' ones (as well as their allies in political circles) is not to be underestimated. Therefore, the most likely general strategy of Russia towards globalization will be formed as the result of a compromise between these two factions of the economic and political elite.

Of course, there are some other important factors which influence and will continue to influence the breadth and 'depth' of Russian companies' integration into the global economy. One of them is the amount and quality of foreign capital inflow and, in particular, the formation of 'partnership' companies (like LukArco) with a significant potential for organizational and technological modernization. Unfortunately, the situation at the time of writing is not encouraging, because the bulk of foreign capital so far invested in Russia is of a speculative character. According to estimates by a reliable expert, there were about 20,000 foreign companies in Russia at the beginning of 2000, but of these, only three to 4% were seriously involved in industrial production and had invested real money in it.[39]

The case study of *Lukoil* is also indicative of some tendencies in corporate social behavior in Russia. As is well known, there are two main rival models of social relations in transnational companies: one model based on the effective participation of its personnel and to some extent of the local community in decision-making (stakeholding company), and the

---

[39] Prokopenko 2000.

other based mainly on the absolute power of the owners and top management (shareholding company). The *Lukoil* case study indicates a very strong possibility that Russian TNCs will be developing, at least in the immediate future, towards the second one (though of course with their own peculiarities). Accordingly, their development will strengthen the position of those who argue for a strong social dimension in corporate activity and for 'corporate citizenship' as a strategic perspective of globalization. Despite the significant economic advantages of the shareholders' model, they are, from the author's point of view, mainly of a transitory character and will grow to be less and less effective at the time when a social and political dimension of the global market and the global economy will become indispensable.

To use Mancur Olson's terminology of 'stationary' and 'roving bandits',[40] this particular actor (*Lukoil*) has from the very beginning behaved as a 'stationary bandit', striving first of all to satisfy its own corporate interests. But its close ties with the state and the 'neo-statist', paternalistic attitudes of its top leadership, as well as its involvement with the loose network of the oil-and-gas industry managerial elite, do not allow it to act as a 'single bandit' who totally ignores the damage which his action may inflict on society.

There is a definite tendency for 'stationary bandits' like *Lukoil*, *Gazprom*, *Surgutneftegaz*, and some others to transform themselves into a 'family of rational stationary bandits' interested in the growth of productivity and the well-being of society. But this tendency is very weak, the main reason being the presence of many influential 'roving bandits' in the oil and some other export-oriented industries. In the last two years, some of their owners have begun to change their 'speculative' orientation as 'robbers' toward a more positive or constructive position and have shown a growing interest in building more stable and effective industrial units (like *Noril'skii Nikel'*, *Iukos* and some others). But this process is very slow and contradictory, and there is some uncertainty as to further developments.

Of course, this development significantly influences the pattern of participation by large Russian export-oriented corporations in the process of globalization. All of them are making substantial efforts to be involved in globalization, but if the 'stationary bandits' are more and more interested in developing along organized international interaction, the 'roving bandits' tend to be orientated toward financial speculation in the global political

---

[40] Olson 1995, 4-6.

economy. The first tendency is, however, obviously getting stronger, and the author is almost sure that in a few years time it will definitely determine the behavior of Russian big business in the global economy.

Conclusion

The main findings of this part of the Project may be summarized as follows: Despite its very short history, the corporate sector of present-day Russia has become the most influential part of its economy and plays an important role in its politics. In the absence of a genuine party-political system, it is now one of the most important participants in the decision-making process, especially in the sphere of economic policy.

The present stage of corporate formation in Russia is characterized by the predominance of export-oriented companies producing mainly raw materials and selling them in the world market.

The big corporations in this group (as the case of *Lukoil* demonstrates) do their best to become an organic part of the network of transnational companies and to occupy a leading position in the process of integrating the Russian economy into the global market. The very fact of their existence, and even their modest success, is of great importance for the process of step-by-step adaptation of the domestic economy to the changes induced by globalization.

'Stationary bandits' like *Lukoil* are gaining the upper hand in the balance between 'stationary' and 'roving bandits' in the corporate sector of the economy, and are in this way enhancing a more positive role for Russian companies in the process of globalization. Both of them are strongly for close integration in the global market, but while the 'stationary bandits' are motivated mainly by national interests and the desire for constructive international cooperation, the 'roving bandits' and their allies in political circles are motivated by cosmopolitan values and are striving for a depoliticized world order.

The imbalance among the Russian participants in the world market in favor of oil, gas and other companies of the fuel and energy complex and metallurgy determines to a large extent the present and future role of Russian corporations in the process of globalization. Not only is there a low turnover of Russian goods on the world market, but also their specific character does not allow Russian corporations to become a substantial part of the global economy.

Nevertheless, their specific social and political characteristics will give some impetus to the formation of a more organized and just global order.

As they participate in the process of globalization, Russian companies are more and more influenced by it. As the case study shows, they are becoming less statist in their general approach and are doing their best to free themselves from state shareholdings. But, at the same time, they are becoming more and more politicized. Stimulated first of all by the large and for some time growing regulatory activities of the Russian state, this tendency may contribute to the strengthening of the political dimension of globalization. As for the Russian state itself, the author is of the opinion that the still substantial amount of its regulatory activity may to some extent hinder the general trend toward decreasing the role of the national state as a result of globalization.

7 The Mining and Metals Industry and Globalization

STEPHEN FORTESCUE

Globalization means many things to many people. In its most radical form, it is the global spread of knowledge and knowledge-based activities, in which geographical location becomes increasingly irrelevant.[1] This form of globalization is of limited relevance to the mining and metals (M&M) industry, in which the location of raw material and energy inputs and means of transport are necessarily of fundamental importance. Naturally, technology and its transfer have an important role to play in the industry, because of technology's influence on competitiveness and, of particular importance in this industry, environmental sustainability. Nevertheless, the industry deals essentially with embodied technologies. Indeed, there are some peculiarities of the Russian resource base that have led to a degree of geographical determination even of Russian M&M technology.

Globalization as 'the increasing integration of world capital and trade flows'[2] is of greater relevance to the global M&M industry, as foreign subsidiaries, cross-border equity relationships and alliances, and foreign investment have increased in importance in recent decades.[3] As this paper is being written, the international industry is going through a new wave of consolidation, often across national boundaries.[4] However, as we will see in this paper, these aspects of globalization, while not entirely absent from the Russian M&M sector, play a relatively minor role.

Most analyses of the international M&M industry in terms of globalization focus heavily on two traditional and even mundane phenomena: international sourcing of raw materials and a large proportion

---

[1] Omae 1990.
[2] *The Economist* (1999), 21 August, 9.
[3] OECD 1996, chapters 6 and 7.
[4] *The Economist* (1999), 14 August, 54 and 28 August, 49-50.

of output entering international trade.⁵ It is precisely here that the most dramatic changes have occurred in the post-Soviet Russian M&M sector. And while in the story of globalization as a whole these aspects may be mundane, in the history of the Soviet Union and Russia they are far from being so. The basic question of whether Russia should become part of global society - particularly one dominated by the West - can be traced back to the old Slavophile-Westernizer debate, a debate which is by no means dead in contemporary Russia. But in the far narrower application relevant to the M&M industry, the question of autonomy of inputs and markets is today no less controversial: can and should Russia strive for self-sufficiency; if it is to be involved in the global economy, in what form; and what will be the consequences of a shift towards or away from the global economy? These are questions which continue to have political and economic resonance in Russia today.

This paper takes the four aspects of globalization that are seen as relevant to the international M&M industry - a large proportion of output entering international trade, international sourcing of outputs, cross-border capital integration, and technology transfer - and applies them to the Russian industry. We will begin by summarizing the situation at the end of the Soviet period and then examine changes in the post-Soviet period. The focus then shifts to an examination of the attitudes towards these various developments, all of which are contentious, of various Russian political and policy actors. Finally, in conclusion, an attempt is made to combine the objective circumstances in which the Russian M&M industry finds itself - raw material reserves, geographical location, transport capacities, markets, etc. - with political and policy trends, to arrive at a prediction of the outlook for globalization and the Russian M&M industry.

The Soviet Period

It is generally accepted that the Soviet economy, and the M&M sector within it, strove for self-sufficiency. In terms of raw material inputs, the ferrous sector was essentially self-sufficient.⁶ With the significant exception of bauxite imports for aluminum producers, on which more below, the same could be said of the non-ferrous sector. The drive for self-sufficiency in raw material inputs was not uncontroversial. In the 1970s, when the

---

⁵ OECD 1996, chapters 6 and 7.
⁶ Rumer 1989, 4.

whole issue of the extent to which the Soviet Union should open itself to the world was a matter of debate, there was a lobby calling for the abandonment of the self-sufficiency goal. It was claimed that self-sufficiency forced the Soviet Union to rely on inferior grade ores in increasingly inaccessible regions, meaning that the opportunity costs were increasingly high. There were calls for a turn to the Third World - a Third World in which the Soviet Union also wanted to exert its political influence - as a source of raw materials for the metals sector. The lobby was not successful, except in the case of bauxite, where essentially there was no choice.[7]

The self-sufficiency debate was primarily over the sourcing of inputs. However, the destination of output, i.e. the extent to which exports should be encouraged, was also an issue. The USSR's demand for metal was proverbially inexhaustible, meaning that very little was available for export. But the need for foreign currency and the existence of foreign trading organizations as lobbyists did create pressure for the release of metal into foreign markets.[8] While the Soviet Union did export metals in reasonable quantities to Eastern Europe, the quantities delivered to non-bloc members were all but negligible.[9] Certainly, the metals sector never became the source of foreign currency and the significant player in world markets that the oil and gas industry became in the 1970s.[10]

Moving beyond international trade in raw material inputs and outputs, technology imports had been a significant factor in the Soviet Union's 1930s industrialization and again in the 1970s. However, such imports were controversial, and the Soviet Union was determined to maintain the capacity to be technologically self-sufficient, both through its own major research and development efforts and through reverse engineering of foreign technologies imported both legally and covertly. Within the M&M

---

[7] Rumer 1989, 128-130. For a concise account of the Soviet debate over interdependence vs. autarchy, see Goldman 1976.
[8] For an example of competition for input, in this case iron ore concentrate from the Olenogorsk Enrichment Plant, between a domestic producer and an exporter, see *Gosudarstvennyi arkhiv ekonomiki*, f. 4732, op. 66, d. 923(1), 63. The domestic producer, the Cherepovetsk Metal Factory, defeated the Ministry of Foreign Trade after appealing to Prime Minister Kosygin.
[9] For data, see Jensen 1983, 263-268, 642.
[10] On the politics of the Soviet oil and gas industry, see Gustafson 1983. It is noteworthy that Rumer's book (1989) on the Soviet steel industry does not have 'exports' in its index.

sector, there was little import of technology for the mining and non-ferrous sub-sectors, but some increase in ferrous technology imports in the 1970s.[11]

As the life of the Soviet Union drew to a close, its metals sector remained an essentially closed, autarchic industry within an essentially closed, autarchic economy. It was clearly showing some of the costs of doing so. Its raw material inputs were increasingly high cost and low quality. This affected not just cost structures, but also technology decisions, with technologies being chosen and adapted for low quality or substitute ores.[12] Although analysts at the time pointed out that in such relatively high-priority and low-tech industries as M&M, Soviet performance was better than in more demanding sectors, they also noted that the technological structure of its industry was increasingly lagging behind world structures. Further, what technology it had, including imported technology, was used inefficiently.[13] That tendency towards inefficiency was strengthened by the peculiarities of the Soviet domestic market, virtually the only market for the industry. The 'deficit economy' meant that suppliers ruled, while perverse planning incentives and indicators encouraged the production not just of poor quality products, but also products which were least in demand, both domestically and internationally.[14]

The consequences of the Soviet Union's self-sufficiency policy remained to be faced by the industry in very different circumstances in post-Soviet Russia. However, the opportunity to overcome them and adopt an entirely new approach to the world was by no means absent.

The Post-Soviet Period

In terms of forcing a revised attitude towards the global market, the most important post-Soviet development was the collapse of domestic demand. In the ferrous sector, between 1990 and 1997 domestic demand for rolled metal, for example, declined by a factor of three, from 45 to 15.6 million tons (mt) per annum,[15] mainly a consequence of the decline in sales within

---

[11] Hanson 1981, 134-35; Rumer 1989, 189-91. There was also a degree of technology export to developing countries.
[12] For some examples, see Sagers 1992, 599-600.
[13] Hanson 1981, 42; Fortescue 1990, 15-18.
[14] Rumer 1989, chapter 2.
[15] *Ekspert* 1998, vol.1, 19.

the Russian machinery and construction sectors (output of the machine-tool sector in 1997 was 37% of the 1990 level).[16] Demand for and consumption of top-end products such as stainless steel have dropped spectacularly.[17] Enterprises with heavy reliance on the defense sector were particularly hard hit. The Volgograd special steels manufacturer, *Krasnyi Oktiabr'*, which in Soviet times delivered up to 70% of its output to the defense sector, saw its output of steel decline from about 2mt in the mid-1970s to 764,000t in 1994 and 85,600t in 1997.[18] The picture in the non-ferrous sector is similar. As can be seen from table 7.1, domestic consumption of primary aluminum more than halved between 1990 and 1993.

Table 7.1 Russian and world steel exports (in mt)

	1992	1993	1994	1995	1996	1997
Russian exports	12.3	17.6	23.0	23.7	25.5	26.1
World exports	115.1	178.3	191.9	191.1	197.5	205.0
Russian as % of world	8.1	9.9	12.0	12.4	12.9	12.7

Source: *Chernaia metallurgiia* (1999), No. 1-2, 4.

Russia is now a low per capita user of metal. Per capita, Russia consumes 122.0kg of rolled steel per annum and 2.7kg of aluminum. The relevant figures for Japan are 595.0 and 17.7; USA 360.0 and 19.7; and Germany 344.0 and 14.4.[19]

Given that the M&M sector had previously served virtually only the domestic market, the implications for enterprises of a collapse in domestic demand were exceptionally serious. The obvious remedy was exports, and since the collapse of the Soviet Union a dramatic increase in metal exports, both ferrous and non-ferrous, has indeed been seen, an increase great enough to have suddenly made Russia a very important, and often disruptive, player in world markets.

---

[16] Ibid., 9. The decline by individual metal-intensive machinery sectors can be seen in *Metallosnabzhenie i sbyt* (1997), No. 4, 41-42.
[17] For stainless steel data, see *Metallosnabzhenie i sbyt* (1999), No. 6, 28-32.
[18] Rumer 1989, 74; Ekspert 1998, vol.1, 352; *Metallurg* (1998), No. 11, 5.
[19] *Chernaia metallurgiia. Biulleten' nauchno-tekhnicheskoi i ekonomicheskoi informatsii* (1997), No. 3-4, 3. Figures for copper and nickel can be found in *Metally Evrazii* (1997), No. 6, 56-57.

Table 7.2 shows primary aluminum exports for the former Soviet Union (FSU) 1988-94 and for Russia 1990-94, along with data for smelter capacity and domestic consumption.[20] The greatly increased importance of exports to the sector is again evident. By 1998 Russia was exporting up to 85% of its aluminum output.[21] Aluminum producers that were once directly subordinate to the defense sector's Ministry of Aviation Industry are now major exporters. Sameko, formerly the Kuibyshev Metallurgical Factory producing for the Ministry of Aviation Industry, raised exports between 1991 and 1995 from 700 to 106,000t, with by the latter date exports taking 70% of output. In 1999 the percentage was 80%, despite the fact that the factory by then was part of Oleg Deripaska's group, with its strategy of domestic market development.[22]

Table 7.2 Production, consumption and exports of primary aluminum from the former Soviet Union (in mt)

	1988	1989	1990	1991	1992	1993	1994
Smelter capacity	3.4	3.5	3.5	3.6	3.6	3.6	3.6
Production	3.2-3.5	3.3-3.5	3.2-3.5	3.1-3.3	3.1-3.2	3.1	2.8
Of that Russia	-	-	-	2.92	2.73	2.73	2.72
Consumption	2.6-2.9	2.5-2.7	2.4-2.7	1.8-2.3	1.6-2.1	1.2	0.9
Of that Russia	-	-	-	2.39	2.06	1.43	1.12
Exports	0.6-0.7	0.6-0.7	0.6-0.7	0.8-0.9	0.95-1.4	1.6-2.0	1.9
Of that Russia	-	-	0.53	0.67	1.29	1.6	1.4

Source: OECD 1996, 273.

For the ferrous sector Russian steel exports are shown in table 7.2, along with total world exports. Although there was a significant decline in 1998 figures, the result of anti-dumping problems in the USA and a slump in demand from Asia,[23] the increase over the decade is nevertheless

---

[20] For data on non-ferrous exports as a whole, see *Metallosnabzhenie i sbyt* (1999), No. 3, 60-61.
[21] *Metally Evrazii* (1998), No. 5, 15.
[22] *Tsvetnye metally* (1997), No. 9, 55-56; *Kommersant"* (1999), 14 April.
[23] *Metallosnabzhenie i sbyt* (1998), No. 6, 6 and (1999), No. 2, 52.

significant.²⁴ If we remember the problems of the *Krasnyi Oktiabr'* plant when military demand for its special steels dried up, by 1995 about 50% of its output went to export.²⁵

The turn to the export market is in and of itself a clear indicator of Russia's entry into the global economy, at least in this one sector. It is a development that has been greeted variously by different audiences. Those audiences will be examined in more detail in a later section.

Inputs

In the previous section we examined the effect of the collapse of the Soviet Union on Russian M&M markets. Here we move to the other end of the production process, in order to examine the effect on inputs of raw materials. As yet other inputs, such as labor, energy and transport are not susceptible to the influence of globalization, since foreign sources of supply are not yet feasible.

The aluminum industry was unusual in the Soviet period in that even then it relied heavily on imports of raw materials, and it is still the sector in which domestic inputs are most problematic. As Soviet aluminum output expanded rapidly through the 1970s and 1980s, imports of raw materials, both bauxite and aluminum, increased from about 12% of the total used to about 50% by 1980. The percentage was still roughly the same in 1991.²⁶

Bauxite came from the 'far abroad', primarily Guinea, where Soviet-era credits financed the development of a major bauxite deposit. Despite continuing discussion in contemporary Russia of the development of the same domestic deposits that were under consideration in the Soviet period, the need for imports is not diminishing. Domestic deposits are generally of poor quality or require uneconomic underground mining. Efforts to develop non-bauxite raw materials for aluminum continue to yield disappointing results.²⁷ Even if the long and much-discussed Timan project were to go

---

[24] Data are not available for the Russian Federation alone before the collapse of the Soviet Union. For the former Soviet Union as a whole, steel exports rose from 7.2mt per year in 1980 to 28.5mt in 1993. In 1980 exports, mostly to Eastern Europe, represented 6.2% of output, in 1993 38.0%. *Trudy Chetvertogo Kongressa Staleplavil'shchikov* 1997, 11.
[25] *Ekspert* 1998, vol.1, 352.
[26] Sagers 1992, 596.
[27] Ibid., 596-598.

ahead profitably,[28] it is unlikely that Russia will be able to forego bauxite imports in the foreseeable future.

The main effect of the collapse of the Soviet Union on bauxite has been on financing methods. The old days of centralized purchase of and payment for imports through a specialized foreign trade organization have gone. Producers are now responsible for their own inputs and that has meant in the aluminum industry the widespread, albeit controversial, adoption of toiling schemes, through which financing is taken on by the international traders who organize the toiling contracts.

In the case of aluminum, the situation is different. Although aluminum imports reached significant levels with the expansion of the Soviet aluminum industry from the mid-1960s (about 1mt in 1975, the last year of official import data),[29] the bulk of the aluminum used in the industry was domestically produced. However, a considerable proportion, about 50%, was produced outside the Russian Federation, in particular at the Pavlodar Aluminum Factory in Kazakhstan and the Nikolaevsk Aluminum Factory in Ukraine. In 1991, 1.8mt of aluminum were imported from the 'far abroad', in which year Russian production was about 2.6mt, with about 2.7mt coming from the rest of the former Soviet Union.[30] Through the 1990s, it was claimed that Russian aluminum producers were able to meet about 57% of domestic needs, but that major declines in output in 1997 reduced that percentage to 34%. That has led to aluminum imports from both the near and far abroad of over 3.6mt per year.[31] The importance of the Pavlodar and Nikolaevsk plants to the Russian industry has meant that their ultimate fate, Nikolaevsk in particular, attracts considerable attention.[32]

---

[28] For a very upbeat account, see *Metally Evrazii* (1998), No. 5, 14-19. For some scepticism, see Sagers 1992, 597-598.
[29] Sagers 1992, 598.
[30] Ibid.
[31] *Metally Evrazii* (1998), No. 5, 15. A table in a Russian journal shows rough estimates of the sources of the aluminum used by the three largest Russian aluminium plants: Bratsk - 30% from Nikolaevsk, 70% from 'export' (one can only assume that this means imports from the 'far abroad'); Krasnoiarsk - 30% from Achinsk, 30% from the Bogoslovo plant, and 30% from 'export'; Saiansk - 50% from Pavlodar and 50% from 'export'. *Ekspert* (1999), 31 May, 39.
[32] For details on Russian reliance on Kazakh and Ukrainian aluminum, as well as the politics of the privatization of the Nikolaevsk plant, see *Ekspert* (1999), 31 May, 38-39 and 14 June, 39. The most recent information suggests that Deipaska's 'Siberian Aluminium' group has at long last obtained a majority shareholding in the Ukrainian plant. *Kommersant''* (2000), 23 March.

Imports of aluminum, even if primarily from the near abroad, are likely to continue at substantial levels.[33]

In the ferrous sector, Russia still has very substantial deposits of the main raw material inputs, iron ore and coal, and indeed could be described as self-sufficient. However, the distances between iron ore deposits, intermediate processors and steel producers have made for some very difficult adjustments. Even in the Soviet period, the exhaustion of iron ore deposits in the Urals and West Siberia led to substantial shipments of ore from the Kursk Magnetic Anomaly (KMA), situated far to the west. What was even then a dubious economic proposition became even more difficult once the eastern steel producers had to meet increased transport costs themselves. Kazakh deposits, six times closer than the KMA, were already being used in Soviet times and continue at substantial levels, but deliveries have not always been reliable.[34] Although rail tariff reductions in 1997 and 1998 on the KMA to Urals and West Siberia routes made domestic ores once again feasible for the eastern Russian steel producers, many commentators see iron ore supply problems as becoming ever more serious.[35] The general director of the Magnitogorsk Metal Combine stated in 1999 that local ores will last only another five or so years, KMA deliveries are extremely expensive in terms of transport costs, and plans to import from Kazakhstan have fallen through.[36]

The other input problem faced by the ferrous sector is unreliable supplies of chrome and manganese, essential inputs into the steel-making process. Soviet-era supplies came largely from Kazakhstan, Ukraine and Georgia, although even then some imports were required from the 'far abroad'. While efforts are continuing to develop Russian sources, the situation is still seen as unsatisfactory.[37]

The loss of 'domestic' access to key metallurgical inputs through the breakup of the Soviet Union is a unique form of globalization, which does not fit the usual definitions of the phenomenon. The consequences for Russian industry are no less serious for that. This author is skeptical that the Soviet Union will be restored, either economically or politically, and

---

[33] Sagers 1992, 598. For reasons of space I have not included here a discussion of the difficulties created for the Russian titanium and copper industries of having traditional domestic ore sources situated outside the boundaries of the Russian Federation.

[34] Sagers 1996, 213-220; *Metally Evrazii* (1998), No. 2, 44-47.

[35] *Gornyi zhurnal* (1998), No. 7, 3-4.

[36] *Ekspert* (1999), 14 June, 42.

[37] Bond 1993, 293-301; *Kommersant"* (1992), 18 December and *Kommersant"* (1995), 13 December; *Informatsiia rukovoditeliu* (1998), No. 3, 3.

FSU imports will soon have to be treated, if they are not already, as no different from imports from the 'far abroad', although with one significant difference. The economic condition of many FSU countries and their energy dependence on Russia means that Russia is in a position to exert pressure on 'near abroad' sources. This can be seen in the case of the Nikolaevsk aluminum plant, where various elements in the Russian ruling elite lobbied the Ukrainians on behalf of their particular Russian business allies.[38]

While Russia's very substantial mineral riches cannot be denied, equally the country faces some serious raw material problems, not just in the form of the complete unavailability of some essential inputs, but also of the poor quality and geographical location of what ores are domestically available. These problems will require Russian producers to think seriously about the sources of their inputs. One could expect imports to become more common, particularly if the industry frees itself of a psychological or national security commitment to self-sufficiency. Nevertheless, Russia's mineral wealth is such that the overall balance will not shift. Russia's essential character will still be that of an exporter.

That finding holds even if one notes increasing imports not just of inputs but also of metal. To a considerable extent, the 'increases' are illusory, since they represent imports from the near abroad, i.e. deliveries that before 1991 would not have been counted as imports. Imports from the far abroad still tend to be of products which are not produced in Russia or which are not of the required quality. These phenomena are most evident in the pipe sector.[39]

Capital Integration

Capital integration in the global M&M industry is highly topical, as a new round of mergers and consolidation proceeds. Consideration of this issue in the Russian context requires looking first at privatization. Russian privatization as a whole has had a very small, for many reformers a distressingly small, foreign element. Foreign investors showed little interest in buying up Russian assets at privatization and, some speculative interest in Russia's very narrow share market aside, have continued to keep away.

---

[38] *Kommersant''* (2000), 26 January and 2 March.
[39] On the pipe sector, see *Metallosnabzhenie i sbyt* (1999), No. 2, 17-18. For some data and commentary on aluminum imports, see *Metallosnabzhenie i sbyt* (1999), No. 1, 28-29.

That general comment does, however, have to be qualified in the case of the metals sector, one in which privatization was both early and extensive. There was significant foreign interest, although not from foreign producers - their equity involvement in the Russian sector is non-existent. It came primarily from international metals traders, initially, it would appear, to ensure supplies of metal for their trading operations after the collapse of the monopoly foreign trading organizations. The best-known and most controversial was the British-based TransWorld Group (TWG). In the Soviet period a relatively small player in metals markets,[40] through and after privatization it obtained equity in both the ferrous and non-ferrous sectors. With time, though, it concentrated its efforts in aluminum, generally in partnership with Lev Chernoi, a controversial former Soviet citizen.[41] It dominated the industry, with major holdings in all the biggest producers. It was always a controversial player, not least because of its extensive use of toiling. It suffered many reverses, including the loss of control in dubious circumstances of the Krasnoiarsk and Saiansk Aluminum Factories. It subsequently regained control in Krasnoairsk, but its one-time protege in Saiansk, Oleg Deripaska, successfully kept the trader at bay over the long term. TWG and its partner Chernoi stunned observers in early 2000 by suddenly selling their holdings to Roman Abramovich, an influential oligarch who controls the oil company *Sibneft'*. The superoligarch, Boris Berezovskii, is also involved with Abramovich and *Sibneft'*.[42] The surprises continued when soon after, Abramovich and Deripaska announced a strategic alliance, which included the Saiansk management moving into Krasnoiarsk.[43] At the same time as this was happening, Deripaska had teamed up with governor Aman Tuleev of Kemerovskaia oblast to drive the Moscow investment firm *MIKOM*, a structure with TWG links, out of the Novokuznetsk Aluminum Factory. That seems to leave out, among the significant producers, only the Bogoslovo plant and the SUAL group, which controls the Irkutsk and Urals Aluminum Factories and which is linked to the influential *Alfa* group.[44]

While TWG had the biggest and most controversial foreign involvement in the Russian M&M industry, other international traders

---

[40] *Finansovye Izvestiia* (1996), 26 November.
[41] For some autobiographical details on Chernoi, see *Kommersant"* (1995), 21 October 1995.
[42] *Ekspert* (1999), 26 April, 46-47; *Kommersant"* (1995), 11 November; Fortescue 1999, chapter 8.
[43] *Russian Regional Report* (2000), vol.5, No. 13, 5 April and vol.5, No.14, 12 April 2000.
[44] *Kommersant"* (2000), 26 January and 11 February.

continue to have equity holdings, often of a controlling nature, in the ferrous sector in particular.[45]

Foreign ownership is clearly not irrelevant to the Russian metals sector, and to that extent the Russian industry can be said to be 'globalized' under the capital integration head of the globalization paradigm. However, it is a very unusual form of capital integration, since the major international producers are not involved at all. And it is not only their lack of equity involvement which is striking. There is also an almost total lack of the cooperative relationships and alliances which are seen as particularly typical of modern globalization. About the only exception, and to the extent that it failed very much the exception which proves the rule, was the joint venture between the Saiansk Aluminum Factory and Reynolds to develop a domestic Russian foil market.[46]

The recent spectacular consolidation of the Russian aluminum industry, if it is maintained, gives the *Sibneft'*-Siberian Aluminum group a considerable share of the world market,[47] although it should be noted that commentators believe that the new consolidation was driven more by concern over access to inputs, primarily aluminum, than a market domination strategy.[48] Because of the Russians' lack of integration with the big Western producers, they are left to concentrate on the spot and short-term contract markets, on which they show every sign of being able to compete on cost. The major Russian plants, in an industry where many of the economies of scale become available at plant level, remain among the largest in the world. While the markets in which the Russians are involved are more volatile than the long-term contract markets to which the big international producers look, it appears probable that they will continue to deal in the volumes needed to keep Russian exports viable.

---

[45] See Fortescue 1999.
[46] *Kommersant"* (1996), 1 June and 6 June.
[47] The four Russian aluminum producers which make up the core of the new alliance have a capacity of over 2mt per year; the planned merger of Alcan, Pechiney and Algroup, if it overcomes anti-trust obstacles, will produce a firm with a capacity of 2.8mt per year. Sagers 1992, 594; *The Economist* (1999), 14 August, 54.
[48] Before the alliance, the two sides were involved in a deadly struggle for control of two major aluminum producers, Nikolaevsk and Achinsk.

Technology

Many globalization theories are linked to the boundary-less nature of technology and modern knowledge-based industries. As mentioned at the very beginning of this paper, the M&M industry, being resource-based and transport dependent, is still essentially geographically and therefore to a considerable extent nationally bounded. But it is also an industry in which technology has a significant role in terms of efficiency and competitiveness. It therefore deserves some attention here.

The Soviet technology base, despite the construction of new facilities using imported technology from the 1970s on, was essentially backward. This was most evident in the ferrous sector, where the Soviet Union continued to rely heavily on open-hearth technology and had a virtually non-existent electric/ mini-mill capacity and low levels of continuous casting.

At first it might have seemed that as it entered foreign markets, the Russian industry had impressive cost advantages that would allow it to be globally competitive using even relatively backward technology. However, as domestic costs rose, particularly for power, the need for improved technology came to be felt. This can be seen in the shift in the technology structure of the Russian steel industry shown in table 6.3. The Russian structure in terms of open-hearth technology, although declining, still has some way to go to reach the international average (7.3% in 1995). The shift to converter technology, which has brought Russia close to the international average (59.7% in 1995), is to a considerable extent the result of shutting down open-hearth furnaces as demand declines rather than replacing them with new converter capacity. Nevertheless, technology replacement programs are by no means rare. Where Russia continues to differ significantly from world practice is in the percentage of electrosteel production and continuous casting. In 1995 the international averages were 33% and 75.7%.[49]

The stagnation of the Russian electrosteel industry, the biggest growth area in the global industry, is particularly striking. The reasons given are increasing power costs and lack of access to the metal scrap, which is the main input into electrosteel production, as the Russian scrap industry

---

[49] *Metallurg* (1998), No. 6, 17. For a table showing Russian vs. foreign levels of technology across the metals sector, see *Metallosnabzhenie i sbyt* (1997), No. 2, 3.

disintegrates and turns to exports.[50] Since it could be argued that mini-mill electrosteel producers, with their greater reliance on relatively local scrap inputs rather than internationally shipped bulk ores and their more limited market range, work against globalization,[51] the effect of the Russian backwardness in this area for our purposes could be said to be ambiguous.

Table 7.3 Technological structure of the Russian steel industry (in %)

	1970	1990	1991	1995	1996	1997	1998
Open-hearth	73.5	53.0	50.6	39.3	34.7	32.5	27.8
Converter	17.2	32.0	35.1	47.5	54.3	55.0	59.8
Electrosteel	9.3	15.0	14.3	13.1	11.0	12.5	12.4
Continuous casting	6.0	23.0	17.9	37.1	-	46.5	-

Sources: Bond 1993, 300; *Metallurg* (1998), No. 6, 6, 17; *Metally Evrazii* (1998), No. 3, 53-54; *Informatsiia rukovoditeliu* (1998), No. 21, 21-22.

Data currently available on the non-ferrous sector do not allow us to present the technology structure in percentage terms. However, Russian technology is recognized as backward,[52] and as mentioned previously, much of its capacity has been designed to process low-quality or substitute ores which seem destined to be always relatively inefficient. Most enterprises proclaim investment programs for the modernization of their electrolysis equipment and the introduction of dry anode technology.

As one would expect of an industry which has come to rely substantially on exports, there is clear pressure to restructure production processes in a way which decreases costs and provides a more marketable product. The collapse of domestic demand has provided the opportunity for a more general restructuring by removing the most inefficient capacity. While this has had some positive effect on the competitiveness of the Russian industry and promises to continue to move it towards a

---

[50] *Informatsiia rukovoditeliu* (1998), No. 3, 5-6. On the problems of the ferrous scrap industry in general, see *Metallosnabzhenie i sbyt* (1997), No. 2, 44-45; *Ekspert* (1999), 11 October, 40-41.
[51] See the internal conflict within NUCOR, the major US mini-mill operator, over whether the company should continue its domestic strategy or become a global company with blast-furnace capacity. *The Economist* (1999), 18 October, 80.
[52] *Finansovye Izvestiia* (1997), 3 July.

technological structure more typical of the global industry, lack of funding slows down the process. Further, as will be discussed later, Russian exports are generally at the lower end of the value-added hierarchy, with many producers dropping higher value items from their catalogues in response to export demands.

One would expect of an industry that was undergoing globalization that funding, and the technology it is paying for, would come from cross-border sources. While the technology - in terms of processes and equipment - is more often than not imported, foreign funding is very limited. As we have already seen, equity involvement, particularly on the part of foreign producers, is at a very low level. Foreign credits are not much more common.[53] When funding sources for investment programs are mentioned, they are generally the enterprise's own resources and depreciation allowances.[54] Some enterprises, generally the biggest, appear to have the internal resources, realized through export sales, to make some progress. But as the case of the Krasnoiarsk Aluminum Factory indicates, even the biggest producers face some dilemmas. The Krasnoiarsk plant underwent a major reconstruction program in cooperation with Kaiser in the mid-1990s. That program has ended,[55] and the Krasnoiarsk management now faces a choice. The plant needs to continue its move to dry anode technology, but to import the technology or to do it themselves is either way very expensive. In the meantime, the plant will have to make do with its existing technology.[56]

Russian producers are able to compete in international markets with their current levels of technology, there are strong signs of the Russian industry moving towards international technological standards and industry technology structures, and what new technology does come into the industry tends to come from abroad. However, international producers and providers of technology show little interest in transferring technology on anything other than a purely commercial, as distinct from cooperative, basis. Given the financial exigencies of the Russian industry and economy as a whole, that represents a serious problem.

---

[53] *Chernaia metallurgiia* (1998), No. 3-4, 7.
[54] In the mid-1990s, about 80% of investment spending came from enterprises' own resources. *Vestnik Komiteta RF po metallurgii* (1994), No. 11-12, 25.
[55] Some sources claim the contract with Kaiser was terminated because of dissatisfaction with the effectiveness of the technology fitted. *Kommersant"* (1998), 22 January.
[56] *Tsvetnye metally* (1998), No. 5, 50-63.

In terms of a single aspect of industrial globalization, a large proportion of outputs entering international trade, the Russian metals industry has very much become part of the global economy, although it has not been a smooth or controversy-free development. In terms of the international sourcing of inputs, much of the movement in the direction of globalization has been unusual, in that it has come about by internal boundaries becoming international with the collapse of the Soviet Union. The response to that, as well as to the current and possibly greater future need to source inputs from the 'far abroad', has been to search for domestic sources, in a way reminiscent of the Soviet era. When producers have turned to imported inputs, the matter has usually been controversial. There has been a response on the part of the industry to its greater involvement in the global economy in terms of technology improvements. However, this has not been, as it would often be in other parts of the world, the basis for an international capital involvement in the Russian industry. Indeed, the integration of world capital into Russian metal production and trade has been conspicuous by its absence. Clearly, one cannot conclude categorically that the Russian M&M sector is not part of the global economy - the trade figures do not allow us to do so. But in any deeper sense - of how the sector is owned and operates - it is still remarkably different and remote from global trends and practices, even in such a relatively traditional industry.

The Politics of Globalization in the Russian Metals Industry

We now look at the attitudes of various political, policy and business actors inside and outside Russia towards the issues so far discussed. Although it is not always easy to do, an effort will be made to line up the forces for and against the globalization of the Russian metals industry. The relevant issues, which serve as indicators of alignment, are: export vs. domestic market orientation, including the debate over toiling; foreign ownership and investment; and trade regime policy, specifically anti-dumping.[57]

---

[57] Another issue relevant to globalization, membership of the WTO, has not featured in debates specifically related to the metals sector sufficiently to allow for serious analysis here. Exchange rate policy is extremely relevant to the M&M industry, since it has become so export-oriented. Certainly, industry spokespeople were bitterly opposed to the strong-ruble policy introduced in 1995. However, to the extent that exchange rate movements do no more than shift the balance between exports and imports, an increase in either of which can

Export vs. Domestic Market Orientation

There are a number of reasons why the major orientation of M&M enterprises towards the export market is controversial. Some domestic manufacturers complain that they are unable to buy domestic metal, particularly aluminum, because it all goes to export.[58] Such complaints often have as a subtext that export-oriented producers are owned or controlled by foreign interests. The trader Glencore attracted considerable criticism for focusing on the export of ore at both the Sredneural'sk Copper Smelting Plant and *Dal'polimetall*, at the expense in the first case of downstream processors unable to get inputs and in the second of alternative development strategies that foresaw investment in downstream activities within the enterprise itself.[59] It is noted that not only does export take ore and metal away from domestic downstream users, but also tends to force the focus onto the lowest value-added products. World markets do not need Russia's generally low-tech, low-quality finished and even semi-finished products. Consequently, in response to the demands of the world market, Russia's integrated producers have reduced their product lines in favor of low value-added products.[60] Even on the domestic market, foreign producers are said to be taking over the supply of high value-added products.[61] Not unexpectedly, such imports produce demands from Russian producers for protection.

In the aluminum sector, the greatest butt of criticism has been the international trader TWG, with its large-scale toiling operations. Toiling is criticized on the grounds just set out, that it takes inputs from domestic users and encourages Russian producers to shift downmarket, but also because it is seen as a monstrous and corrupt drain on government receipts. The tax breaks that make it profitable are said to cost the treasury US$400mn per year. The fact that the traders who run the toiling schemes also control the aluminum producers provides the perfect opportunity for

---

be seen as opening Russia to the global economy, it is a globalization-neutral issue. For a useful discussion of the exchange rate policy debate, see Woodruff 1998, 73-76.

[58] *Financial Times* (1993), 11 February, 32; *Metal Bulletin* (1992), 24 September; *Metallurg* (1998), No. 8, 10.

[59] *Kommersant''* (1996), 13 March and 31 August.

[60] *Ekonomika i zhizn'* (1994), No. 51, 4; *Kommersant''* (1996), 13 March; *Metallurg* (1998), No. 11, 5. The last reference deals with the *Krasnyi Oktiabr'* plant, which as we have already seen lost its domestic market for special steels with the collapse of defense industry orders.

[61] *Metallosnabzhenie i sbyt* (1998), No. 6, 15-16.

capital flight through the artificial lowering of processing charges. The proponents of toiling respond that, given the processors' lack of operating capital and access to credit on reasonable terms, they have no choice but to accept a scheme under which they do not have to pay for their material inputs.[62] For many years the arguments of the toilers held sway. However, at the end of 1999, after considerable debate, the decision was made not to renew for 2000 the tax regime that makes toiling feasible.

Even among producers, there are some who are uneasy at over-reliance on the export market, for the reasons just outlined and also on the grounds that such markets are extremely volatile and that Russian exports are highly susceptible to anti-dumping actions. The aluminum and steel industries have experienced both in full measure during the 1990s. Further, under the Russian government's strong ruble policy, exports were often at best of marginal profitability.

Oleg Deripaska of the Saiansk Aluminum Factory is the most prominent representative of producers looking towards the domestic market. He forswears toiling and thereby, he claims, is able to retain the profits from aluminum exports, profits which are then used to finance the development of the domestic market. By development of the domestic market he means downstream integration, i.e. purchasing semi- and finished product producers and then shipping primary metal to them.[63]

Foreign Ownership and Investment

As already mentioned, it is implied in much of the criticism of an excessive export orientation, particularly in the form of toiling schemes, that such an orientation tends to be imposed by foreign owners. This adds an extra dimension to the already controversial issue of privatization. The metals sector was one of the most quickly and most fully privatized industrial sectors. The sector has also been characterized by an unusually high level of foreign ownership, as already suggested, by international traders, rather than foreign producers.

Not only has foreign interest in the Russian M&M sector been overwhelmingly on the part of traders rather than producers; it has also

---

[62] The different arguments are set out well in *Kommersant"* (1999), 1 December 1999.
[63] Fortescue 1999, 229-230. For a diagrammatic representation of the group's holdings, see *Metallosnabzhenie i sbyt* (1999), No. 1, 31. This source indicates a significant decline in the group's exports of primary aluminum, but an increase in the exports of its downstream producers.

been overwhelmingly in existing enterprises rather than in development projects. It is presumably because of this lack of interest in development projects that foreign investment legislation, most particularly production sharing legislation, which has been so controversial in the oil and gas sector, has attracted very little attention in the M&M sector.

Trade Regimes

Russian export activities have produced furious reactions among foreign producers, in both the ferrous and non-ferrous sectors. The disruptions brought to international aluminum markets in the mid-1990s by Russian exports led to the 1994 Memorandum of Understanding, in which all producers, Russian and Western, agreed to cut capacity.[64] The EU imposed wide-ranging quotas on Russian steel imports in the mid-1990s, leading to 'managed trade' agreements in 1995 and 1997.[65] The opening of anti-dumping investigations against Russian steel imports into the US in 1998 led to agreed quotas on a whole range of Russian ferrous products.[66]

If these are the issues which can be used as indicators of orientation towards globalization, who are the actors involved? The following are involved in the debate in one way or another: international traders; enterprise managers; international producers; the government, consisting of the central government leadership and the sectoral M&M bureaucracy; regional elites; and a vague category of 'nationalist' forces.

The positions of some of the actors are unequivocal. The international traders are clearly in favor of the integration of the Russian industry into the global economy, at least in terms of the export of primary metal and the import of raw materials, usually through toiling. Because they stand outside the mainstream of global M&M production, their 'globalization' is of a limited nature. They tend to buy inputs and sell metal on the spot markets, rather than be tied into long-term relationships, whether of equity, alliance or contract form. They are also relatively uninterested in technology transfer or even the import into Russia of management personnel and

---

[64] OECD 1996, 286-87; Fortescue 1999, 214.
[65] *Delovoi mir*, 11-14 April 1997; *Jamestown Monitor* (1997), vol.3, No. 70, 9 April.
[66] The text of the formal agreement can be found in *Metallosnabzhenie i sbyt* (1999), No. 5, 80-88; and the Russian Ministry of Trade instructions and procedures for allocating quotas in *Metallosnabzhenie i sbyt* (1999), No. 6, 87-89. For background commentary, see Winters, Rubin and Bond 1998, 183-224.

techniques. The traditional production-oriented management suits them well.

Unequivocally on the other side are, unsurprisingly, the 'nationalist' forces. Their slogan is 'raw material appendage', the fate they foresee for a Russia which abandons itself entirely to the global market. That involves not just foreigners taking over all the choicest parts of the Russian patrimony, but also, as already described, the degradation of Russian industry as raw materials are sent for export in low value-added form. Thus far, it has to be said, the nationalists have had limited success translating such arguments into popular and particularly electoral support. The chief ideologist of the raw material appendage argument, Sergei Glaz'ev, was totally unable to build a political career out of it.[67] Such forces are strong enough in parliament to block significant progress in such things as production sharing legislation, but as already mentioned, that legislation has aroused little interest in the M&M sector.

Generally, among the most vehement opponents of globalization are regional political elites. They are opposed to any outsiders, even those from no further field than Moscow, owning or controlling local enterprises, since they want to be able to ensure that enterprises follow their preferred social policies, i.e. that they maintain employment, that they pay taxes locally rather than centrally, and that they make funds available for the regional governor's reelection campaign. It is a commonplace of contemporary Russian politics that power has shifted from the center to the regions. One might therefore expect regional administrations to be very successfully gaining control of local enterprises and then implementing corporate strategies that stress regional goals at the expense of international competitiveness and a globalizing orientation. Particularly since August 1998, regional administrations have indeed moved in a very determined way to gain control of local enterprises.

However, regions are able to gain control of enterprises primarily through insolvency proceedings, by having local courts appoint administrators to their liking in insolvent enterprises.[68] But those enterprises successfully engaged in the global economy are the least likely to be insolvent. Successfully involved is not just a matter of having an export

---

[67] Fortescue 1997, 117, 134. In December 1999, he was elected to parliament on the Communist Party ticket, and has been appointed head of the Duma's Economic Policy Committee. He recently called for increased taxes on the resource sector. *RFE/RL Newsline* (2000), 3 February.
[68] *Ekspert* (1998), 2 November, 20-22 and *Ekspert* (1999), 18 January, 28-30.

orientation, since many exporters have found themselves insolvent. Nevertheless, enterprises such as the big aluminum toilers have generally been able to resist regional pressure.[69] Indeed, some governors, Lebed' not currently among them, feel obliged to provide lobbying support for toiling enterprises in their region. Thus, in the late-1999 debate over toiling Eduard Rossel', governor of Sverdlovskaia oblast and as determined a protector of regional interests as one could wish to find, supported the practice, because the region is home for bauxite mines providing ore under 'internal toiling' schemes (under which the toilers purchase their inputs domestically, but enjoy the same tax breaks as if they had imported them). Konstantin Titov, governor of Samarskaia oblast, in which Deripaska's 'Siberian Aluminum' has investments in downstream capacity, was opposed.[70] It is no great discovery to find that regional elites are pragmatic in a narrowly self-interested way.

For the same reasons, the presence of international producers in the anti-globalization category will surely seem only momentarily paradoxical. Without here attempting to determine one way or another whether Russian producers are truly guilty of dumping, one should hardly be surprised that Western producers counter the Russian threat to their markets with anti-dumping actions, particularly when they themselves have no equity involvement in Russian producers. They have been in practice perhaps the greatest impediment to Russian involvement in world markets.

The other way in which it could be said that foreign producers fail to contribute to the globalization of the Russian M&M industry, is their almost total failure to invest in that industry, or even show any interest in alliances and other forms of cooperation. That failure is presumably not due to fundamental opposition to that form of globalization, since it has become an increasingly important feature of the international industry.[71] The most obvious reason is that Russia is a thoroughly unattractive place in which to

---

[69] A smaller player, the Moscow investment firm *MIKOM*, has been unable to resist the pressure of Kemerovskaia oblast's governor Tuleev. A good relationship was soured when *MIKOM* refused to pay into the governor's slush fund. In response, Tuleev had local courts insert his own administrators into two *MIKOM* enterprises, the Kuznetsk Metal Combine and the Novokuznetsk Aluminium Factory. In the latter case, not without the assistance of Oleg Deripasks, the classic stratagem was used of having the local electricity company impose unpayable increases for electricity in order to drive the enterprise into insolvency. *Kommersant"* (1999), 27 November; *Kommersant"* (2000), 20 January, 26 January and 10 February.
[70] *Kommersant"* (1999), 8 December.
[71] *The Economist* (1999), 28 August, 49-50.

invest. But it is almost inherent to the metals industry that it invests in unattractive parts of the world, since it is such a resource- and therefore geography-based industry. Further, the lack of interest of metal producers contrasts sharply with the other resource sector, the oil and gas industry, which does not find its Russian involvement easy going, but nevertheless feels obliged to maintain a presence.

One suspects that the more important reason for the lack of interest is that, as has been already mentioned, in a number of key areas Russia is not overly well-endowed with raw material resources, having serious quantity, quality and location problems. Russian processing capacity, whether primary or secondary, is of no interest.

The remaining two groups of actors in the globalization debate - managers and the government - are hard to place. Different managers proclaim different opinions and it is difficult to discern any pattern of alignment. It can be tentatively claimed that older, more traditional managers have been somewhat more willing to accept foreign involvement and the export orientation that goes with it than one might have expected. The very rapid inroads made by outsiders, despite the predictions of the consequences of 'management privatization', suggest this.

This is not what one might have expected of 'Red directors'. A major reason seems, initially at least, to have been desperation. Managers were desperate for investment and even more urgently for operating capital to enable them to purchase essential raw material inputs. The arrangements could then become nicely lucrative, one imagines, for the small group of top Russian managers prepared to cooperate. One could also argue that the 'Red directors' did not have the entrepreneurial spirit of some of their younger colleagues, to be described below, to enable them to come up with and implement alternatives to the trader-toiling approach. An example of a traditional 'Red director' is Anatolii Sysoev, general director of the Bogoslovo Aluminum Factory, typically 'beginning as a worker in the electrolysis shop and moving up all the steps of the ladder ... and who sees things differently from some 'new Russian' who cannot feel the earth beneath his feet and does not know the value of each hard-earned kopeck.'[72] He has extremely traditional anti-reform views,[73] and yet has worked with TWG and strongly defends toiling.[74] Those traditional managers who did take the traders on did so more in order to copy their strategy - to maintain

---

[72] *Metally Evrazii* (1997), No. 1, 68.
[73] *Metally Evrazii* (1997), No. 6, 8-12.
[74] *Kommersant''* (1999), 1 December.

the export orientation but to reallocate trading contracts to traders more directly controlled by them - rather than to replace it.[75]

Among what could be called the 'new' managers - young entrepreneurial types who, if not coming from entirely outside the industry, at least clearly owe their current positions entirely to post-Soviet developments - the picture is quite confused. Some, such as Vasilii Anisimov and the very controversial Anatolii Bykov, were quite prepared to work with TWG at the Krasnoiarsk Aluminum Factory.[76] Vladimir Lisin at the Novolipetsk Metal Combine helped remove his erstwhile patron TWG from the enterprise but has maintained an export orientation and remained unenthusiastic about the domestic market.[77] Mikhail Zhivilo, another TWG protege at the Novokuznetsk Aluminum Factory, maintained a strong export orientation both there and at the neighboring steel producer, the Kuznetsk Metal Combine, while he had control of them.[78] Others, most noticeably Oleg Deripaska, while unable to foreswear the export market altogether, determinedly find their own financing in order to escape the toilers,[79] and use the proceeds to implement their main strategy of development of the domestic market through downstream integration with semi- and finished product manufacturers.

Also ambiguous in its attitude is the sectoral bureaucracy within the central government. One might have expected traditional values among the bureaucrats of the various successor bodies to the Soviet-era Ministries of Ferrous and Non-Ferrous Metallurgy. The Committee for Metallurgy indeed expressed concern over and dissatisfaction with privatization, and yet the sector was one of the most rapid privatizers.[80] As part of its criticism of privatization, the Committee warned about the excessive interest of 'dubious commercial structures' in Russian metal enterprises,[81] and yet it and its successors, as well as the 'Aluminum' company, the corporatized successor to the chief aluminum administration of the Ministry of Non-Ferrous Metallurgy, have been consistent supporters of toiling.[82]

---

[75] Iurii Kolpakov at the Krasnoiarsk Aluminium Factory is a good example. *Delovoi mir* (1997), 19 June.
[76] *Ekspert* (1999), 26 April, 46-47.
[77] *Ekspert* (1998), 10 August, 34.
[78] *Kommersant"* (1995), 11 November 1995; *Ekspert* (1998), 21 December 1998, 29.
[79] On Deripaska's credit lines, see *Ekspert* (1999), 8 February, 27-28 and 12 July, 35.
[80] *Vestnik Komiteta RF po metallurgii* (1994), No. 3-4, 26-28.
[81] *Metallurg* (1996), No. 3, 7-8.
[82] Fortescue 1997, 95; *Kommersant"* (1994), 31 August, 3 and *Kommersant"* (1995), 23 March, 10; *Tsvetnye metally* (1997), No. 11-12, 78.

There is a considerable similarity in their position and that of a 'Red director' such as Anatolii Sysoev. Quite possibly the reasons for the sectoral bureaucracy's acquiescence to 'globalizing' tendencies, albeit of a distorted kind, are the same as were described above with regard to the traditional managers: desperation, material gain, and a lack of capacity to come up with alternatives.

When we move to trade regime policy, we see a slightly different picture. Representatives from both the sectoral bureaucracy and the Ministry of Trade have been prepared to imply, if not openly admit, that complaints of dumping are justified even as negotiations are getting underway,[83] and in the most recent US actions against Russian steel they earned the ire of Russian producers who considered that they agreed to a deal which gave far too much away to the Americans.[84]

Perhaps this was a case of experienced people coming to a sensible conclusion that there was no point fighting too hard for a hopeless cause and that a conciliatory approach would bring the best results. There is, however, a suspicion that the official negotiators, as representatives of state bureaucracies, are far happier with 'managed trade' than free trade, because it gives them the opportunity to collect cost and price data and to impose and enforce quotas and capacity reductions, in a word, to get their hands on some of the old administrative levers.[85]

Among managers and bureaucrats with a traditional background, one can find the comments skeptical of the market and reform that one would expect. But they avoid the 'raw material appendage' language of their 'nationalist' cousins. Although support for toiling and managed trade is hardly an indication of a commitment to unfettered markets, it does at least put them in the camp of the supporters of globalization Russian-style.

One political actor remains unaccounted for, and that is the central government. It would be easy, but too facetious, to state that the central government is too weak to have any influence on matters, and leave it at that. In fact, it was the 'weak' but radically reforming government of Egor Gaidar that laid the foundations for any globalization that might have occurred by floating the currency, greatly liberalizing the granting of export

---

[83] *Finansovye Izvestiia* (1997), 10 June, 1; *Metally Evrazii* (1997), No. 6, 9 and (1998), No. 4, 110; *Metallosnabzhenie i sbyt* (1997), No. 4, 8-9.
[84] For example, see the complaints of Vladimir Lisin of the Novolipetsk Metal Combine. *Ekspert* (1998), 14 December, 29. For other examples, see *Metallosnabzhenie i sbyt* (1999), No. 2, 8, 23.
[85] *Kommersant"* (1995), 28 March.

licenses, and allowing foreign involvement in privatization. Central government can still, virtually at a stroke of the pen, exert enormous influence on the operations and prospects of industry. The ruble corridor of 1995 transformed the profitability of the metals sector; the government-induced crisis of August 1998 had major ownership implications by breaking the backs of the Russian banks; the abolition of VAT exemptions for toiling schemes has major implications for aluminum exports.

Given all that, has the government been pro- or anti-globalization? Clearly, to the extent that all post-Soviet Russian governments, whether voluntarily or under pressure of the IMF, have been essentially reform oriented, they have maintained the basic institutions necessary for globalization. However, often the commitment has been grudging. Sometimes, this has clearly been because domestic opposition, particularly in the parliament, has made it difficult to get the necessary legislation through, foreign investment legislation being most prominent.

But on other occasions the government has adopted policies unhelpful to globalization without such obvious domestic opposition. One notes the constant threats to toiling, the strong ruble policy (which, while having its harshest effects on domestic manufacturers, certainly did not help exporters), and the willingness to set export duties and to demand conversion of foreign exchange earnings (*valiutnaia vyruchka*). There is no intention here to suggest that these policies were devised as specifically anti-globalization policies. What is suggested is that they were driven by other, essentially macroeconomic priorities. The government's fundamental priority has been to keep inflation and monetary emission under control. Essentially the government will do anything it can to get hold of money, and the export sectors tend to have the money. While a willingness to soak exporters is not necessarily the same as being anti-globalization, it does at least suggest other priorities.

Conclusion

We will conclude by summing up the discussion in terms of two questions related to the main divisions of the paper: is the Russian M&M industry globalized? and who determines whether it is or not?

The answer to the first question is a qualified yes. Russia clearly meets the requirement of a large part of output entering international trade. While some Russian producers might have a reasonable desire to develop domestic markets, it is hard to see the export orientation fading in the foreseeable future. Russia less clearly meets the requirement of the international sourcing of raw materials. When it has no choice it does source raw materials internationally, but it still shows signs of hankering for self-sufficiency even when the costs of doing so are considerable. Whether that hankering will fade with time, depends not just on politico-psychological developments, but also on developments in technology and mineral exploration. If these developments are not in favor of domestic inputs, the industry will have no choice but to globalize its raw material inputs.

In terms of the third aspect of globalization, the Russian industry is undergoing a significant restructuring of its technological structure, to bring it more into line with global models. This restructuring, to the extent that it is not brought about simply by the withdrawal of outdated capacity, usually uses imported technology. However, it is often self-funded and appears not to entail truly integrating cross-border technological cooperation.

The final aspect of globalization in the international metals industry, the integration of international capital and trade flows, is one where there has been very little movement in the Russian case. International traders have acquired major equity interests in the Russian industry and used them to promote their form of trade. But in global terms, the traders are small-scale and their form of trade limits the degree of cross-border capital integration. Perhaps most significant is that the lack of integration of the Russian industry with world capital is largely due to the lack of interest of world producers in such integration. This is perhaps due not just to an uninviting Russian investment climate, something which theoretically can be changed, but also to inherent resource base problems that cannot be changed simply by changes in government policy or corporate strategy. That makes one think that this aspect of globalization might well be the hardest for the Russian industry to come to terms with.

If the Russian industry is globalized only to a qualified degree, and it appears possible that it will not in the near future move towards the levels of globalization that rule on average in the international industry, how is such an outcome determined? As long as there is a commitment to an economy which is anywhere on the market side of a full command economy, Russia's economy is likely to remain heavily resource based with an export orientation. Such a commitment could be questioned by the current or a new political leadership. But it is hard to see any government being able to do so in a significant or radical way. Vladimir Putin, recently elected president, seems to fit the trend. While not averse to 'raw material appendage' statements, albeit in bland form, he has in his actions been more pro than against the resource sector, for example in refusing to extend the 5% export levy on metal exports, dropping the ban on platinum exports, and failing to support the government's push to require exporters to convert all their currency earnings into rubles.[86] Until domestic demand picks up significantly and sustainably - unlikely to be a short-term development - M&M enterprises have no choice but to export. But even when domestic manufacturing revives, comparative advantage and balance of trade considerations are likely to ensure the maintenance of exports at significant levels. At the same time, weaknesses in the resource base, on the one hand, push Russia towards the globalization of its inputs, but on the other reduce the interest of foreign producers in integrating Russia into their world-wide operations. This suggests that to a considerable extent globalization is determined not by policy and strategy but by objective circumstances of resource base and geographical location.

This means that actors have relatively little room for maneuver. Nevertheless, the key shapers of the Russian industry's place in the world are international traders, corporate managers, central government, and international producers, the latter through their lack of investment and their willingness to resort to anti-dumping tactics. The place of the international traders is always vulnerable, and indeed with TWG's departure greatly reduced. It will be interesting to see whether the new dominance of domestic entrepreneurs in the aluminum industry produces some movement away from TWG's limited model of globalization, in the form of some withdrawal from international markets and greater reliance on domestically sourced raw materials. Possible movement in this direction is limited. Even in the absence of the traders, Russian managers and government would find themselves obliged to maintain something of the traders' approach. And while international producers choose to keep themselves out of Russia, and at times to keep Russia out of the world, the degree of globalization is unable to move beyond the traders' limited form.

What does this mean for the Russian industry? In the short or even medium term there appears to be a solid and profitable niche for a relatively non-globalized, low-cost metals industry. Longer-term viability without further integration into the global industry is more open to doubt. At the very least it would require keeping in touch technologically on a

---

[86] *RFE/RL Newsline* (2000), 7 and 13 January.

self-funded basis, the continued existence of reasonably large world spot and short-term markets, assured supplies of cheap raw materials, and probably a significant shakeout of Russian producers in order to improve economies of scale and market clout. Not all of these can be guaranteed in the long term.

8 The Banking Sector and its International Involvement

ARTOS G. SARKISIANTS

Most Russian credit institutions are not banks by western standards. At the same time, they cannot avoid the global integration process and worldwide changes, and must adapt to them. This is shown by the growing relations with foreign partners, the use of new instruments on international financial markets, and by participation in world development programs.

The process of international involvement of a nation's banking sector is always complicated, and eight years is a very short period for such a huge country as Russia. One could say that the existence of international ratings of Russian banks and the attention paid to them by foreign business and financial circles is evidence that Russian banks have become part of the world financial system. Yes and no. The reputation of the Russian banking sector is dependent on the fact that it is very young and was formed in only three years (1989-92), during which more than 2,500 commercial credit institutions were born: there has been no comparable experience in world history.

On the other hand, a review using international accounting standards shows us that the total liabilities of the top twenty Russian banks are about US$15.0bn, against US$5.5bn in assets.[1] The overall capital shortfall of these banks is mainly due to bad loans (34%), losses on forward currency contracts with foreign institutions (28%), and losses on short-term government debt (13%),[2] on which Russia defaulted in 1998, when it also declared a moratorium on the payment of commercial debt and decided to let the ruble float. At the same time, the value of the short-term debt portfolio (with a market price of a few kopeks on the ruble) was increased from 10% to 50% of face value, and the provisions for bad loans were

---

[1] Tsentral'nyi Bank Rossiiskoi Federatsii (2000), *Biulleten' bankovskoi statistiki No. 1*, 63.
[2] Schaic 1999, 254.

lowered. Total negative capital for the banks amounted to about US$3.5bn.[3] Less than 1,000 of Russia's 1,300 banks are in stable financial condition.[4] These are mostly smaller and medium-sized banks in the regions. So far, there are no clear criteria for reforming the sector, apart from the Central Bank's statement that it is official policy to keep strategically important banks alive. In practice, this will mean that politically well-connected banks will be allowed to limp on.

This article demonstrates the peculiarity of the Russian banks and their relations with international financial and credit institutions.

The Main Differences of the Russian Banking Sector from International Standards

Banking is a key part of the economy in most emerging markets, but Russian banking is still in its infancy. What is readily apparent, though, is the rapid pace of change, the increasing differentiation among banks, and the emergence of a premier league of 20 institutions, which concentrate about 60% of the assets in the banking system.[5] However, even for the largest Russian banks survival is not assured. Most remain small by international standards: 85% of them have capital less than EUR5bn.[6] From the outside, it is not possible to predict the eventual winners and losers. But a first-tier group of private-sector banks has emerged, and the eventual survivors are likely to come from among these.

The Russian banking system is disproportionately small in relation to the economy. The ratio of bank lending to GDP is only 16%, and the ratio of private sector lending was only half that. In Poland, Hungary, and the Czech Republic, the ratio for total lending ranges from 40% to 102%.[7] The picture is similar for deposits. The ratio of total deposits to GDP is only 12% in Russia, compared with 35% to 75% in the three central European countries.[8] So far, no clear pattern has emerged from the turmoil of Russian banking, but it is increasingly diverse and specialized, with intensifying competition for the retail market, as well for the blue-chip corporations.

---

[3] Tsentral'nyi Bank Rossiiskoi Federatsii (2000), *Biulleten' bankovskoi statistiki No. 1*, 68.
[4] 'Psevdobanki', in *Vedomosti* (2000), 28 February.
[5] Tsentral'nyi Bank Rossiiskoi Federatsii (2000), *Biulleten' bankovskoi statistiki No. 1*, 68.
[6] Ibid.
[7] Westlake 1998, 20.
[8] Ibid.

The Russian banking system, excluding the savings institution *Sberbank*, is equal to about 2.5 US regional banks (there are nearly 10,000 banks in US), or about the same size as the 30th bank in the USA (by total assets).[9]

The banking system was first rocked by a liquidity crisis in August 1995, and the Central Bank has admitted that less than half of all banks are financially reliable. Banking crises were common, too, when western countries, notably the USA, were developing market economies in the 19th century. As for developing economies, almost a quarter have had a banking crisis, and over half had significant banking problems short of a crisis since the 1980s.[10]

The Russian banking system had two wellsprings. First, there were several specialized banks created out of the Soviet *Gosbank* structure. This monobank was responsible for all the various internal banking activities, while the Bank for Foreign Trade of the USSR handled external operations. Then, after 1988, many companies took advantage of rules allowing them to set up in-house 'pocket' banks. In subsequent years, groups of entrepreneurs, often politically well-connected, also established banks (in those days you could set up a bank with a few thousand dollars). Most of these institutions were not banks by western standards, doing little lending or deposit-taking. In many cases, they were set up to capture a share of government budget funds, which were distributed through the banking system. Frequently, banks used these funds for extended periods before channeling them to their intended beneficiaries; in some instances, the money never reached its intended destination.[11]

It was common practice to speculate in the foreign exchange market during the early days; and later, to trade in *GKO*s (Treasury bills), which delivered yields of 200-250%[12] for a time (for example, before the presidential elections). Moreover, for the past few years, many Russian banks had effectively been operating like hedge funds, borrowing money abroad to invest in high-yield Russian Eurobonds, MinFins and Brady bonds.[13] As prices crashed in July-August 1998, the banks were obliged to liquidate their positions to meet margin calls.

---

[9] 'Statistics on Banking', in *Federal Reserve Bulletin* (1999).
[10] See Goodhart, Hartmann, Llewelynn, Rojas-Suarez and Weisbord 1998; Frydl 1999, 35-60.
[11] Aleksashenko et al. 1999, 13.
[12] *GKO* (*Gosudarstvennye Kratkosrochnye Obligatsii*) - Short-term Government Bonds. Tsentral'nyi Bank Rossiiskoi Federatsii (1999), *Biulleten' bankovskoi statistiki No. 1*, 44.
[13] MinFins - Long-term foreign currency bonds of the Ministry of Finance of the Russian Federation. Brady Bonds - new bonds, in which the previous debt of less development

Many banks also stand to realize large losses on the non-deliverable forward (NDF) contracts they wrote with foreign investors wanting to cover their ruble exposure. Outstanding currency forward exposure was estimated at US$15bn at the time of the above-mentioned moratorium, with a distribution sufficient to bankrupt several banks.[14] The problem was not limited to the Moscow banks. NDF fever affected the smaller, regional institutions as well as the better-known, Moscow-based names since the larger banks had covered themselves by writing contracts with smaller institutions that often left their own positions uncovered.

Curiously, the largest banks, such as *Sberbank*, which holds 75% of retail deposits,[15] and *Vneshtorgbank* were ready to fulfill all their obligations. But the Central Bank was not in a mood to accept such dissent. It warned the banks not to break the moratorium, threatening consequences that reportedly could include the withdrawal of their licenses. In a parallel attempt to shore up the banks on the domestic front, the Central Bank promised to guarantee individuals' deposits at all banks, so long as those deposits were transferred to *Sberbank*. It also set up a payment pool to support the 12 most important institutions. The chosen few were all well known to Western bankers: *Oneksim, Most, Inkombank, SBS-Agro, Rossiiskii Kredit,* National Reserve Bank, *Sberbank, Vneshtorgbank, Menatep, Alfa, Vneshekonombank* and the Bank of Moscow. This small group has since been reduced, with the announcement of plans to merge several of the biggest names.

The current crisis in the Russian banking sector is all the more surprising since government sources initially portrayed the August 1998 financial package (moratorium and devaluation) as designed to protect the country's banks from a spiraling financial crisis. The developments of 17 August 1998 delivered a double blow to the Russian banking system, because the largest banks held a large proportion of their total assets as government securities, and because of the scale of their foreign currency liabilities, including those derived from forward foreign exchange contracts. Moreover, in addition to their highly speculative activities in securities and foreign exchange markets, most Russian banks have close links with their business clients and the government. In particular, a large number of banks belong to the so-called financial and industrial groups

---

countries is restructured in the frame of a plan of the former US Treasury Secretary Nicolas Brady.
[14] Farrow 1998, 152.
[15] Ibid.

(FIGs), which have large shareholdings and exposures to the industrial sector and high levels of connected lending, and which rely on a few large corporate accounts for funding.

By the end of 1999, 75 FIGs were registered with the state register (comprising about 1,500 enterprises and organizations, and about 100 credit and financial institutions). In reality, there are about 150 amalgamations of business units (banking-industrial holdings),which, although not always officially meeting the formal criteria of financial-industrial groups, might aspire to be called so.[16] There are many aspects to the formation of Russian financial-industrial groups in 1993-99 and the crisis in which many of them find themselves today. The first institutional crisis in the Russian economy was connected with the disappearance of trade at the beginning of the 1990s; the second with the sharp decrease in the number of banks in the mid-1990s; and the third is the crisis of management in the giant financial-industrial groups in 1998-99. Even during the pre-crisis period, the role of banks in corporate governance caused many complaints from outside shareholders, as seen in *Iukos'* transfer prices in the *Menatep* bank group, the transfer of funds from *Sidanko* within the *Oneksim* group, and the monopolization of commodity flows to subsidiaries by *Inkombank* and other owner-banks. To understand the post-1998 management crisis, it is also necessary to take into account the whole set of macroeconomic problems of 1998-99, including the level of world prices for raw materials, government regulation, and the specifics of corporate relations in Russia. Below is a review of only those aspects of the crisis of Russian financial industrial groups which have a bearing on the prospect of property rights redistribution for industrial sector companies.

The 1998 banking crisis sharply aggravated the problems of liquidity and insolvency in connection with the default on *GKO*s, forward contracts, eurobond debt, foreign loans etc. At the time of the default, the holdings of *GKO-OFZ*[17] by Russian banks (excluding *Sberbank*) stood at about Rbl40bn. The Russian banks which were hedging the exchange rate risks of the foreign investors are estimated to have lost US$10-22bn as a result of the collapse of the ruble.[18] The debt of the 20 largest borrowers against foreign commercial loans was about US$1.3bn.[19] This crisis created a clear tendency towards contraction of the ownership share of a number of the

---

[16] Tsentral'nyi Bank Rossiiskoi Federatsii (2000), *Biulleten' bankovskoi statistiki No. 1*, 15.
[17] *OFZ (Obligatsii Federalnogo Zayma)* - Federal Bonds.
[18] Tsentral'nyi Bank Rossiiskoi Federatsii (2000), *Biulleten' bankovskoi statistiki No. 1*.
[19] Ibid.

largest formal and informal groups, at the core of which were the commercial banks. At the same time, it should be pointed out that some Russian banks, which did not actively participate in the corporate expansion, reached an understanding with Western creditors concerning the restructuring of their debts (excluding the forward contracts). Among these are: *Avtobank, Konvers,* National Reserve Bank, *Roseksim,* and *Promstroibank-St.Petersburg.* (In this last case, the debt under forward contracts was included.)

In general, the situation in 1998-99 has the following specific features. First, as early as the beginning of 1998, the leaders of the largest Russian financial groups, which had actively participated in the redistribution of property during the 1990s, declared that their groups were entering the stage of efficient management of their acquired assets, or 'putting their business in order'. Now that conditions have changed, we can speak about the transition from the stage of property grabbing to the stage of asset-dumping and crisis survival, thus bypassing the stage of corporate reorganization in order to increase overall efficiency. Second, the weakening of the former leaders means an increased possibility of aggression from their smaller but better-off competitors, as well as from regional authorities, which previously could not afford to engage in a tug of war with 'Muscovite' financial groups. The trend toward growing regionalization of ownership creates potential grounds for a new spectrum of corporate conflicts. Third, the reorganization of big business in 2000-01 could also be connected with the financial-industrial groups' considerable loss of opportunities to work with government money, and their subsequent need to enter the private capital market for new sources of financing. This, in particular, would lead to a redistribution of ownership in exchange for financial resources. Fourth, the crisis faced by some of the largest banks and financial groups may lead to an increase in the power of the federal natural monopolies and other 'autonomous empires', initially oriented towards 'self-sufficiency', which suffered little during the financial crisis. Of course, this strengthening may proceed largely at the expense of the assets and influence of former rivals. Fifth is the attempt to reanimate the state holding companies in strategic branches of the economy. To a large extent, this is possible only by redistributing the ownership shares in large Russian corporations. Finally, we may witness a series of mergers and friendly alliances between companies from the crisis-ridden financial groups, most probably aimed at strengthening their overall defensive positions or restoring past lobbying clout, and not at achieving economic efficiency of the corporations and production operations involved. This also explains why all such intentions are very shaky. Thus, given the otherwise unchanged conditions, we can expect the formation during 2000-01 of new large financial entities and an overall change in the disposition of forces in the political economy.

It will be difficult for any new government to unravel the intricate web of dependencies between commercial banks and the Central Bank, which was woven shortly after the August crisis. The Central Bank handed out Rbl18bn in stabilization loans to get the payment system going.[20] Among the recipients were *SBS-Agro, Promstroibank, Vozrozhdenie and Avtobank*, which all pledged 75% plus one share of their capital to the Central Bank as collateral. The Central Bank also allowed a number of unnamed banks, reportedly including all the bigger ones, to swap some of their frozen short-term government debt for at least Rbl65bn in Lombard credits to provide liquidity for the sector.[21] These back-room deals, paid for with taxpayers' money or specially printed rubles, basically ensure all these banks' future existence and make a major overhaul less likely.

In this political vacuum, the larger commercial banks took it upon themselves to resurrect their empires. They moved their assets to new entities, called bridge banks or shadow banks, leaving their liabilities in the old shells. Many experts doubt that the bridge banks are serious about repaying foreign creditors. *SBS-Agro* has set up the *Soiuz* group and the First Mutual Credit Society where its VIP clients can park assets. The significance of the government's having revoked *Menatep*'s license is blunted by the fact that the bank had already transferred its major assets to *Menatep St. Peterburg*, and to the Trust and Investment Bank. At the time it lost its license, *Menatep* had been negotiating with foreign creditors and had agreed with them that a possible debt repayment would be taken over by its affiliates *Rosprom* and *Iukos*. *Oneksim* created a new entity called *Rosbank*, which received a new banking license from the Central Bank within two weeks of applying. *Rossiiskii Kredit* transferred its assets to *Impeks*. The Moskovskaia oblast bank *Unikom*, which also lost its license in May 1999, formerly handled the budget funds for the Moskovskaia oblast government. When it got into difficulties, its assets were swallowed by *Guta* Bank, an institution affiliated with the Moscow city government. This moving of assets is legal according to the letter of the Russian law.[22]

---

[20] Schaic 1999, 255.
[21] Ibid.
[22] *Vedomosti* (2000), 28 Februaury.

Meanwhile, troubled banks have taken assets off their already bleak balance sheets by rewriting contracts. New contracts show a new owner, for example an offshore company controlled by the bank's shareholders, while the bank's balance sheet still shows the liability. With creditors knocking on their doors, Russian bankers are as inventive in hiding their assets as they were in exaggerating them when they wanted loans. Russian banks have always inflated their capital. They did it because they wanted to look more important and because it made their ratios look much better. In some instances, capital was overstated by 50% to 80%.[23] This is the very essence of the Russian banking problem. The banks were also hiding risky investments. A widely used trick was to buy a stake in an affiliated fake company, which would then reinvest the money in high-yielding short-term debt or elsewhere. This would keep the banks' published market investments under the required 10% limit.

International Activity of Russian Commercial Banks

Undercapitalized Russian banks that wanted to grow had three choices: they could increase profits, merge with another bank, or go to the international capital markets. However, the potential of traditional banking business as a source of higher profits was strictly limited. Before the crisis, balance sheets had improved and the level of non-performing loans reduced (thanks to high *GKO* yields), but the bad-loan ratios ranged from 6% to 49%.[24] Those banks big enough thus turned to activities on international capital markets.

The history of international borrowing for Russian commercial banks covers only about three years, and 90% of it took place in 1997-98. There were two main forms: eurobonds and syndicated loans (in a ratio of on eto three). Foreign loans, mostly from German, Austrian, and British credit institutions, became common for Russian banks before the August 1998 crisis. The most aggressive were *Rossiiskii Kredit, Inkombank, Tokobank, Mosbiznessbank* and *Vneshtorgbank*. The main 'donors' were Bayerische Vereinsbank AG (7 loans); London Forfaiting Asia Ltd (7), Citibank (7); Bayerische Landesbank (6), Komercni Banka (6); Raiffeisen Zentralbank Österreich AG (5), Bank Austria AG (5), Die Erste Österreichische

---

[23] Schaic 1999, 257.
[24] Tsentral'nyi Bank Rossiiskoi Federatsii (2000), *Biulleten' bankovskoi statistiki No. 1*, 43.

SparCasse (5); West Merchant Bank (4), Dresdner Bank Luxembourg SA (4); Dresdner Bank (2), United Bank of Switzerland (2), CS First Boston (2), and Berliner Bank AG (2). The average weighted volume, interest rate over LIBOR[25] and term were US$40mn, 4.5%, and 10 months, respectively. As a group, Russian commercial banks have received more than 50 loans, totaling more than US$2.5bn.[26] The debt problems of Russian banks could thus have a profound effect on German banks, which have the largest exposure to the Russian loan market. Moreover, if the German banks take sufficiently heavy losses, it will curtail their other lending, and the potential impact on the syndicated loan market in Europe would be immense. This would not only render distribution extremely difficult, but would greatly accelerate the rise in pricing.

The last year before the crisis also witnessed a trickle of Russian bank paper. 1997 alone produced three Eurobonds from *Oneksim*, *Alfa* bank and *SBS-Agro*. The last issued a US$200mn, three-year Eurobond at 425 bp[27] over the US treasury rate (led by JP Morgan).[28] There has also been a floating rate note, Euro commercial paper issues (ECP),[29] and three American depository receipt (ADR) offerings,[30] as well as a raft of syndicated loans. The *Vozrozhdenie* bank, for example, has issued level-one ADRs (a repackaging of existing shares) up to the maximum 3% of its share capital, as have both *Inkombank* and *Menatep*. The ADR prices for these banks were reported to have risen by about 100%, 250%, and 60% respectively, although virtually no trading took place. *Oneksim* undertook a private ECP placement. *Inkombank* was the first local bank to publicly issue Euro commercial paper (US$200mn ECP was arranged by SBC Warburg). Russian bank euros were issued in all three years. And several other Russian banks were planning ADR or debt issues.[31]

---

[25] LIBOR (London Interbank Offered Rate) - the rate at which prime banks offer to make Eurocurrency deposits with other prime banks for a given maturity, which can range from overnight to five years in London.

[26] Tsentral'nyi Bank Rossiiskoi Federatsii (2000), *Biulleten' bankovskoi statistiki No. 1*, 70.

[27] Basis point (bp) - 1/100 of 1%, i.e. 0.01%. Used to express yield spread or differential.

[28] Tsentral'nyi Bank Rossiiskoi Federatsii (2000), *Biulleten' bankovskoi statistiki No. 1*, 15.

[29] Short-term note or draft of a government agency, bank or corporation issued on a discount basis, the proceeds of which are typically used for current transactions (usually an unsecured promissory note issued for short-term credit needs).

[30] American Depository Receipt (ADR) - a depository receipt issued by an American bank to promote trading in a foreign stock of share (the bank holds the underlying securities and an ADR is issued against them).

[31] Tsentral'nyi Bank Rossiiskoi Federatsii (2000), *Biulleten' bankovskoi statistiki No. 1*, 16.

One place where investors could hedge their exposure was on the Chicago Mercantile Exchange (CME), which since April 1998 became the first - and so far, only - institution to offer ruble contracts outside Russia. The CME clearing house protects all market participants against counter party risk. In less than six weeks of trading, the contract had broken all existing records: the number of open contracts, each worth US$82,000, reached 5,000.[32] In mid-May, only weeks after the CME launched the ruble contract, the collapse of *Tokobank*, one of the 20 largest banks, dealt a nearly fatal blow to the domestic forward market. The failure was a shock to one well-known Wall Street firm, which had hedged much of its currency risk through *Tokobank*.

Russian bank activity in the international capital markets became increasingly desperate over the summer of 1998, as it became clear that, while the burden of domestic debt was unsustainable, the appetite of international investors also had its limits. It is estimated that Russian banks combined owe foreign creditors US$10-12bn, excluding up to US$5bn in forward contracts. Some analysts believe that foreign creditors could expect repayment offers of 25% of the outstanding debt.[33]

To conclude this overview of the international activities of the Russian banking sector, one might mention that 70 Russian banks have together about 100 subsidiaries and representative offices about. However, their total liabilities exceed their assets by five to six times.[34] Five international banks owned by the Russian state, all dating from the Soviet era, serve as important nodes in trade-finance relations with Western Europe. These institutions are based in London (*Moskovskii Narodnyi Bank*), Paris (Banque Commerciale pour l'Europe du Nord), Frankfurt-on-Main (Ost-West Handelsbank AG), Vienna (Donau-Bank AG) and Luxembourg (East-West United Bank). The most active among these are the first, due to its position in the center of international capital movement; the second, which is universal in the character of its operations (including offering non-deliverable forward to foreign investors wanting to cover their exposure to the ruble); and the third, which plays a considerable role in economic ties between Germany and Russia.

---

[32] Davidson 1998, 28-29.
[33] Schaic 1999, 258.
[34] Tsentral'nyi Bank Rossiiskoi Federatsii (2000), *Biulleten' bankovskoi statistiki No. 1*, 55.

Restructuring the Banking Sector

The problems of the Russian banking sector were well-known long before last year's crisis and efforts to restructure the sector date from pre-crisis times and were driven on by the World Bank and the European Bank of Reconstruction and Development (EBRD), who were well-informed about the banking sector's structural flaws. They had in-depth access to banks' books since 1995, through their Financial Institutions Development Project (FIDP). This program was set up to help banks develop their structures and stimulate automation. Before banks were admitted to the program, they were checked for fitness. This was done by the Bank Review Unit, a part of the FIDP. The review unit functioned as a mini central bank, arranging banking inspections of its own. The technology component of this program was widely used and yielded good results, but not the development side. Each Russian bank was supposed to team up with a foreign, twinning, bank, which would assist with its development. The beneficiaries were not willing to accept the support. Only three of the 41 banks in the FIDP have completed the twinning program. In the final analysis, the twinning system was a complete failure, shaming the World Bank and the EBRD.

Fundamental flaws in the banking system were ignored, in the hope that they could be overcome later. After a slow start, the FIDP program went ahead and signed up 41 commercial banks, representing nearly all the commercial capital in the sector. These were destined to become the core of the new Russian banking system, setting them apart from the fly-by-night speculators that called themselves banks. However, audits by the Bank Restructuring Unit indicated that most banks were not as reliable as their public picture suggested. The World Bank and the EBRD did not push them into action, because they did not want to infuriate their clients. This was a time of rapid transition in Russia. Given the volatility in the sector, foreign banks considered FIDP participants to be the most reliable partners in the country. Cunning Russian banks were eager to display their FIDP membership as an international seal of reliability. With all parties eager to lend and to borrow, few questions were asked. The FIDP program became a license to kill banks.

Post-crisis restructuring has been in Russian hands. In 1999, a new bank restructuring agency with the Russian acronym *ARKO* was established jointly by the Central Bank and the government to provide capital to banks under rehabilitation, acquire bank shares, manage bank operations, manage bad assets, arrange for mergers and acquisitions, initiate and oversee liquidations, etc. In principle, *ARKO* is not a bad idea. For, example, helping regional banks is the right way to go, because it is easier to figure out what is going on in smaller banks. But many of these banks are closely connected to regional authorities. Some might be taken over by the state, some restructured, others will stand alone. With only Rbl4bn available, *ARKO* is unlikely to make a difference.

Russian financial ethics (first of all transparency) are different from those in the West, and so is its system. It is therefore difficult to base financial decisions on financial reports only. But even aside from the question of corruption, proper supervision of commercial Russian banks is virtually impossible. Other steps have to be taken, such as better legislation and effective law enforcement. And bank restructuring will have to form part of an economic program, which in turn will help restore confidence. Without a functioning banking system, there can be no economic growth. Banks are the main nucleus for economic growth.

Rebuilding confidence will be the cornerstone of banking reconstruction. Although it will be politically hard to swallow, Russia will have to rely on foreign banks to restore trust in the sector. Commercial banking is not going to be revived in Russia unless internationally renowned banks such as Deutsche Bank or Citibank open a branch on Main Street. The share of 'foreigners' in the total capital of Russian banks is not currently high - about 12%, as compared with about 50% in Hungary. There are 21 banks with 100% foreign capital and eleven banks with over 50%.[35] The big investment banks all say that they have a presence, that they've not abandoned Russia, but this may mean two men in a small office. It would be amazing if any of them had budgeted for revenues from Russia in the immediate future. Banks with foreign capital in Russia (about 135) accumulated more than 50% of assets of the whole Russian banking community.[36] This is one more proof of the weakness of the national banking sector. Changes in banks' ownership can lead to corporate restructuring and improvements in financial and operating performance. Foreign investors have played a key role in restructuring domestic banks and firms in the transition economies of Central and Eastern Europe and the former Soviet Union. For example, foreign investment institutions in the Czech Republic, Poland, and Hungary over the 1992-95 period were faster in restructuring and had a higher propensity to invest.[37]

---

[35] Ibid.
[36] Ibid.
[37] See Hunya 1997.

Conclusion

We can thus conclude that the gravest shortcomings of the Russian banking system are: first, the very small dimension of capital of the most Russian banks; second, the very low quality of capital; third, the lack of development of the regional banks; fourth, the misbalance of assets; fifth, the low efficiency of asset management; sixth, the low quality of liabilities; seventh, minimum tax receipts from the banking sector; eighth, basic mistakes of the Central Bank in the policy of the development of the Russian banking system. The process of reconstruction of the Russian banking sector will sooner or later have to look for external stimulants in the forms of foreign investment.

9 Financial Groups and the Development of Market Institutions

GRIGORII V. KRASNOV

As the decade draws to a close, observers fiercely compete to identify and classify significant recent trends in the post-Soviet space, to provide certain closure to what has undoubtedly been one of the most remarkable periods in recent time. The assessments range from declaring the 1990s the most revolutionary decade in Russian history to likening it to the 'lost decade' of Brazil. If this author were to join the line of those attempting to pass judgment on the topic, he would single out Russian privatization as one of the most stunning achievements of the 1990s. Chubais' grand 'fire sale' resulted in a massive redistribution of assets within the country, yielding unimaginable economic gains to those skillful and ruthless enough to take advantage of the immense opportunities offered. At the same time, it represented one of the most fascinating experiments in modern history, providing the academic community with a broad canvass of political, social, and economic dislocations to address, analyze, categorize, and ultimately seek a solution to.

The decade has also seen the evolution of Financial-Industrial Groups (FIGs) as key actors on Russian economic scene. With origins in the insider-dominated privatization auctions, FIGs have been leveraging their newly-found economic power to exert considerable political influence and rapidly grow their asset bases largely at the expense of the Russian state, thereby gaining an unsavory reputation in the West.[1] Today, with the

---

[1] Formation of industrial groups on the back of a number of individual enterprises has been developing on an ad hoc basis since the early 1990s, although it was not until the Law on the Financial-Industrial Groups of 1994 that the concept received widespread acceptance. For example, Starodubrovskaya (1995) mentions *AO Konsensus* and *AO Rosneftegazstroi* as typical examples of such early FIGs.

privatization opportunities having diminished, Russia's FIGs have entered a new stage, in which the mentality of the 'asset-grab' stage by necessity is increasingly giving way to considerations of return on assets. At the same time, Russia is struggling to develop stable market institutions to support further development. Some of these processes possess self-reinforcing properties, raising issues of path dependencies and creating potential roadblocks on Russia's path towards democracy and free markets.

This paper argues that the ongoing process of FIG reorientation towards profit-based performance benchmarks in Russia is closely intertwined with the development of market institutions, and that the FIGs are affecting this development it in two major ways. Firstly, by having preempted and internalized the development of market institutions, FIGs are able to offer significant economic benefits to other economic entities, creating strong incentives for continued industrial consolidation around the core groups. Secondly, by virtue of their economic dominance, the FIGs are serving as powerful agents for institutional change, including profoundly affecting such fundamental market institutions as property rights, business ethic, and market infrastructure.

In the latter process in particular, the FIGs have become one of the main conduits of values associated with the effective integration of the Russian economy into the global marketplace. There is significant human and intellectual capital currently being accumulated within the FIGs as a result of their frequent interactions with business counterparts outside of the post-Soviet realm. This accumulation is starting to spill over into space external to FIGs existing structures, and within this context, the FIGs are having a strong globalizing influence on the Russian society at large.

The key methodological question of relevance to the entire inquiry is to what extent one can consider an FIG as an independent actor, determining the behavior of its constituent parts (including individuals) and to what extent the individual actors determine FIG behavior. As argued below, significant explanatory benefits can be gained by viewing FIGs as organizations within the framework of institutional economics, which is the approach adopted in this paper. This approach leads to the viewing of organizations as agglomerations of individuals with certain constraints imposed on their behavior by the umbrella of broader organizational interests. Because such constraints are backed by internal enforcement mechanisms, the fulfillment of organizational objectives can be achieved.

This path of thinking leads to an examination of the inherent alignment of individual interests with those of the organization, and to this end a distinction must be drawn between two sets of individuals functioning within the organizational structures, namely owners and employees. The objectives of owners are closely aligned with those of an organization. In fact, by virtue of exercising ownership control, this group of individuals is in a position to shape organizational structures and incentives to ensure an ever-closer alignment of the organizational interests with their own. On the other hand, the objectives of employees may not be aligned with those of the organization as a result of a classical agent-principal conflict. Some companies seek to overcome this deficiency by motivating employees through profit-related bonus structures. However, these types of incentives are rarely applied beyond the top layer of management, and even then they often fail to overcome an individual manager's other preferences related to job security, maximization of short-term financial gain, and the extension of personal power.

Thus, the question of the direction of behavioral determination can largely be reduced to the analysis of FIG ownership, also with some important consequences for the choice of a relevant unit of analysis. The presumed primacy of the ownership vectors leads to the choice of the concept of a 'market participant' as a primary unit, which is defined broadly to include both individual and corporate entities.[2]

The paper seeks to address the above themes in four parts. Firstly, the analytical tools of institutional economics are offered for the evaluation of FIG formation and behavior. Secondly, these tools are applied to examine the potential benefits and the resultant incentives provided to individual enterprises by FIG affiliation. Thirdly, the mechanisms for the application of these forces are analyzed in a case study of a segment of the petrochemical industry. And finally, the impact of these developments on the future evolution of market institutions in Russia is assessed.

---

[2] This perspective is clearly limited to the examination of economic phenomena by relying on an implicit assumption of economically rational actors. This assumption, however, is consistent with this paper's primary focus on analyzing the economic dimension of FIGs within the context of market institutions, as further discussed below.

Theoretical Framework

In the developed countries, there has been a growing trend questioning the efficiency of diversified conglomerates. With the notable exception of General Electric corporation, conglomerates tend to trade at lower multiples of earnings then their more focused counterparts, reflecting the fact that the capital markets view these companies as suffering from excessive agency costs created by the empire-building ambitions of their managers.[3]

By comparison, the proliferation of insider lending arrangements in transition economies is a well-documented phenomenon, with a substantial body of scholarly literature in existence on the topic covering the USA, Europe, Japan, Taiwan, China, Hong Kong, India, Singapore, and several Latin American countries.[4] Starting with the early days of the US financial system, insider lending seems to be a near-universal phenomenon in transition markets, where, in absence of a formal financial system, insider lending can mitigate information asymmetries and reduce transaction costs, thus potentially facilitating improved firm performance.[5] In essence, institutional economics has become the leading framework for analyzing emerging-market conglomerates.

A number of authors have sought, directly or indirectly, to understand the formation of the Russian financial-industrial groups (FIGs) in terms of institutional economics.[6] Originating with the seminal work by Coase, institutional economics stipulates that under the conditions of non-zero transaction costs, an incentive exists for market participants to create institutions.[7]

According to North, institutions can be defined as 'humanly devised constraints that structure human interaction.'[8] In order to lower their transaction costs in an exchange, individuals resort to entering into contracts, which are formal agreements outlining the terms of an exchange. The strength of the contracts, and therefore the level of transaction costs associated with an exchange, are largely determined by the institutional

---

[3] Jensen 1986.
[4] An excellent review of comparative literature on insider lending is contained in Keister 1997.
[5] Lamoreaux 1994.
[6] Including Prokop 1995, Perotti and Gelfer 1998, Thornton 1998, Kuznetsov 1998 and Klimov 1999.
[7] Coase 1937.
[8] North 1996, 344.

environment. Under institutional economics, an organization, according to Eggertson is a 'set of actors who cooperate or act jointly in production.'[9] By means of internalizing control over resources, organizations minimize transaction costs associated with exchanges. Actors are incentivized to enter into organizations by the existing institutions. At the same time, organizations influence the prevalent institutions, creating the conditions for institutional development.

The theoretical framework applied in this paper begs the issue of units of analysis. Various grouping methodologies can be and have been historically applied to actors in transition economies, largely based on the perceived alignments of political, economic, and social preferences of these actors. The scope of this paper is to analyze the economic dimension of FIGs within the context of market institutions. Thus, by definition, this paper adopts an assumption of actor behavior motivated primarily by economic considerations.

This assumption has profound implications for the unit of analysis framework deployed. A distinction between a physical and a legal entity that is the beneficial owner of an asset becomes less meaningful when analyzing the logic of industrial consolidation. As a result, a relevant unit of analysis becomes 'the market participant', which is defined as an economic unit acting rationally in its own self-interest, and can include individuals as well as commercial organizations. While admittedly limited in scope, this approach is reflective of the economic focus of this analysis.

This analysis does not negate one of the leading approaches historically used for explaining the formation of FIG's, i.e. the one emphasizing the rent-seeking behavior of actors in the economic and political arena. In fact, it is acknowledged by this author that the behavior of such actors in Russia, in particular in the early stages of reform, has been driven by considerations of leveraging political access for the achievement of personal objectives. However, it has to be pointed out that the institutional economics approach largely subsumes the issue of rent- or profit-oriented behavior by relying on the assumption of economically rational units acting in the environment of institutional vacuum, while introducing a further interpretive dimension to the analysis. For example, normative judgments notwithstanding, the swapping of political influence for equity in privatized companies by a bank (a clear example of rent-seeking behavior) would be interpreted as the optimal economic outcome under the conditions of non-zero cost of ownership, i.e. when the potential

---

[9] Egertsson 1996, 9.

political disruptions from the competitors for the equity are factored into the equation. From this perspective, the logic of institutional economics supersedes the traditional analysis by incorporating the economic value of political influence.

A traditional definition of markets as 'a setting within which exchanges may take place'[10] leads one to the examination of the preconditions for the carrying out of such exchanges, e.g. the component parts of what is broadly termed 'market institutions'. Firstly, this would include the existence and the possibility for the impartial enforcement of contracts and property rights. This precondition directly relates to the perceived strength of the state as an entity possessing the 'monopoly on violence' in a society, in accordance with Max Weber's classical definition. Secondly, this relates to the universally accepted informal set of behavioral norms and constraints targeted at establishing credibility in the market place, e.g. what can be termed as a 'business ethic'. Thirdly, organizational infrastructure facilitating the efficient allocation of resources, which is taken for granted in the developed markets, can be also considered as an important market institution. This would include service organizations providing support for market-based activity, including market research, executive search capabilities, business plan development, financial intermediary, and other types of 'consulting' services. The third category can be referred to as 'formal' institutions, while the first two are better described as 'informal' institutions.

In the initial conditions of a transition economy, both the formal and the informal institutions comprising what can be broadly defined as capitalist markets are lacking. As summarized by Thornton, 'in the pre-reform era, state controls supplanted much of the institutional infrastructure of the market economy'.[11] Polishchuk argues with some degree of success that of Balcerowicz's classic LSI transformation reform triad (Liberalization, Stabilization, Institutional Reform)[12] only the first two items were actively pursued in Russia. Thus Russia became 'a gigantic laboratory, testing the "organic growth" model of economic and political institutions'.[13]

The emergence of market institutions in post-Soviet space was inevitably conditioned by both the domestic and the global contexts within

---

[10] Tordjman 1998, 2.
[11] Thornton 1998, 2.
[12] Balcerowicz 1994.
[13] Polishchuk 1998, 84.

which the transformations were taking place. The domestic context included the development of new economic actors, such as the organizations led by the newly developed finance and trading interests. The lifting of government controls created exceptional opportunities for individuals with broad industrial connections to arbitrage the severe information asymmetries, which arose due to the lack of market institutions. This resulted in robust capital accumulation through supernormal profits enjoyed by the 'new management' interests active in finance and trade. Acting within the environment which lacked market institutions, these actors undertook to create such institutions in order to facilitate further wealth accumulation.[14] Because of the grass-roots origin of this development, most of the market institutions arising in this manner retained their proprietary nature, remaining effectively shared by a limited number of economic entities as opposed to belonging to the society at large.

In addition to the domestic drivers, the global context exerted a strong influence on the process of building market mechanisms in Russia. The country was particularly strongly affected by the worldwide trends of globalization, which remains in many respects primarily an economics-driven phenomenon related to the rise of what has been termed by some observers as 'supra-territorial capitalism'. For example, Scholte argues that the six most visible manifestations of globalization include the areas of communications, organizations, trade, finance, ecology, and consciousness.[15] The importance of globalization to the development of market institutions can be derived from the relating of these areas to the three components of market institutions as outlined above. In absence of a strong state, the functionality of contract enforcement is provided by organizations, especially if the latter are viewed within the context of incomplete contracts. Consciousness and communications relate directly to the concept of business ethic. Finally, trade and finance are facilitated by the existence of an organizational infrastructure of markets, such as the trade and financial intermediaries. Thus, of Scholte's six key globalization areas, five are of direct relevance to the formation of market institutions.

As discussed above, the institutional vacuum arising in Russia following the initial implementation of market reforms led to preemptive grass-roots moves by economic actors to develop proprietary market

---

[14] According to Freinkman 1995, this capital concentration in the financial and trade sectors subsequently became one of the driving forces behind the formation of industrial conglomerates known as FIGs.
[15] Scholte 1997, 3.

institutions. In absence of well-developed independent institutions provided as a collective good by the state, these institutions presently remain embedded in the organizational structures of the FIGs, creating strong economic incentives for other enterprises to continue joining FIGs, as analyzed below.

Consolidation Drivers

It can be argued that the financial-industrial consolidation through FIG formation in Russia fulfilled two broadly defined functionalities which in the developed economies are normally provided by the infrastructure of the broader markets. Firstly, it reduced the contract monitoring and enforcement costs for the participants, thus facilitating intra-group trade and providing effective product markets. Secondly, it partially replaced capital markets by establishing the mechanism for the management of liquid resources within the group, allocating capital between the entities, and facilitating the participants' access to external sources of finance, including foreign direct investment and Western capital markets.

The importance of these drivers in the stages of initial formation varied between the two main types of FIGs. As argued by Johnson, industry-centered groups are a category of FIGs distinct from the bank-centered groups.[16] Gorbatova examines the mechanisms of formation of the two types of groups in greater detail.[17] She finds that industrial enterprises found the concept of an FIG, as articulated by the 1993 legislation, significantly more attractive then banks: while 30% of enterprises surveyed said they wanted to participate in the creation of an FIG, only 7% of the

---

[16] Johnson 1997.

[17] While Gorbatova (1995) considers Regional FIGs and Special Investment Purpose FIGs as separate categories, the distinction hardly survives the test of time. The first (regional) category has typically been related to either a regional bank leveraging political influence to achieve priority treatment in privatization, or to an agglomeration of regional enterprises forming part of a technological chain. Thus the category is largely subsumed within the bank-related and industry-related FIG definition. Furthermore, the only FIG falling into the second category (special investment purpose) according to Gorbatova (1995) is AVVA, which is in fact a clear example of an industry-related FIG. Therefore, extrapolating from Freinkman 1995, an analysis of the sources of capital that is applied for the acquisition of assets (e.g. trade-related or finance-related capital) provides much greater explanatory powers vis-à-vis both the mechanisms of privatization/consolidation and the corresponding embedded incentives.

banks surveyed acknowledged any familiarity with the statute.[18] These findings are not surprising, since, as is not abundantly clear, most of the bank-centered FIGs were formed de-facto through the acquisition of shares by the banks in privatization, only to be formalized as FIGs in compliance with the legislation much later.

The discrepancy is easily explained by examining the intent of the 1993 legislation, which focused on the creation of 'vertically integrated financial-industrial groups with a closed production cycle [which] can form islands of stabilization in a sea of chaos.'[19] For the enterprise directors, the re-establishment of former production links served as one of the most powerful motivators for their enterprises joining into an FIG. Therefore, industry-led FIGs would arise as a result of the manager-owners recognizing the need for closer cooperation with their suppliers and customers. On the other hand, an affiliation with a bank would provide an enterprise potentially with greater access to capital, but with much less in terms of supply chain benefits. The discussion below, therefore, focuses on the two drivers in turns. First, evidence for the 'product market' benefits to a number of industry FIG-affiliated enterprises in the automotive industry is examined. Secondly, the 'capital markets' benefits accruing to companies affiliated with bank-led FIGs are analyzed.

The automotive industry provides an excellent case study on the value of inter-enterprise cooperation to the preservation of the market position of participating companies. The choice of the automotive industry as a case study is explained by its relative transparency, as well the high complexity of the automotive supply chain which highlights the transaction costs component of the economic 'value subtracted', thereby making a transaction costs-based analysis particularly applicable. The table above summarizes the historical market-share trends for the three leading Russian automotive producers, including *AvtoVAZ*, *GAZ*, and *AZLK*. As can be seen, considerably different trends can be observed, which can be tied to the different degree of linkage that these manufacturers have with their suppliers and customers.

---

[18] Gorbatova 1995, 27.
[19] Starodubrovskaya 1995, 5.

Table 9.1 Market share of leading Russian auto producers, 1993-99

	1993	1994	1995	1996	1997	1998E	1999E
AvtoVAZ	69%	67%	73%	78%	75%	74%	73%
GAZ	11%	15%	14%	14%	13%	13%	13%
AZLK	10%	9%	5%	0%	2%	5%	5%
Other	10%	10%	8%	7%	10%	8%	9%
Total	100%	100%	100%	100%	100%	100%	100%
Total units produced	955,954	798,109	834,779	867,298	981,887	914,894	926,106
Change in units produced		-17%	5%	4%	13%	-7%	1%

Abbreviations of the Russian automotive producers names stand for the following:
AvtoVAZ = *Volzhskii Avtomobil'nyi Zavod*; GAZ = *Gorkovskii Avtomobil'nyi Zavod*;
AZLK = *Avtomobil'nyi Zavod imeni Leninskogo Komsomola*.

Note: E = estimated.

Sources: Troika Dialog, ASM-Holding.

AvtoVAZ fell under the effective control of the FIG led by *LogoVaz*, the Company's national dealership network accounting for bulk of *AvtoVAZ*'s sales. By integrating the production and the distribution of the *Lada* cars, the *LogoVaz* consortium was able to maintain production at the plant stable. While the plant's financial situation remains difficult, this is probably not a direct reflection of the company's underlying profitability, but can rather be attributed to the transfer pricing arrangements under which most of the sales value is captured at the level of the dealerships, where they can be more directly controlled by *LogoVaz* shareholders. The ability of *LogoVaz*-related interests to finance significant further acquisitions in a variety of industries, including transport, non-ferrous metals and oil production, provides circumstantial but convincing evidence of the *VAZ-LogoVaz* value transfers that took place in the early days of Russian reform.

The situation at *GAZ* differed from that at *AvtoVAZ*. Importantly, *GAZ* benefited from a massive investment program amounting to close to US$1bn, which was undertaken by the Soviet government in the late

1980s.[20] This program allowed the producer to introduce the light truck model *Gazelle*, whose popularity in a previously non-existent niche provided a strong boost to sales. However, and more importantly, *GAZ* has undertaken steps to establish close relationships with its suppliers and customers. On the distribution side, *GAZ* proceeded to aggressively restructure its service network to take on a broader role of a captive dealership system with more than 150 points of presence across Russia.[21] Additionally, and equally important, *GAZ*'s production has been from the start characterized by a very high degree of vertical integration, with over 70% of parts manufactured in-house.[22] The initiation of a FIG *Nizhegorodskie Avtomobili* in 1994 strengthened the manufacturer's relationships with the rest of the suppliers and secured the cooperation of such leading banking institutions as *Menatep* and *Avtobank*. The combination of these measures is widely acclaimed by the analysts as having been responsible for *GAZ*'s survival.

In contrast, the *AZLK-Moskvich* plant remained under government control, with no measures taken to re-establish the distribution and supply links. Distribution problems were compounded by the perception of low quality that *Moskvich* had in the eyes of the consumer. And, using in excess of 1,200 parts for the production of its vehicles, with most of these sourced externally, supplier relationships were much more critical to *Moskvich* than to *GAZ*.[23] As a result, the company's production declined dramatically, reaching its nadir in 1996, the year in which *AZLK* produced 3,000 vehicles in a plant that produced 189,000 units in 1985.[24]

The involvement of the Moscow city government helped to reanimate the company. In 1997, the City of Moscow undertook to buy a controlling stake in the enterprise from the federal government, and used municipal orders to start filling up capacity at the plant.[25] In parallel, discussions were held with Renault for the production of its *Megane* model at the *AZLK* facilities from knock-down kits in a US$420mn project.[26] As a result of these measures, the plant is returning to life, after escaping bankruptcy proceedings by a narrow margin. Effectively, it can be said that *AZLK*'s ultimate rescue was a result of joining the de-facto FIG constituted by the

---

[20] Shashenkov 1996.
[21] Ibid.
[22] Oganesian 1998.
[23] *Nezavisimaia gazeta* (1998), 16 April.
[24] *Moskovskie novosti* (1999), 16 March.
[25] *Moskovskaia pravda* (1998), 22 October.
[26] *Automotive News Europe* (1998), 14 September.

business interests related to the administration of the City of Moscow. The City of Moscow's position as a 'FIG in disguise' is persuasively argued by Jensen.[27]

In summary, the comparison of the performance of the top three Russian automotive producers supports the view that under the conditions of institutional vacuum, mechanisms for inter-enterprise cooperation furnished by the FIGs were of critical importance to the well-being of the participating entities. The mechanisms for capital reallocation provided by the FIGs were a further incentive for the enterprises to join.

Improving allocation of capital among enterprises within the group is one of the key reasons for the existence of diversified groups in the emerging markets that is cited by researchers. The reasons that groups may allocate capital more efficiently can be summarized in relation to the three functions of market institutions discussed previously. Firstly, lacking a strong legal system which protects the rights of minority equity investors and lenders, project profitability becomes a less important determinant of capital allocation than majority equity control. Secondly, an investor must possess a reasonable level of comfort with the intangible agreement between the investor and the manager on the strategy to maximize shareholder value. Lacking a universal business ethic, such understanding is best achieved by exercising effective control over the investor, even to the extent of replacing existing management with tested individuals the investor knows through previous experience. Finally, a single group is more efficient at overcoming the obstacles of accounting intransparency and incomplete market information than the more dispersed shareholder set characteristic of the public markets.

The mechanisms for capital reallocation at the leading FIGs are well-established and are embedded in the organizational structure. The structure of the *Onexim* bank holding serves as a good example of this point. FIG *Interros* is at the core of the holding, incorporating close to thirty of the 'traditional' industrial enterprises under the group's control, including such leading companies as *Norilskii Nickel* (non-ferrous metals), *Sidanko* (oil production), *Perm Motors* (engineering), and *Khimvolokno* (petrochemicals). The management committee of the group includes the directors of other companies *Interros* is an investor in, including the leasing, travel agency, pension fund, and insurance businesses (*Interros-Finkom*), real estate (*Interros-Estate*), investment banking (MFK-

---

[27] Jensen 1998.

Renaissance), and media and publishing (*Prof Media*).[28] Additionally, Sputnik Funds, an affiliate of MFK-Renaissance carries out the principal investment activity, relying both on the *Interros* group's own funds and on the funds raised for direct investments from Western financial institutions, such as pension funds and university endowments. Sputnik's portfolio includes investments in such growth industries as mobile telephony (Techinfo Communications, *Kyivstar GSM*), branded consumer food products (*Dovgan* Holding), and radio (*Evropa Plus*).[29]

A recent study by Perotti and Gelfer[30] specifically focuses on the role of the Russian FIGs as substitutes for the capital markets in allocating capital between the net savers and the net borrowers within the group. By comparing the internal cash-flow-to-investment relationship among the FIG-affiliated and the independent companies, the authors find that the relationship is largely negative for the former and largely positive for the latter. From this, the authors conclude that FIGs do in fact serve as capital reallocators, utilizing some companies within the group as 'cash cows' to fund other, less profitable but more promising entities. Additional testing of the relationship between the market-expected profitability of firms and the level of investment provides further support to their hypothesis that, within the Russian context of weak capital markets, groups do serve as more efficient allocators of capital.

The conclusions that Perotti and Gelfer[31] draw appear somewhat tainted in view of the negative experience of the FIGs in the aftermath of Russia's devaluation and default. The events of August-September 1998 revealed the depth of the risk management problem that the leading FIGs faced. As the banking system crumbled, many an observer bemoaned the 'excessive' control enjoyed by the banks over the industrial enterprises. It has been argued that this control has led to the redirection of liquidity into speculation on the capital and currency markets, leading to further exacerbation of the industrial liquidity crunch when the markets collapsed.

It is difficult to disagree with the fact of the large-scale liquidity redirection by the FIGs, with all the logical implications of such a stance vis-à-vis the moral fabric of the Russian business environment. At the same time, this author would like to point out that such redirection was also strongly affected by the high real interest rates on government obligations.

---

[28] *Interros*, <www.interros.ru>, accessed 5 June 1999.
[29] *@-daily* (1999), 2 July; *RosBalt* (1998), 1 July; Telenor Press Release, 30 March 1998.
[30] Perotti and Gelfer 1998.
[31] Ibid.

Combined with the lack of overall political and economic stability and the enormity of the distortions introduced by the Russian system of corporate taxation, the FIGs were being effectively penalized for investing in industrial projects, encouraging short-term speculative behavior. In a sense, the capital allocation decisions taken by the FIGs were at least as much a function of the broader motivational context of their environment as of the individual morality and professional judgment of the decision-makers, and, given the context in which they were taken, were strongly rational.

The apparent impact of the high degree of FIG exposure to the international portfolio capital flows leads to a discussion which directly relates to one of the more controversial aspects of globalization. Namely, it is often expressed that the globalization of international finance underpinned by the ongoing technological and telecommunications revolutions exposes the emerging market economies to a new kind of economic hazard. This problem relates to the extraordinary mobility of speculative capital, which today can overpower the financial abilities of governments. This view, as most recently prominently expressed by the Malaysian Prime Minister Mohammed Mahathir is implicitly supported, among others by George Soros, the engineer and the prime benefactor of the infamous run on the British pound leading to the disintegration of the European Exchange Rate Mechanism.[32]

Indeed, for the FIGs led by sizeable banks, such as *Onexim, Menatep, Rossiiskii Kredit*, and others, the ruble forward contracts were among the leading financial instruments bringing these banks into closer cooperation with their Western peers. As such, these instruments served to enhance the integration of the Russian banks into the international financial community, thus exerting a strong 'globalizing' influence. However, as the August 1998 events demonstrated, this has also exposed the FIGs involved to the risk of a sustained speculative run on the ruble. For example, at the start of October 1998, Thomson Bank Watch estimated *Onexim* bank's obligations on the ruble/dollar forward contracts to be in the range of US$1.9bn, eclipsing the rest of the bank's foreign debt in the amount of US$525mn.[33] While government's default on obligations was the primary cause in the sinking of these institutions, ruble devaluation also played a large role highlighting a potential danger for an emerging-market group of pursuing

---

[32] Soros's implicit support of the view is particularly curious given the fact that his funds were among the prime targets of Mahathir's latest outburst against the currency speculators. For further discussion, see Soros 1998, 45.

[33] *Moskovskie novosti* (1998), 17 November.

globalizing strategies through exposure to the highly mobile portfolio investment flows.

In addition to serving as capital allocators to the enterprises within a group, FIGs also often serve as the focal points for the raising of capital for its member-companies. For example, the hydrocarbon industry FIGs, such as *Lukoil* and *Gazprom*, are of critical importance for raising external finance for their subsidiaries, which included tapping the Western syndicated loan and bond market. Even before the crisis, it was extremely difficult for a Russian industrial company with US$100-$200mn in sales without a major FIG affiliation to raise external finance. Membership in an FIG clearly provides a company with enhanced access to capital, which it would not be able to enjoy otherwise, serving as an additional incentive for industrial consolidation around the leading FIGs.

The combination of the demonstrated benefits to the member-companies from participating in a financial-industrial formation continues to drive the consolidation of the Russian industrial landscape. This consolidation leads to an effective oligopolization of Russia's leading industries, as examined below.

Consolidation Mechanics

As discussed above, development of market institutions in Russia follows a grass-roots route of natural selection and is directly connected with the organizational landscape and the FIGs. With most of the institutions being embedded in the FIG organizations, evolution of these entities and the analysis of the industrial control patterns provide useful insight into the process of institutional formation in Russia. One of the most interesting examples of such evolution is provided by the experience of the petrochemicals industry.

The tire segment of the petrochemical industry is among the most prominent examples of a consolidation that was initiated by the trading interests. Based on in-place capacity, Russia's tire industry would be considered the world's sixth largest.[34] However, since the early 1990's the industry's condition has deteriorated markedly, with production falling from 48 million units in 1990 to only 19 million in 1995.[35] The breaking down of the previous production chains with the industry's privatization

---

[34] *Rubber and Plastics News* (1998), 7 September, 20.
[35] *European Rubber Journal. Global Tire Report* (1998), 24.

was one of the leading causes of this decline. These difficulties were compounded by the severe capital flight which plagued the Russian industry at the time, robbing the plants of working capital, and thus preventing the productive capacities from being utilized.

Table 9.2 Russian and Ukrainian automotive tire production trends, 1995-97 (in million units)

Company	Estimated Capacity	1995	1996	1997	1997 Prod. Share	Affiliation
Nizhnekamsk	12.0	7.7	8.4	9.4	27%	*Neftekhimprom*
Rosava (Ukraine)	6.4	5.1	5.1	5.1	15%	*Neftekhimprom*
Dneproshina (Ukraine)	5.2	3.7	3.7	3.7	11%	*Neftekhimprom*
Iaroslavl'	5.4	2.0	2.9	3.3	10%	*Gazprom*
Volzhskii	2.5	1.2	1.8	2.6	8%	*Management*
Kirov	2.5	1.0	1.5	1.9	6%	*Management*
Barnaul	2.0	1.1	1.3	1.8	5%	*Neftekhimprom*
Voronezh	2.5	0.4	1.1	1.6	5%	*Iukos-Rosprom*
Moscow	3.0	1.6	1.1	1.6	5%	*Iukos-Rosprom*
Omsk	3.0	0.9	1.1	1.5	4%	*Iukos-Rosprom*
Ekaterinburg	1.0	0.8	0.8	1.0	3%	*Iukos-Rosprom*
Krasnoiarsk	2.0	0.4	0.7	0.9	3%	*Iukos-Rosprom*
Total	47.5	25.8	29.5	34.4	100%	

Sources: *European Rubber Journal*; *Russkie Investory*; Wood & Co., author's estimates.

At the start of privatization, two groups took an active interest in the industry. *Rosshina*, a financial group affiliated with Bank *Menatep* and boasting several top ex-tire-industry managers, consolidated control of five factories, including Iaroslavl', and Omsk, and established close relations with the plants in Moscow, Ekaterinburg, and Krasnoiarsk. *Neftekhimprom*, whose management team was previously known as *Maxim* group of companies, established effective control of the Dneproshina plant and close relationships with Nizhnekamsk, Rosava, and Barnaul plants in Russia and the Ukraine. The management of both groups initially gained commercial experience in tire distribution, and subsequently pursued downstream integration into tire manufacturing.

Rosshina undertook to establish equity control over the tire production companies, accumulating equity stakes at or immediately post-privatization. Subsequently, the group would seek to restructure these companies and fill up the production lines. By comparison, *Neftekhimprom* sought to work with the management of the tire companies by providing both a supply and a distribution solution through its direct equity control of tire company suppliers and the *Shintorg* tire dealership network. *Neftekhimprom*'s strategy included being a 'one-source' provider to the tire producers, which also led it to develop and introduce its own 'Forward' brand of tires. *Neftekhimprom*-controlled petrochemical entities today include the Novomoskovsk Organic Synthesis plant, *Kurskkhimvolokno*, *Nimpromtex*, and the Barnaul Carbon Black Plant, and for almost two years included the Novokuibyshev Petrochemical Plant and *Sintezkauchuk* of Togliatti.[36]

The strategy for both *Rosshina* and *Neftekhimprom* consisted of rapid growth through highly leveraged acquisitions, in the hope that the resultant synergies and restructuring benefits would allow them to repay the incurred debts. This risky strategy inevitably led to some losses. Of the two companies, *Rosshina* was the hardest hit. Following a period of unsuccessful restructuring, including a period of flirtation with Nokian Tires (Finland), *Rosshina* managers fully sold out to the *Iukos-Rosprom* FIG linked with Bank *Menatep*.[37] One of the largest oil production companies in Russia, *Iukos* has recognized the necessity to add further value to its production, and is therefore assembling a holding in the petrochemical industry, of which *Rosshina* became a part. The enterprises in the *IukosSibir* petrochemical subsidiary include the Omsk and Voronezh tire plants, as well as the Otradnenskii and Neftegorskii oil processing plants.[38]

Faced with a formidable competitor, *Neftekhimprom* found itself under considerable pressure. In late 1997, *Neftekhimprom* had to give up ownership of two of its flagship 'founding' enterprises, *Sintezkauchuk* and the Novokuibyshev Petrochemical Plant, both suppliers to the tire industry. As *Neftekhimprom*'s shares in the enterprises were collateralized to secure the debts the two enterprises had, following the unsuccessful restructuring

---

[36] *Delovoi mir* (1997), 17 July; *Izvestiia* (1997), 23 October.
[37] *Kommersant"* (1998), 26 May; *European Rubber Journal* (1998), March.
[38] *Samarskoe obozrenie* (1998), 1 June.

these shares had to be given up to the creditors.[39] The main benefactor of the repossession was FIG *Volgopromgaz*, one of the leading financial-industrial groups of the Samaraskaia oblast.[40] The group's strength comes from its origins in natural gas distribution. Formed by four principals originally as a construction contractor for gas distribution infrastructure, the company has evolved to control a large portion of gas distribution in the region.[41]

Volgopromgaz has strong connections with the regional administration, with the governor's son of the Samarskaia oblast serving on the board of one of the group's banks.[42] This position has allowed the group to diversify into other areas, including services, hydrocarbon processing, publishing, and finance.[43] *Volgopromgaz* counts *Samaratransgaz*, *Gazprom*'s subsidiary, among the founding shareholders.[44] The company maintains close connections with *Gazprom*, and one of the founding partners presently holds a senior management position with the local *Gazprom* subsidiary.[45]

Following protracted negotiations, *Volgopromgaz* reached an agreement with *Iukos*, in accordance with which a joint venture would be established between the two entities for cooperation in the petrochemical industry. *Volgopromgaz* would contribute the Novokuibyshev Petrochemical Plant, *Sintezkauchuk*, and the Samara Synthetic Alcohol Plant.[46] While the terms of the agreement were not disclosed, a statement by the *Volgopromgaz* executive implies that *Iukos-Rosprom*'s contribution to the venture includes oil raw material deliveries, guaranteed sales volumes to its tire producing plants, as well as negotiating power with the other suppliers.[47]

The competition for petrochemical assets has recently been intensified by *Gazprom*'s aggressive entry into the field. In May 1999, *Gazprom* declared the establishment of a petrochemical holding company on the basis of *Sibur*, a petrochemical and pipeline company acquired by *Gazprom*

---

[39] Ibid. (1997), 1 December.
[40] Ibid.
[41] Ibid. (1998), 20 August.
[42] *Vremya MN* (1999), 1 September.
[43] *Delo* (Samara) (1997), No. 45, 24 December.
[44] *Samarskoe obozrenie* (1999), 6 July.
[45] Ibid. (1998), 20 August.
[46] Ibid. (1998), 2 March.
[47] Ibid.

in a December 1998 privatization auction.[48] The acquisition of *Sibur* gave *Gazprom*, among other things, control over 30% of Russia's rubber production.[49] Serendipitously, *Sibur*'s assets include a 35% stake in the Novokuibyshev Petrochemical Plant, which, following the signing of the *Volgopromgaz-Iukos* agreement fell under the effective control of *Iukos-Rosprom*.[50] In June 1999, *Sibur* carried out its first add-on acquisition, purchasing the shares of the bankrupt Iaroslavl' Tire Plant from the *Iukos-Rosprom* owned *Rosshina*.[51] The Iaroslavl' Tire Plant is located close to the rubber production plant in Iaroslavl', which is jointly controlled by *Sibur* and *Gazprom* (SK Premier plant). The proximity of the two facilities both geographically and within the technological chain makes them a nice match. Given the relatively passive role taken by *Sibur* in Novokuibyshev Petrochemical Plant, it is not inconceivable that this passivity was traded off in a broader deal between *Gazprom* and *Menatep-Iukos* that included control over the Iaroslavl' tire plant.

The petrochemical industry example demonstrates an important trend. The relatively small groups, such as *Rosshina* and *Neftekhimprom*, which led the initial consolidation, are being clearly marginalized by the larger players. By bringing to the table a stronger financial and political muscle, management expertise, and, most importantly, industrial connections, the larger groups, such as *Rosprom-Iukos* and *Gazprom* are increasingly driving the consolidation of the industries that fall within their chosen areas of strategic focus. The petrochemical industry, in this case, is demonstrative of a broader trend towards the oligopolization of the Russian industrial space. Other prominent examples of this trend include the metals industry, and the oil industry, where in excess of 50% of Russia's crude oil output is controlled by five FIGs.[52] In the oil industry in particular, the battle between *Alfa* and *Onexim* for the control of *Sidanko*'s subsidiaries *Kondpetroleum* and *Chernogorneft* appears likely to lead to further consolidation in the near future. This oligopolization presents an interesting set of problems with respect to the development of broader market institutions in Russia, which is examined separately below.

---

[48] *Moskovskie novosti* (1999), 11 May.
[49] Ibid.
[50] '*OAO Sibneftegazpererabotka*', Russkie Investory Equity Research, 1998.
[51] *Kommersant"* (1999), 9 July.
[52] Krasnov 1997.

FIGs and Institutional Development

Organizations do not arise in a vacuum, and are shaped and conditioned by their environment. As argued above, for business organizations, their competitive environment is what determines the form organizations adopt. At the same time, organizations have the ability to influence their environment, both as a result of a deliberate strategy and by virtue of their existence alone.

The development of market institutions independent of the FIGs is an important roadblock on the way to an open, transparent economy in Russia. The role of the FIGs in shaping such institutions therefore becomes of critical importance. For example, Kuznetsov argues that the evolution of a number of highly diversified economic groups that are economic agents at the macro rather than micro level represents a so-called 'institutional lock-in'. Under this scenario an 'inefficient institutional structure based on networks perpetuating extensive entry barriers rather than contestable markets becomes the stable equilibrium'.[53] The problem can be tackled in parts, in accordance with the three component parts of market institutions discussed above, namely property rights, business ethic, and market infrastructure, with the latter two being strongly interconnected.

Firstly, much of the appeal of the FIGs to their participants today is a direct function of the lack of unambiguous enforcement of property rights in Russia. The problem is mostly a political, rather than an economic one, although its effects are clearly felt in the economic sphere. As was recently very clearly shown by a series of scandals, Russia is plagued by corruption at the highest levels of government. Sadly, the statement made by one of the oligarchs a few years ago that politics is the best business in Russia remains true.[54] Privatization of justice and contract enforcement that has been undertaken by the FIGs is likely to continue for some time.

The government's interest in providing a stronger system of contract enforcement and unambiguous property rights represents an interesting collective choice dilemma. On one hand, in the long-run the society at large would benefit from re-nationalization and de-oligopolization of property rights enforcement. On the other hand, the continued growth of the large national FIGs points to the existence of a strong path dependency, whereby

---

[53] Kuznetsov 1998, 181.
[54] This sentiment expressed by the head of the *Menatep-Rosprom* group was quoted in *Euromoney* (1999), April, 74.

the preferences of the individual actors towards property rights and contract enforcement are met by joining an ever-larger FIG.

It can be argued that the current stance of the FIGs will continue so long as the opportunity cost of a strong government does not offset the benefits gained by extending their influence. In other words, given the fact that the development of market institutions in Russia is occurring in a grass-roots evolutionary manner, the preferences of agents vis-à-vis having an independent arbiter will not manifest themselves into political action until industry reaches a high level of consolidation. At this level of concentration, competition among the large groups for 'independent' assets will intensify due to the lower supply of such assets. Given the higher level of competition, the benefits to be gained from preserving and restructuring the existing assets will offset the benefits to be gained from incremental asset additions. The achievement of the described saturation point will thus strengthen the relative appeal for the agents of having an independent arbiter in the form of a state, causing a shift in the lobbying preferences.

The suggested line of reasoning is, in fact, reminiscent of Mancur Olson's classical discussion of 'roving' vs. 'stationary' bandits, which deduces that the size of the community in which a criminal operates relative to the size of the crime committed becomes a decisive factor in the evolution of the criminal's preferences. By virtue of becoming a significant institutor of incentives and motivations for economic activity, as well as indirectly benefiting from this activity, a Mafia head may be inclined to steal less percentage-wise in order to promote the economic well-being of the community.[55]

The point at which this condition will be reached in Russia is difficult to predict. However, it has clearly been delayed by the crisis of 1998. In 1996, experts were estimating that between 25% and 30% of Russia's Gross National Product was controlled by the eight largest FIGs.[56] While this number may have increased due to continued consolidation in the more recent period, such an increase would have been offset by the collapse of a number of these empires following the events of August 1998. The assets previously controlled by these groups, including *SBS Agro* and *Inkombank*, are now back 'in play'. For example, in a pre-bankruptcy scramble for liquidity, *Inkombank* sold *Novosibirski Zhirovoy Kombinat* to enterprises associated with the aluminum industry FIG Trans-World Group in April

---

[55] Olson 1996.
[56] Jensen 1998.

1999.[57] The step took place in anticipation of the bank's takeover by the National Reserve Bank, itself controlled by *Gazprom*, which announced plans to buy the several hundred million dollars of *Inkombank*'s debts with the eventual goal of converting these debts into a controlling equity stake.[58]

The second of the mentioned institutions is the business ethic, which as a socio-psychological phenomenon is nevertheless of great importance to the effective functioning of markets. In absence of a strong legal system, which allows for the enforcement of contracts, the existence of a shared business ethic incorporating transparency and credibility as strong values is more important than ever for open markets. By providing the shared set of values, a positive business ethic reduces transaction costs, thus facilitating exchange.

As argued by Raiser, Russia's informal market institutions are dramatically different from those in the West. The rising of the current business leaders from the former black market operators imbued these individuals with the moral values that highly value official corruption and utilization of violence for the resolution of conflicts. In Raiser's view, 'the path dependence of informal institutions and the considerable private business interests associated with the present predatory system are likely to mean that the accumulation of social capital in support of the transition may take a considerable amount of time'.[59]

When viewed as mechanisms for reducing transaction costs, informal institutions revolve around the concept of 'trust', presenting a classical 'prisoners' dilemma'. In order for costs to be reduced, the social norms of the business environment have to suggest that an average counter party to the transaction can be 'trusted'. However, the development of social norms is highly reflexive, in that the norms are reinforced by the encountered behavior. Thus, supporting Raiser's proposition, the existence of the current business ethic in Russia does in fact create a strong path dependency, the overcoming of which is driven by the learning process of the individuals involved in exchange.

The centrality of the self-reinforcing social values points to the importance of the opening of the Russian business environment to global economic forces. The growth in the number of transactions with 'trustworthy' multinational counter parties will enhance the acceptance of international business norms within the Russian business community, thus

---

[57] *Kommersant"* (1999), 23 April.
[58] *Moskovskie novosti* (1999), 1 March.
[59] Raiser 1997, 21.

facilitating the development of market institutions that are FIG-independent. An additional force for change is introduced through the entry into senior management positions in Russia of individuals whose education or experience have exposed them to and made them skilled at the type of behavior demanded by the international business ethic.

On both counts, FIGs serve as powerful agents for the alteration of the informal market institutions. Their control of much of the export-oriented industries provides their employees with the international cultural expertise through frequent contact with foreign business entities. Furthermore, the leading FIGs have been actively recruiting foreign managers to head their operations. For example, of the top twelve managers at MFK-Renaissance, all have had considerable experience working at the top Western financial institutions and five are foreign-born.[60] In another example, since February 1998, Tiumen Oil has been headed by a Harvard-educated US citizen who was brought in by *Alfa* Bank, Tiumen's controlling shareholder.

Thus, due to a number of factors, individuals working at leading FIGs have the opportunity to experience the international business ethic first-hand. This cumulative expertise benefits the economy at large, as individuals move out of the Russian 'corporate scene' to pursue attractive opportunities in the non-FIG segments of the economy. For example, in the last two years, *Menatep* and *Inkombank* have suffered defections of their entire investment banking teams, who left to set up their own *Russkie Investory* and KFP Capital investment boutiques respectively.

Conclusion

As argued above, the Russian economy is undergoing a process of grass-roots institutional development. Due to the lack of active state participation in this process, key market institutions, such as property rights, business ethic, and market infrastructure have been emerging in an evolutionary manner, with the FIGs largely monopolizing the emergence of these institutions. By being able to offer the economic benefits of participating in these institutions, the leading FIGs continue increasing their size, thus driving the ongoing consolidation of the Russian economic landscape.

The tremendous political power wielded by the leading FIGs is of obvious concern to the observers. However, at the same time, the FIGs are fulfilling a number of positive functions. Firstly, by offering their

---

[60] *Kommersant"* (1998), 16 January.

proprietary infrastructure for the facilitation of exchanges and capital flows, the FIGs are fulfilling the need for market-led reallocation of resources leading to industrial restructuring. Secondly, the FIGs are at present nurturing the very base of human capital that, with the passage of time, is going to serve as a foundation for the opening of the Russian economy. Within this context, the FIGs are serving the function of globalizers, transmitting the international business ethic and the corporate know-how into the Russian environment.

As the Russian economy continues to develop, these skills will be increasingly leaving the FIGs to more directly reap the financial benefits that are commensurate with their level of added value. This phenomenon is already observable, and will be growing as the base of human capital within FIGs accumulates. The opening up of parts of the market infrastructure will take over the historical FIG prerogative of serving as valves between external capital and the growth sectors in the economy, leading to a further weakening of the FIG positions.

The major remaining obstacle to the emergence of this scenario is the question of property rights. The deterioration of the contract enforcement power of the Russian state coincided with the effective privatization of this functionality by the FIGs. Thus, in the future, the effective functioning of an open market economy in Russia will depend on the state's ability to regain its dominance as the provider of the collective good of property rights enforcement. Ultimately, this will be the most critical issue determining the fate of the Russian economy both regarding its efficiency and its integration into the global economy.

10 The Mass Media between Political Instrumentalization, Economic Concentration and Global Assimilation

IVAN I. ZASURSKII

The study of post-Soviet change would be incomplete without an inquiry into the development of the media sector. The mass media were deeply transformed by the sweeping process of change, while at the same time helping to shape it. The role of the media in the political history of the 1990s was profound, while the media themselves were subjected to tremendous influence by relevant groups and important economic actors.

In this analysis, we will try to trace the trajectory of that change, to follow the actors and define the strategies that produced it. In fact, the media sector provides such a wealth of information and examples that we will be able to present our answers to the central questions posed by this study.

The transformation of the Russian media in the 1990s provides us with a number of extremely elucidating clues to the rules of the game, the interplay of global and local factors, actors and strategies; it gives us an insight into a number of impulses to which the actors had to react, and generally provides us with a guide to the economic and political history of the 1990s. Through the media, the relevant groups defined their interests and the important actors secured their positions, initiating the highly politicized process of the concentration of the media.

We shall examine this and many other issues in detail, and certainly we shall seek our own answer to the hypothesis of this research project - that traditional political institutions and power arrangements, especially the state, are giving way to new settings that are still taking shape, presumably in the form of a patchwork, or of a number of networks.

This article consists of two parts. In the first part we shall trace the trajectory of change through the decade, in both the global and local contexts. We shall also examine the transformation of the media system and its role in society, as well as its influence on the public communication process. In the second part of the article, we shall concentrate more on the actors and strategies - local as well as global - that shaped this process of change. In the conclusion, we shall look at the results of our inquiry and provide our answer to the hypothesis of this research project.

Tracing the Trajectory: the Driving Factors of Change

The First Period (1986-90)

The development of the new Russian press can be divided roughly into five periods. One, starting under the initiative of Mikhail Gorbachev and the Communist Party, lasted from 1986 to 1990, when the first Media Law was introduced in the Soviet Union. Widely advertised and familiar to everybody under the labels of *glasnost* and *perestroika*, this period was essentially a grand effort to build a public sphere in place of that administered by the CPSU propaganda machine. It was a time of intellectual discussion and emotional upheaval, marked by increased interest in literature and philosophy. Freedom of speech was promoted vigorously throughout the country, and even Jürgen Habermas, who paid a visit to Moscow in the late 1980s, was impressed enough to recognize the contours of a public sphere and the opportunities for true democracy opened up by the CPSU policy.[1] It was fun living and reading in those days, and these times will remain a paradise lost for intellectuals and the *intelligentsia* for generations to come - until this era is lost in memory or transformed into a tale of the distant past.

The culmination of these processes was a *putsch* that took place in August 1991 and was defeated by a public uprising. The putsch saw the first truly independent newspaper, *Obshchaia gazeta*, published by the united editorial boards of a dozen publications that had been closed by order of the *putschists*. In fact, it also initiated a very important process that is often overlooked: it brought about the first wave of privatization - of the media.

---

[1] Habermas 1995, 13.

Under Soviet media law, the publications, radio stations and TV channels did not have owners, but founders - various social institutions that were responsible for their mass media, totally controlled or directly accountable to the CPSU. Under the policy of democratization, the importance and the independence (and popularity) of the press grew to such an extent that in effect no pressure could be put upon it without provoking public outrage, and thus threatening the general line of the CPSU.

After the putsch, there were moves to ban the CPSU altogether, and certainly it was unthinkable to keep the media directly accountable to Soviet-era institutions, both useless and dangerous at the time. Thus, the press and some radio stations became truly independent, and control over TV was relaxed for a while, although the 'state'[2] still controlled the broadcasting industry at large. Boris El'tsin swore to stand by the independent media, and thus became their key ally in their defense against the previous owners and 'communist party revenge'.

The Second Period (1990-92)

A change in media content came about as, little by little, the media started to embrace the global media culture. As defined by Denis McQuail,[3] 'global media culture' means the genres, styles and formats of commercial media adopted worldwide as a result of the development of media systems in similar environments.

The Soviet school of journalism was a very specific tradition with functions stemming from its social duty to enlighten and organize. As the USSR was a project built around ideology, it is hardly surprising that the media were very literary, and television was underdeveloped.

Soviet publications, even the most popular and pioneering, were dull by design. In the mixed Gutenberg-Marconi Galaxy of Soviet media, with little or no commercial sense, entertainment was in deficit and so were colors. Since the whole industry of mass communication was basically an ideological propaganda mechanism, facts were reported too little, too late,

---

[2] Here and later, I will put the state in single quote marks, since the formal meaning of the word, while necessary, is deceiving (and was used originally precisely for that purpose). What state in single quotes means is the executive branch of power, or the party of power and other arrangements that are a part of the general patchwork as defined by the editors of this volume.

[3] McQuail 1994, 89.

and most of the space was devoted to feature articles. These, in turn, dealt more with rhetorical structures than with facts, figures or personalities.

As the press was liberalized at the beginning of the 1990s, it was the ideological bias of the texts that started to change prior to the style of presentation. Of course, a couple of good new shows and a load of Mexican soap operas appeared on TV, but the print publications stayed basically the same. The articles now dealt with hot topics, a lot of new material was released from the archives, and lots of issues were uncovered. But in the twilight of the USSR, the press corps simply switched from promoting one ideology to promoting another. In fact, 'market fundamentalism' was as much their creation as that of liberal economists. While most of the other social institutions were in ruins, the media enjoyed an unprecedented amount of attention, prosperity and influence. The new Russian authorities depended exclusively on good will, and there were no owners aside from the journalists' collectives. All this explains why the fourth power concept was so widely shared among journalists at the time. And certainly, even when circulation started to fall and the economy slipped into gloomy crisis, the traditional mass circulation newspapers saw no need to reform themselves, but approached the state for support and received it. And some of them even obtained special gifts - like *Izvestiia*, which was given the building on Pushkinskaia Square, a perfect real estate outlet that afterwards became an important source of income and helped the newspaper to stay afloat independently until as late as 1997.

It was due to the new publications that the media landscape started to change and global media culture was introduced to the Russian audience. With it came a separation between reporting and analysis, the news culture, and the general adoption of commercial media standards - the influx of pictures and graphics, as well as general criteria for what is considered important (e.g. spectacular or newsworthy). The new newspapers, seeking to differentiate themselves from their aging rivals, were sometimes modeled on their Western prototypes: for example, *Nezavisimaia gazeta* (est. 1990) owes much to Le Monde and the Independent; *Segodnia* (est. 1992) - to Le Figaro and the Times; *Kommersant"* to the Financial Times, etc.

Entirely new emerging markets were explored, and thus new formats emerged: the business newspaper (*Delovoi mir*, *Kommersant"*, *Ekonomicheskaia gazeta*), erotic magazines (*Mr. X*, *Eshche*), and tabloids (*Megapolis-Ekspress*), etc.

It should, however, be noted that imitation was by no means a recipe for success. On the contrary, a number of copycat publications failed - for example, the color weekly *My/Moi* (a joint venture of *Izvestiia* and Hearst) and the business paper *Delovaia sreda* (which went so far as to copy the front page design of the Wall Street Journal), to name just a few examples.

On the contrary, the most successful start-ups possessed a distinct formula - like the weekly *Argumenty i Facty*, the monthly *Sovershenno Sekretno* and *Speed-info*. These three success stories have in common a multi-million readership and unique marketing strategies. This reminds us once more that while thinking globally, one must act locally.

In fact, it was among the politicized and business elite that the global media culture originally took hold (*Nezavisimaia Gazeta*, *Segodnia* and *Kommersant"* were printed precisely for this audience), only gradually making progress in the mass-circulation markets.

With television it was a different story, though the trajectory remained the same. Here, news bulletins came about first. At the beginning of the 1990s, advertising first appeared, becoming the major source of income and investment in both TV and radio. TV-shows and TV-game shows were introduced by Donahue and Pozner in the late 1980s, but until the beginning of the 1990s they were a rare event, the cloned shows ('Field of Miracles' - a Russian analogue to the 'Wheel of Fortune', 'Guess the Melody', 'Love at First Sight', etc.) arriving only in the middle of the 1990s, and infotainment programs coming along by the end of decade.

The Third Period (1992-96)

By the summer of 1992, the golden years of the independent press were finally suppressed by the economic crisis, a sharp decline in income, inflation, and general destabilization. The first financial difficulties began after the collapse of the USSR and the introduction of Gaidar's reforms - that is, after so-called price liberalization. This liberalization, carried out in order to do away with disproportions in prices and with shortages of goods, resulted in an explosion of inflation that was without precedent in peacetime. The savings of the population were wiped out, along with the greater part of effective monetary demand. The effect was to create a huge disproportion between the prices of raw materials (which quickly reached world levels) on the one hand, and the prices of Russia's technologically unsophisticated manufactured goods on the other. Living standards collapsed.

Opposition commentators in the early 1990s dubbed this the scissors effect. On the one side were the monopolies, and on the other were the country's citizens and consumer-oriented businesses. The whole of Russian industry found itself between the scissors-blades. The press encountered spiraling prices for heavily monopolized newsprint, typographical and postal services, while at the same time the strong competition meant that publishers could not pass on increased costs to the consumer. Due to the rising costs of transportation, the centralized Soviet-era newspaper system was at last dismantled. Consequently, the role of regional media and newspapers in particular rose, but the printed word never made a comeback, leaving the provision of information exclusively to broadcasting, primarily television. The dominant influence thus became television with its floating succession of images, creating a more emotional than reasoned response. By the middle of the 1990s, Russia became a part of the global 'McLuhan Galaxy' as defined by Manuel Castells,[4] and thus the development of the media system was synchronized with the global transformation process.

Because of the low definition of TV, McLuhan argued, viewers have to fill in the gaps in the image, thus becoming more emotionally involved in viewing. Such involvement does not contradict the hypothesis of least effort, because TV appeals to the associative/lyrical mind, not involving the psychological effort of information retrieval and analysis. This is why Neil Postman, a leading media scholar, considers that television represents an historical rupture with the typographic mind. To make the distinction sharply, in his own words:

> Typography has the strongest possible bias towards exposition: a sophisticated ability to think conceptually, deductively and sequentially; a high valuation of reason and order; an abhorrence of contradiction; a large capacity for detachment and objectivity; and a tolerance for a delayed response. ... [E]ntertainment is supra-ideology of all discourse on television. No matter what is depicted or from what point of view, the overarching presumption is that it is there for our amusement and pleasure.[5]

Based on these conclusions, one could argue that television is not capable of transmitting a coherent ideology - especially if compared to the typography-based Soviet propaganda machine. But to stop here would

---

[4] Castells 1996, 330.
[5] Postman 1985, 87, cited by Castells 1996, 330.

mean to oversimplify the matter. A single ideology is possible only when there is a single center of power - while in the patchwork structure of the post-Soviet state, such power centers were multiple and even multiplying. What television creates is a single ideological space which functions along the lines defined by the medium.

Beyond the discrepancies in the social/ political implications of this analysis, from McLuhan's belief about the universal communitarian potential of television to the Luddite attitudes of Jerry Mander and some other critics of mass culture, the diagnoses converge on two fundamental points: television has become the cultural epicenter of our societies; and the television modality of communication is a fundamentally new medium, characterized by its seductiveness, its sensual simulation of reality, and its easy communicability along the lines of least psychological effort.[6]

If a single power center creates a dominant ideology, then the patchwork of intertwining power arrangements reassembled in the TV galaxy turns into the dominant mythology where the heroes, heroines, enemies (Saddam Hussein, Milosevic, Chechen rebels or anarchists) and mystic forces (such as natural disasters, an occasional industrial catastrophe, or a plane crash) clash in a highly ritualized public spectacle. The patterns of these conflicts and their outcomes determine the unspoken laws of the universe where Mexican serials or 'Santa Barbara' stand for normality, and the borders are set and experienced through the bloodshed of violent cop stories or the mysticism of 'X-files'.

The years 1992 and 1993 were a time of political conflict and of economic difficulty for the mass media; the future of the media organs was in many ways determined by the struggle with these problems. The independent *Nezavisimaia gazeta* suffered a split, with a part of its staff of journalists using money from the *Most* financial group to begin putting out the newspaper *Segodnia*, the first publication in what was to become one of the two largest Russian media-holdings. For the first time during this period, a clear difference emerged between the development of the central and of the regional press, a difference that would only become bigger as time went on. Except for communist and nationalist publications, the regional press took its distance from politics, and was now an observer of the federal political mechanism rather than a participant in it. Partly because of its closeness to local elites, a closeness that appeared in the most diverse forms from sponsorship to subsidies or effective ownership, the

---

[6] Castells 1996, 332-333.

local press began to elevate regional interests to the highest level of importance.

From 1993 and after, the press was bought by political and/or financial capital, little by little losing its independence, but gaining investments in return, with a small number of publications succeeding in staying afloat on their own. The newly independent media sprang up only to become the future victims of politically and financially motivated takeovers, or to form the centers of independent press consortia and publishing houses that remain an influential minority among Russian publishers nowadays.

It would be an almost unthinkable task to provide an overview of the history of the new Russian media in the context of global transformation without imposing certain limits on the universe of facts and events of the last decade. It seems that the best way to give an idea of how the new Russian media were born and what they look like today would be to combine the basic conclusions and a more detailed time-table of these processes with a snapshot of the concentration and economic structures of the Russian press, while displaying the motives and the political and economic processes that influenced the way the Russian mass-media have developed.

My belief is that the new Russian television and quality press have been shaped so far at least as much by politics as by commerce. While enthusiastic Russian journalists at the beginning of the 1990s hailed the coming of the information market, it was effectively the market of political influence which provided the vast sums of money and where control over TV channels was decided. In fact, political and commercial interests shaped the Russian media system in somewhat different ways, the former helping to keep afloat Moscow-based politicized newspapers, the latter leading to the spread of specialized publications. Sometimes, however, they went hand-in-hand, as in the case of both central and regional TV, or in the process of concentration, which was usually of a mixed character.

On the one hand, the concentration of media ownership led to exploring the benefits of the economy of scale; at the same time, it increased the political influence of the media-holdings. In the context of the never-ending power struggle characteristic of the 1990s, this influence was a currency in itself that, in the heat of the political battle, could be exchanged for access to privatized property. This issue will be explored later in some detail, but one thing we should mention here is that the interests of those participating in the process of privatization were concentrated in the raw-materials and refining industries; this was, in fact, a common strategy of large-scale economic agents of that time. In essence, it was nothing other than a primitive, still globally-oriented strategy that sometimes promised immediate, but always tremendous, returns (whether in oil, aluminum or steel).

This probably explains to a large extent the bloodshed among the 'globalization pioneers' at that time - and the proliferation of gangster-type arrangements that turned out to be a helpful, if sometimes fatal, backbone for ordinary 'grab-it-and-run' privatization schemes.[7] Once the right to property or access to resources was secured, the enterprise and the state were robbed (through tax evasion) to provide the necessary investment, or profit. Later, transnational corporations were approached for purposes of investment partnership or sales. The reselling of privatized enterprises was one of the leading businesses for a number of years, and the capital accumulated was sufficient to create a number of oligarchs, for example the *Alfa* group.

The processes in the media sector at the center resemble another global trend of the concentration of media ownership. The rise of transnational media-corporations, stimulated by the needs of their key advertisers - transnational companies selling mass-produced goods all over the world - is very similar to what happened in Russia in the 1990s. In fact, for the central TV channels, local politicized capital was mingled with the revenues coming from the same transnational advertisers that provided a sound financial base for the construction of the new propaganda machine. There were no contradictions between the demands of the advertisers and the interests of the party in power in Russia. As observed by Robert McChesney, all over the globe, transnational media holdings are becoming larger and work exclusively for profit, effectively subverting active political culture and thus presenting a threat to democracy.[8] The extent to which central TV relied on the support of the transnationals up until the crisis of 1998 is evident from the statistic that up to 90% of the advertising revenue of the central TV channels came from transnational corporations (some of it through the transnational advertising networks).[9]

---

[7] Indeed, while the system of property rights was not yet institutionalized, problems were often solved on the personal level. The assassination contract costs were US$5,000 to US$50,000, it was often cheaper to kill then to pay off - especially considering that kill-under-contract plots are the most complicated and the least solved cases of homicide.
[8] McChesney 1997.
[9] 'Sredstva massovoi informatsii v Rossii, 1997 god', a paper by the Union of Journalists, 1997.

We could generalize further by saying that whenever we speak about mass media, we address the phenomenon that first appeared in the middle of the nineteenth century, when mass-circulation newspapers sold cheaply because they advertised mass-produced goods. The mass media dealt primarily with a market of influence, albeit not always a political one. One can wonder, though, whether there is such a great difference. Or rather, the same function of mass communication and control simply manifests itself in different ways in varying local environments and in constant interplay with the audience - which accepts, resists or even rejects it according to the message, its context, and the cultural codes embedded in it and in the audience as it exists as the lonely crowd.

By the middle of the third period, from 1994 to mid-1995, there was a marked decline in the influence of politicized capital (in November 1994, *Nezavisimaia gazeta* cut the number of its pages in half, and in May 1995 ceased to appear altogether). Even taking into account the fact that the transformation of the Russian economy implied a strengthening of the role of the mass media and an increase in the demand for information services, the positive tendencies (including such long-term factors as the development of a market for information services) could not compensate for the economic problems. The market for the print media did not become broader on a mass scale, and the print runs of virtually all publications declined, although some publishers managed to expand their operations by targeting new niche markets. Against the general background of difficulties, a dynamic development of information capital began in niches of the newspaper and electronic media markets that were new to Russia. The *Kommersant"* publishing house, which launched new publishing projects, one after another; the group founded by the traditional leader among mass-circulation dailies, *Komsomol'skaia pravda*; and numerous private television and radio companies, including large ones, generally flourished during this period.

From 1995 on, the process of concentration of politicized capital gathered pace as the parliamentary elections of the winter of 1995 and the presidential election of the summer of 1996 were approaching. The motor of this process was financial and commercial-industrial capital, represented by the *Most* financial group, Boris Berezovskii's *LogoVAZ*, and numerous other enterprises.

The beginning of the Berezovskii media holding can be traced back to the founding of *ORT*.[10] In this, as well as in his other media ventures (such

---

[10] *ORT* means Public Russian TV, people call it 'channel one'.

as sacking Poptsov from *RTR*[11] and appointing Sagalaev), he was empowered as a fixer on the part of the President. The establishment of ORT (as a Channel One operator instead of a bankrupted *Ostankino*) had begun in February-March 1995; the founding of *ORT* was initiated early, so that the underlying motives would not be too obvious. In mid-1995, Berezovskii also obtained *Nezavisimaia gazeta*, which was in financial difficulties due to its total unprofitability in general and the lack of private subsidies in particular.

The press slowly reoriented itself towards commercially-styled information on celebrities and mass-culture, gradually losing its influence, with the Chechen war in 1994-96 becoming the last victory of public opinion over the state. The fact that the media (including the state-owned TV) could get so much out of step with the authorities on the eve of presidential elections made the rebuilding of the state-media relationship inevitable. For the journalists, this was probably the last time they acted according to their self-proclaimed 'fourth power' concept. Although the threat of 'communist revenge' made them swing back to support Boris El'tsin, and some clever political technologies ensured his victory, the honeymoon was over.

The new techniques of manipulation, imported from the USA with a couple of experts and energetically developed locally, proved to be effective instruments for molding public opinion, especially if conducted by, or in cooperation with, the media owners. These techniques of the information war consisted mostly in adapting the strategies of political and economic players to commercial media standards. The scripting of public events, skillful character assassination, and carefully plotted sabotage entered the Russian media system as new means of controlling public life which, under the pervasive influence of television, became a kind of spectacle.

Once tested in the elections, they spread widely throughout the media system, as the participants in the campaign settled back into their positions as the leaders of the Russian business community and PR companies. In fact, as it turned out later, owning a medium was not an indispensable prerequisite for the utilization of these techniques. The rising sector of semi-independent commercial media provided a milieu for such operations, regardless of ownership rights. Another discovery made by the PR experts was that these techniques could also be used regardless of a journalist's

---

[11] *RTR* stands for Russian Television, or 'channel two'. It is a part of *VGTRK*, which is All-Russian Television and Broadcasting company.

views on a subject, since influence here consisted not in the media's insisting on this or that point, but on its delivering the 'factual' message to the audience. The messages were designed, so to speak, to 'work' regardless of the commentary and context of the news program or the editorial position of the publication: after they had reached the audience, they were to be disseminated by viewers through their informal social networks until penetration was complete. And the strength of the newly emerged Russian PR industry is also a global feature in mass communications systems felt all over the world today (McChesney et al.), or, in different words, all over the McLuhan Galaxy.

The Fourth Period (1996-98)

Actually, after the elections the amount of politicized capital invested in the press remained basically at the same level, while the large-scale political battle over the Russian presidency turned into a number of relatively small-scale fights among Russian financial groups and the government. This was the epoch of the information wars. Most of the time, the only thing that made this routine struggle political was the fact that it was fought out in public: none of the fights were ever transformed into political debates, nor was any feed-back expected from the audience. Perhaps the only exception was the newspaper war over the *Sviazinvest* holding company, declared and promoted by Berezovskii and Gusinskii together.

This unprecedented media campaign was not actually a war - it was an act of revenge. The government, faced with huge salary debts to state sector employees, auctioned off 25% of the *Sviazinvest* holding company to the highest bidder - i.e. George Soros and his partners, who were local oligarchs themselves (*Oneksim*). Berezovskii and Gusinskii tried to capitalize on their political influence and thus were not able to collect the sum sufficient to beat their rivals. For two weeks after the auction was held, their press - two out of the three national TV channels, two daily newspapers and two news magazines - operated as the instrument of a centralized propaganda campaign that accompanied a political intrigue in the corridors of the Kremlin. Their victims were two members of the Russian government, Boris Nemtsov and Anatolii Chubais, responsible for the fair play auction policy that replaced the tradition of special investment tenders, where enterprises were sold for promises of future investment (and in exchange for special favors, e.g. media campaigns).

The results of this campaign are rather controversial and should be assessed in full. The practical results were the weakening of Anatolii Chubais and his allies in the government - but this was accompanied by the long-anticipated resignation of Berezovskii as deputy chief of the Security Council: i.e., the war was neither won nor lost. Indeed, Russian media moguls had managed to manifest their power, but at the same time, their campaign (and *Oneksim*'s large-scale counter-offensive) served as an education program for the Russian public, providing the initial course of instruction in media literacy to whoever was paying attention. The competing media outlets jumped at the opportunity to restore the value of independent editorial policy and provided basic knowledge on who owns what for the public, to the benefit of the reading public. Needless to say, TV viewers remained media-illiterate even after this.

What happened in fact after the 1996 elections showed the power of the media and illustrated the benefits one could reap while wielding the power of a media holding company, so the process of concentration once more gathered speed, leading to the final division of the media system along the lines of property rights obtained through politicized investments fuelled by the political ambitions of some, and the defensive reactions of others.

The result was that a number of holding companies came into being, and a lot of large economic agents started to invest money in the media: *Oneksim*, *Lukoil*, *Gazprom* and *Alfa*, to name just a few. Others acted on behalf of political players - like *AFK-Sistema*, which helped Moscow mayor Iuri Luzhkov to assemble a media power base which, along with the media outlets financed directly by the city budget, made its presence felt all through the latter part of the 1990s.

Douglas Gomery of the University of Maryland finds that there are three ways of maximizing profits that explain the concentration in the media: the desire to use all the benefits of the economy of scale, vertical integration, and the diversification of capital.[12] While all three do explain the global viability of the media-holding model, it is due to a fourth reason - the political weight derived from concentration - that this model has proliferated in Russia at the end of the 1990s. But this model also has its limitations, since the media in politicized holdings were not a source of profits, but also a burden. That is why these holding companies were so vulnerable and why some of them did not survive the crisis of 1998.

---

[12] Gomery 1998.

The years 1997-98 were also boom years for the commercial media and the Internet, while the advertising market blossomed. The Internet provided another opportunity for the public sphere concept to resurface in media studies in the modified fashion of cyberspace collective conscience utopias,[13] but this was marginal and elitist compared to the beginning of the 1990s. And, we should add here, rather short-lived.

In the same period, the adoption of a new global strategy by mature Russian businesses started to take shape - from the not widely publicized local partnerships between Berezovskii and Murdoch in the field of advertising and FM-radio, to the expansion of the *Most-Media* holding company by Vladimir Gusinskii, who acquired a stake in the important Israeli newspaper, Maariv, in the spring of 1998.

News America Inc., a part of the News Corporation run by Rupert Murdoch, bought a stake in the PLD-Telecom holding company, which holds shares of various mobile phone operators, including Cable and Wireless.

The Fifth Period (1998-2000)

When things at last seemed to be settling in place under a clear sky, and new horizons for the media sector (like satellite TV systems and prospects of across-the-border expansion) were opening up, and globalization at last seemed to have triumphed, the after-effects of the Asian crisis made themselves felt in August 1998, and the system of state debt collapsed, leading to a default that had a strong and immediate effect on the media sector. The transnational advertisers panicked and withdrew, new projects were postponed, and a number of the already established ones collapsed.

The small-scale, power-hungry investors withdrew from the media market, advertising revenue fell by 50% to 70% according to different assessments, and a reshuffle of the spheres of influence then followed. The largest TV advertising market before the crisis was controlled by the cartel of two major players, *Premier-SV* and *Video International*, and one minor player, *Maxima*, which served the interests of the Moscow-based media holding company (especially the central TV channel). After the default and crash, the *Premier-SV* crumbled and collapsed, while *Video International* became more powerful - to such an extent that in the middle of 1999, it abandoned its long-term client *NTV* in favor of the *ORT* (first channel),

---

[13] For example, visit the intellectual 'Russian journal' at <http://www.russ.ru> or the enthusiastic E-zine at <http://www.zhurnal.ru>, named after its Internet address.

while keeping its exclusive rights to the second channel (*RTR*). It should be no surprise, then, that the chairman of *Video International*, Michael Lesin, became Minister of Information in the Putin government and has kept this post up to this day with little protest from the media. With an iron hand and some help from his colleagues like Sergei Iastrzembskii, he guided the Russian media coverage of the second Chechen campaign through the heat of the battle, issuing official warnings to the media left and right and only stopping just short of closing some of them down.

The *Kommersant"* publishing house, the flagship of independent media, was sold to Berezovskii. Generally, by the end of the decade, political investment intensified as the media system was structured along the lines of the power struggle. The state media were somewhat revitalized by vigorous investment, and other media holding companies just played the game, making their bets and hoping to win the Jackpot. Although the parliamentary election battle was rather hot, the presidential elections were expected to be much hotter still, and this is precisely why everybody felt deceived when, on 31 December, Boris El'tsin resigned.

After the victory of the obscure pro-government *Edinstvo* block in the parliamentary elections and the successful coverage of the second Chechen campaign, Putin's chances were already high. But as the elections moved to the spring and Putin proceeded to carry out the last of the Great Rituals reserved to presidents - New Year's congratulations to the Russian people, everybody understood that the fate of the elections was already decided.

To summarize, let me just state that the popular war effort and the New Year ritual unleashed a profound and surprising support for Yeltsin's hand-picked successor, Vladimir Putin, which was absolutely incompatible with his public profile. The reason for this is perhaps that a politician, like any other character, can never be himself in public - it is always someone else he is taken for. And, luckily for Vladimir Putin, he was accepted as a reincarnation of the classic TV-series icon and popular hero, Standartenführer Stirlietz, a Soviet spy in the Gestapo - a strong, self-sacrificing personality.

Let this be a perfect illustration of the laws of the McLuhan Galaxy, and of what is real in the global culture of 'real virtuality', as Castells would put it.[14] The image of Stirlietz is written in the codes of the culture as a system of preferences: order instead of chaos, mastery instead of drift, duty instead of freedom, law against power, and a strong state instead of a weak one. And these are indeed the preferences of the public, according to

---

[14] Ibid.

every survey. Hence the evocation of this image and the triumph of theophany over the Gutenberg mind.

The commercial development of the media effectively shaped the media system wherever it was not overpowered and exempted from this mainstream development by the political process. It must be said that in the second part of the decade, the influence of political history over the development of the media continued to diminish, becoming an important, yet isolated, factor - not the rule, but the exception. The development of the Internet seems to have reinforced the logic of this process.

Starting as an enthusiastic endeavor, the net quickly became commercialized - although not due to profits, but to expectations. Even here, one of the first virtual media holding companies, built by Gleb Pavlovskii - a former dissident, but also a 1996 presidential campaign veteran and a prominent political consultant for the presidential administration - was also financed by 'political money', though more for profit than for influence.

By the middle of the year 2000, however, we can state that there is an increasing similarity in the way the development of the net is financed in Russia and abroad, with lots of local and international investors, developers, and venture capitalists lurking about in search of areas of potential profit. This example illustrates probably more clearly than any other to what extent global trends have penetrated the media sector in Russia and the way this system is about to develop in the future.

Defining Actors and Strategies

Such is the historical map of the development of the press in the context of post-*perestroika* Russian politics. However, it is impossible to speak of a general fate of the Russian mass media under the new conditions. Of course, some events were so important that they affected a great many publications. But in any case, we can in the end by and large confirm the impression that from a free yet chaotic information space, the new Russian media have been reassembled into some kind of system resembling the Soviet one to a large extent, mostly due to its predictability. Yet, as explored in part one of this article, it is certainly totally different.

As can be seen at the end of the decade, the Russian media can be divided into two parts: the politicized and the commercial groups, although the lines of division are sometimes blurred. However, it is still the case that most of the TV networks and quality newspapers are better treated as politicized media, while magazines, music channels and tabloids - as exclusively commercial. They both share the same media culture, but the politicized media can be described as a media-political system, where various media holding companies play roles somewhat similar to those of the political parties. Whether this is a local or a global trend is for the reader to judge. What may (or may not) be labeled as a local specific, however, is the special role enjoyed by the executive branch of the state. In Russia, as we shall see, the government and presidential administration not only have a number of extremely important media outlets at their disposal, but also exert a preponderant influence on agenda-setting. Every high official is a newsmaker by default, and it is no problem in fact for the executive branch of power to introduce into the public scene issues it considers important. Control over what happened to these issues next was rather weak throughout the decade (excluding election times), but at the end of the 1990s this has changed, as well.

The Executive Power Usurps Control

The 'state' has retained a significant part of its influence in Russia. From the federal and republican levels to those of the province, city or region, almost everywhere administrations still control media organs, or have the ability to influence the press in one way or another. Of course, this participation by the authorities in the mass media is not to be compared in any way with the absolute power the Soviet state used to wield over the press, requiring it to carry out the propaganda tasks of the Communist Party of the Soviet Union. Nevertheless, the influence of the 'state' is extremely significant, as are the sums of taxpayers' money that go to support the 'state' media organs that, in practice, are controlled by the party in power.

The 'state' has a controlling stake in the joint stock company Russian Public Television *ORT* (which is de-facto run by Berezovskii[15]), and also

---

[15] While handing in the article I was confronted with the question from the editor, why does Berezovskii control the channel if 51% of shares belong to the government? Why indeed? It is a question that has bothered the Russian political elite for half a decade, and still, no definite answer exists. However, there is a number of insightful guesses that should be presented here. One of the reasons was that Berezovskii served as an intermediary during the election campaign in 1996 and it was his job to provide the media support. This is why the *ORT* was founded in the first place and why two of his companies received 16%, and a number of shares went to his business partners. However, he never controlled more than 30% of shares but still was able to shape the *ORT* coverage long after the elections. Here we

has complete control of *VGTRK* (including the recently founded Culture channel) - that is, it controls the first, second and fifth channels of 'state' television. The Moscow television channel has already been turned into a joint stock company, but here the City Duma, the mayor's office, and also the provincial authorities have shares. On the federal level, the channels *NTV* and *TV6* can be considered commercial and independent of the state in the full sense of the word, as can the private, joint-stock local and cable television channels. However, the role of 'state' television broadcasting in Russia remains paramount. The position of the 'state' in radio broadcasting is just as substantial.[16] The 'state' has retained ownership of Russia's largest information agencies, *Itar-Tass* and *RIA-Novosti*. There is no longer a monopoly in the market for information; new organizations are subjecting the 'state'-owned agencies to powerful competition. These new bodies include *Interfax*, which arose from within *Gosteleradio*; Postfactum; National News Service, and also countless specialized information agencies and services. Of course, there exist other forms of control besides ownership. For example, Interfax president Comissar did not hesitate to take a post in the presidential administration when it was offered to him.

Finally, the federal authorities also have their enclave in the newspaper market, with the newspapers *Rossiiskie vesti* and *Rossiiskaia gazeta* - although the former has been closed down. The remaining newspaper, *Rossiiskaia gazeta (RG)*, was founded by the Supreme Soviet of Russia in 1992. At the time of the conflict between the Supreme Soviet and President El'tsin which broke out in March 1993, the newspaper was the mouthpiece of the parliament. According to figures from the European Media Institute, the cost of maintaining the newspaper in 1993 came to Rbl2.6bn, at that time a more than significant sum.

Later, after the events of 3-4 October 1993 and the parliamentary elections, *RG* was placed under the control of the Russian government. In

---

come across the much-rumored invention of Boris Berezovsky that helped him get the most out of privatization. In fact he discovered that it is always cheaper to privatize management, than a company. If management is privatized, the company can be stripped of assets pretty fast and some of these assets (not all of them, certainly) can be used to buy it when it is almost bankrupt. There is evidence that the *ORT* management was privatized and kept under control by the complex schemes of zero-tax-salaries ranging from US$3,000 to US$50,000 per month.

[16] The overwhelming majority of non-'state' radio companies operate in the ultra-short waveband, although with the help of satellites, some private companies such as Radio 101, Europe Plus, Radio Nostalgie, Radio Maximum and so on have managed to extend their broadcasting to the provinces.

this capacity, the newspaper also distinguished itself, publishing materials that unmasked the sinister scheme of the *Most* group aimed at seizing power under the patronage of the mayor of Moscow (with the sensational article entitled 'Snow is Falling').[17] In political circles, people spoke of an intrigue by then presidential security service chief Alexander Korzhakov. This was confirmed in exquisite fashion after the famous operation carried out by the presidential security service against security guards of the *Most* group. The operation did not succeed in provoking the guards to fight back, but it resulted in their being forced to lie in the snow next to the Moscow mayor's office, and to remain there under the muzzles of automatic rifles. After *RG*'s chief editor Natal'ia Polezhaeva had been replaced by former *Rabochaia tribuna* editor Iurkov, the newspaper ceased to participate in such excesses. But the direct subordination of a press organ to the government always carries the danger that the organ will be used in someone's narrow interests, particularly in moments of political crisis - or war.

The need of the authorities to usurp control over the 'state'-owned mass media, a need that appeared so clearly in the political conflicts described above, has persisted since the events of October 1993. However, the most revealing element here has not been the fate of the newspapers published by the government and the presidential administration, but the scandalous process through which the first channel of Russian television was turned into a joint stock company. As a result of this process, the executive power won control over property belonging to the state as a whole. Though, as it turned out after the elections, the channel was privatized not by the authorities, but by Boris Berezovskii and his business partners, whose role earlier was regarded as purely instrumental.

The story of the creation of the closed joint stock company *ORT* begins in the autumn of 1994. On 5 December 1994, a board of trustees of the shareholding company *ORT* was set up, with Boris El'tsin as its chairperson. On 1 January 1995, a resolution of the government was issued, containing a list of state representatives in *ORT*'s organs of management. On 24 January, a founding meeting of the shareholding company took

---

[17] It should be noted here that this kind of articles are common to the new Russian press. Another example of that sort of media manipulation is the headline, run by *Nezavisimaia gazeta* on 29 September 1997 in the heat of *Svyaz'invest* campaign, 'Will Potanin become Russian president' (by notorious Rustam Narzikulov and Tatiana Koshkareva). All these publications share the same goal: to destabilize someone's position in the establishment and irritate existing power players by exposing someone's excessive ambitions. Or, if the speculation is deliberately insane - to justify possible actions by the power players.

place. Subsequent events developed just as rapidly and dramatically, with the most intense struggle evidently shifting to the sphere of influence of the large advertising firms. Almost nothing is known about this conflict, but it was crucial for deciding subsequent events.

Against a background of a long drawn-out intrigue among the advertisers, *ORT* was registered in Moscow on 28 February 1995. On 1 March the channel's chief executive, Vladislav List'ev, was murdered.[18] A search was made of Boris Berezovskii's office. The murder of List'ev became a topic of extensive speculation. The television industry declared a period of mourning; entertainment programs were suspended, and portraits of the popular television personality were broadcasted for several days. List'ev was the pioneer entertainment celebrity on Russian TV: the programs he launched on Russian TV - various TV-games, TV-shows and news shows - still get high ratings. The sorrow over his death was a Russian equivalent of mourning for Princess Diana (or any Kennedy, for the American public) - another emotional outburst so characteristic of the TV galaxy, and another indication of the extent to which these images are a part of people's lives. The murder still has not been solved, but the fact that such methods were used shows better than anything else how tense the struggle around the first television channel had become.

Back in 1995, the political motives underlying the changes that took place in the first channel before the elections to the State Duma (these elections took place some six months after the appointments had been made) turned *ORT* into a target for numerous critical articles and caused an uproar in the parliament. It seems, however, that the founders' choice of this television channel was correct - the political criticism did not hinder the work of the new channel in the lead-up to the 1995 elections. Nor was *ORT* troubled by the appearance in *Pravda* and *Moskovskii komsomolets* of convincing information concerning abuses in the channel on the eve of the presidential elections.

ORT represented the most notorious instance in which the authorities moved to exert control over 'state' television on the eve of the presidential elections, but it was far from being the only such case. For informed

---

[18] Vladislav List'ev was one of the most popular personalities in the whole history of Russian television. A graduate of the journalism faculty at Moscow State University, he was one of the hosts of the program *Vzgliad* ('Glance'), which during the Gorbachev period had the highest rating on central television. Later he revealed himself to be a talented producer. To this day some of the programs he was involved with (We, Field of Marvels, Peak Hour and others) continue to enjoy top ratings in the field of entertainment broadcasting.

Moscow analysts, just as clear a move was the replacement of second channel head Oleg Poptsov by Eduard Sagalaev, director of *TV6* and a shareholder in that body. In the view of an anonymous commentator[19] examining the state of affairs in the Russian media before the parliamentary elections, Poptsov managed to put himself in the position of someone who had to be reckoned with, not only government officials in charge of the broadcasting committee and the 'state'-controlled press, but also by the top political leaders of the Russian Federation. In fact, Russian television was a highly reliable source of information, even while remaining loyal to the regime; this was especially evident in its reporting of events in Chechnia. El'tsin stated that the reason for Poptsov's sacking was excessively negative coverage.

In 1997, however, a corruption scandal followed by a split in mid-level management led to Sagalaev's resignation, which he later attributed to the high level of politicization of the 'state' television. Svanidze, a notorious political commentator, took his place. The party in power could hardly have found a more convinced supporter among intellectuals. Svanidze is unique: the sincerity of his views combined with the boldness of his positions, dominated by a strong state ideal, have allowed him a fantastic career; the head of the second channel was a low-ranking researcher less then 10 years ago.

A year later Svanidze stepped down, and Minister of Culture Michael Shvydkoi became the CEO of the company, to be replaced by ex-director of *NTV* newscasts Oleg Dobrodeev last winter, during the war in Chechnia, in a move aimed at strengthening the 'state' TV in a time of war effort.

Concentration: the Heavyweights

As mentioned earlier in this article, by June 1996 - that is, by the time of the Russian presidential elections - only two politicized media groups existed alongside the 'state' media machine. These were the press group controlled by the *Most* financial group, and another formation consisting of several media enterprises partly managed and financed by the *LogoVAZ* company. Russian politicians and journalists had already dubbed these groups the empires, respectively, of Vladimir Gusinskii (the *Most* group) and Boris Berezovskii (*LogoVAZ* and *Sibneft '*).

By the way the *Most* group presents its participation in the media, it is possible to see the mark of the strategic investor who understands the

---

[19] *Sreda* (1995), No. 3.

inherent value of the information empire that is being assembled. The secretiveness of his main rival leaves no doubt that Berezovskii has seen no need until quite recently to put his motives up for show, and that he is trying to avoid attracting attention to himself, even at the price of losing the benefits that would flow from a coordinated market strategy by the enterprises under his control.

Since Berezovskii himself remains silent, we can only guess at the real motives for his behavior. It is possible that as a political influence-broker, this media mogul - unlike Gusinskii - is not in a position to conduct any general advertising campaign for the media holding company he has built around himself. As a trader in influence, Berezovskii has a clear interest in ensuring that the media organs he controls retain their independent status. For him to advertise his participation in the media would mean waving a red flag in the face of his political rivals, arousing suspicion and mistrust among readers, and also accepting responsibility for all the material that appears in the publications or on the television channels that the company effectively controls.

Berezovskii's media group is thus unique not only because it was put together primarily for reasons of political expediency, something that is itself remarkable in the late twentieth century, but also because it was built through political intrigue, on which the central node of his holding - the *ORT* - continues to depend. He could lose his share in the first channel (*ORT*) overnight if confronted with enough resolve. If this has not happened yet, it speaks volumes about the new administration.

Berezovskii has concentrated in his hands a large proportion of the shares of two television channels (the first channel of Russian Public Television and the Moscow channel *TV6*, which is actively expanding its presence in the Russian television market), as well as the journal *Ogonek*. Berezovskii also controls *Nezavisimaia gazeta* and, according to rumor, *Novye Izvestiia*. He has also made some investments in the FM radio market (*Nashe Radio*) and created one of the strong Internet providers (Cityline).

His latest acquisition - the *Kommersant"* publishing house - is one of the most impressive, since this is a strong media holding by itself that has in the past set a standard of independent, quality journalism against which the performance of other business and quality publications could be judged.

The outlines of the Berezovskii empire are blurred, and the details of Berezovskii's involvement in various enterprises are difficult to obtain, since they are publicized not because of the wishes of the empire's founder, but despite them. For example, the list of the founders of *ORT* was published for the first time in the Communist newspaper, *Sovetskaia Rossiia*.

The media organs united beneath the control of the Most group might seem to amount to a civilized and flourishing media conglomerate, especially if we keep in mind the comparison with Berezovskii's empire, which is more like the stronghold of a powerful political faction than a media group of the late twentieth century. This is so especially since, at the beginning of 1997, Gusinskii separated his media-holding from the group, thus establishing a new company called *Most-Media*. His empire stood rather firm until May 2000 (the time of writing), when it was attacked by the key shareholder *Gazprom*, the gas monopoly that, according to rumor, is acting on behalf of the new President Vladimir Putin. The reasons are clear, since so far it has been the only media holding company to offer powerful, and at times damaging, criticism of the second Chechen campaign.

While *Most-Media*'s future is somewhat unclear, we have to acknowledge that Vladimir Gusinskii was almost set to become a Russian Murdoch after he became the first Russian media mogul to develop satellite broadcasting,[20] a US$170mn project promoted by *NTV-Plus* company. To finance the launch of the first Russian pay-TV network, Gusinskii actually had to sell a 30% stake in the *NTV* channel to *Gazprom* for US$120mn. It is ironic that at the time the deal was struck, it was considered part of a pay-off package for supporting Boris El'tsin during the elections (another part was broadening the scope of the license for the fourth channel, thus enabling uninterrupted broadcasting of *NTV* at the expense of the daytime educational channel).

Berezovskii profited from his media interests mostly through gaining favors from the authorities for himself and his partners. But is there enough of a basis for us to conclude that the *Most* media group came into being as the result of a process of political concentration? In the case of the *Most* group, the picture is more complicated; because of politicized concentration, the group has received dividends mostly in the field of the mass media. Who knows whether Vladimir Gusinskii would have won control of *NTV* had he not had the newspaper *Segodnia*? Or whether NTV would have obtained the fourth channel's full license had Igor Malashenko (the CEO of the company) not been involved in El'tsin's election campaign?

---

[20] 'Russian networks race for the sky', *The Moscow Times* (1996), 10 September.

By now, however, Gusinskii and Berezovskii are far from being the only collectors of press organs. Iurii Luzhkov, the mayor of Moscow and founder of the *Otechestvo - Vsya Rossiia* political bloc - the only serious rival of the party in power during both parliamentary and presidential elections - has built an impressive empire, financed by the Bank of Moscow, the operator of the city budget. Today, he controls two television channels, *TV-tsentr* and *Stolitsa*, as well as a dozen local city newspapers and a country-wide weekly *Literaturnaia gazeta*. He also helped to finance a number of regional projects for Moscow-based publications on the eve of elections.

As a serious rival, he was under attack for the last year and a half from the Kremlin authorities and has become so far the most powerful of their victims. His limited success in the parliamentary elections and the decision of his candidate, former premier Evgenii Primakov, not to participate in the presidential elections led to the decline of his influence. There are threats that the license of the *TV-tsentr* channel might be revoked. If this happens, it would be the first major threat to his hold on Moscow.

Among other foci of concentration is the *Oneksim-Rosbank* group (after default), which founded the weekly economic magazine *Ekspert*, intercepted *Gazprom*'s 20% share in *Komsomolskaia pravda* and bought a controlling stake in *Izvestiia* in a scandalous (although commonplace) power struggle back in 1997. The *Komsomolskaia pravda-Segodnia* group is a large company in itself - it controls a huge network of regional publications.

Within the print media, there are numerous other foci of concentration which are not so striking because the spheres of influence of the large companies involved do not encompass television, as is the case with Berezovskii, the *Most* group and the Luzhkov holding. *Argumenty i fakty*, which has a strong position in the market for weekly newspapers, is one such focus, and there are others. A typical example of such concentration is provided by the Independent Media. Independent Media is a private company, founded by two editors from the Netherlands and financed by foreign private capital. This company was a success story for foreign investment in Russia, and certainly it conveyed a mass of global media *culture* into the Russian market. To truly assess the value of this holding, we might add that, as a result of a correct marketing strategy, IM has managed to gain first place, as judged by advertising revenue in the print media market, leaving even the *Kommersant"* publishing house far behind. In 1997, IM's budget was US$26.85mn, compared to US$24.9mn for

Kommersant". Together, these two groups controlled almost 40% of the entire print media market before the crisis. What is the reason for this success? IM is involved in publishing Russian language editions of Cosmopolitan, Playboy, Good Housekeeping, and Harper's Bazaar, as well as English language newspapers in Moscow and St. Petersburg, a financial news agency, and so on. The Russian bank *Menatep* has acquired 10% of the company.

There are other success stories regarding foreign investment in the media, even in television. For example, the American Peter Harvey created the large TV holding company, Story First, comprising the eighth channel in Moscow (*STS*), as well as a number of regional stations, from scratch. He started with a small-scale FM-radio project. However, Ted Turner was not so lucky in Moscow. He was behind the project of the *TV6* channel, which he started with the above-mentioned Eduard Sagalaev way back at the beginning of the 1990s. Since the law did not provide for the ownership of major media by foreign investors, he made a gentleman's agreement with Sagalaev to buy out his share when legally possible, granting in return the rights to the large TNT movie archives, which filled most of the station's airtime after it was launched.

When the channel had achieved popularity, Sagalaev approached Turner for more investment, but Turner asked for a controlling interest in return. Sagalaev refused and broke off the partnership, raising suspicions that this had been his intention from the start. After the conflict, the shares were redistributed among local investors: the Moscow government, Berezovskii and *Lukoil* got 25% each.

In the media during the 1990s, the smaller the scale of the project, and the farther from the 'media of influence', the more likely the success of the international investor. But this appears to be the case in many media systems, giving foreign investors all the more reason to embrace new media and the 'new economy' - in Russia as well as everywhere else.

There is some evidence, though, that things are changing. The newspaper *Vedomosti* was started last year as a joint venture between 'Independent Media', 'The Financial Times' and 'The Wall-Street Journal', where each has an equal stake. As soon as it was launched, it was recognized as obviously the best newspaper in Moscow. The advertisement on billboards with the newspaper logo said: 'Any oligarch can buy this newspaper. In a kiosk'. One of the reasons for the success of this venture may lie precisely in the fact that *Kommersant"* - the other leading business daily - now belongs to Berezovskii and has thus lost the credibility necessary for a business newspaper. Unfortunately, this small, elitist market of business publications is the only one where independence can be considered a big advantage, and corporate concentration is not seen as a threat (after all, every member of this joint venture is a heavyweight).

Conclusion

Let us recall our findings. As we have seen, the media system was the first sector to experience privatization, and was the one with the hottest competition. The effects of globalization could be described as the adoption of global media culture - a set of formats, genres and styles characteristic of the commercial media, worldwide.

While the Soviet media system was based on newspapers, the newly-born Russian media system is dominated by television, making it a part of the McLuhan Galaxy, as defined by Manuel Castells. One of the principal features of this system is the existence of a fine-tuned industry that manufactures public opinion, operating in the symbolic space of the media, and appealing more to the emotions and subconscious of the audience, according to the laws of public spectacle. Instead of a public sphere, there is a public scene.

As appears from our analysis, the privatization process proceeded according to the primitive, yet highly efficient and globally-oriented, strategy of the new-born economic agents, who secured natural resources for the global markets. While access to these resources was determined by the 'state' (the executive branch, or 'the party in power') according to the rules of the game, it was exchanged for favors. Since the party in power was primarily interested in staying in power, i.e. controlling the elections, access to resources was often traded for political influence that, in the de-institutionalized public space, was exerted primarily by the media, leading to the construction of a media-political system in place of the underdeveloped system of political parties. This explains the influx of politicized capital in the media and the concentration of media ownership for political ends.

The influence of foreign capital on the new media system was limited to spheres with little or no political meaning, such as the magazine-publishing business or TV-entertainment. Efforts to penetrate important TV networks were blocked and discouraged. However, good management and a sound financial base have turned enterprises financed by foreign investment into the leaders of the advertising markets, securing a base for further expansion.

In general, it is my belief that we have found the answers to the central questions of this study in this article, so we now turn to the main hypothesis of this research project.

The hypothesis of this research project is that traditional political institutions and power arrangements, and the state in particular, are becoming less and less effective and are giving way to something else.

On the basis of our inquiry, we can claim that this holds true for the history of Russian media in the 1990s. Indeed, all through this article the words, state and 'state' (in single quotation marks), have been used with different meanings. The term, state, stood for the state 'in general', as it is traditionally used to describe the totality of administrative units that control and represent a given geographic territory, i.e. the idea of the state. Whereas 'state' in single quotation marks was used here to describe one of the relevant groups, in particular the executive branch on the federal level - probably the most important and influential group, but only one of them, acting in the framework of multiplying structural limitations imposed by the state debt, international markets, the local business climate, pressure groups and even individual actors with political (or media) clout.

But simply to agree with this would mean ignoring the desperate efforts of the new administration to reverse this trend and impose a new order - a different pattern of normalization - in reaction to this state of affairs. The first steps of the new administration - the Chechen war, administrative reform, the construction of the new patriotic ideology, and the attempt to convert the media-political system into a number of party structures - all aim in this direction of trying to build a solid state and to institutionalize the patchwork into some kind of stable arrangement.

11 The Telecommunications Sector: Signs of Liberalization and Globalization

ELENA K. RYTSAREVA

Having shown stable qualitative and quantitative growth for years, telecommunications are now seen as one of the most fast-developing branches of the Russian economy. The losses from the August 1998 crisis have nearly been offset in full by the subsequent growth of industrial production in Russia, which stimulated demand for telecommunications services. In the course of ten years, Russian telecommunications progressed from one monopolist state-owned provider to a multi-actor industry with 8,000 different service providers (from post to satellite communications).[1] Now private enterprises account for more than 40% of industry income, according to the Ministry of Economics. The telecommunications industry is going to play a greater role in Russia's national economy in the future than it has so far. The Minister of Telecommunications, Leonid Reiman, has expressed the opinion that 'to ensure a percentage point of economic growth in Russia today, a 3% growth in the telecommunications industry is needed'.[2]

The global trends typical of the communications sphere in particular and of economic development in general have affected the Russian telecommunications industry to an ever greater extent. The globalization process inevitably affected Russian telecommunications for the following reasons. The first arises from the very nature of telecommunications, which presupposes constant contact with foreign service providers and other countries' communications infrastructure. Such integration is impossible without a certain degree of unification of technologies, standards and business processes; since globalization is understood to mean the

---

[1] Popov 2000.
[2] *Interfax* (2000), 17 May.

impossibility of isolated development,[3] globalization of telecommunications cannot be avoided. Second, Russia with its vast territory has the world's seventh largest telephone network,[4] with a total operational capacity of over 32 million numbers. This huge network is connected to the networks of other countries and makes up a significant part of the global telecommunications infrastructure. Russia's geographical location increases the importance of the last factor. The shortest trunk line from Asia to Western Europe goes through Russia. Third, there was a considerable demand for new lines and affordable conventional communications services, which is a very important factor in a country whose national economy is in transition. The conventional telephone network is affordable for a vast majority of Russia's 145 million inhabitants. To a certain extent, such services can be seen as a mass consumption product, but at the same time, their availability is insufficient. The potential for growth in years to come has attracted foreign companies to telecommunications and encouraged transnational corporations to penetrate the market, a typical symptom of globalization. Over the past five to seven years, 1-2 million lines have been added to the communications network annually, with most of the growth financed from foreign investments.

In this article, we try to trace global trends and consider the factors that stimulate and hinder this process. First, we analyze the penetration of transnational service providers, market liberalization and the role of regulators in this process.

Paradoxes of the Development of Telecommunications in Russia

One of the specific features of Russia's present political and economic environment is the simultaneous existence of a multitude of diverse and sometimes contradictory processes, and of a multitude of service providers, any of which may gain considerable weight or lose its importance entirely at any time. One may well apply to the situation the comparison to patchwork originally devised by its author, Klaus Segbers, for the entire post-Soviet world.[5] On the telecommunications services market, this applies, in particular, to the lack of uniformity in the development of

---

[3] Segbers 1999.
[4] 'Global Telecommunications Map', in *Financial Times* (1999), 8 October.
[5] Segbers 1999.

communication networks, and the presence of different forms of ownership within the same sectors of the telecommunications market. There is no single object for study within the branch, while the relationships between different actors change all the time.

The basic indexes observed within the branch show that telecommunications in Russia are currently in a stage of transition, and that in development they lag considerably behind not only West European, but also East European telecommunications. For instance, the networks operated by the *Sviaz'invest* holding (mixed state-private ownership which includes 86 regional businesses and the national long-distance communication carrier, the *Rostelekom* Joint-Stock Company) are 53% digitized, compared to levels of 100% in Western Europe. According to the Russian Ministry of Telecommunications, there are 21.2 traditional wire main telephone lines, 1 cellular phone and 0.3 pagers per 100 residents.[6] Besides, telephone services are not available to everyone who wants them: Russia still has the Soviet-era atavism of waiting lists, with as many as six million citizens currently in line.

In the Soviet era, the government paid little attention to development of the telephone network, notably for political reasons. For instance, all traffic between the USSR and other countries was channeled through a single exchange situated in Moscow, whose capacity amounted to only a thousand channels. Of the USSR's population of 250 million, just a thousand people could make a call abroad simultaneously. At present, practically all international communication problems have been solved; the Russian Federation's national long-distance telephone service provider, which serves Russia's entire population of 145 million, has an operational capacity of 98,000 channels, which is plenty. At the same time, local networks' capacities remain insufficient.

Moreover, the average indexes cannot give one an idea of the great range in levels of development and income of different actors in various sectors of the telecommunications services market. While the number of cellular telephone users in Russia doubled last year, and the volume of Internet services grew by 300%,[7] according to the Ministry of Communications, in 54,000 populated localities no telephone services are available at all. Paradoxes are to be observed even within regions. In Moscow, for instance, there are about one million cellular telephone users (according to the Ministry of Communications). The percentage of cellular

---

[6] Timoshenko 2000; Goskomstat 1999b, 430-434.
[7] 'Itogi raboty otrasli za 1999 god', in *Vestnik sviazi* (2000), No. 3, 18-39.

telephone users among Moscow residents (about 10%) is about the same as the percentage of cellular telephone users in Eastern European countries. At the same time, 60,000 residents of Moscow are on waiting lists for installation of wire telephone lines, while in Moskovskaia oblast the number of people on such lists has topped 600,000. Some have been waiting for 20 or even 30 years.[8]

Technologically, levels of development also differ vastly. For instance, the network operated by the *Elektrosviaz'* Joint-Stock Company in Tulskaia oblast (south of Moscow) is fully digitized, while digitization of some networks operated by *Sviaz'invest* daughters amounts to 10-15%. The national long-distance telephone service provider, *Rostelekom* Joint-Stock Company, boasts a powerful ground digital network, whose fiber-optic channels have a total length of 39,000km, while the orbital satellite telecommunications system has been decaying, 9 of the 11 satellites are past their service life span, and television channels have problems with transmission of the signal to distant areas.

Another factor that makes the situation 'patchworky' is heterogeneity of the forms of ownership. Telecommunications services in Russia are offered by Russian joint state-private ventures, altogether private enterprises, and the leading international telecommunications service providers.

Thus, Russian telecommunications companies are not now merely the object of political games. But the low level of infrastructure development will play a role in economic and social life. The heterogeneous structure of telecommunications shows that this market is not stable. On the one hand, instability scares off investors; on the other hand, open niches on the market attract foreign companies.

Foreign Penetration

For a long time, the geographic principle was crucial to the development of telecommunications companies' organizational structure, trademarks and business in general. At present, as has been noted, in particular, by experts of the PriceWaterhouseCoopers consulting company, the old geographic divisions have been replaced by the new geographic structures of a world embraced by a single network, a world in which developments will be determined by sectors or groups of service users, rather than by national or

---

[8] Parfenov 2000.

regional boundaries.[9] In Russia, that global trend is seen particularly vividly in the expansion of major national service providers and transnational corporations.

Penetration of the Russian telecommunications services market by private capital started back in 1990. At first, Russia attracted mainly Western investors specializing in developing markets, with most investments going to the cellular telephone communication sphere, which was particularly profitable at the time. Cellular telephone communication, which has been Russian telecommunications' leading growth sector for years,[10] has in general served as a catalyst for the development of the private sector of the Russian telecommunications services market. At the initial stage, service providers whose presence on developed countries' markets was scarcely noticeable or nonexistent, such as Millicom International Cellular, US West, RTDC and *PLD Telekom*, played a considerable role in cellular communication in Russia. Of late, however, Russian private companies in telecommunications have begun to receive investment from leading world actors on the telecommunications market. Just after the 1998 crisis, for instance, the Norwegian service provider Telenor purchased 25% of the stock of *Vympelkom*, the leading Russian cellular telephone communication service provider, while late in 1999, *PLD Telekom* was acquired by the American service provider Metromedia. The US-based MCT Corp. has purchased the former RTDC's assets; Telia has acquired about 15% of the St. Petersburg-based holding company *Telekominvest*. In March 2000, Finland's Sonera made operational a fiber-optic communication line running from Moscow to Helsinki; in May, a joint venture of Sonera and Central Telegraph (an associate of *Sviaz'invest*) applied for a cellular license in Moskovskaia oblast. The company aims to build a GSM[11] mobile network in the Moscow area.

The number of foreign ground communication service providers on the Russian market has grown. In particular, there are some joint ventures with the participation of AT&T, Metromedia, GTS and Millicom International Cellular (all US-based); Telia, Sonera, Telenor, GN Great Nordic (all Scandinavian); and Deutsche Telekom and Global One (based in Germany). Among prospective investors, Scandinavian service providers should be singled out. Their countries' domestic markets for

---

[9] 'Telecom Great Divide', PriceWaterhouseCoopers, 2000.
[10] Ibid.
[11] GSM (Global System for Mobile Telecommunications) - the most widespread cellular standard. GSM networks are used in all European countries, America and Asia.

telecommunications services have long been flooded. Finland is the world frontrunner in availability of cellular telephone communication services, and Sweden's performance in that sphere is nearly as impressive. Expansion abroad is the only means of development available to the local service providers. As a large neighbor country, Russia has invariably attracted their attention since 1993. First, investment went to St. Petersburg communication companies; then to those operating in other regions of Russia. It cannot be said, however, that investment has poured in. International communications companies' expansion of their presence on the market has been hampered by political and economic risks.

Penetration of capital has been by no means a one-way street. Following the entry of foreign companies to the Russian Federation, Russian communication service providers started looking for investments on foreign markets. That process was pioneered by the Moscow-based cellular telephone communication service provider *Vympelkom*, which placed its stock on the New York Stock Exchange as far back as 1996, becoming the first Russian company - in telecommunications or otherwise - to do so. Later, the national long-distance telephone communication provider, the *Rostelekom* Joint-Stock Company, also entered the stock market. Late in 1999, shares of Golden Telecom, a branch company of US-based GTS that was oriented toward CIS markets, were placed with the National Association of Securities Dealers Automated Quotations (NASDAQ) system.

Both the processes described above are likely to continue this year. Another Moscow cellular telephone communication provider, MobileTeleSystems, intends to place its shares on foreign stock exchanges. The St. Petersburg-based holding company *Telekominvest* proposes to sell about 50% of its stock; *Vympelkom* has also carried out an additional issue of shares.

In communication services exports, *Rostelekom* is the leader among Russian companies. Since the fiber-optic line from Moscow to Khabarovsk was made operational late in 1999, that company has had among its assets a trunk line running all the way from Russia's western to eastern borders - a trunk that is shorter than any of the similar lines run by Western service providers. *Rostelekom* proposes to make the trunk available for Western service providers' traffic between Europe and Asia.

Geographical expansion typical of the telecommunications world in general can be observed so far mostly among private Russian companies on the interregional level.[12] There are three major holding companies on the market, *Sistema-Telekom*, *Vympelkom* (both Moscow-based) and *Telekominvest* (based in St. Petersburg), whose operations have long spread beyond the regions where they were originally established.[13] *Vympelkom* is licensed to offer cellular communication services in more than 60% of the territory of Russia; *Sistema-Telekom* has been licensed to offer such services throughout European Russia and also in some regions beyond the Urals; while *Telekominvest* fully controls the market throughout the Northwest, has acquired some companies operating in the Volga region, and will probably spread its operations to Moscow in the future.

Thus, mergers, alliances and acquisitions in the global telecommunications industry, which accelerated in the last two or three years, are also typical of the Russian market.[14] Foreign service providers will acquire Russian service providers, especially on the fast developing cellular and Internet markets. Also, mergers will occur, when the strong Moscow or St. Petersburg companies will buy up small service providers.

The State Role in Liberalization

Integration of wire communication companies and attraction of investment to finance them have been less extensive than in the case of the cellular telecommunications sector. The reason is simple: the state currently has a majority stake in the public voice telephone service providers (local and long-distance). Competition on this market is low.

In the mid-1990s, most European regulators were faced with the same difficult problems. They decided to de-monopolize the European telecommunications market. The role of state in the liberalization process was very significant. Over the last three years, most European countries have liberalized the provision of public voice telephone service. In some countries, licensing requirements and connections to the 'public telecommunications network' were the barriers to open competition.[15] Now, Russia is beginning to liberalize its wire market, and the success or failure of this process depends mostly on state policy.

---

[12] 'Telecom Great Divide', PriceWaterhouseCoopers, 2000.
[13] Rytsareva 1999.
[14] 'Mergers, Alliances, and Acquisitions: the Regional Report', in *Financial Times Telecoms World*, third quarter 1999, 66-72.
[15] Ryan 1999.

The state's role in regulating the economy in general and the telecommunications sphere in particular remains significant in Russia. It has, however, undergone some transformation lately; formerly rather chaotic actions have given way to more purposeful regulatory measures. After Leonid Reiman, a communication engineer from St. Petersburg, formerly first deputy to the general director of St. Petersburg Telephone and a member of the Putin team, assumed leadership of the industry in 1999, the work of the Ministry of Telecommunications became more efficient. Moreover, a clear-cut policy goal was established - to create a competitive environment with a view to stimulating the establishment of sound companies offering up-to-date high tech services at reasonable prices. That objective was first made public at the Geneva Telecom '99 World Fair in October 1999.[16] As a regulator, the state has begun to pursue a more considered policy, while as the owner of many telecommunications enterprises, it has taken measures to improve the efficiency of their management.

The de-monopolization of long-distance service and restructuring and sale of the *Sviaz'invest* state holding are part of the immediate plans of the Ministry. If the Ministry copes with this task, Russian telecommunications companies will have taken a dramatic step toward a fully competitive European telecommunications marketplace.[17]

Sviaz'invest

Denationalization of the local public service networks began in the mid-1990s, and corporate ownership dates from that time. Each of the 89 regions has seen the establishment of at least one local JSC *Elektrosviaz'* operator, and a single national long-distance telephone service provider, *Rostelekom*, has been established. Over 50% of those companies' voting shares belong to the state, while the rest have gone to private investors or been sold on the domestic stock market. The state-owned blocks of shares have been held by the *Sviaz'invest* holding.

At a competitive sale in July 1997, a block of *Sviaz'invest* shares amounting to 25% of its capital plus one share was sold for US$1.875bn to Cyprus-based Mustcom, which acted on behalf of the Russian oligarch Potanin and the well-known US financier George Soros. It may have been the most significant step in liberalization of the local telephone market. In

---

[16] 'V zheneve gostelekom uvidel tsel'', in *Ekspert* (1999), 18 October, 4-5.
[17] Ryan 1999.

this year, there were similar auctions in Brazil (Telebraz) and other Latin American countries (Peru, Chile). The strategic partners, first of all Telefónica de España, invested hundreds of millions of dollars, and the telecommunications industry in these countries developed dramatically.[18] However, the wire communication sphere in Russia did not greatly benefit from the *Sviaz'invest* sale, since 90% of that money went to the state budget. Most of the freely quoted local *Electrosviaz'* companies' shares have found their way into the hands of stock speculators.

Both the attraction of strategic investors and development of free competition in the sphere of wire communications have been hampered by a vestige of the Soviet era - cross-subsidizing: under existing arrangements extremely low rates for the use of local telephone lines (in Moscow, for instance, private telephone users are charged just 50 rubles, that is, less than US$2) are offset by very high international rates (for instance, a call to the United States during the workday costs about US$1 per minute).

Last year, after a long period of inactivity, the Ministry of Telecommunications resumed its efforts to lobby for and promote in other state bodies resolutions and bills meant to form a civilized communication services market - in particular, by doing away with the vestiges of the Soviet era in the sphere of pricing. In Russia, charges for the services of local communications networks are still determined by the state and approved by the Ministry of Anti-monopoly Policy and the Support of Private Enterprise, because regional *Elektrosviaz'* branches' share of the local markets exceeds 50% in each and every one of the regions, and in most regions it even amounts to 80-90%. Under Russian law, if a company's market share is that high, its charges are subject to state control. However, as communication services play, among other things, an important role in social welfare, the charges for home telephone users and state-run companies have been kept below cost. Thanks to efforts by the Ministry of Communications, that situation has begun to be rectified. Now, charges for local telephone calls have begun to increase every quarter, but they are still lower than the prime cost.[19]

To make the holding more attractive, the state is improving the efficiency of *Sviaz'invest*'s management. Although the holding was established as far back as 1995, its structure started to take shape only after its first block of shares was sold in 1997. Until recently, the state hardly

---

[18] 'Mergers, Alliances, and Acquisitions: the Regional Report', in *Financial Times Telecoms World*, third quarter 1999, 66-72; Sergeev 2000.
[19] Rytsareva 2000a.

received any payments at all out of the income its enterprises made. According to the Ministry of State Property, AO *Sviaz'invest* paid a mere US$700,000 in dividends for the year of 1997 on blocks of shares belonging to the state, while the holding's net profit that year amounted to US$9mn. In 1998, the holding's profit dropped dramatically due to the general economic crisis: According to preliminary estimates, it amounted to Rbl85mn, of which amount the Ministry of State Property got almost nothing.[20] In 1999, the state's income from its telecommunications establishments was not much greater.

At the same time, the management of *Sviaz'invest* has launched a number of measures to raise the industry's efficiency. At present, *Sviaz'invest* branch companies are being consolidated with an eye to forming eight to twelve large regional companies instead of the existing 86. According to architects of that plan, in particular the company's general director Valerii Iashin, that measure is expected to increase the holding's capitalization and make it generally more attractive to investors.[21]

Because of low charges, market capitalization of *Sviazinvest* is still very small. However, the state wants to sell 25% minus two shares at the end of this year or at the beginning of the next (presently, the state holds 75% of the holding's shares minus one share). The plan and rules for the further privatization of *Sviaz'invest* have not been approved. But now, according to experts, rather than selling its shares to banks or stock speculators, the state wants a strategic investor, probably a large European service provider. Only in this way can *Sviaz'invest*'s integration into the global market increase.

Rostelekom Ceases to be a Monopolist

Ever greater diversity among the actors is another global trend that has affected Russian telecommunications. That global process has not yet reached the long-distance communication services, but is expected to do so in the near future. In the 1990s, that sector was de-monopolized in most European countries. This policy and the simultaneous upgrading of transmission technologies have brought about a considerable drop in international call charges.

Russia has also begun de-monopolization of the long-distance communication services market. The Ministry of Communications is to

---

[20] Svetlova 1999.
[21] 'Itogi raboty otrasli za 1999 god', in *Vestnik sviazi* (2000), No. 3, 18-39.

develop guidelines for entry into the market of new service providers.[22] So far, *Rostelekom*, a branch of the *Sviaz'invest* Joint-Stock Company, has been exclusively licensed to offer such services. On the Moscow to St. Petersburg stretch, Rascom and Sonera also run fiber-optic communication lines, and *Transtelekom* has built a trunk to connect Moscow to Novorossiisk on the Black Sea, but otherwise *Rostelekom* has no rivals in its line of business. Service users no longer benefit from *Rostelekom*'s monopolist situation, nor has it been of much use to *Rostelekom* itself, especially when the long-term perspective is taken into account.

At present, some of *Rostelekom*'s charges are 50-100% higher than those charged by Western companies for similar services. Not only do customers have to pay through the nose in the absence of alternative services, but *Rostelekom*'s monopoly has caused the company itself to stagnate. It has been slow in introducing new services, and those that have been introduced have not been made available to retail users. *Rostelekom* has been active mostly on the business-to-business market, while leaving the ISP and multimedia markets (which are also quite profitable) to other service providers.

Thus, liberalization is long overdue. It is obvious, however, that the contestants for another long-distance communications license (or licenses) will not be private companies, but companies with mixed state-private capital, sometimes called 'natural monopolists': the giant *Gazprom* (whose main line of business is gas production), United Energy System (*EES*), the electricity utility, and the Ministry of Railways (*MPS*). The procedure for the de-monopolization process has not yet been formulated, but the rival parties' lobbyists are already at work. It must be noted that there are some grounds for the ambitions of *Gazprom*, *EES* and *MPS* to get licenses for national operation. All three of them already have vast communication networks of their own.

Besides, if any real competition is to be faced by *Rostelekom*, the prospective competitor should be able to put up enough funds to build a communication network comparable in scale. According to estimates, such a project may cost around US$1bn. Only very few Russian companies can afford this kind of spending, and the 'natural monopolists' are among them. Each of these parties has specific features as far as infrastructure is concerned, and these are expected to determine their future roles in Russian telecommunications.

---

[22] Rytsareva 2000a.

The Ministry of Railways has set up a branch company, *Transtelekom*, which plans to build a mainline fiber-optic network in Russia with a total length of 35,000km within the next three years. Railway poles have been used to suspend fiber-optic cable. According to *MPS*, US$800mn is to be invested in that project. In September 1999, the first Moscow to Novorossiisk line was made operational, after which construction work seemed to slow down. *Transtelekom* interests used to be defended by the Minister of Railways, Nikolai Aksenenko, who held the office of vice premier in 1999. Upon Aksenenko's discharge, *Transtelekom* lost some of its influence. The company has been looking for a strategic foreign investor, to which it would sell 49% of its stock.

EES has not yet proclaimed any plans as ambitious as *Transtelekom*'s, but late last year it announced that it had established a company, *Enifkom*, whose functions seem similar. It should be noted that *EES* regional branches have amassed some experience in the creation of communications infrastructure. They have cooperated with *Rostelekom* in the construction of fiber-optic mainlines in Siberia, and with Finnish Sonera in the construction of a similar line to link Moscow to St. Petersburg, with the cable suspended from power transmission line supports. Some of the communication line capacities have been left at the *EES* branches' disposal. Thus, *EES* has already acquired some communication lines that may in the future form part of its own network.

The gas production monopolist, *Gazprom*, is the only member of the triumvirate with a communications satellite (*Iamal*) of its own. Though the company's ground infrastructure is not very extensive so far, there are plans to build and make operational a fiber-optic trunk from Moscow to Berlin (the project will be realized by *Gazprom*'s branch company, *Gaztelekom*).

Apparently, none of the three is going to concentrate on retail services at the initial stage of their development. Instead they will make their facilities available for transit traffic. It is obvious that it will be difficult for any of the three new actors to compete with *Rostelekom*, since the latter already has a digital network spread throughout Russia, while its rivals have still to create theirs.

Other factors also suggest that the competition on the long-distance communication services market is going to be tough. In the first place, long-distance and international traffic in many sectors even of the existing network has been slack. Some of *Rostelekom*'s facilities have been used at only 50% of their capacity. The company has considerable unused capacities which are unlikely to be exhausted until 2003 or even 2005. According to the Ministry of Communications, international traffic grew by 20% in 1999.[23] Though this growth was considerable, it still does not create sufficient additional demand for such services as to ensure use of another service provider's facilities. Thus, competition among various service providers is going to be pretty tight.

Moreover, the various budding actors are in opposition to one another. *Rostelekom* spokesmen have already spoken many a harsh word about *Transtelekom* in the media,[24] while Chubais's *EES* has been in constant conflict with Viakhirev's *Gazprom*. It should also be borne in mind that *Gazprom* and *EES* have viewed their telecommunications-related activities as a secondary line of business, and it is well known that in the highly personalized Russian economy no project can be carried out promptly without direct attention from top levels.

Yet in general terms, de-monopolization of the long-distance communication sphere should be seen as a positive development. It is true that even with such a 'de-monopolization', no private companies will be able to enter the market, which will remain reserved for companies with mixed state-private ownership. But it should be remembered that such a phenomenon is also to be observed elsewhere, particularly in Eastern European countries (although there, it has affected other spheres than telecommunications). The state's role as a unitary actor is thus undermined and various groups' interests assume supreme importance.[25]

Globalization Policy

Many Russian political and economic circles hold a negative view of globalization.[26] There is no clear-cut state approach to the matter. The latest statement by Leonid Reiman, however, shows that in the sphere of telecommunications, a positive stance has been taken on the matter in favor of globalization. Reiman has been quoted by Interfax News Agency saying that

---

[23] 'Itogi raboty otrasli za 1999 god', in *Vestnik sviazi* (2000), No. 3, 18-39.
[24] Rytsareva 1999.
[25] Segbers 1999.
[26] Mikheev 1999.

development of information technologies within the framework of the world information space [was] a most important aspect of Russia's social and economic strategy. ... Russia's telecommunications infrastructure must be developed in such a way as to be able to become part of the world information space in the future.[27]

That position of the state, represented by the Ministry of Communications, is clearly reflected in the technology policy currently being followed. The process is particularly obvious in the area of cellular communications. Due to lobbying by various Western producers and a lack of a firm and consistent stand on the standards issue by the Ministry of Telecommunications, the Russian market was penetrated in the early and mid-1990s by networks using AMPS[28] and CDMA[29] standards (which are not in use in Europe). Today, the ministry is seeking to phase out such technologies and promote wider use of the European standard, GSM. At present, GSM network capacities in Russia, just as elsewhere in the world, have already exceeded the capacities of networks using other standards. According to the Ministry of Telecommunications, the number of GSM network subscribers in Russia more than doubled in 1999, while the number of AMPS network subscribers and analog NMT-450[30] network subscribers grew by 60% and 25%, respectively. This clearly shows that in Russia, the same technological trends are observed as elsewhere in the world.

Another illustrative example of the liberalization process was the abolition in February 2000 of the atavistic requirement for a special permit to use radiophones. Before that time, each cellular telephone user in Russia was required to carry such a permit at all times on the grounds that mobile phones were transmitting devices. Until recently, the spy-obsessed state security organs and the police insisted that such permits were necessary. The opening months of the year 2000 also saw such a memorable development as the closing of the technological gap in the sphere of

---

[27] *Interfax* (2000), 17 May.
[28] AMPS (Advanced Mobile Phone Service) - a cellular standard. The first AMPS network was launched in 1983 in the USA. Now, AMPS networks cover the entire United States and nearly 30 countries, mainly in North and South America.
[29] CDMA (Code Division Multiply Access) - a form of cellular technology for modems. The first CDMA network was launched in 1995 in Hong Kong. CDMA technology will be used in the third generation of mobile communication.
[30] NMT-450 (Nordic Mobile Telephony) - the first cellular standard (analog). NMT networks are in operation in more than 40 countries around the world, especially in Scandinavia and Eastern Europe.

cellular communications between Russia and the more advanced countries. (It is to be noted that cellular networks appeared in Russia ten years later than in Europe.) Today, the latest technologies, including mobile Internet access and other multimedia, are being introduced in Russia at the same time as in Europe.

The effects of the current global convergence of telecommunications technologies, the Internet, the computer industry and entertainment will also affect the Russian market to an ever greater extent. Already now, there is on the Russian market a distinct tendency towards greater universality of services and provision of the whole complex of technologies to their ultimate users by a single service provider.[31] In the mobile phone business, cellular service providers have already started to provide access to the Internet. *Most-Media*, which owns some newspapers, magazines and the broadcast companies NTV and TNT, has also developed new markets. The television company NTV+ has offered access to the Internet by means of satellite dishes. The Moscow telephone service provider *Komkor*, in cooperation with US investors, has built extensive wide-band multifunctional cable networks. It plans a switchover to digital television and radio, Internet access, and voice transmission.[32] Experts expect the appearance of new players on this emerging market. The traditional Russian telecommunications service providers (e.g., the subsidiary of US Global Telesystems Group, Moscow's *Sistema*) are also investing in providers and preparing for a global convergence.

It is noteworthy that until recently global trends penetrated Russian telecommunications 'naturally', so to speak, without any deliberate encouragement from the nation's political leadership. The government's current stance will, no doubt, give a new impetus to that process.

Conclusion

Russia is in the mainstream of global developments in the telecommunications industry. The main trends are present also in the Russian market. There are many foreign companies, and market liberalization is accelerating. The convergence of technologies has begun.

Globalization, however, has been hindered by the shortcomings typical of Russia's ever-changing national economy in general and of the

---

[31] 'Telecom Great Divide', PriceWaterhouseCoopers, 2000.
[32] Rytsareva 2000b.

telecommunications sphere in particular: insufficient and heterogeneous infrastructure, the low efficiency typical of state ownership, the resulting inflexibility of state-owned businesses, and the lack of clear-cut rules.

Further denationalization of the industry and a clear regulatory policy will improve competition on the market and help to attract multinational service providers. Further development of competition in telecommunications will open up new prospects to innovation-orientated companies. On the other hand, all technological innovations of today are aimed at least to some extent at creating a common information and technology space. Thus, the process of globalization is bound to increase in Russia, and the telecommunications industry is going to be one of its major driving forces.

12 High-Technology Defense Production: The Move into Foreign Markets

RUSLAN N. PUKHOV

Characteristics of the Soviet Military-Industrial Complex

The Soviet military-industrial complex (MIC) was an almost completely isolated system with practically no connections to the world economy. The USSR was capable of producing virtually the whole spectrum of armaments and military equipment needed by the Soviet Army.[1] There were only a few individual examples of cooperation and division of labor between the Warsaw Pact (WP) states. They all had to do with different kinds of training and related equipment. In the 1950s, a political decision was made to produce training aircraft in Czechoslovakia. The USSR obviously had the necessary scientific and industrial capabilities to build its own aircraft for the advanced training of military pilots, if necessary. A specific motive for rationalizing the Soviet military industry through development of cooperative relations with the WP allies was completely lacking. The decision to do so is explainable partly by the general wish to create a self-sufficient military-industrial complex, and partly by a failure to take into account the problems of foreign military security costs reduction and the economic rationalization of military production.

The principal mechanism for military and technical interaction with the WP allies was the transfer of licenses for the production of armaments systems which the Warsaw Pact armies needed in especially large quantities. The most vivid example is the transfer of the license for

---

[1] The most complete and up-to-date information on the functioning of the Soviet military-industrial complex is contained in Maslukov and Glubokov 1999, 82-129 and also in Kuzyk 1999.

production of the T-72 main battle tank to Poland, Rumania and Czechoslovakia.[2]

In general, arms transfers had military and political, rather than commercial, goals. For example, at the end of the 1980s, the USSR is thought to have exported armaments worth US$25bn a year; however, the real hard-currency proceeds were only about US$1.5bn.[3] These proceeds had neither a financial nor a technological effect on the Soviet MIC. The USSR almost always refrained from the transfer of its most modern armaments systems to its WP allies and Third World clients. The armaments delivered to the countries of Asia, Africa and Latin America were usually taken from the reserves of the Ministry of Defense. The armaments taken from the Army were replaced by more advanced systems from the industry. This policy resulted in a situation where the purchasers of Soviet arms were equipped with less advanced systems than their military and political enemies. For example, on the eve of the Yom Kippur war, Egyptian and Syrian air forces had second post-war generation aircraft (MiG-21 fighters and Su-17 attack aircraft), while Israel was armed with the American F-4 Phantom-2 bombers with third generation characteristics. Moscow declined all requests by Cairo and Damascus to provide them with the more advanced third-generation MiG-23 and MiG-25 fighters.[4] Thus, foreign military and technical relations had little effect on Soviet MIC technological policy and did not in any way affect its financial status.

But even with an isolated economy and an orientation toward military-industrial self-sufficiency, the USSR still failed to create an absolutely autarchic MIC. In the 1970s and 1980s, the Soviet lag in high-tech mechanical engineering and microelectronics became quite obvious. This is why the USSR made efforts through its intelligence services or dummy firms to gain access to Western technologies and to dual- or general-use equipment. The Soviet microelectronic industry was completely based on copying obsolete samples from the West. Machines and supercomputers imported from Japan and Europe helped considerably to reduce the lag in the acoustic protection of Soviet nuclear submarines. It is clear that in this case we can speak about integration - though of a peculiar kind - into the world economy. But these examples show that, despite its isolation, the USSR failed to make its defense industry fully autarchic.

---

[2] The Soviet arms export mechanism is described in detail in Kuzyk 2000.
[3] Ibid.
[4] *La guerre israelo-arabe d'octobre 1973*, Ed. Economica 1999, 31-32.

Preconditions of the Development of the Globalization Process in the Russian MIC

The whole post-Soviet political and economic context has promoted the active integration of the plants of the military-industrial complex into the world economy. The basic preconditions in the post-Soviet era of the development of the globalization process in the Russian scientific and industrial complex are the export orientation of the Russian MIC, which had been formed by 1995, and the institutional restructuring of the military-industrial complex.

MIC Export Orientation

Since 1993, there has been a considerable reduction in the Russian Ministry of Defense's expenses for armaments and military equipment (AME) purchases and R&D. In the first place, the drop in the country's GNP from 1989 to 1998 resulted in a large reduction in the resource base for securing the country's defensive capability. Second, within existing budgets the priority was not armaments and military equipment purchases, but support of the troops.

Between 1992 and August 1998, production in the defense industry dropped to one-eleventh of its former volume.[5] In 1997, it amounted to only 8.7% of the 1991 index.[6] Until 1999, expenses for armaments and military equipment purchases were the first to be cut if the profitable part of the federal budget was not being met. For example, in 1996, 86% of the planned expenses for troop support were approved, and in 1997, 90%. At the same time, in 1996 only 62% of the amount budgeted for purchases of armaments and military equipment was spent, and in 1997 just 14%. The corresponding figures for R&D are 32% and 4.5%.[7] The general targets in the Russian military budget for AME development and purchase fell from 47-50% in 1991 to 27-28% in 1997-98,[8] while the real expenditures (as mentioned above) were very different from the ones stipulated by law.

At the very same time the Ministry of Defense was reducing its purchases in the second half of the 1990s, the MIC was increasing the income from sales of its products abroad. Since armaments exports reached

---

[5] *Vek* (1998), 7-13 August.
[6] *Nesavisimoe voennoe obozrenie* (1998), 31 July-6 August.
[7] Ibid.
[8] See <http://www.vpk.ru>.

their minimal level of US$1.7bn in 1994, they grew by 65% to US$3.1bn in 1995 and reached their highest figure of US$3.6bn in 1996.[9] As a result of the Asian and the Russian crises in 1997 and 1998, exports remained at the lower level of US$2.6bn for the two years, but in 1999, they grew to US$3.4bn again.[10] This index is expected to reach US$4.3bn in the year 2000.[11]

Thus, in 1995 the Russian MIC had begun to work exclusively for the foreign market. The disproportion in the sources of MIC financing affected the correlation of particular supplies for export and for the Russian Ministry of Defense. The following table illustrates this correlation.

Table 12.1 Comparison of the volume of some AME purchased by the Ministry of Defense of Russia and exported by *Rosvooruzhenie* company in 1996 (in units)

Armament type	A	B	C	D	E	F	G	H
Export supplies	100	60	22	14	18	6	2	1
Min. of Defense purchase	25	18	11	2	0	0	0	0
Export share in total production	80%	77%	67%	88%	100%	100%	100%	100%

A - AIFV BMP-3
B - MBT T-80
C - Fighter Su-27
D - ADS Tor-M1

E - MLRS Smerch
F - MDS Tunguska
G - ADS S-300PMU-1
H - Submarine, 877EKM project

Source: AST center's conventional weapons database.

The existing export orientation of the Russian MIC has two important consequences for its technological development. On the one hand, the need to enter the foreign market with its extremely strong competition promotes adaptation to the market by Russian plants and design bureaus. This is especially clearly seen in aviation. The Soviet Air Force was always

---

[9] Database on conventional arms trade, Center for Analysis of Strategies and Technologies.
[10] Ibid.
[11] INFO-TASS electronic bank, 'Vega' database, 8 March 2000.

oriented toward purchasing special interceptors, fighters for gaining air superiority, ground attack aircraft, etc. But in the 1990s, the market generally demanded multifunctional aircraft capable of performing all of these tasks under all weather conditions and at all times. As a result, the united design bureau *Sukhoi* and the Moscow Aviation Production Organization (*MAPO*) made efforts to develop multifunctional versions of battle aircraft (they were the Su-30MK in different modifications, and the MiG-29SM and MiG-29SMT versions).[12]

On the other hand, the export orientation leads to a significant deformation of the national defense industrial complex's structure. Under the rule of comparative preference, only the most competitive plants and design bureaus have facilities for development. Among them are the designers and constructors of air defense systems, battle aircraft platforms, helicopter platforms, diesel-electric submarines, and anti-ship missiles. The less competitive plants producing avionics; ship and tank engines; electronic warfare systems; systems for transmitting, receiving, and processing information; and reconnaissance, control and communications systems are becoming outsiders in the market.[13]

It can actually be stated that the Russian military-industrial complex has turned into a fully open system working exclusively for the interests of the world market with all the advantages and disadvantages of this situation. The predicted increase in expenditures for new armaments and military equipment that was expected due to the Yugoslav crisis did not really happen. Although a 50% increase in expenditures for these purposes was planned in the 2000 budget, at the moment of writing, there is no information that the Ministry of Defense has placed additional orders for the army groups in the Caucasus.[14] Accordingly, the dominant tendency - i.e. production mainly for export - remains unaltered.

Institutional Restructuring of the Defense Industrial Complex

The second basic precondition for the development of the globalization process in the Russian MIC is the institutional restructuring of the Russian

---

[12] Concerning the innovative dynamics of the Russian MIC and its adaptation to the demand of the world arms market, see Pukhov 1997 and Pukhov and Makienko 1998.
[13] This tendency was first noted and described by Facon, Huet and Ben Ouagham 1997.
[14] In August 2000, the expenditures of the Ministry of Defense made up just 17% of the amount stipulated by the law. It should be noted that such dynamics of army financing exist under conditions of the military actions in the Caucasus and the unprecedentedly good financial situation in Russia caused by high world market prices for energy resources.

defense-industrial complex, which has by now promoted the emergence of economic entities capable of integrating efficiently into world economic relations. Three types of such actors have appeared up to the present: first, integrated military-industrial corporations; second, diversified holding companies that own the share packages of military plants and design bureaus; and, third, small, completely private, venture companies working primarily in the field of military software and development of certain electronic equipment.

In general, the restructuring process of the Russian defense complex can be divided into two stages. The founding of vertically integrated multi-profile corporations with significant export capabilities dominated the first stage. After the 1998 crisis, the main tendency has been the founding of diversified holding companies that manage the industrial assets of different plants and design bureaus.

In the mid-1990s, active attempts were undertaken in the aviation, missile and shipbuilding industries to create large economic structures that integrated the designers and the producers of military products. It should be noted that, in the USSR, design bureaus and manufacturing plants used to be different legal persons. Under conditions of a planned economy, this division between production and R&D was insignificant; however, under market conditions it made no sense from the outset. The process of founding new corporations developed most actively in those industrial sectors that were the most competitive in the world market - aviation, missile construction and shipbuilding. In 1994-97, the theorist and the organizer of the corporate foundation process were, respectively, President Boris El'tsin's assistant for military and technical cooperation, Boris Kuzyk, and Iakov Urinson (Minister of Economics from 1997 to 1998).

In 1994-1996, a few holding companies were established, such as the military-industrial complex *MAPO*;[15] the aviation military-industrial complex *Sukhoi*;[16] the financial and industrial group Defense Systems,[17] producers of ADMC S-300PMU-1/-2; the *Antei* concern, producers of

---

[15] Military-industrial complex here is the legal organizational form of state-owned consortiums for military production, not to be confused with the military-industrial complex as a designation of the sector. MIC *MAPO* genesis and development process are described in 'Sistema "MiG": transformatziia v postsovetskii period', in *Export vooruzhnii* (1999), No. 4, X-XX.
[16] About *Sukhoi* development see 'Sistema "Sukhoi": transformatziia v postsovetskii period', *Export vooruzhnii* (1999), No. 5, IX-XVI.
[17] For more details about FIG *Oboronitelnye sistemy* see *Export vooruzhnii* (2000), No. 3, on <http:www.cast.ru>.

ADMC S-300V, Antey-2500 and Tor-1M; and the financial and industrial group Naval Technology, producers of the 877EKM project and Kilo class diesel-electric submarines. The correlation between corporate genesis and export expansion displayed its negative side as well: namely, the immediate emergence of a serious crisis as soon as export income fell.

These large corporations were supposed to be highly competitive in a world class context, to possess large financial reserves, and to have considerable political influence exercised through lobbying with the executive and legislative bodies in the capital and in provinces. But it can now be stated that in the 1990s, the development of the military-industrial corporations was in crisis. In almost all associations there were serious disagreements between the managing companies and the other associated entities.[18] The disagreements between designers and serial producers that existed in the Soviet period were preserved. The associations became the target for the struggle among the financial and information groups of the oligarchs, and on some occasions among political forces.[19]

There are several reasons for the emergence of conflicts inside the military-industrial associations. First, Russia has large, superfluous industrial facilities. There are not enough existing orders to keep all plants included in a corporation busy. For example, the Chinese, Indian and Vietnamese orders received in the 1990s could be filled by a single *Sukhoi* plant, though the association includes three such plants. The Irkutsk and the Komsomolsk-na-Amure plants naturally began to compete for orders. (The Novosibirsk production association did not show enough dynamism and energy in this competition.) Competition attracts the intervention of local power centers, lobbying structures on the federal level, and political and criminal groups.

Second, since they are state property, these superfluous facilities cannot economically be properly restructured. In 1998, the expected privatization of *MAPO* and *Sukhoi* did not take place because of the financial crisis that emerged in August that year and destroyed the financial and industrial empires of the large Russian banks capable of participating

---

[18] There was a conflict between the managing company and *MAPO* plant in MIC *MAPO* in 1996 and the beginning of 1997. The conflict between the managing company and *Sukhoi*'s UDB that was supported by the serial plant in Komsomolsk-na-Amure, has continued from the moment of *Sukhoi* foundation. The disagreement between the holding company and the scientific and production complex *Almaz* emerged in FIG *Oboronitelnye sistemy* in August 1999.

[19] For example, for a long time, the *Oneksim* bank group and *Inkombank* competed for *Sukhoi*.

in the privatization of the military-industrial companies. The preservation of state property while the state is extremely weak promotes corruption and the inefficient management of industrial facilities.

Finally, neither corporations nor other economic entities can function normally under conditions of permanent personnel and institutional instability. Since 1995, the system of MIC state administration, and the chiefs of the respective ministries and organizations, have changed practically every year. In the three years that *MAPO* has existed, the association has changed its general director four times. *Sukhoi* has changed its general director twice. Under such conditions, the MIC plants cannot work out an intelligent strategy for their economic and technological development.

Simultaneous with the founding of vertically integrated state corporations in the first half of the 1990s, some defense plants and design bureaus were privatized. At that time, Russian bank groups and foreign investors had the opportunity to buy theoretically rather attractive assets at a very low price, compared to world prices. On the eve of the financial crisis in the summer of 1998, 40% of defense-industrial complex plants were joint-stock companies where the state had neither a controlling nor a blocking share.[20] Thus, the objective basis was created for founding corporate economic entities of a new kind - diversified industrial holding companies with non-state property that have prospects for developing independent foreign economic activity. In 1998, four non-state economic entities - *Oneksim* bank, *Inkombank*, the *Belukha* joint-stock company (later transformed to the *Kaskol* group of companies) and the Oppenheimer fund - actively participated in the Russian MIC. In the spring and summer of 1998, the large oligarchic empires were actively being divided into banking, industrial and mass-media components. The *Oneksim* bank that turned over its industrial assets to the *Interros* group before the crisis on 17 August 1998, was an active participant, or rather the initiator of this process. It should be noted that in 1998, *Oneksim* bank controlled 60% of all share assets of the Russian military-industrial complex.[21] That is why the military-industrial holding company based on the bank's assets was the most active and successful. In April 1998, a decision in principle was made to unite the *Oneksim* bank's military-industrial assets in a separate holding

---

[20] Kuzyk 2000, 136.
[21] Author's interview with the Chief of Armaments of the Russian Armed Forces Brigadier General Anatoly Sitnov.

company. Such a company, named New Programs and Concepts (*NPK*), was finally founded in the autumn of 1998.[22]

The *Inkombank* also turned over its military-industrial assets to the Cyprus offshore companies. But the situation regarding the share packages that belonged to the *Inkombank*, which went bankrupt after the 1998 financial crisis, remains unclear at the moment (spring 2000). Today, there are two industrial holding companies with a significant share package of the military-industrial plants and design bureaus active in Russia. They are the industrial company *NPK* and the *Kaskol* group of companies mentioned above.

The asset of the *NPK* holding company with the best prospects is the controlling share of the Northern Shipyards shipbuilding plant, where one of the largest military export contracts for two *Sovremennyi* class destroyers for China at a price of about US$1bn is being filled. Among Russian engineering plants, the shipyard became the largest exporter in 1999 with a supply volume of US$320.3mn.[23] In February 2000, the group was reported to have acquired an 80% share in the North-West Sea Line, allowing the holding company to create a closed ship construction and operation circle within a single ownership.[24] The holding company also owns shares in plants producing air defense systems, anti-tank missile systems, optical devices, small arms and military aircraft.

The *Kaskol* group of companies combines the activities of 20 companies working in the aviation and shipbuilding industries, as well as in the fields of information and management technologies and foreign trade. Today, the *Kaskol* group has share packages and the power to participate through the Boards of Directors in the management of a number of aircraft and helicopter construction plants, including such large ones as the Nizhnyi Novgorod *Sokol* aircraft construction plant (construction and modernization of MiG-29UB and civil aircraft equipment), *Rostvertol* (Mi-26 and Mi-24 civilian and military helicopters), and *Gidromash* (Russia's monopolist in hydraulics and chassis for the aerospace industry, where the *Kaskol* group has a controlling share package). In June 2000, the *Kaskol* group bought from the Oppenheimer Fund 18.59% of *Sokol* shares, in addition to the package of 19.79% it already possessed, thus becoming the owner of one of

---

[22] For more details about *Novye programmy i kontzeptzii* holding company see *Eksport vooruzhnii* (2000), No.4.
[23] *Ekspert* (2000), 26 June, 54.
[24] Mikhailova 2000.

the Russian aviation construction plants with the best prospects for the future.[25]

The activities of diversified holding companies differ qualitatively from those of vertically integrated corporations. First, as compared to military-industrial corporations, the management of holding companies has a more highly developed commercial culture, including competence in the financial markets, which remain *terra incognita* for the staffs of military-industrial corporations. Second, the holding companies were originally founded as structures with a predominant or at least significant share of their production and sales volume devoted to non-military markets. Third, the importation of high-tech machine engineering production, software and hardware into Russia has a significant place, besides exports, in the structure of the holding companies' economic activity. Thus, since the military-industrial corporations are being integrated into the world economy under pressure of the changing political and economic environment, the holding companies were a priori founded in the new market environment and, due to this fact, are able to cope with it.

Finally, from the beginning of the 1990s, small venture companies belonging to private individuals began to appear. In most cases, the founders of these companies were medium-level MIC managers or designers formerly working in the electronics or the aviation industry. The specific features of these venture firms are the following: first, activity in the field of high technologies, most often in the field of military software, electronic equipment for aviation and shipbuilding, and the design of electronic warfare devices; second, active work in the foreign market and with para-military bodies independent of the Ministry of Defense and the General Staff (the Federal Border Service, the Ministry of Internal Affairs, the Ministry of Emergencies, the Federal Security Service) and promotion of their own products as dual-use products or technologies; third, cooperation with the administration and bureaucratic groups, and with financial and industrial clans having connections to the liberal and right-of-center political spectrum.

This type of economic actor most often remains unknown to a wider audience. Information about their activity appears in the press only under extraordinary circumstances. During the last year, the Russian press has written much about the activity of the Russian Avionics company due to the conflict between the Vice-Premier for Defense Industry, Iliia Klebanov,

---

[25] *Interfax* (2000), 5 June.

and the Ministry of Defense over MiG-29 modernization.[26] The company was founded in the early 1990s by a few former *Mikoian* design bureau designers. It filled Ministry of Defense orders to equip the Russian aircraft that flew over NATO countries under the 'Open Skies' program. Thereafter, Russian Avionics conducted MiG-29 modernization for the Malaysian Air Force within the contract for the 18 fighters supplied to that country. The company is doubling its income annually and is also rapidly increasing its resources for influencing political bodies.

The private companies operate in an unusually aggressive financial-economic and political-legislative environment, and, as a result, have a large capacity for adaptation, flexibility and aggressiveness. The rapid expansion of firms like Russian Avionics can be expected if the financial situation in Russia is stabilized, taxes reduced, and corruption decreased. Today, the private military-industrial businesses are already integrated into a wide network of international relations. In the world market of particular systems and components, high-quality basic elements are purchased and the final products are then sold. Russian private military-industrial businesses are thus an ordinary link in a long chain of, for example, the production of navigation systems, starting in Taiwan where the basic elements are produced and ending in West European and American dockyards and aircraft plants.

Forms of Russian MIC Integration into World Economy

Integrated Corporate Structures

The first efforts to integrate the Russian military-industrial complex were taken on governmental level as early as the beginning of the 1990s. At that time, a number of international programs in the aircraft and missile industry with the participation of Russian and West European firms started. The economic entities that had joined the vertically integrated corporate associations participated in them from the Russian side. Decisions on all these programs were taken on political grounds. Technological considerations were also taken into account, but to a lesser degree. As time

---

[26] *Vremia MN* (1999), 29 November; Kukushkin 1999; 'Minoborony uzurpiruet promyshlennost'', Interview of MIC *MAPO* General Director Nikolai Nikitin, in *Nesavisimoe voennoe obozrenie* (1999), 3 December.

passed, most of the projects initiated at the beginning of the 1990s failed commercially.

Russia made the largest effort to establish military and technical cooperation with French defense plants. A number of political, economic and even psychological factors explains the choice of French partners. In Europe, France has the largest and best-developed military-industrial complex, working on the basis of principles similar to Russian ones. These include a significant participation by the state, a tendency to preserve to the maximum its military-industrial facilities, and delays in the process of mergers within the MIC. Since the end of the Cold War, Russia considers France to be one of the few states daring modestly to oppose the USA. The Ministry of Defense and the State Committee on the Defense Industry supposed that two poles of geopolitical opposition to American domination would inevitably be drawn together, including their military and technical potential. During the last century, Russia and France felt a military and political attraction to each other even in the years when both states belonged to opposite worlds. A Franco-Russian rapprochement also looks logical because Paris is the undoubted leader and the driving force in the establishment of a united European defense and industrial area in which Moscow cannot help but be interested. All of this created a favorable political and psychological background for the initiation of Franco-Russian military and technical relations.[27]

Under the 1994 intergovernmental agreement on military and technical cooperation, French and Russian organizations carry out about twenty joint programs on armaments production or modernization. One of the first Franco-Russian projects was the construction of a new generation MiG-AT training aircraft. The *Mikoian* design bureau that became a part of *MAPO* (since February 2000 renamed the Russian aircraft construction corporation *MiG*) participates in the program from the Russian side. Snecma, producing aircraft engines, and Sextant Aviniques, supplying modern avionics, participate in the project from the French side. Currently, at least two aircraft prototypes have been constructed and are being tested. The credits received from the French government are supposed to be spent for the fifteen engines and the avionics needed to construct the first lot of training aircraft.

From the beginning of the project up to the present, its commercial prospects remain unclear. The French Air Force generally did not plan in the early 1990s, and does not plan now, to purchase new training planes.

---

[27] For more details about the Russian-French MTC see Pukhov 1998, 33-35.

The Russian Air Force has not yet made a clear choice between two competing airplanes - the MiG-AT or the Yak-130. Additionally, the Air Force command has made it clear that the national Air Force would prefer to purchase aircraft with no foreign components. The MiG-AT prototype with Russian Avionics already exists and is being tested. Simultaneously, two Russian and one Ukrainian firm are developing engines to substitute for the French Snecma's Larzac engine installed on existing prototypes. The MiG-AT program could succeed as a joint Franco-Russian project if a third country purchased a large number of this aircraft. India (where both Russia and France traditionally have strong positions), Venezuela, Egypt and South Africa were originally expected to import MiG-AT aircraft. By now, however, all these countries have already made their choice in favor of the Hawk training aircraft, the Italian Mb-339 or the Sino-Pakistani K-8. The MiG-AT project was particularly strongly threatened after the Indian Air Force decided to purchase 60 Hawk-100 training aircraft for about US$1.5bn.[28] With no foreign customers, either the joint part of the MiG-AT program or its purely Russian part is likely to be suspended because the Russian Air Force can choose the less expensive option of the modernized L-39 it already possesses.

Although the Russian participants in the project prefer not to talk about it, they certainly expected that their French partners would make their own contribution to promoting the MiG-AT in foreign markets. Meanwhile, France was in reality completely passive in this respect and, according to some information, even tried to promote its obsolete Alpha Jet training aircraft, thus competing with the French-Russian joint project. Russia and France have made no coordinated efforts to market the aircraft in foreign markets. Most likely, nobody in Russia was thinking about a serious commercial rationale for the project when it started in the beginning of the 1990s. Political and technological reasons dominated. Most probably, the Russian side also hoped without foundation that French participation would ease the project's financing.

The second large Franco-Russian project - the modernization of missiles for the Grad multiple launch rocket systems carried out by the *Splav* association and the Selerg group - is approximately at the same stage of design completion and search for customers to start the commercial part of the program. As the result of the work carried out by the engineers of the two countries, the 122mm missile's range was increased from 22km to 36km, and the warhead yield and operational effectiveness were increased

---

[28] *ITAR-TASS* (2000), 20 April.

by 500%. The new missiles are supposed to reduce the damage to *Splav* caused by the illegal producers of Grad. The realization of this project would also prove that the two military-industrial complexes are technologically complementary at a low level of commercial profitability for the bilateral program.[29]

Although the third largest joint project - the construction of the Mi-38 medium transport helicopter - is in some financial difficulty, the first prototype is about to be finished, and the next step is flight tests. In this program the participants are the Franco-German Eurocopter association (the largest helicopter producer in the world), the Kazan helicopter construction plant, and the Moscow *Mil* helicopter construction plant. The Mi-38 project has some advantages a priori, compared to MiG-AT. First, the Russian Armed Forces are already reported to intend becoming the major customer for the new helicopter. This strongly reduces the program's commercial risks and makes it independent from export sales. Besides, the Armed Forces or other state organizations and commercial firms are interested in purchasing a transport helicopter that is initially a dual-use product, as against an assault weapon. This expands the potential market for the product and makes its commercial future brighter.

The major problem for the realization of the project is insufficient financing, leading to constant delays in the schedule. In addition, since the start of the second war in the Caucasus, Franco-Russian relations have became more complicated in a deteriorating psychological and political environment.

The largest-scale Russian-European joint project without French participation is the Russian-Italian-Slovak Yak-130 training aircraft program. As the major competitor to MiG-AT, Yak-130 resembles the Franco-Russian program in many ways. The Russian side is responsible for the aircraft platform construction and the general systems integration. The Italian firm Aermacci designs the avionics. The Slovak side is to deal with the engine construction. As in the case of MiG-AT, the lack of a customer remains the main obstacle for the project development.

---

[29] It is significant that after the R&D on Grad modernization was completed, the general director of the *Splav* group that designed and produced these systems strongly criticized the leaders of the Russian export companies *Rosvoorouzhenie* and *Promexport* for their inability to promote the upgraded MLRS on the foreign market. 'Rossiya teriaet pozitzii na mirovom rynke modernizatzii RSZO', Statement of General Director of *Splav* State Research and Production Plant Nikolai Makaravets in his interview to *ITAR-TASS* (2000), 2 March.

Finally, the construction of the An-70X tactical military transport airplane could become one of the most promising projects, with the participation of Russia, Ukraine and a number of European countries. Germany was the European country most interested in including Russia and Ukraine in the European project. France, which supports the more expensive and technologically risky A-400 project, strongly opposes it. At present, the situation remains uncertain, but the A-400 has more advantages, and the An-70X has fewer chances. However, the situation could change if the governments of Russia and Ukraine find the facilities to develop serial production of even a small number of this aircraft for national Air Force needs. The chances of finishing the An-70X project will also grow if the number of European states wishing to purchase the American C-130J increases. Then, fewer states will participate in the Airbus Military Aircraft consortium that is to develop and produce the A-400, and the project's economic profitability will become doubtful.[30]

Thus, it can be stated that at present, the European-Russian projects based on political motives, and to a lesser degree on technological cooperation between the Russian and the European military-industrial complexes, are in crisis. Projects involving hybrid arms systems constructed according to the customer's particular wishes have much better prospects. The best-known and most promising such programs are the Su-30MKI multifunctional fighter and the Ka-50-2 Erdogan attack helicopter construction projects. The Su-30MKI fighter is being constructed by the joint efforts of the *Sukhoi* design bureau, the Irkutsk aircraft construction association and the French firm Sextant at the request of the Indian Air Force. In November 1996, a contract was signed to supply 32 completely Russian-made aircraft of this type and eight more simple fighters at a price of about US$1.8bn.[31] Later, the Su-30K fighters, whose number reached 18 after an additional contract to supply 10 more planes had been signed, are to be upgraded to the Su-30MKI version.[32] Delivery of Su-30MKI aircraft is expected to start in 2001. The difference between the Su-30MKI project and the above-mentioned programs is that this plane is being constructed from the outset at the specific request of a particular customer. That is why

---

[30] On 9 June 2000, the German Ministry of Defense officially supported the European decision on the new transport aircraft. Thus, An-7X has no further prospects on the European market.
[31] *Interfax* (1996), 3 December.
[32] INFO-TASS electronic bank, 'Vega' database, 18 December 1998.

the program has a guaranteed sales market for at least 50 units from the beginning.

The joint work to construct the Erdogan attack helicopter on the basis of the Russian Ka-50 platform, carried out by the *Kamov* helicopter design bureau and the Israeli IAI group, is riskier but still has rather good commercial prospects. The helicopter was constructed to fulfill the tender made by the Turkish Army, which intended to purchase 145 helicopters for a minimum of US$4.5bn. At the tender committee's request, the *Kamov* firm and the IAI group actually constructed a new helicopter. As compared to the single-seated Ka-50, Erdogan is a two-seated attack helicopter with seats positioned in tandem, Israeli onboard equipment and missile weapons, and also with French air cannon. It is currently reported that the Israeli-Russian helicopter has reached the final stage of the tender, having surpassed such competing offers as the American AH-64D Apache Longbow helicopter and the Franco-German Tiger attack helicopter. The Ka-50-2 modifications will be offered for tender in South Korea, as well as in China and India, in the future.[33] Although at the time the project started, the Ka-50-2 helicopter, as compared to the Su-30MKI, had no guaranteed customer, it was still being constructed according to the customer's specific request. The project was not initiated on the state level, but as the result of the negotiations between *Kamov*'s general director Sergey Mikheev and the representatives of the IAI group during the Le Bourget aerospace exhibition in June 1997.[34] Initially, commercial success was the only goal of the program. Either the Russian or the Israeli side actively participates in marketing. The *Kamov* representatives confessed that neither access to the tender's final nor participation in it would be possible for the Russian side without Israeli technological and marketing participation. At the end of July 2000, it became known that the American King Cobra helicopter had won the tender of the Turkish armed forces. Thus, neither the technological attractiveness of the Russian-Israeli offer nor the capabilities of the Israeli lobby in Turkey were enough to compete successfully with the American firms.

Finally, the construction of a new Il-76 platform-based early warning radar system ordered by the Chinese Air Force became the third such project. Taking part in the project are both the *Beriev Taganrog* aviation scientific and technical complex that prepares the Il-76 plane for the radar's aerial installation from the Russian side, and the Elta company that

---

[33] Kukushkin 2000.
[34] Kozyrev 2000.

constructed the Falcon radar and the data processing and display equipment from the Israeli side. One complex costs about US$250mn, 90% of which goes to the Israeli participants in the project. The initial plans to produce four units of the radar early warning planes for the Chinese Air Force may be subject to change because of US pressure on Israel to suspend Sino-Israeli cooperation in the field of military command, control, communications and intelligence high technologies.

Most likely, only joint programs for the construction of hybrid armament systems involving installation of Western or Israeli onboard systems, armaments and sometimes engines on cheap and rather simple Russian platforms at the specific request of a customer will develop in the future. Earlier projects, such as the MiG-AT and the Yak-130 training aircraft, the Grad multiple launch rocket system ammunition, and perhaps the Mi-38 helicopter, will either be frozen or transformed into purely Russian programs. They will be resumed as international ones only if customers from third countries are found, something that is almost impossible for both trainer aircraft projects, but is more likely to be possible for the ammunition and Mi-38 helicopter programs. The chances for the An-70X to be developed as the European medium-class transport plane should also be estimated as low, mainly thanks to the tough position of France which is undoubtedly striving for the launch of the A-400 program. France will most probably be able to influence the position of Germany, which is still hesitating.

Except for such commercially successful projects, initially motivated by market demand, the prospects for Russian-European military-industrial cooperation seem to be rather modest. The experience of Franco-Russian military and technical relations, as of wider Euro-Russian cooperation, seem to be quite disappointing. In our view, the reason for this is the structural identity of the problems of both the Russian and the French (and in a more extended sense - the European) MIC. Both military-industrial complexes actually have powerful industrial, scientific and technological facilities that became superfluous after the end of the Cold War, and at the same time they need new financial resources and new markets. In order to develop any joint project, the first problem to be confronted is the source of financing, the second - whose industrial facilities will be used. Neither France nor - even less - Russia has the money. There is also a natural competition for the limited markets of third countries. It should be noted that, even though the French were interested in the Su-30MKI program development, they made an effort at the same time to revise the contract for the supply of Su fighters supply to India in order to promote sales of their own Mirage 2000-5 or Mirage 2000-9 there.

Political competition is also unfavorable for the development of Euro-Russian military-industrial cooperation. Participation in international military programs requires the highest level of confidence among the partners because they become mutually dependent in the most sensitive field - the guarantee of national security. Under conditions of NATO enlargement to the East, such a level of confidence between Russia and Western Europe hardly exists. Since the participation of European countries in the strikes on Yugoslavia, Russia has realized that Europe and the USA are not ready to accept it as an equal partner sharing the values of a common civilization with the West. Moreover, Moscow has begun to fear that, because of its increasing weakness in the future, it could become the object of similar NATO military actions as against Yugoslavia. That is why there can be no discussion about Western components in systems in service in the Russian army.

The Asian Alternative

Against the background of the Russian-European military-industrial cooperation crisis, the problem of searching for foreign partners remains extremely acute for the Russian MIC. The internationalization of the military industry, a process in which Russia cannot be left out, is a global trend. This phenomenon is based on the impetuous growth of armaments and military equipment design and production costs. Today, the second post-war generation fighter (MiG-21, MirageF1) costs US$5-7mn on the world market, the fourth generation aircraft from US$25mn (MiG-29) to US$60mn (Mirage 2000-5). The price forecast for the fifth generation F-22 fighter is more than US$100mn.

Military equipment costs grow considerably faster than the economic and financial capacity of the major armaments producing countries. Today, only the USA is still capable of developing and producing the whole spectrum of armaments and military equipment alone. The tendency to internationalize military production was precisely the result of the rise in the cost of armaments. International military programs allow their participants to share the risks and the financial burden and also to manufacture products in large series that reduce the cost of a single unit of equipment. In addition, cooperation among the MICs of several countries makes it unnecessary to maintain national military-industrial facilities that manufacture the full range of military products.

The necessity to seek partners for military-industrial cooperation is especially acute for Russia because of the particularly strong disproportion between its economic potential and military development needs. At present, it is obvious that the country does not have the economic capacity to carry through development and start production of major new generation systems, including first of all fifth generation combat aircraft based on the MFI and S-37 projects; the S-400 anti-aircraft systems; a new main battle tank; and command, control, communications and intelligence systems based on satellite navigation technology. In this situation, China and India and, to a lesser extent, some countries of South-East Asia and the Middle East become the most likely military-industrial partners of Russia.

The preconditions for Russo-Chinese and Russo-Indian cooperation are the following: first, that all three countries have similar main tactical armaments systems; second, that there is a possibility of integrating the sub-strategic armaments system of all three countries,; third, that there is a possible transition from the trade-mediator type of Russo-Chinese and Russo-Indian military and technical cooperation to a cooperative one in the next few years.

Since the mid-1960s, the Indian Army, Air Force and, to a lesser extent, Navy have been armed with Soviet/Russian armaments and military equipment. Earlier, beginning with the 1950s, the Chinese Army was also armed with Soviet armaments. The break in Sino-Soviet relations did not in any case affect the military and technological policy of China. Until the end of the 1970s, the Chinese military-industrial complex continued to copy and develop the Soviet models. An attempt to change to Western technologies was suspended after the events in Beijing in 1989, and since the early 1990s China again started purchasing mainly Soviet/Russian armaments. Thus, it can be stated that today the three largest non-Western countries of the world intending to preserve their military and political independence are equipped, to a great extent, with closely related tactical armaments systems. This fact does not mean much in itself, however. The genetic military and technical proximity of the Soviet, Chinese and Indian armies existed already during the Cold war, but this fact did not make these countries military and political allies or military-industrial partners. Nevertheless, at the beginning of the twenty-first century, the related armaments of China, Russia and India exist in a qualitatively new geostrategic context. Besides, if at an earlier time there was a gap of one or two armaments generations between the Soviet Armed Forces and the Chinese and the Indian armies, such a gap does not exist now. Finally, in 1999, the first signs appeared that either the tactical armaments of the three countries or the substrategic ones would be similar in the next decade.

In the summer and autumn of 1999, it was reported that China and India would possibly purchase the substrategic armaments that had hardly been available on the market earlier. For example, India was reported to intend renting some Tu-22M3 bombers,[35] and there were rumors that the Akula atomic submarines of the project 971 would possibly be sold to this country.[36] The negotiations on the transfer of the Gorshkov aircraft carrier to the Indian Navy are approaching the final stage. The export of these systems to India is impossible in principle without deliveries of the same or similar armaments to China, but there is always less information about potential sales to Beijing than about the prospect of military and technical cooperation with Delhi. That China is also interested in such armaments was indirectly confirmed by a false report from a Hong-Kong newspaper about the forthcoming sale of two strategic Typhoon submarines of project 941 to China.[37] In reality, the submarines taken for Typhoon by the Hong-Kong press are most likely to be the 971 project submarines, in which the Indians are also interested.

Nuclear submarines, bombers and aircraft carriers designed to fight carrier strike groups, and Tomahawk missile naval carriers are possessed by just one country of the world - the USA. The USA has used these very weapons as one of the major military and technical means in its operations against Yugoslavia, Iraq, Bin Laden's bases in Afghanistan, and targets in Sudan. The experience of recent years shows that the USA can simultaneously launch hundreds of such missiles. It is a technically difficult and expensive task for air and anti-missile defense to repel such massive strikes. That is why the destruction of missile carriers is the most effective means of repelling massive cruise missiles strikes.

After the American operations in Kosovo, Afghanistan, Sudan and Iraq, China and India obviously decided to accelerate the deployment of a basis of defense against massive sea- and air-launched cruise missile strikes. The 971 project submarines equipped with new armaments and the Tu-22M3 bombers may in particular be the first elements of such a defensive system. Negotiations on the purchase of such expensive systems

---

[35] *Interfax* (1999), 27 August.
[36] *Kommersant''* (1999), 20 March.
[37] AP Agency with reference to the *Sing Tao* newspaper.

have been conducted for years, so it is not certain that the appearance of related information is connected to the strikes on Yugoslavia. But the Balkan events have obviously created a more than favorable background for accelerating the trade in Russian-Indian and Russian-Chinese substrategic armaments systems. The possible interpretation by Beijing and Delhi of the air strikes on Yugoslavia as signaling the Western Alliance's aspiration towards military expansion was confirmed when the USA de facto abandoned the ABM treaty.

If the hypothesis about the beginnings of an anti-sea-based missile and aircraft defense deployment on the Indian peninsula and continental China is true, then the purchase of MiG-31M fighters to fight the B-52 bomber air-launched cruise missile carriers could be the next stage. The Kirov-class heavy nuclear missile cruisers that could be delivered to China and India from the Russian Navy reserve would perfectly match such a defense system.

A number of difficult financial and international law problems need to be resolved in order to create an effective continental defense system against massive cruise missile and aircraft strikes. First, in order to deploy such a defense in China and India with Russia's help, Moscow would need to pull out of the Missile Technology Control Regime (MTCR) and the ISRM treaty. The Russian anti-aircraft carrier group defense system is based on the Granit sub-strategic missile that has a flying range of 500 km. The 949 project submarines that hunt aircraft carriers, as well as the Kirov class missile cruiser (*Petr Velikii* is the latest and most famous of this series), are equipped with these very missiles. The export of Granit, however, is impossible because of MTCR limitations. As an alternative, Russia offers for the market the carrier-integrated Yahont missile and the new ZM-54E cruise missile designed by the Ekaterinburg *Novator* design bureau. Both missiles have the declared flying range of 300 km. that is the upper limit under the MTCR restrictions. In the short- and medium-term perspective, such technical parameters can be considered satisfactory, but sooner or later, China and India will need to strongly increase the range of the missiles deployed for defense against US aircraft and sea-launched missile carrier groups. In the early 1980s, R&D were being conducted on the development of reconnaissance and attack systems to destroy US aircraft carrier and large submarine groups approaching the Eurasian continent. The means of destruction included long-range cruise missiles and even the medium-range SS-20 Pioneer ballistic missiles that were banned later under the Washington IRSM treaty. It is interesting that in the specialized press some authors have carefully begun to hint that Russia is interested in reviving production of medium-range missiles in a non-nuclear version. This make it necessary to secure the country's withdrawal from either the Missile Technology Control Regime or the IRSM treaty by diplomatic means.[38]

The second problem is the very high cost of the systems mentioned above. Besides the missiles and missile launchers themselves, they include the expensive families of satellites dealing with detection and missile guidance. The Soviet researches on the above-mentioned reconnaissance and attack system confirmed in principle the feasibility of deploying it, but work was suspended precisely because of its unacceptable cost and, in part, because of the medium-range missile negotiations. Today none of the countries resisting Western influence is capable of constructing such expensive and complicated complexes alone. The integration of the financial, industrial and research capacities of Russia, China, India and, probably, some Muslim countries can solve this problem. Thus, the fundamental preconditions are being created to start such military-industrial cooperation as the alternative to Russian-European cooperation.

During the 1990s, Russian-Chinese and Russian-Indian military and technical cooperation took the rather simple form of the direct supply of armaments from Russia, paid for in hard currency or through a clearing system. The most complicated deal conducted within this trade-centered MTC model was the 200-unit Su-27SK production license sale to China in 1996. Now talks are being conducted to sell the production licenses for the T-90S main battle tank and 100 multifunctional Su-30MKI units to India. The contract for this aircraft production license sale will most likely be signed after the contract on the Su-30MKK supply to China is fulfilled by 2003-04.

The sales of Russian licenses for the production of high technological armament systems promote the further integration of the three countries' military-industrial complexes, and in this way, they prepare the transition from the trade-mediator MTC paradigm to the cooperative model of military and technical relations. As compared with the situation in Russian-European military-industrial cooperation, the structures of the Russian and Chinese military-industrial complexes complement each other. China has the requisite financial and industrial capacity, and Russia has the scientific and technological capability. Such a combination of Russian scientific and

---

[38] For more details about the problems of the export of substrategical armament systems, see Makienko 1999.

technical potential, Chinese finance, cheap and disciplined labor, and industrial facilities, as well as Indian capabilities in the field of microelectronics and software, makes possible the necessary coordination for mastering the complicated and expensive projects to develop the new generation of armaments.[39]

Because of the extreme secrecy of the Chinese side, little is known about the Russian-Chinese joint projects. The Chinese were reported to have proposed financing the construction of the fifth generation heavy fighter, based on the Russian *MiG* aircraft construction corporation's 1.42 project (also known as MFI).[40] Subsequently, however, the corporation's representatives denied this information. In addition, there are rumors in Russian journalist and expert circles that China will possibly participate in the operation of the GLONASS satellite navigation system, similar to the American NAVSTAR. At present, this system can use just 30% of its planned functional resources because of the lack of financing. The launch of at least ten new satellites, as well as significant investments in ground infrastructure and the production of receivers, would put it into fully operational condition.[41] If China does join the GLONASS program, it will have real revolutionary consequences. The major consequence would inevitably be Russian-Chinese mutual dependence in the field of new generation, high-accuracy, stellar-guided weapons construction. This, in turn, would mean the conceptual and the technological proximity of the two countries in preparing their armed forces for the wars of the sixth generation.

In addition, it has been reported recently that China may finance the R&D of the new, modified air-to-air medium range R-77 missile that can compete with the American ABRAAM missile and the European Meteor missile.[42]

Thus, even under conditions of the information vacuum that surrounds Russian-Chinese military and technical cooperation, it is obvious that a transition is now taking place from the simple trade forms of MIC to a new stage where Russian-Chinese military-industrial cooperation will be created.

---

[39] About the Russian-Chinese military and technical cooperation see Makienko 1998.
[40] Korotchenko 1998.
[41] Golotuk 2000.
[42] *Jane's Defence Weekly* (2000), vol. 33, No. 20, 17 May.

Conclusion

The present status of the integration of the Russian military-industrial complex into the global economic context consists in the following.

Three types of economic entity affected by the globalization of military-industrial production have appeared in Russia over the past decade. These are: vertically integrated military-industrial corporations, diversified industrial holding companies that own or manage large (sometimes controlling) share packages of military plants and design bureaus, and private venture companies working in the field of high technologies, primarily microelectronics and software.

All of these actors participate to some extent in a number of Russian-European, mostly Franco-Russian, military-industrial projects. The most significant programs are the MiG-AT and the Yak-130 trainer aircraft, the Mi-38 medium helicopter, the ammunition for the Grad multiple launch rocket system, and the An-70X medium military transport aircraft. Because of the lack of political confidence between the parties and the structural identity of the Russian and European military-industrial complexes, all of these projects are in crisis. Programs involving the construction of hybrid arms systems according to a particular customer's requirements, when Western electronic subsystems are installed on Russian platforms, have a good future. The largest and best-known programs of this kind are the Su-30MKI multifunctional fighter and the Erdogan Ka-50-2 attack helicopter projects.

Russia will most probably conduct large-scale R&D and new generation armament production programs together with China and, to a lesser extent, India. The development of a Russian-Chinese fifth generation fighter and cooperation between the two countries on the rehabilitation and following joint operation of the GLONASS space navigation system could become the first such projects.

13 Defense Industry Managers and the Dynamics of Intra-Sectoral Divergence

LEONID I. KOSALS, ROZALINA V. RYVKINA

This article focuses on the changes in the status of directors of defense enterprises and on shifts in their relationship to the state in the context of the transition to a market economy. Russia's success or failure in its transition to the market depends mainly on changes in the status of many social actors in the current socio-economic networks. Enterprise directors are one of the main actors during this transition period. In the Soviet system, their status was determined mainly by the state and depended on relations between them and the state, whereas in the market system, their status is in many ways the result of individual initiative and the ability to take advantage of the new opportunities arising from privatization and the introduction of private ownership. Accordingly, the status of directors of defense enterprises was determined in the 1990s by three factors: first, by the level of their activity in the sphere of privatization; second, by the efficiency of their enterprises - i.e., whether they achieved economic profitability or not; and, finally, by the general conditions (economic, political, social) that developed as a result of reforms.

For purposes of this research, we have chosen directors of defense enterprises as a social group for two reasons. First of all, during the Soviet era, the defense industry was the most significant sector of Russian industry in general, and had accumulated the bulk of Russian technological and scientific potential.[1] Hence, the situation in this industry may serve as a sample for assessing the results of the reforms, enabling us to judge

---

[1] For example, as Gaddy has calculated, people whose livelihoods depended on the defense complex comprised 15-18% of the total workforce in Soviet era, that was four times as many as in the United States. Gaddy 1996, 24.

whether they brought prosperity to the Russian economy or whether, on the contrary, they caused an economic decline, and whether the reforms will give rise to a new and transformed economy or will lead to decay. If the reform succeeds through downsizing and conversion of military production, Russia could reap a 'peace dividend', fostering growth of production and technological development.[2] Aside from this, directors of enterprises belong to the social group that basically found itself in the most favorable position, as compared to other actors, upon implementation of reforms in Russia. They virtually controlled the privatization process in their own enterprises, and they enjoyed many privileges from the very start of privatization in the early 1990s in exchange for political loyalty (actually, it was labor which was entitled to the privileges, but it was the directors who took advantage of them first and foremost).

This article is based on seven surveys of directors of defense enterprises conducted all over Russia by means of questionnaires addressed to the directors (the last such survey was conducted in December 1999 on results for that year). Between 150 and 220 directors replied to the questionnaires. These surveys focused on specific questions dealing with such matters as increases or decreases in production, changes in the financial position of enterprises, privatization, conversion, changes in technological potential, the social infrastructure of enterprises, employment and wages, as well as the attitude of directors of enterprises to government economic policies. A special section of the questionnaire dealt with the status and strategy of the director: e.g., was he the proprietor of the enterprise or a hired manager? Was he satisfied with his status? etc. It is to the current status of directors of defense enterprises as the result of developments in the second half of the 1990s that we turn to now.

Economic Role of Directors of Defense Enterprise in the Second Half of the 1990s

The status of directors of industrial enterprises in post-Soviet Russia has changed drastically, compared to the Soviet epoch: they have gained considerably more freedom. These changes are reflected in the new roles the directors play under the new circumstances at their reformed enterprises. In order to track these changes, we have analyzed the answers we received to the following question: 'What is your role at your enterprise

---

[2] On the 'Peace Dividend' see Intriligator 1998.

- are you an official proprietor, an actual proprietor (though not legalized), or just a hired manager?' The answers are presented in table 13.1.

Table 13.1 Roles of directors at their enterprises (in %)

	1996	1997	1998	1999
Official proprietor	9	15	16	20
Actual proprietor, though not legalized	10	9	11	18
Hired manager	81	76	73	62
Total	100	100	100	100

Evidently, the status of directors changed considerably during the second half of the 1990s: the percentage of formal and informal owners grew drastically. Today, it amounts to 38%, more than twice the 1996 figure. Moreover, the number of legalized owners more than doubled. The proportion of hired managers fell correspondingly: it is now less than two-thirds. However, the idea of a 'proprietor' can imply different meanings. A director can consider himself a proprietor in either of two cases: if he actually controls his enterprise, or if he both controls and owns it (that is, if he is either a co-owner or the single owner). Thus, there can be two different kinds of director: (1) a director-manager and (2) a director-owner.

A director-manager controls the enterprise on a day-to-day basis and makes all the key decisions, but he is not the owner of the business. However, in the Soviet period, when there was no private property as such, but directors suffered from the incompetent interference of the state in management, an unusual understanding of the concept of 'owner' came into being. This understanding implied that a director 'could do whatever he wanted', without heeding any instructions 'from state bodies'. As a result, the directors of defense enterprises (most of whom have in many respects a 'Soviet mentality') do not judge their role according to the size of their shareholdings in the enterprise. More important to them is the extent to which their decisions are carried out, and whether they have enough influence to impose their will on their employees.

When a director claims to be the proprietor of his enterprise, he most likely implies his autonomy from state bodies and, at the same time, the extent of his control over the staff of the enterprise. If the director is independent and controls his subordinates, then he considers himself a 'de-facto' proprietor, even if the enterprise is state-owned, or - if privatized - he owns no shares in the enterprise. In order to single out managers who regard themselves as proprietors but are not legal owners, we studied the answers to the question: what role do directors of state and private enterprises play in their enterprises (see table 13.2)?

Table 13.2   Roles of directors at enterprises with different ownership structures as of 1999 (in %)

	Director's role			
	Official proprietor	Proprietor, though not legalized	Hired Manager	Total
State-owned	14	12	74	100
Mixed ownership (Joint-stock company with a state share)	30	25	45	100
Private (Joint-stock company without state share)	16	16	68	100
Total	20	18	62	100

It turned out that one-fourth of the directors heading state enterprises consider themselves as proprietors; more than half of these answered that they are the formal proprietors. Indeed, a large number of directors in post-Soviet Russia have good grounds for considering themselves owners of their enterprises, as state policy towards state enterprises has not yet been determined. They exercise full authority in their enterprises and make all key decisions. They manage all the revenues of their enterprises; they can appropriate these revenues as they wish. They can start or halt privatization procedures. In addition, they are responsible for the considerable remaining social obligations of defense enterprises to their workforce and, quite often, to the residents of the city where the enterprise is located. This is why many directors of state enterprises have good reason to regard themselves as proprietors. One-tenth of directors of the organizations covered within the present research, state enterprises included, belong to the above group. Thus, as noted in table 13.2 above, 38% of directors are the formal or informal proprietors of their enterprise; within this group, 27% of directors are co-owners of private and mixed enterprises, whereas the remaining

11% are managers of state enterprises who consider themselves owners of those enterprises.

A director-proprietor is the legal owner (or co-owner) of an enterprise's capital, who can simultaneously act as manager. As such, he considers himself to be the proprietor of the enterprise a fortiori. Without analyzing the reasons, we would like to state that such a combination of roles damages the enterprise's operation and can result in embezzlement of funds, especially when a business has several co-owners.[3]

The biggest percentage - more than half - of director-owners are directors of mixed enterprises (see table 13.2). We believe that this figure should be regarded as an indicator of the inefficiency of the economic system in post-Soviet Russia, where there is a lack of institutions needed for the efficient management of private property.

Having analyzed the forgoing tables and interviewed a number of enterprise directors, we conclude that directors nowadays play virtually five basic roles, each of them associated with a certain social status. Following is the distribution of those roles:

Table 13.3 Distribution of directors' roles (in %)

State enterprises	
managers	32
directors regarding themselves as proprietors of their enterprises	12
Private enterprises	
official proprietors	14
unofficial proprietors	12
hired managers	30

The analysis shows that directors of defense enterprises are not a homogeneous group of actors at the moment. An intensive process of socio-economic stratification is underway. Among the directors are the director-owners who combine two roles - owner and manager. On the other hand, some directors have evolved fully into hired managers. They do not belong to 'the lower strata of the *nomenklatura*' but work on a contract basis either for a private owner or for the state. At the same time, there is a

---

[3] Experts stress that insiders have too much control over the enterprises in Russia. See Blasi 1995, 24-32.

group of 'shadow' directors with implicit roles. These are the informal, unofficial proprietors of enterprises where, legally, they are just managers. Different from hired managers, they have a number of additional status features that characterize them as the informal proprietors of enterprises. These features are as follows: (1) The director controls a considerable block of shares in the enterprise, which may be held via relatives, trustees, etc. It is essential that he have virtual control of the shares and, if necessary, can use them to assert his status. (2) He controls financial flows and income distribution with the opportunity of appropriating a sizeable income, using different tricks to re-direct financial flows and incomes into 'shadow' areas (offshore companies, etc.). (3) He controls the enterprise staff and the production cycle (relations with suppliers, consumers, etc.). (4) He enjoys the support of the local authorities, who recognize his property rights and can act to protect them, if necessary. (5) He has the support and recognition of political forces and criminal groups who control the region. (6) He has the support and recognition of the federal authorities.

It is not necessary for a director to possess all six of the above informal status characteristics to be regarded as the de-facto owner of the enterprise. He may have only one of the six, e.g. control of financial flows, or the support of the local authorities. The point is that, in case of '*force-majeur*' circumstances (a hostile takeover attempt, intimidation by the authorities, etc.), the director can use his 'resources' to protect and assert his informal owner status.

We have studied the differences among the five directors' roles noted above, in particular the different attitudes of directors towards their work as well as the characteristics of enterprises controlled by directors with different statuses. We have discovered a number of essential differences (see table 13.4).

Private enterprises controlled by unofficial proprietors show the best outcomes: their directors are the most satisfied and do not intend to give up their jobs. At the same time, these enterprises received the least inflow of investment in the past year. Hence, it is highly probable that these managers are pursuing short-term goals and are trying to 'squeeze' as much as possible out of their enterprises, without regard to the long-term prospects. In state enterprises run by managers who consider themselves proprietors, the situation is different. Although these enterprises are developing less successfully than the others, they attract new investments more frequently. Directors of the remaining categories are satisfied with their jobs and, as a rule, do not intend to change them. Obviously, these managers are motivated by the prospect of privatizing the enterprises where they are already informal proprietors. This is why they engage themselves in increasing production.

Table 13.4 Differences in directors' attitude towards their work and in the position of enterprises run by directors with different social roles (in %)

	Satisfied with the job	Stable (do not want to resign)	Situation in enterprise run by these directors has improved in the last year	Attracted investments during 1999
Managers of state enterprises	48	83	61	31
Managers of state enterprises regarding themselves as proprietors	67	90	63	40
Official proprietors of private enterprises	73	96	78	26
Unofficial proprietors of private enterprises	48	100	80	20
Hired managers of private enterprises	30	88	60	32
Average	48	89	66	30

The private enterprises controlled by hired managers are in the worst position. Results are lower than average, and their directors are not satisfied with their jobs. At the same time, these enterprises attract average-level investments, they are rather stable, and the managers are not planning to quit. Probably, these managers are unhappy with their status because they find themselves in a less advantageous position than the director-owners of private enterprises. Almost three-fourths of the latter are satisfied with their status. The overwhelming majority of them do not intend to change jobs, which is not surprising, given that the situation of their enterprises is better than average. However, it is a paradox that the level of investments at such enterprises is lower than average. Finally, the position of state enterprise directors who regard themselves as hired managers is close to average.

Meanwhile, they attract investments more frequently than the director-owners of private enterprises.

We believe that the forgoing structure of the status of directors vividly reflects the unstable, transitional stage of development of the Russian economy. For example, under normal, relatively stable, circumstances it would usually be the director-owners of private enterprises, rather than the hired managers of state organizations, who sought investments for their enterprises. However, taking into consideration the high degree of uncertainty and the risks associated with this stage of economic development, it is more reasonable for private owners to keep their investments at a minimum. After all, they are venturing their own money, not state funds. That is why they are unwilling to invest in increased production, choosing rather to save their money abroad - not in Russia - until the situation changes for the better. On the other hand, it is not just the owners of enterprises who can implement this strategy in the current situation. This is one of the reasons why many directors of private enterprises appointed as hired managers are unwilling to change their status.

Why Would Directors Not Like to Become Owners?

In order to find out about the status of directors, it is equally important to learn their personal attitude towards the roles that they could potentially play at their enterprises, including that of 'official proprietor'. Our questionnaire contained a series of questions concerning this point. In particular, we asked whether the director would like to become 'an official proprietor' and, if not, why not. In answering this question, the respondents split into two almost equal groups: 54% of the directors said they would like to become official proprietors, while 46% of them said they would not.[4] With respect to the latter group, their reasoning changed between 1996 and 1999 (see table 13.5).

---

[4] On difficulties of privatization leading to this reluctance to assume the role of proprietor see Nellis 1999; Åslund 1999b.

Table 13.5 Why directors said they would not like to become official proprietors of their enterprises in 1996-1999 (directors' estimates, in %)

	1996	1998	1999
Chaos, disorganization in society and the economy	65	75	57
Very high taxes and the extra burden of responsibility	7	9	24
The enterprise is in very poor condition	12	19	3
My relations with labor are deteriorating	12	16	27
This would not increase my income	7	15	11
Risk of racketeering	1	6	0

Note: Since every respondent could give more than one answer, the total percentage in each column differs from 100%.

The percentage of directors referring to disorganization at their enterprises declined considerably between 1996 and 1999, whereas the number of those mentioning high taxes and similar problems as a reason not to become the official proprietor of the enterprise increased four times. This kind of reason is quite common and corresponds to the actual situation in Russian society and the economy. The number of directors explaining their unwillingness to become owners by their deteriorating relationships with labor has more than doubled. This is the second motive. It reflects the negative attitude of a considerable part of Russian society towards private ownership of large industrial enterprises (while the population is more positive about private ownership of small and middle-sized enterprises). This negative attitude has not faded with time but serves as a factor slowing down the rate of expansion of private ownership in the Russian industry.

The 'poor position of the enterprise' factor has lost much of its weight. Indeed, defense enterprises have managed to adjust themselves better to the market and to undergo spontaneous restructuring from the ground up. Although this restructuring has not converted defense enterprises into efficient, self-sufficient market agents that can survive without state assistance, the process of primary adaptation to the market has taken place. Apart from this, changes called forth by the August 1998 crisis have played an important role, since many defense enterprises took advantage of these changes to step up production and to win new markets.

Thus, there are good reasons for the seemingly odd unwillingness of directors of large industrial enterprises (defense enterprises among them) to change their status and become legal owners. Under current social and economic conditions in Russia, it is not worthwhile for the majority of potential proprietors (and enterprise directors are the first-line potential proprietors) to assume the status of official, legal owners of enterprises. It is wiser for them to preserve an undefined, 'marginal' status, remaining de-facto owners and appropriating a considerable part of the profits, but avoiding legalization of their status.[5] We assume that the aforementioned conditions result in very high expenses associated with the maintenance of legal proprietor status. Moreover, this maintenance implies not only the direct spending required for company registration, registration of shares, etc., but also socio-political expenditures. First of all, a large number of industrial enterprises still have to fulfill certain social obligations. To give an example, one-third of the enterprises studied here have to foresee accommodation costs in their budget, and 18% have to provide for preschools. By retreating into the shadows, an owner reduces social spending, which is still rather high for many defense enterprises (the percentage of social costs in overall expenditures has remained constant or has even grown since 1992 for one-third of enterprises). The director assigns welfare expenses to the parent company and takes advantage of his rights of ownership through a chain of affiliated companies (thus earning profits, realizing investments, etc.). Second, by remaining in the shadows, a proprietor hedges against possible attacks by criminal groups or pressure from the state authorities. Moreover, this status can help a director-owner to relax the hostility of labor and local residents towards him (according to the statistics cited above, one-fourth of the directors who were polled would not like to become owners because of the hostile attitude of labor). Third, when no one knows for sure who the real owner of the enterprise is, it is hard for outside contenders for ownership to take action. But in the event the real owner legalizes his status, he will be exposed to the potential attacks of those who actually want to (and theoretically can) seize a share of the property.

---

[5] The researchers outline that privatization led to many specific troubles for the enterprises. For example, Baumgarten writes about nine problems emerging because of the privatization of defense enterprises - from the decline of production to decay of the social services (Baumgarten 1996). Surely, a lot of troubles arose from privatization and were the prime cause of the director's fear to become the official proprietor.

The situation may grow even more complicated when the de-jure owner is not the de-facto owner. We will call him the 'nominal owner'. Usually, such owners belong to one of the following categories: (1) the state; (2) labor; (3) foreign entrepreneurs and companies. In 1999, the percentage of nominal owners (of joint-stock companies both with and without state participation) in each of these three categories were 19%, 37% and less than 1%, respectively (in 1998, the last figure totaled 3%). In other words, more than half of the overall capital of private enterprises is in fact in the 'gray zone' where nominal owners have no real opportunity to realize their property rights. A major part of this capital is controlled by directors of enterprises (this statement is based on the results of other research, interviews, and on mass media sources). What is more, the directors prefer to remain in the shadows in order not to show off their wealth and to hedge against possible resentment and even violence by labor, criminal groups, etc. This risk is always present in Russia, where the population has always had negative feelings towards wealth and property. Indeed, when the real proprietor is unknown, and when shares have different legal and actual holders, an attempt to buy a block of shares can meet with stiff resistance from 'shadow forces' which often resort to 'non-economic' methods (use of private guards, the police, etc.) to prevent the purchase.

Moreover, the current situation frequently leads to disputes, and even to armed conflicts, among different owners when it is not clear who controls how much of the capital. At any rate, the numerous examples of such disputes (for instance, conflicts at Lomonosov Porcelain Factory, Kochkanarsk Mining Combine, etc.) prove that arguments over enterprise ownership result in legalization of the real proprietor, who sometimes resorts both to legal procedures and to force. This situation derives from the absence of an ownership doctrine in the USSR/Russia, and from the market transition policy being pursued by the state. This policy can be summed up as 'property in exchange for the political loyalty of enterprise directors'. The directors were granted 'freedom to privatize' their enterprises provided they did not oppose the government's market transition and democratization policy. To understand this, we need to analyze the relationship between enterprise directors and the state.

Relationship Between Directors and the State: New Trends

After decades of tight central planning of the Soviet economy, when enterprises and their directors were under daily pressure by the state, and the latter kept an eye on directors' operations (supervising how they met plan targets, how they used resources, etc.), these relations have changed radically today. Thus, the question arises: what is the relationship between the state and directors of Russian enterprises today, in the year 2000, and what changes has this relationship undergone?

The transition of the Russian economy to the market system was characterized by the overall privatization of state property, which was basically completed by the late 1990s. As this was a very rapid and very large-scale process (130,000 enterprises were privatized between 1992-97:[6] i.e., 1,500 enterprises a month on average), it caused many problems in Russian society and in the economy. Although, in a formal sense, the private sector is dominant in the Russian economy (73% of all enterprises and organizations were in private hands as of early 1998),[7] the public sector still comprises a considerable proportion: there are 13,786 enterprises fully owned by the state, 2,500 joint-stock companies where more than a quarter of the shares belong to the state, and 580 joint-stock companies where the state holds a so-called 'golden share' (allowing the state to block decisions unsatisfactory to it).[8] Among these companies are the so-called 'strategic enterprises': that is, enterprises which play a key role for national security, as well as for the export and the long-term development prospects of the Russian economy.

One of the major problems arising out of the rapid and large-scale privatization is the lack of clear rules for relations between the state and all kinds of enterprises. On the one hand, this leads to unsolicited actions by enterprise management, which sometimes results in embezzlement of funds. On the other hand, this lack of clear rules enables state officials at different levels to take arbitrary actions against enterprises without effective legal safeguards to protect themselves from outside interference. This is why the development of a stable regulation of relations between the

---

[6] Goskomstat 1999a, 362.
[7] Ibid., 341.
[8] These data are from the government resolution No. 1024 of 9 September 1999 'O Kontseptsii upravleniia gosudarstvennym i privatizatsii v Rossiiskoi Federatsii'. We are not referring to the state property in general, but only to 'federal-level' enterprises. Non-profit state organizations, real estate and natural resources are not considered, either. Thus, the real scope of the public sector in the Russian economy is even larger.

state and enterprises is one of the major challenges facing the Russian economy today. It is often emphasized in academic literature that the state should create and maintain stable and legalized 'rules of the game'.[9] This is important for every sector of society, but it is particularly true for relations between the state and state-owned enterprises. With regard to such relations, enterprises do not 'automatically' operate efficiently on the market, as there is no owner who can lose his own property if a company is poorly managed.

Although there are no stable and legalized rules regulating relations between the state and enterprises, certain mechanisms have been shaped and are in use nowadays. (1) Directors seek the spontaneous privatization of enterprise assets to their own benefit, transferring these assets to their private accounts in offshore zones. (2) The strategy of the state is, on the one hand, to turn these enterprises into extra sources of income for state officials earning low legal wages; on the other hand, to ignore the most urgent needs of enterprises, making little or no effort to solve their most difficult problems, and to delay the adoption of key decisions in economic policy.

To give one example, the state has virtually neglected its duty to carry out much needed restructuring in the defense industry, a procedure that cannot be conducted 'at grassroots level'. The government granted enterprises the freedom to manipulate their property, but, in turn, disclaimed its liabilities to the enterprises. This policy was dictated by the situation in Russia at that time. In particular, the government strategy was dictated by a shortage of funds for restructuring industry (first of all, the defense industry). As a result, the state pursued a 'neither peace nor war' policy regarding the defense industry. On the one hand, the state gave advances to enterprises: it promised large orders that would have provided a full workload for all defense enterprises, thus encouraging them to continue cooperating with the state. On the other hand, the government kept reducing the amount of its orders during the year, depending on budget revenues. As for the directors, their behavior was dictated by the new opportunity to make important economic decisions independently (after decades of full government control) and to appropriate funds and material resources.

The government strategy in the 1990s described above was reflected in state economic policy and, above all, in the particular policy for allocation of orders by the state. According to the data we have acquired, the average

---

[9] See, for example, Sachs 1994a, chapter 12.

level of production, as compared to productive capacity, remained the same from 1995 to 1999, amounting to 49%. Meanwhile, the percentage of state orders was reduced from 29% to 22% (see table 13.6).

Table 13.6 State orders and exploitation of productive capacity (in %)

	1995	1996	1997	1998	1999
Exploitation of productive capacity (100% corresponds to full use of productive capacity)	49	43	44	43	49
Percentage of state orders (100% corresponds to the full use of productive capacity)	-	-	29	17	22

This policy inevitably resulted in a growing government debt to the defense industry. The amount of this debt is hard to calculate because each year, the value of the orders was repeatedly revised. Aside from this, the state and the enterprise would handle a state order in different ways. The state preferred to calculate the final figures on the basis of minimal figures, whereas an enterprise would use the initial figures - the figures it had referred to when negotiating with suppliers and banks on the expansion of production. Obviously, such a mechanism (NB: not accidental errors, but a mechanism) results in state indebtedness and makes it difficult for defense enterprises and the state to reconcile the amount of indebtedness and to make payments. Consequently, cooperation between the different partners becomes difficult.

According to our data (which, as far as we are aware, are similar to those cited by the managers of defense enterprises), the average outstanding receivable debt is approximately Rbl49mn per defense enterprise as of 1999. The total debt receivable by the defense industry, which currently includes 1,520 enterprises, is Rbl74bn, of which Rbl35bn are owed by the state (or an average of Rbl23mn per enterprise). This means that Rbl25,000 (around US$900) are due to each employee, Rbl12,000 (over US$400) of which is owned by the state. This is almost half of what it was in 1998. However, given that the ruble lost three-fourths of its value during 1999, we can state that the outstanding government debt to defense enterprises actually doubled in real terms.

At the same time, defense enterprises owe money to banks, suppliers and other partners, including the state. We have calculated the balance of debt in order to find out whether it is the enterprises that owe money to the state, or vice versa. We estimated the accounts payable by the enterprises to the state without penalty fees and fines for tax evasion. The reason for this is that the state does not add any penalty fees to its own debt. Moreover, by charging huge penalty fees which can total more than half of the outstanding sum (according to our data), the government can effectively drive any enterprise into the position of a bad debtor. According to the data, an average enterprise owes over Rbl15mn to the state, or a bit more than Rbl8,000 per employee (fees and fines excluded), as of 1999. This means that the balance of debt will total approximately Rbl8mn per enterprise. Hence, the state owes over Rbl4,000 on the average to each employee, which is more than three times his monthly salary. The net government debt to the defense industry amounts to more than Rbl12bn, or over US$400mn.

At present, this policy is undergoing transformation. After a long period of unrestricted interference in enterprises' activities, the state intends to regulate its relationship with them, first of all with the public-sector enterprises. The government is working on stable rules of the game for building new relations with the enterprises. The state is supposed finally to set the tasks for the enterprises: that is, to tell them exactly what it expects from them. It intends to develop and implement a new mechanism for governing state enterprises. This mechanism is intended to reconcile both state and enterprise interests in the market, where the enterprises are already market agents. This mechanism is to include a contract with the director; a charter approved by a federal executive body; a fair audit procedure; a set of criteria approved at the federal level for assessing the performance of enterprises, etc. It is vitally important for the government to set up a stable and efficient system for governing the state enterprise sector in order to demonstrate its ability to enhance its governance of society in general, and to raise public confidence in government. The market will never work efficiently without public confidence in government; crime will increase, capital will continue to 'flow' abroad, and the investments will fall.

The principles of this new policy are laid down in the 'Concept of governing state property and privatization in the Russian Federation' adopted by the government resolution No. 1024 of 9 September 1999. These principles are dealt with in detail in almost 30 statutes or draft statutes at different stages of development and approval. For instance, one of the most innovative resolutions adopted within the context of the new state policy of interaction between the state and directors is the government resolution No. 234, 'On the appointment of directors of industrial enterprises in Russia' of 16 February 2000. This resolution is applicable to all state-owned enterprises and includes a standard contract form that specifies: (1) the procedure for advertising a vacancy in the position of an enterprise director, (2) the priorities to be considered when selecting a candidate; and (3) appointment and confirmation procedures. A number of attempts have been made since the reforms were launched to regulate the selection of management bodies and to specify in legal form the authority and duties of a director. However, there have been no standard regulations (or contracts) until recently. Today, both a standard contract and a legal basis for it have been created. In spite of some bureaucratic 'traps', the standard contract which has now been adopted will fundamentally change the nature of the relationship between the state and enterprise directors existing in the former USSR and the post-Soviet Russia of the 1990s. This change is a big step towards more civilized relations. It seems that the new policy of cooperation between the state and enterprises proves that the state is willing to put an end to the 'period of chaos' in those relations.

However, there are certain obstacles in the existing relations between directors and the state to the implementation of the new policy. There are two groups of such obstacles. First is the inertia of current economic policy, more or less settled during the last eight years: priorities representing the interests of particular financial and production groups have been set and are taken into account when federal and local budgets are considered and approved; certain financial flows processed by particular banks have taken shape; certain foreign trade rules have been established, etc. The second group of obstacles arises from various patterns of relations between enterprises and numerous government bodies. In what follows, we elaborate on each of the groups mentioned above.

Directors' Attitudes towards State Economic Policy

The drawbacks of economic policy implementation by the Russian government have been analyzed in a number of publications. In this paper we will cover only those drawbacks that have a detrimental affect on the position of defense enterprises. In order to research this issue we asked directors the following question: 'What do you think are the main drawbacks of government policy preventing the defense industry from operating efficiently?' The answers are presented in table 13.7.

Table 13.7 Main drawbacks of government policy (in %)

Defense enterprises are overtaxed	73
The state regularly defaults on its obligations with regard to orders by the state	67
No restructuring and military conversion have been conducted	50
Incessant reorganizations prevent efficient management	34
Economic errors (e.g. extra mobilization of production capacities)	20
Wrong privatization policy	17
Too many barriers to export of military production	15

Note: The total percentage is greater than 100% because the respondents could specify more than one policy drawback.

Directors are especially concerned about the drawbacks of the tax system. The existing tax system has serious defects because it was developed with two main objectives in view: to achieve financial stability and to increase budget revenues (in order to collect enough funds for further allocation). At the same time, such liberal goals as the creation of favorable conditions for private entrepreneurship, or protecting property rights, savings, and investment were ignored. Such a fiscally oriented tax system has suppressed private entrepreneurship activity, encouraged entrepreneurship by the *nomenklatura,* and boosted the development of a shadow economy. These defects are among the main factors preventing the development of a workable competitive market economy in Russia (although there are certainly other obstacles). Apart from other drawbacks, the existing system of taxation entails extraordinary tax rates, reducing companies' incomes by 60-80%, or even more. These rates do not take into account the actual solvency of enterprises and the amount of taxes that directors are prepared to pay. We have asked the directors this question and learned that they are ready to pay 30-32%, or roughly one-third of enterprises' income.

We have written, above, about the breach of state obligations on state orders. Obviously, these are not accidental errors or miscalculations, but an essential feature of the current system of governing, where the state has deep obligations in the spheres of the economy and social welfare. Since the state does not want to cut back these obligations (the reasons for this are a separate subject for research, beyond the scope of this article), the state allocates orders for armaments and other products and deals with enterprises in a manner resulting in severe indebtedness.

The third grave defect of government policy is that no restructuring and conversion to civilian production have been conducted in the defense industry. Indeed, the reformers consciously avoided such a serious sociopolitical challenge as the real reduction and restructuring of the defense industry. They believed that the employees of defense enterprises were against reforms and would oppose the transition to a market system. That is why, in order to avoid political problems and social conflicts, the reformers chose an easy way out: they cut down federal spending for the defense industry without introducing any structural or institutional reforms.[10]

Meanwhile, according to polls conducted regularly (by the authors of the present article) among the directors of Russian defense enterprises, they were fully prepared for a 50% reduction and the further restructuring of the defense industry in 1992-94. Thus, in 1992-93, the government could have developed a reduction and restructuring program that would have been approved by the majority of defense enterprises - a program that could have been implemented within four to five years without serious disturbances and completed by 1998-99. Instead, none of the key problems of the defense industry that emerged in the early 1990s was solved during the eight years of market reforms. Moreover, there is no prospect that these problems will be solved in the near future.[11]

The remaining three defects of government economic policy are of lesser importance, as fewer than half of the directors mentioned them at all. Still, judging from these defects, we can assume that the existing economic policy seriously affects the relationship between directors and the state.

---

[10] The only exception was conversion from military production that was partially financed during the first phase of market reforms. Later, the funding was reduced and then - in 1997 - cancelled.

[11] By the end of 1997, a government program for defense industry restructuring was developed (under the guidance of the then Minster of Economics Iakov Urinson) and approved by the government. That program envisaged reduction of the number of defense enterprises in order to concentrate state orders within the remaining ones, conversion of some enterprises from military to civilian production; their partial transfer to the non-defense industry, preservation of a small number of full state enterprises, further conversion, etc. However, a new political crisis (which resulted in Urinson's resignation) prevented this and other reforms from implementation. At present, neither this program has been revived, nor a new one is being developed.

Certain economic and social mechanisms have been established in Russian society as a result of this policy. Thus, it will take time to get rid of them and to re-shape the relationship between directors and the state.

Yet, what does the concept of the 'state' imply? With whom, exactly, are the directors of enterprises unhappy? Actually, it is not a universal power structure that is to be blamed for inefficient economic policy, but a number of the particular state agencies the enterprises have to deal with. Thus, all the forgoing defects are associated with specific bodies. We have attempted to find out which among these bodies the directors are especially dissatisfied with.

Directors' Assessment of Relations among Enterprises, State Bodies and Natural Monopolies

A large number of explicit and implicit conflicts have occurred between enterprises and numerous social actors during the period of transition in Russia. Judging by our interviews with directors, the main conflicts are concentrated in the area of relations between defense enterprises and state agencies, on the one hand; and defense enterprises and natural monopolies (*Gazprom*, etc.), on the other hand. The description of relations between directors and the state, as well as directors' attitudes to state economic policy, would be incomplete if we did not mention what directors think about the many state agencies and 'natural monopolies' that carry out state economic policy and by their actions cause directors to be discontented with this policy. Obviously, the negative attitude of directors towards state policy is the result of their negative experience with some state bodies and natural monopolies - the units of state machinery that implement policy.

On the basis of the foregoing, we asked directors the following question: 'How do you assess the attitude of different authorities (federal and regional) and of Russian corporations towards your enterprise? Which of them create favorable conditions for your work, which of them create obstacles, and which ones do not affect your enterprise at all?'[12] We provided a list of 21 items for assessment. In table 13.8, we group them according to the impact they have on enterprises.

---

[12] Since the natural monopolies are operating as 'Russian Joint-Stock Companies' (*Gazprom* and United Energy System) or state ministries (Ministry of Railways), we asked the directors to estimate enterprise relations with state agencies and 'Russian Joint-Stock Corporations'.

Table 13.8 Impact of state bodies and natural monopolies on enterprises' operation (directors' estimate, in %)

	Creates favorable conditions	Creates obstacles	No impact	Total
Federal organs (president, government, etc.)	8	30	62	100
Economic ministries (Ministry of Finance, Ministry of Economics, etc.)	6	51	100	100
Power ministries (Ministry of Defense, Ministry of Internal Affairs, etc.)	19	21	60	100
Natural monopolies (*EES, Gazprom, MPS*)	3	52	45	100
Social security foundations (pension fund, employment fund, etc.)	2	76	22	100
Local authorities (Republican, regional, city, municipal authorities)	40	28	32	100
Average	10	38	52	100

As can be seen, enterprises are not very dependent on the federal organs. More than half of the directors believe that federal organs have no impact on the operation of their enterprises. 60% said the same about the power ministries, and 51% about the economic ministries. This is a very important point. Although various explanations are possible, it is obvious that enterprises are no longer dependent on state bodies, as they were before the reforms were launched. To cite a specific reason for this increasing independence, we would mention first of all that some defense enterprises survive mainly on arms exports and are thus (within limits, of course) not dependent on changes occurring within Russia. In addition, some enterprises have restructured themselves from the ground up, setting up an efficient internal system of management and regularly launching new, saleable articles according to market demand. This is why these enterprises are relatively independent of resolutions adopted by state regulatory bodies. This independence, however, can also have negative causes. In particular, some directors think that their enterprises are in such poor condition that no resolutions or measures taken by state bodies can help to remedy the situation. Finally, many directors no longer believe that the authorities can do anything useful for enterprises.

Most of the directors who provided some kind of assessment of the impact of government bodies on their enterprises sounded negative. Four times as many directors stated that the authorities 'created obstacles' as said that state bodies created 'favorable conditions'. The directors were particularly unhappy about their relations with social security foundations (pension, employment and mandatory medical insurance foundations). They viewed these organizations as a kind of 'state racket': enterprises have to pay high fees to the state (about 40% of an employee's wages), but do not receive the appropriate services in return. These heavy payments are one of the major reasons for the development of the shadow economy and the practice of paying wages in cash (when managers prefer to pay unofficially between 15% and 60% of the salary, and even more, in order to avoid social security taxes).[13]

The second most important source of problems for enterprises is the natural monopolies. Indeed, high charges for gas, electricity, and transportation services have always been mentioned by directors among the main obstacles to increasing production. The so-called 'natural monopolies' are in fact former Soviet branch ministries which were privatized entirely by certain groups of the old Soviet and the new *nomenklatura*.[14] Pro forma or 'shadow' privatization enabled these groups to avoid restructuring these organizations and turning them into genuine private companies able to operate efficiently on the market. Today, the state cannot control these organizations because they are 'private', and neither can the market - because they are 'monopolies'. They virtually own the major part of the Russian economy and have a huge amount of political power, both on the federal and local levels. The degree of this influence is comparable with that of the government. Therefore, a single enterprise cannot deal with any of these companies on equal terms, and in case of a conflict, the 'natural monopoly' will certainly gain the upper hand.

---

[13] Probably these rates are normal for a European country with stable market economy, but they are purely unacceptable under market transition when enterprises have to bear huge expenses arising from the shortcomings of the economic system. This, by the way, is reflected in the foregoing assessment of the negative influence of the socio-economic environment on enterprises.

[14] Although the Ministry of Railways is not privatized formally, it has been privatized de-facto through a branch of affiliated private companies controlled by relatives and trustees of Ministry heads.

The next group of bodies creating problems for enterprises is comprised of economic departments - The Ministry of Finance, The Ministry of Economics, etc. The directors regard them as the main source of various kinds of economic aggression and injustice. Negative assessments exceed positive ones by a factor of more than seven. The Federal Assembly and the president and his administration, it should be noted here, are regarded with equanimity. Though negative assessments of their activities exceed positive ones, the majority believes that they have no impact at all on the business of their organizations. The power ministries also are regarded as having on the whole a neutral impact on the defense industry. Enterprises are generally rather independent of them, whereas the proportions of positive and negative assessments are almost equal. Directors are positive about the Ministry of Defense and the Federal Security Service and negative about the Ministry of Internal Affairs, which runs the militia, and Ministry of Justice. The main complaint about the Ministry of Internal Affairs is that it does not provide protection against crime. As for the Ministry of Justice, it raises obstacles to military exports.

The directors were rather positive about local authorities - there are one and a half times as many positive as negative assessments. Although there were some complaints, on the whole, the directors thought they had established good relations with local authorities, in contrast to relations with federal ones.[15] In their view, local authorities create favorable social and economic conditions for the enterprises, help to solve many social problems, assist in conversion from military to civilian production, and protect the enterprises from competitors in the event of property disputes.

By the year 2000, a new socio-economic and political situation had developed in Russia. This situation can affect the status of enterprise directors. The key factor is the second war in Chechnia, which has stepped up military production.[16] In turn, this production growth has resulted in an increase in state orders for defense enterprises and provided new development opportunities for those enterprises. On the other hand, the Putin government has reaffirmed its attitude toward the 'structural

---

[15] For instance, almost two-thirds of directors think that local taxes are too high; 35% complain that local authorities do not provide funding for schools, kindergartens, other social services; 34% criticize the authorities for failing to maintain stable supplies of energy, gas, etc.
[16] We are leaving out the moral and political assessment of both Chechen wars, as well as their macroeconomic consequences. This analysis is out of scope of the present article. However, we would like to mention that the negative consequences of these wars will undoubtedly outweigh any gain for Russia.

transformation' of the Russian economy, further privatization, and the consolidation of market institutions. This means that enterprises should make further efforts and take advantage of the new carte blanche in order to carry on their economic activity. Their future will depend a good deal on how hard they try to make the most of the new favorable political and economic situation in the country. In the meantime, this new situation acts as an umbrella for the defense enterprises, and will protect them a little bit from international competition. If so, we can expect this factor to have a weakening influence on Russia's defense enterprises and on the status of their directors in the near future.

Conclusion

Directors of defense enterprises have been powerful actors in the Russian economy during the post-Soviet period. Developing formal and informal relations with federal and local authorities, controlling labor, maintaining contact with criminal groups, they have mostly determined the process of privatization within the military-industrial sector. Taking into account the fact that this was the most developed sector of the Soviet/Russian industry, these actors have played one of the key roles in the privatization of Russian industry in general.

In the course of the market transformation, the director's status has shifted radically. The equality of all executives under state bodies has changed: their positions now vary greatly, according to many economic and social indicators. A 'multi-role' phenomenon has emerged within the framework of the position of directors. This phenomenon includes five different executive roles, from hired manager to official and unofficial (though formally unrecorded) proprietor. This variation in itself shows that there have been significant changes at the institutional and microeconomic levels under the pressure of market reforms in Russia.

The social consequences of the new variations in the position of directors are rather contradictory. On the one hand, this is an indicator of the drive to privatization, as well as a manifestation of directors' adaptation to the specifically Russian market system. On the other hand, the ensemble of the new roles of directors is an indicator of the inefficiency of this system, because it fails to attract new investments and prevents diffusion of technological innovations: on the contrary, it promotes both legal and illegal capital outflows and misappropriation of enterprise assets.

Directors of Russian defense enterprises are involved in the global economy and in global society in three ways. First are the legal operations of the enterprise in the international market: selling products (military and civilian), buying technologies, establishing joint ventures, etc. Here, the director focuses on the everyday functioning of the enterprise, because almost three-fourths of defense enterprises are now involved in the international market in one form or another. Both sides - the defense enterprises as well as their foreign partners - are fruitfully involved. The second way in which defense enterprises are globally involved is the development of directors' 'shadow' activities outside Russia. A significant part of this activity takes place abroad because the economic activities of Russian firms abroad are totally uncontrolled by the state and society in present-day Russia. At the same time, reliable domestic information on the genesis and functioning of Russian firms is almost completely unavailable to foreign law enforcement agencies. As a result, because of the lack of state supervision, some of Russia's companies are in effect functioning as anonymous entities, especially in the financial markets, in real estate and some other areas. Finally, in a third aspect of global involvement, directors save their money in foreign banks and send family members. They prefer foreign banks to protect their personal savings, they want to provide an education for their children at elite universities in the USA and Europe, and they want to have an additional residence abroad in case of troubles in the motherland. These three types of global engagement are tentative and rather restricted forms of actor involvement in globalization. In future, they may possibly be further developed and expanded.

In the current Putin era, the status of directors of defense enterprises has risen. The government has promised to increase state procurements (though as of 1 June 2000, only about 6.5% of state orders were covered under the annual plan).[17] The new policy, if it is really implemented, could restructure the current status-system of directors, a system which has been formed in the defense sector over the past eight years. What will be the main lines of this restructuring? We will receive the answer in the near future.

---

[17] *Izvestiia* (2000), 7 June.

14 Actors in Agro-Food Policy: Who Shapes Outcomes?

EVGENIIA V. SEROVA

As a rule, agriculture is the most protected sector of a nation's economy. In the developed countries, the agricultural population represents an insignificant part of the total population, and its lobbying possibilities are quite restricted. However, the up- and downstream sectors have a strong economic interest in state support of agriculture. It is their pressure which determines agrarian protectionism. The role of interest groups in agriculture is well studied, but the post-socialist countries have specific features in this respect. What are the driving forces in the formation of agrarian policy in transition countries? To whose interest are the measures of agro-food policy addressed? These issues are the focus of the present article.

At the start of reforms, Russia was confronted with the process of worldwide economic integration. The opening of markets for foreign goods, services, and actors has affected the Russian economy and its domestic actors significantly during the last decade. No actor in the Russian agro-food sector today can ignore these world processes. The transformation of the agro-food chain and policy in accordance with this economic challenge is one of the most evident results of this opening to the world. Absolutely new actors, who did not exist in the centrally planned economy, have appeared in Russian society. The emergence of classical interest groups in this sector in Russia, and their institutionalization, are further effects of the reforms. Russia's application to world organizations, in particular to the WTO, will further contribute to the internationalization of the Russian agro-food sector and the Russian economy in general.

Therefore, we will examine the emergence of these new actors and structures in Russian agro-food sector.

Specific Features of Agro-food Policy in Russia

The concept of agro-food policy is new. In Russia, as in almost all other post-socialist countries, this policy has passed through two stages of evolution irrespective of other transformations in agriculture. The first stage in Russia began with price liberalization, reduction or abolition of state purchases of agro-food commodities, and an end to state direct plans for farms. Food subsidies and privileges for agriculture were lifted. This confronted agro-food policy makers with a vast number of unexpected problems, which could not be solved with the traditional measures of the centrally planned economy. As a result, agro-food policy was formed *ad hoc*: problems which arose were fought spontaneously, very often with the tools of the previous economic paradigm. The government tended to control prices, and price controls were continued for a large set of foodstuffs for some time after the start of liberalization. Russia maintained a trade policy typical of economies with food shortages: promoting agro-food imports and limiting agro-food exports. Thus, Russia in the first stage of reform experienced a severe decline in state support for agriculture. At the same time, economic liberalization led to a deterioration of the sector, as expressed in the following trends: a fall in the real income of the population, and corresponding shrinkage of the agro-food market; a rapid worsening of terms of trade for agriculture, and a decline of the sector's share in the national economy; the collapse of the Committee for Mutual Economic Assistance (Comecon), leading to further shrinkage of the market for agriculture; rapid exit of the state from the agro-food distribution field, and lack of sound market infrastructure, which led to a growth in transaction costs and further decline in demand; financial crisis on farms, aggravated by the lack of a relevant agricultural credit system, and the corresponding deterioration of assets and fall in sector efficiency.

In the second stage, agrarian protectionism has started to substitute for the euphoria of liberalization. Russia since 1993 has launched minimum guaranteed prices, import duties and quotas, and export subsidies. However, this policy is still influenced by the previous paradigm. For instance, the minimum guaranteed prices are set above actual market prices, which means that they are set at inefficient levels and not used for real market interventions. However, with the development of the reforms, policy makers gained market experience and began to be aware of market performance. Russia, like other post-socialist countries, has adopted special laws on state support for agriculture. These laws usually copied the common agricultural policy (CAP) legislation of the European Union. All over the region, export subsidies were being introduced, and import duties were being increased.

In addition to the common problems of post-socialist countries, Russia has its own specific problems influencing agrarian policy. First, Russia is a federation in which the federal power is quite weak. As a result, agrarian policy is formed more in the regions than on the federal level, and varies significantly from region to region. Thus, land tenure legislation differs from one region to another, sometimes radically: in one group of regions private land ownership is strictly prohibited while another group of regions has adopted regional land codes with rather liberal land tenure regimes. Second, the high level of paternalistic expectations among the population and economic players, on the one hand, and the high inclination of bureaucrats to reproduce the traditional Soviet distribution system, on the other, determine the transformation of every measure of market regulation into traditional administrative measures. Finally, Russian reforms have proceeded rather slowly. The period of growing protectionism in agrarian policy has coincided with a period of financial instability and an under-restructured agro-food sector. In such circumstances, protectionism creates impediments to further reforms.

Institutional Structure of Interest Groups in the Russian Agro-food Sector

Analysis of Russia's agro-food policy during the past decade leads to the conclusion that it was not the farms who were the major beneficiaries of this policy.[1] Nevertheless, the main programs of this policy were maintained year after year, with significant budget expenditures for their implementation. This suggests that certain interest groups lobbied effectively for these programs. These interest groups should be institutionally organized.

During the Soviet era, the Communist Party of the Soviet Union (CPSU) was the absolute driving force in agrarian policy. All decisions were made, implemented, and controlled by the CPSU through its republic, regional and local branches. This situation was radically changed during the reforms, when the ruling role of the CPSU was eliminated.

---

[1] OECD 1998; Gaidar 1998; Serova 1999; Braun, Serova, Seeth and Melukhina 1996; Wehrheim, Serova and Frohberg 2000.

At the beginning of the reforms, the main driving forces of agro-food policy were based on political contradictions, which can be roughly described as the opposition of liberals and conservatives. Economic interest groups were not yet formed. In these circumstances, policy was formed mostly in accordance with the dominance of one or another political group - reformers or anti-reformers - in the government, as well as following the spontaneous reactions of the population. As the reforms progressed and the market began to take root, new interest groups began to emerge and to play a more and more important role in the development of agro-food sector policy. At the same time, centralization in decision making was yielding to the pressure of regionalization. This was especially evident in the agro-food sector. Political groups and parties began to reflect the economic interests of various social groups, rather than political and ideological perceptions, as they initially had. During this process, a number of forces impacting on agro-food policy development were established in Russia.

Federal and Regional Governments

The federal government remains the major player in agro-food policy formation. As in any other country, the Ministry of Agriculture is the sector's major lobbyist in relation to the Ministry of Finance and the Cabinet as a whole. The size of the agrarian budget reflects the power of the ministerial bureaucracy; therefore, they strive to increase their share of the national budgetary pie. Severe budget constraints are characteristic of Russia as a transition country. In this respect, the Ministry of Agriculture cannot pretend to a significant budget share, but instead tends to approve support programs which are accompanied by inputs distribution: such programs enlarge bureaucratic power.

The federal government formulates the major rules of the game in the agro-food sector: taxes, trade regulations, types of subsidies, etc. At the same time, its role is steadily diminishing. Thus, at the beginning of the reforms, the federal budget supplied 40% of agricultural support payments (with the remainder coming from the budgets of the constituent members of the federation. Currently, this share is around one third while the regions provide two thirds of total expenditures for this sector.

Diagram 14.1 Share of the federal budget in financing the agro-food sector

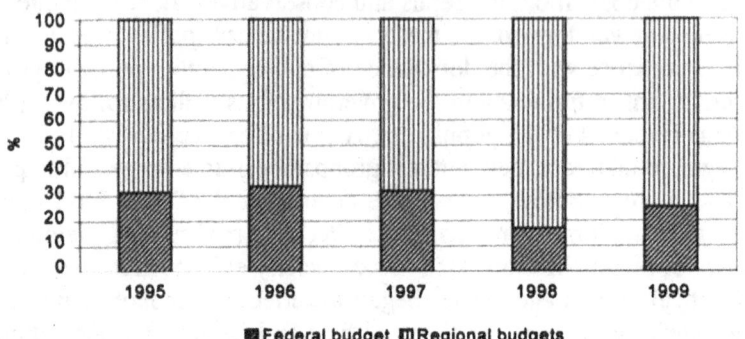

Source: Goskomstat.

Purchases of agro-food commodities for federal reserves have decreased from year to year, and are now an insignificant share of total sales. At the same time, regional reserves are rather large, and their share in sales has barely decreased (Figure 14.2 illustrates this for grain reserves).

Diagram 14.2 Federal and regional grain reserves (mt)

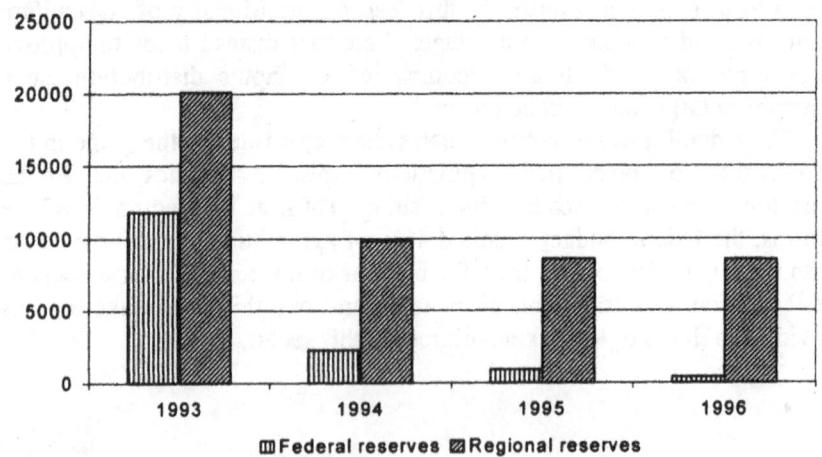

Source: Goskomstat.

The center of agro-food policy formation is shifting towards the regional authorities. This trend is manifested not only in the growing share of regional budget support to the sector. At the beginning of the reforms, the regional authorities were still inclined to use policy tools inherited from the centrally planned economy. They tended to distribute inputs and output, and to regulate financial and labor flows in the agro-food sector. Within the first few years, regional policy-makers began to be aware of the futility of their efforts to regulate the sector in the old manner. This period was followed by a period of full deregulation in most Russian regions. Later, however, policy-makers came to an understanding of market rules and began to apply more or less adequate policy tools.

Since 1993, the regional governments have maintained livestock subsidies, which are the second largest program in agriculture. Regions have significant rights in the privatization plans for the agriculture and food industries, which also have a substantial impact on countrywide agro-food policy. Some regional governments maintain price regulation for both the retail and agricultural markets. The regionalization of agro-food policy increased significantly after the 1998 crisis. Faced with a sudden increase in demand for foodstuffs, many regional authorities introduced price regulations, trade barriers, and retail network control.

Land tenure provides another example of the regional influence on Russian agrarian policy. The Constitution assigns land tenure regulation to authorities at both the federal and regional levels. In practice, several regions have adopted their own land legislation, which contradicts federal laws. Thus, twelve constituent members of the federation have prohibited private land ownership, although this is against the Constitution and federal land legislation. In contrast, a few other regions have adopted their own land codes, with private land ownership, while there is still no new land code at the federal level.

Along with allocating most subsidies to agricultural producers, the regional governments also impose inter-regional trade barriers. One can distinguish three types of such barriers: first, there are temporary bans on exporting the most liquid agricultural commodities (grain and some others). The local administrations in this way reduce farm-gate prices for these commodities, contribute to their artificial shortage in the net-importing regions, and accumulate stocks at lower prices and later export them at increased prices. The price gap is a regional revenue. About 20 members of the federation currently impose such barriers. Second, there are temporary bans on exports of staple foodstuffs. This is mostly connected with excise commodities, such as spirits, because excises are transferred to the regional budgets. However, such temporary bans can be imposed when there is danger of food shortages, as was the case after the crisis of 1998. There are barriers to importing foodstuffs, in order to protect local producers. At the beginning of the reforms, several subjects of the federation imposed their own import duties, in addition to the national ones. All these barriers are illegal, contradicting the Constitution, the antitrust law, and the law on competition. However, federal power is not strong enough to stop regional trade barriers, legislation, or other activity which contradicts federal laws. Therefore, the agro-food situation in the country today is under strong influence from regional authorities. The regional governors are one of the driving forces behind Russia's agro-food policy today. A number of constituent members of the federation have formed regional associations and unions, such as Siberian Accord, Urals union, Association of the Center, etc. Most of these associations have their own agrarian programs.

The Federal Legislature

The Federal Assembly is another arena of policy-making and lobbying in agro-food policy. The Duma impacts federal agro-food policy mostly through the budget process. The agrarian group in the parliament, supported by the Communist faction, has managed to insist on a rather high share for agriculture in total budget expenditures. However, agrarian group activity toward creating an agro-food sector legal system has been much less effective. The Duma has been known for its opposition to any reform-oriented initiatives by the government. Laws adopted by the Duma regarding the agro-food sector have been mostly declarative. Thus, during the years of the reform, the Duma has adopted such laws as 'On grain', 'On state regulation of the agro-industrial sector', 'On price parity', etc. with no impact on real life, some of which were later repealed. In the new, third, Duma there are 35 Agrarian deputies, just enough to set up a faction. At the first session of the new Duma, however, the Agrarian deputies had already split into two groups: a more conservative group, closely related to the Communists, and a more pragmatic group. There are hopes that the new Duma will be more supportive of progressive legal work in the agricultural arena.

The upper house of the Russian parliament, the Federation Council, consists of the leaders of the regional governments and legislatures, and demonstrates a more considered strategy. The acquisition of power over the distribution of federal financial flows to the agro-food sector seems to be a major objective of these regional leaders, at which they have so far been quite successful.

Political Parties

The manifestos and other documents of the different political parties take very different positions on agrarian policy issues. Almost all political parties taking part in the 1999 legislative elections had their own agrarian programs. However, the Agrarian Party of Russia (*APR*) counts as the major representative of the economic and social interests of Russia's rural population. The constitutive forum of the *APR* took place in February 1993. The Agrarian Union of Russia, the Union of Agro-industrial Workers of the Russian Federation, the Russian Council of *Kolkhozes*, and former deputies of the Supreme Soviet of the Russian Soviet Federated Socialist Republic were the initiators and co-founders of the *APR*. *APR* leader Mikhail Lapshin - a former *sovkhoz* director - is a very successful agrarian lobbyist. The backbone of the *APR* consists of the former Soviet agrarian-sector *nomenklatura*, directors of *kolkhozes* and *sovkhozes* and their deputies, and local administrators. Ordinary employees of agricultural enterprises, private family farmers, owners of private household plots, and other elements of the rural population are very thinly represented. The *APR* has a three-tier structure at the federal, regional and local/primary levels. It has branches in 80 out of 89 regions. The *APR* has its own regular national newspaper, *Rossiiskaia zemlia*, published since April 1996, as well as some regional *APR* newspapers. During the parliamentary election campaign, the Agrarian Party of Russia split into two parties, one of which joined the political bloc *Fatherland - All Russia*, while the other remained in the Communists' political bloc. The first, more flexible, part of the Agrarian party was led by Mikhail Lapshin and Gennadii Kulik (a vice-premier in Primakov's cabinet). The second, more conservative, part was headed by Nikolai Kharitonov, the head of the Agrarian Committee in the second Duma.

In the survey mentioned above, experts were asked to estimate the real role of this party in representing rural interests. More than 60% of experts believe that this party does not (or probably does not) truly represent the rural and agricultural population.

Diagram 14.3 Distribution of experts' responses to the question 'Do you believe the Agrarian party represents the economic and social interests of the rural and agricultural population?'[2]

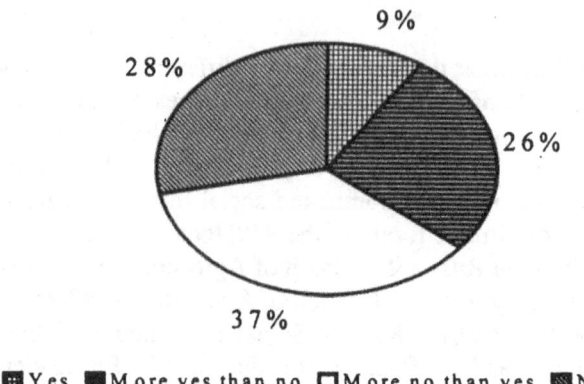

■ Yes ■ More yes than no □ More no than yes ▩ No

Farm managers and scientists, who are presumably the major contingent of the Agrarian party, are slightly less likely to believe that the Agrarian party does not represent the interests of the rural population (58%). Less than 50% of those on the left agreed with this conclusion. Older experts are more convinced of the rural representativity of this party. At the same time, the extreme right, traditional opponents of the Agrarian party, and the mass media are more certain that the Agrarian party reflects the interests of rural people (48%). It is notable that the center-right is the most skeptical regarding the coincidence of interests of rural people and the Agrarian party (66% of these respondents believe that this party does not represent the interests of the rural population).

Despite a certain variation in their responses, it is obvious that the major part of the agrarian establishment does not consider the Agrarian Party a real political force standing for the interests of the agricultural and rural population. This means that the failure of the reforms and the worsening of living standards in rural areas are not being brought into the political arena in a structured way. This may be one important reason for the failure of agrarian reform in Russia. Also, it can suggest the need for further party building in society in order to reflect the interests of

---

[2] See also Norsworthy 2000.

agriculture and of rural residents in politics. Radical transformation of the existing Agrarian party would be another possibility (this process has made a partial start, as the party begins to drift to the right of the Communist Party).

Public Organizations

Besides the Agrarian Party, there are numerous public organizations representing the interests of the various strata in agriculture. These non-commercial organizations have no political purposes in their charters. One of the most influential is the Agro-Industrial Union of Russia (*RAPS*), which is a successor to the Agrarian Union of Russia. Among the members of *RAPS* are representatives of agricultural enterprises, processors, storage and transport enterprises, machinery stations, producers of fertilizers and agricultural chemicals, and service and scientific organizations. However, the majority consists of representatives of large agricultural enterprises (there are only two private farmers as of 1998).

The predecessor of *RAPS*, the Agrarian Union, was created in 1990 to lobby the Government for the interests of the 'red' agricultural directorate, and to prepare for the first Parliamentary elections. Its membership consisted of legal entities in the agro-food sector. The role of the Agrarian Union (AU) has decreased since the establishment in 1993 of the Agrarian Party, to whom the Union has gradually delegated most of its political functions. *RAPS* was created in April 1997 to replace the AU, because the Charter of the AU contradicts the 1995 Civil Code, which clearly states that social organizations should consist only of physical persons. *RAPS* signs an annual agreement with the federal government. This agreement has a declarative character, however, and *RAPS* has never achieved one of its goals, obtaining budgetary funds for its activity. *RAPS* has branches in all constituent members of the federation except Chechnia. The main body of *RAPS* is the Forum, which is convened no less than once every three years.

The other influential social organization is the Association of Private Farms and Co-operatives of Russia (*AKKOR*), created in 1990 at the initiative of the new-born group of private farmers. In contrast to *RAPS*, *AKKOR* has a very progressive and democratic image. It is considered one of the most market-oriented organizations in agriculture since the *perestroika* era, lobbying for private ownership of land. The major goals of *AKKOR* are to protect the civil, political, economic, and cultural rights and freedoms of private farmers; to promote agrarian reform and private initiatives in agrarian development; to support the legal power in designing land and agrarian legislation, etc. In order to achieve these goals, *AKKOR* takes part in launching proposals for the Government and participates in discussions on the agrarian budget. It also maintains contacts with political parties and movements, and with religious and social organizations on questions regarding the social and economic development of Russia, the continuation of economic reforms, and the sovereignty of Russia. The main body of *AKKOR* is the Forum, which is convened no less than once a year. *AKKOR* is a member of various international organizations, such as the International Federation of Agricultural Producers.

In the beginning, *AKKOR* also engaged in some economic activities: its branches disbursed the first financial support for the private farmers, and it attempted to organize cooperative banks and insurance companies. These attempts failed, and *AKKOR* now minimizes its economic activity. *AKKOR* initiated the annual agricultural fair of family farms, *Russian Farmer (Rossiiskii Fermer)*, which has taken place in St. Petersburg during the last week of August every year since 1992. This fair is considered quite important, since many top governmental officials as well as representatives of foreign governments and international organizations generally participate in it. Many decisions and announcements are often made during this fair.

A number of other agrarian social organizations (Agro-Industrial Union, Russian Union of Rural Women, Russian Agrarian Union of Youth, Russian Peasant Foundation, Union of Landowners, Movement of Women-Farmers, Union of Small Agricultural Producers, Union of Rural Credit Co-operatives, etc.) have been organized to fit current political ambitions, but have little impact on Russian social and political life.

Business and Producers' Associations

It has already been mentioned that agro-business is the chief beneficiary of the current agro-food policy in Russia. Of course, the biggest representatives of this business are important actors in the formation of agro-food policy. In 1997-98, one of the biggest Russia banks, *SBS-Agro*, controlled the largest share of the agricultural budget, and accordingly impacted policy in its interest. The financial groups *Alfa* and *Menatep* also had a strong interest in agribusiness, especially in sugar imports. They also actively lobbied their interests before the government. Since the 1998 crisis, the array of major lobbyists has changed significantly, and it is difficult to say which actors play the major roles today.

Besides the giant lobbyists from agribusiness, there are also small and medium-sized firms with interests in agro-food policy, but little individual power to impact it. Lobbying organizations of these firms have been formed. The great majority of these organizations represent processors and traders, rather than farmers. The most successful of these groups so far are the Grain, Sugar, Tea, and Meat unions. Business and Producer's Associations (BPA) have begun to emerge since the privatization of the food-processing sector.

The Grain Union of Russia was the first, organized in 1994 by the federal corporation *Roskhleboprodukt*, the joint-stock company *Eksportkhleb*, *Mosoblkhleboprodukt* corporation, trading company *OGO*, the Russian Grain Exchange, Moscow Trade Exchange, and others. The main chartered goals of the Grain Union are to interact with the Government on the issues of grain market regulation; to elaborate and monitor laws and instructions concerning the grain business; to provide members of the union with information on grain market trends, etc. The Grain Union is open to membership by legal entities in grain purchase, storage, processing and trade, commodity exchanges, and other facets of the grain trade.

The Sugar Union was organized in 1996 for the effective resolution of the problems of the sugar industry and sugar market of the Russian Federation; the representation and protection of the interests of sugar plants and operators of sugar markets in governmental structures, social organizations, and other organizations, including those abroad; and the strengthening of united action and mutual assistance. Russian Sugar corporation and the joint-stock companies Lipetsk Sugar, Tula Sugar, *RosSakhar*, and *Alfa-Eco* are the main co-founders. The goal of the Sugar Union is to establish a sugar regime which favors domestic sugar producers. The introduction of high import tariffs in 1997 was the direct result of Sugar Union lobbying. The Sugar Union has agreements with many international sugar unions. The most important is with Ukraine, Russia's primary competitor in cheap sugar production. The Sugar Union unites a total 96 sugar plants throughout the country, and is one of the most successful in lobbying the government for the interests of its members.

The Meat Union was organized in Russia in November 1998 at the initiative of the Committee of Economic Security of the Meat and Meat-products Market, under the auspices of the Trade and Industry Chamber of the Russian Federation, the Association of Meat Processors of Russia, the Veterinary Association of Russia, the trade-industrial companies *Rosmiasomoltorg* and *Rosmiasomolprom*, the agro-industrial enterprise *Cherkizovskii* (Moscow), the share company *Samson* (St. Petersburg), and other well-known organizations. The total membership of the Meat Union is 272 enterprises, representing 72 regions. The Ministry of Agriculture supported the idea. The main tasks of the Meat Union are to promote favorable conditions for domestic producers and processors, to develop the infrastructure of the meat market, and to eliminate unscrupulous competition between domestic and foreign companies. The Meat Union intends to present regular proposals to the government. Among its first proposals was the reduction of import tariffs on raw meat for the processing industry, since imports became critical after the August financial crisis.

Other business associations are being formed, such as the Tea Union, the Alcoholic Beverages Producers Association, etc. Recently, the Union of Food Exporters was set up to promote exports of Russian food commodities. In late December 1999, a few big food companies in Russia set up the Export Union to promote Russian food exports and to lobby for exporter interests. The biggest Russian food producers, such as *Wimm Bill Dann* (dairy and juices), *Trade House of Smirnoff's Successors* (alcohol), and *Crystal* (alcohol) established the Union, and a number of lesser known Russian food and export companies have joined. The organizers explained the Union's establishment by the shrinking of the domestic food market in Russia, which has forced producers to seek new markets. After the 1998 crisis, the Ruble was devalued by a factor of four, promoting Russian exports, including food. Under current conditions, the main constraints on food exports, in the organizers' opinion, are created by an unsound tax policy. Therefore, the Union intends to attain tax concessions for food exporters. In addition, the Union will seek direct contacts with the western companies that control 80% of the world food market.

To a large extent, the business associations' influence on policy is concentrated on trade regulation. Studies show that the effective import tariff on agro-food commodities in Russia favors processors, but not farmers. Thus, for several years the sugar producers have managed to keep high import tariffs on white sugar and low tariffs for raw sugar, and meat processors insist on lowering raw meat import tariffs. Agribusiness is much better organized than farmers. They have capital and contacts among policy-makers, facilitating their lobbying capacity with governments and legislatures, on both the federal and the regional levels.

The current government supports the emergence and development of these business and producer's associations. In the outline of federal agro-food policy through 2010, which is being elaborated for the new Cabinet, the establishment of such unions is considered a priority of government tasks in the agro-food field. The government intends to extend some administrative functions to them. The Duma is drafting the legislation for these unions.

Research and Consulting Organizations

Research and consulting organizations have a certain influence on agrarian policy development. Agricultural research institutes work under the auspices of the Russian Academy of Agricultural Sciences (*RASN*) (the Presidium of *RASN* is a nest of ultra-radical left opposition, with most of its members belonging to the Communist Party). *RASN* unites 199 research institutes, 24 experimental agricultural stations, 47 selection and biotechnological centers, and the central agricultural library. *RASN* finances its institutes, and can thus influence their research and conclusions.

There are a few independent research institutions providing expertise for policy makers in the agro-food area. The Institute of Agrarian Issues and Informational Sciences (the Agrarian Institute) is one of the most important in this respect. Set up in 1991 by the liberal-oriented President of the Soviet Academy of Agricultural Sciences, Alexander Nikonov, it is the most liberal research institute, where the basic concepts and legal acts initiating agrarian reform in Russia were drafted. The agricultural division of Gaidar's Institute for the Economy in Transition (with a newly established Analytical Center for Agro-Food Economics) is a respected research institution that produces numerous recommendations for policy-makers. The Saratov Institute for Agricultural Economics is a regionally important research body.

The *RASN* has a network of economic institutes in the regions. Some of them, including the Novosibirsk, Rostov, and St. Petersburg institutes, have had a notable impact on regional agrarian policy. In 1997, the Foundation for Support of Agrarian Reform and Rural Development (*RosAgroFond*) was founded. *RosAgroFond* is famous for the development and dissemination of the Land Privatization and Farm Reorganization Model in Nizhny Novgorod. *RosAgroFond* provides legal and economic consultation to federal, regional and local administrations, farm directors, and other populations participating in agrarian reform. Similar consulting foundations were created in Orlovskaia, Nizhnegorodskaia, Rostovskaia and Volgogradskaia oblasts. Foundations for promoting agrarian reform are united into the Association of Agrarian Foundations, *AGRO*, founded in 1999.

The Impact of Globalization on Domestic Agro-food Policy

Globalization is a broad process in the contemporary world. We will consider the impact of two elements of this process on Russian agro-food policy - the WTO and the creation of a common agricultural market within the framework of the CIS.

For the last several years, accession to the WTO has remained a strategic objective of Russia. The necessity of WTO membership is determined by the tasks of further integration into the world economy, creation of more preferential terms of access to world markets, elimination of discriminatory conditions for domestic exporters, promotion of know-how transfers, and attraction of foreign investments. In mid-1992, the Russian Federation was granted the status of observer in the GATT, formally inheriting this status from the USSR, which had it since 1990. In June 1993, Russian President El'tsin gave the official government statement of Russia's intention to join this organization to the GATT Director General. This was the starting point in the long process of Russian accession. However, until 1996, the activity of the Russian government regarding WTO accession was led more by ideological motivations than by practical ones. Accession was considered a symbolic step towards the international economy, not a procedure for the elaboration of the most preferential terms of trade for domestic producers. This approach determined the numerous attempts to accelerate accession, to achieve it by a fixed date, and so on. In 1997, there was a real change in government activity: the government has started to seek guarantees of national benefits under minimum concessions, that is, minimum losses for domestic producers.

Russia's accession to the WTO provides an uneven balance of benefits and costs for the domestic export and import-substituting sectors (table 14.1). The agro-food sector is expected to be on the losing side in the short term, and that unavoidably impacts agro-food policy.

Table 14.1 The balance of benefits and losses from accession to the WTO for Russia's major export and import commodities

Neutral balance	Potential beneficiaries	Potential losers
Exports		
Crude oil and oil products	Ferrous metals (rolled metal, pipes, etc.)	
Natural gas	Mineral fertilizers	
Wood	Furs	
Cellulose and paper	Machinery and equipment	
Non-ferrous metals		
Seafood		
Imports		
Raw sugar	Services (the major branches)	Agricultural products (major items)
Pitch and polymers		Textile and clothes
		Alcohol and tobacco
		Footwear
		Cosmetics and perfumery
		Electronics
		Cars
		Medicine

Source: Biuro ekonomichekogo analiza (1998), 342.

Nevertheless, the Russian government keeps negotiating on accession. There are some contradictions with negotiating partners regarding bound tariffs, and the reference level of support. There is some continuing work on harmonizing sanitary and phytosanitary measures. However, so far there has been no explicit legislation issued in this connection.

The break-up of the USSR resulted in the creation of the Commonwealth of Independent States (CIS). In 1996, an Agreement on the Common Agro-Food Market (CAM) was drafted within the framework of the CIS. The Agreement was aimed at setting up a common market for agricultural and food commodities within the CIS, protecting the internal CAM from third-country imports, and promoting exports. To stabilize the CAM, a Common Agro-Food Reserve was supposed to be established, financed from the Fund on Orientation and Development. The last was to be formed from annual fees of the member countries, as high as 0.5% of the gross agricultural output for the previous year.

However, efforts to create a regional free trade area within the CIS framework have not been very successful, and are not a substitute for the WTO accession process. The slow development of the CAM generally follows the liberalization trend of the Agricultural Agreement of the WTO Uruguay Round. There is no risk that the CAM will become a closed regional market, well insulated from third countries. First of all, the member countries of the CAM tend to participate in other international trade agreements and associations, especially the WTO. Secondly, the CIS countries have neither the financial resources for high protectionism on the international level, nor the will for sufficient coordination of national agro-food policies with other CIS members. Moreover, the levels of market development in each country are too different for deep integration.

Another side of globalization is represented by foreign direct investment (FDI) in agriculture and agribusiness. Transnational corporations potentially play a significant role in domestic policy formation. However, Russia as yet has a rather insignificant share of FDI in this sector, and these corporations are only slightly represented in the market (table 14.2).

Table 14.2 Foreign direct investments in the agriculture and food industry (annually, in million US$)

	1995	1996	1997	1998
Agriculture	296.0	779.0	704.0	1473.0
Food industry	-	3.7	5.5	4.2

Source: Goskomstat; Journal of Economics, Higher School of Economics (1999), vol. 3, No. 4, 631; 633.

Thus, the global processes considered here have not yet had a very significant impact on domestic agro-food policy in Russia, although WTO accession could play an important role in the future. In contrast, integration within the CIS will have little direct influence on Russian policy.

Conclusion

Agro-food policy in Russia, as in the rest of the world, is formed under the influence of various interest groups, which have been actively institutionalized in recent years. Globalization still is not notably reflected in domestic policy. The major trends in the driving forces of agro-food policy in Russia are the following: first, the shift of policy-making from the federal to the regional level; second, growing concord among different groups within the agricultural establishment, especially regarding an increase in protectionism; third, emergence of agribusiness interest groups and formation of their institutions; fourth, weak representation of farmers' interest on the political level; and, finally, lack of faith in near-term recovery of the sector.

15 Agrarian Actors in the Localities

ZEMFIRA I. KALUGINA

Globalization and internationalization of production, structural changes in the world economy, and economic and financial crises in the world exercise an increasing influence over both the Russian economy as a whole and the development of its separate sectors. The economic reforms of the 1990s and foreign trade, including liberalization, have contributed to the openness of the Russian economy, and created certain preconditions for integration of the country into the world economic system. The disintegration of the world socialist system and of the USSR's united economic complex have sped up all these processes.

The Russian agricultural sector, an integral part of the economic system, underwent not unambiguous changes during these years. In this period, the following measures were undertaken: privatization of land, reorganization of the collective farms, formation of a multi-structural economy in the agricultural sector, and increase in freedom of managers and other economic actors. However, these measures have not resulted in the revival and increase of efficiency in agricultural production. The country was compelled to import a considerable share of its foodstuffs.

Besides a plunge in the volume of domestic production, the main reasons for the growth of food imports were the ruble's overvaluation in relation to the dollar and the low weighted rate of customs duties, averaging 15%, which was not a serious barrier to imports of foodstuffs and agricultural raw materials. In the mid-1990s, their growth achieved a critical mass. They made up more than one third of the commodity structure of the Russian Federation's imports;[1] for some products the share of imports reached 40% to 70%.[2]

---

[1] Goskomstat 1999b, 569.
[2] Shcherbak 1998, 7.

The financial crisis of August 1998 had an ambiguous effect on the development of the country's agricultural sector. On the one hand, it sharply reduced the capacity of the managers and other actors to buy foreign machinery, resources, and materials. On the other, it gave domestic producers a unique opportunity to occupy the vacant niche on the internal food market. In this period the instability of the ruble and booming consumer demand for Russian produce caused the prices of food products to shoot up. According to calculations of the Department of Regional Monitoring of the Ministry of Regional Policy, the cost of a basket of 25 basic food products increased more than 30% on average in September 1998. In particular, the prices of imported foodstuffs and goods manufactured from imported raw materials have risen by 50%. The decline in imports from the Russian market opened a market niche of about US$35bn, according to expert estimates, and that has resulted in the revival of production and the strengthening of Russian producer's position on the internal food market. Changing market conditions and conditions of management have required changes in agrarian actors' economic and social strategies.[3]

This article analyzes the main institutional transformations in the Russian agricultural sector during the 1990s, evaluates their social and economic consequences, and seeks to explain some of their failures. Attention is paid predominantly to the role of local actors. The paper is based on data from statistics, sociological surveys - conducted under the author's direction and with her participation in rural Siberia from 1991 to 1999, and secondary sources.

The Main Institutional Transformations in the Agricultural Sector, 1991-99

The Situation in the Agricultural Sector and Ideas for its Reform

At the end of the century, many of Russia's social problems, including that of food provision, remain unsolved. The rate of growth in food production in the 1980s was too low to provide a full and balanced diet for the national population. In a number of areas, food distribution was rationed. Attempts to improve the situation in the administrative-command system by superficial adjustments proved futile in the long run. The underlying reason

---

[3] Savchenko 2000, 4.

was that social and economic innovations such as intrafarm cost-benefit analysis, various types of contracts, intensive technologies etc., did not reach the heart of the problem. They yielded only short-lived improvements, and then only within specially chosen experimental farms, artificially created and enjoying conditions more favorable than elsewhere. After each campaign everything returned to usual. The socialist system rejected market elements alien to it. For the situation to be changed, radical reforms were needed. The radical economic transformation undertaken at the beginning of the 1990s was aimed at constructive changes in the national agricultural sector. It included land reform, reorganization of collective and state farms - the dominant form of socialist agriculture - and the development of autonomous private farms.

The main purposes of the land reform were land redistribution among economic agents, equal development of different forms of economic activity, and rational use of lands on Russia's territory. The Land Reform Law passed in December 1990 repudiated the state monopoly on land throughout the national territory and reinstated the institution of private ownership of land.[4] The right to private land ownership was established in the Constitution of the Russian Federation. But in the same year, 1990, the Second (Extraordinary) Congress of People's Deputies introduced a ten-year moratorium on the sale and purchase of land. This suspension remains in force despite decrees by the Russian president designed to protect citizens' constitutional rights to land and to cancel the moratorium.[5] Debates over the free sale and purchase of land continue.

At the end of December 1991, the Russian government provided for the reorganization of collective and state farms, and the order of their privatization.[6] These measures were meant to change the organizational and legal status of collective enterprises, giving workers the right to choose a form of entrepreneurship freely, and endowing them with shares of assets and land along with the right to exit from the collective enterprise without permission. The reorganization was to affect every collective enterprise, profitable or unprofitable. On this basis, various partnerships, joint stock companies, agricultural production cooperatives, privately run autonomous

---

[4] 'O zemel'noi reforme' (1992), in Rossisko-amerikanskii universitet, *Kak poluchit' zemliu? Sbornik osnovykh dokumentov po zemel'noi reforme v Rossii*, SP Lexica, Moscow, 19-24.
[5] 'O regulirovanii zemel'nykh otnoshenii i uskorenii realizatsii zemel'noi reformy', in *Sobranie Aktov Prezidenta i Pravitel'stva RF* (1993), No. 44; 'O realizatsii konstitutsionykh prav grazhdan na zemliu', in *Sobranie Aktov Prezidenta i Pravitel'stva RF* (1996), No. 121.
[6] 'O poriadke reorganizatsii kolkhozov i sovkhozov', in *Sobranie Postanovlenii Pravitel'stva RF* (1992), No. 1-2.

farms and their associations could be set up. The working collectives were allowed to maintain, if desired, the collective form of economic activity. Reorganization was to be completed by the end of 1992.

The development of a privately run, autonomous farm sector began with the adoption in December 1990 of the federal Law 'On Autonomous Farms', which laid the economic, social and legal foundations for the organization and activity of privately operated farms and their associations as a form of free enterprise run on the basis of economic gain.[7] Thus, in the early 1990s, the legislative basis for the formation in the agricultural sector of a mixed economy and for every rural worker's free choice of land management was established.

Trends in the Agricultural Economy during the Reform Process

Reorganization of collective agricultural enterprises The reorganization of collective and state farms was practically completed by the beginning of 1994, when 95% of collective enterprises had been re-registered. As a result of this reorganization, 66% of collective agricultural enterprises changed their organizational and legal status, and 34% exercised their right to retain their collective form. After reorganization, 300 open joint-stock companies appeared, 11,500 partnerships of all types, 19,000 agricultural cooperatives, 400 sideline farms of industrial and other institutions, 900 associations of autonomous farms, and 2,300 with other organizational forms. 3,600 state and 6,000 collective farms retained their previous status. State-owned enterprises made up 26.6% of the total; municipally-owned enterprises, 1.5%; privately owned enterprises, 66.8%; and enterprises of mixed ownership 5.1%.[8] Thus, the reorganization of collective enterprises was the first step towards the creation of a mixed agricultural economy based on equality of all forms of ownership and of land management.

Unfortunately, neither greater efficiency nor higher output resulted from this reorganization. Agricultural output and the share of agricultural enterprises - as opposed to household plots - contributing to it are in steady decline. While in 1990 agricultural enterprises accounted for 74% of total output, they produced only 41% in 1998 (table 15.1, 15.2, diagram 15.1).

---

[7] 'O krest'ianskom (fermerskom) khoziaistve' (1992), in Rossisko-amerikanskii universitet, *Kak poluchit' zemliu? Sbornik osnovykh dokumentov po zemel'noi reforme v Rossii*, SP Lexica, Moscow, 25-46.
[8] Goskomstat 1995b, 48-49; 57.

Table 15.1 Index of Russia's agricultural output by farm category, 1991-97 (comparable prices, percentage of previous year)

	All categories of farms	Collective enterprises	Household plots	Private farms
1991	95.5	91.0	108.7	-
1992	90.6	82.7	108.1	in 5.7 times
1993	95.6	90.9	102.7	166.7
1994	88.0	83.9	95.3	86.2
1995	92.0	84.6	103.4	97.4
1996	94.9	89.9	100.4	95.2
1997	101.3	102.4	99.2	126.2

Source: Goskomstat 1998b, 443.

Diagram 15.1 Percentage of different farm categories in the agricultural output of Russia in 1970-96 (in prices of that time)

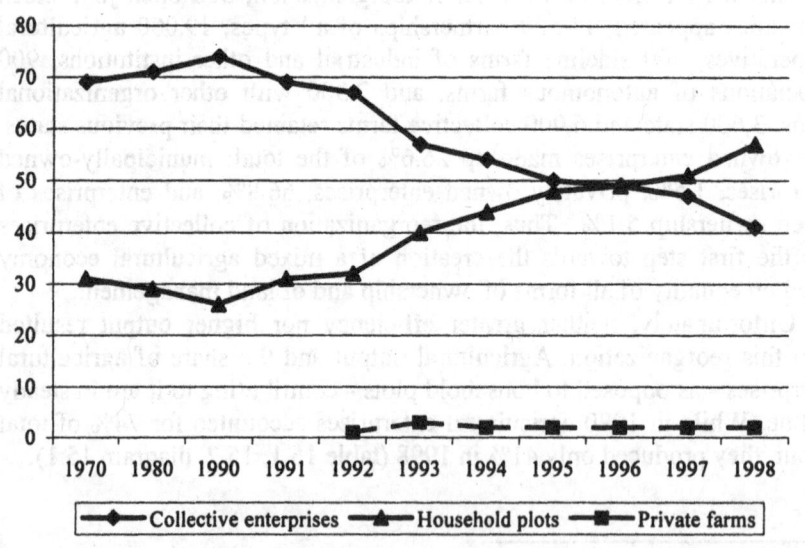

Sources: Goskomstat 1997b. 379; Goskomstat 1999b, 203.

The number of livestock and productivity in this category of agricultural enterprise continues to decrease. Most are in a critical economic position.

While at the end of 1991, they enjoyed 43% profitability, in 1995, it was -2%, and in 1996, -20.5%.[9]

Table 15.2 Structure of agricultural production in Russia by categories of farms (at prices of that time, in %)

	Household plots	Private farms	Collective enterprises
1990	26	-	74
1998	57	2	41

Source: Goskomstat 1997b, 379; Goskomstat 1999b, 203.

Specialists attribute this situation in Russian agriculture to the constantly increasing disparity between the prices of agricultural products and those of material-technical resources used for their production, extremely low state subsidies, low purchase prices, delays in the settlement of the accounts for products sold, and the monopoly of processing, procurement and service-supplying enterprises and organizations.[10] But in each Russian region some agricultural enterprises can be found that are successfully functioning under the current unfavorable conditions. Such farms have adjusted promptly to the new economic conditions by studying the market situation, identifying the most profitable channels through which to sell their products, restructuring their production according to market requirements, successfully developing the processing of agricultural products, and selling them through a network of their own stores, retail markets or trusted wholesale agents at better prices.

Some of these farms became founders of large commercial structures and have set up modern agro-industrial companies. They can become centers of scientific-technological progress in the countryside to show other

---

[9] Stroev 1997, 43.
[10] Khlystun 1997, 7.

farms how to work under market conditions. But such farms in Russia, according to experts' estimates, make up no more than 5-7% of the total.[11]

The development of privately run autonomous farms Since the adoption of the federal Law on Autonomous Farms and the reorganization of collective and state farms, Russian peasants have gained a real opportunity to become independent economic agents. The quantitative development of autonomous farms in Russia show that at the beginning of the reforms the country did possess a social base for the development of the private sector in the agricultural economy. Between 1991 and 1997, the number of privately-run farms grew to 279,000. But in 1994, their rate of growth began to decrease (table 15.3). And the process of bankruptcies and closures is increasing. In 1992, the number of closures was 5,100; in 1993, 19,100; and in 1994, 45,900. In the second half of 1994, the number of closures for the first time exceeded the number of newly created farms.[12]

Table 15.3 Autonomous farms and land plots allotted to them in Russia in 1991-98

	1991	1992	1993	1994	1995	1996	1997	1998
Autonomous farms (thousands)	4.4	49.0	182.8	270.0	179.2	280.1	278.6	274.3
Land plots allotted (thousands of hectares)	181	2068	7804	11342	11870	12011	12237	13045

Source: Goskomstat 1997b, 383; Goskomstat 1998a, 217.

Studies conducted in the country's regions show that the main causes of instability among autonomous farms in Russia are extremely high taxes, exorbitant prices for agricultural equipment, fuels and other resources, violations of owners' rights, low subsidies from the state, allotment of lands of low quality distant from the center of the settlement and the lack of

---

[11] Poshkus 1997, 14.
[12] Petrikov 1995, 108; Goskomstat 1995b, 53.

roads and communications.[13] Part of the failures must be attributed to subjective causes - to Russian peasants' lack of experience in independent economic activity, lack of knowledge, and unpreparedness to work under economic and social risk.

As of 1 January 1997, there were 279,000 autonomous farms with a land area of 12.2 million hectares (44 hectares per farm), compared with 280,000 autonomous farms as of 1 January 1996. Agricultural lands in autonomous farms occupy 11.3 million hectares (93% of allotted lands), including 8.3 million hectares (68%) of arable lands. Autonomous farmers occupied 5.3% of agricultural lands and 6.3% of arable lands in the Russian Federation. More than half of autonomous farms were of 20 hectares or less, and a fifth of 21-50 hectares. No more than 9% exceeded 100 hectares.[14] The share of autonomous farms in total agricultural output remains low and does not exceed 2%.

Back in 1991, when comparing the necessary conditions for the development of autonomous farms with those in fact at hand, we concluded that blanket decollectivization would be rash. Considering the public's mentality, the level of industrial potential, the legislative base, and the sociopolitical situation, and taking into account that for the transition to a market economy a long time would be needed, we reached the conclusion that in the foreseeable future, autonomous farms could not become a dominant form of agricultural production in the Russian countryside. It was possible to say with confidence only that the prerequisites existed for the establishment of a mixed agricultural economy, with autonomous farms as one of its sectors.[15] These predictions were fulfilled.

Development of part-time farming (household plots) Part-time farming (*Lichnoe podsobnoe khoziaistvo, LPKh*) is a specific segment of the agricultural economy based on the use of the resources and labor potential of rural families. Household plots as a special form of production under socialism had appeared at the end of the 1920s in the process of socialization of individual peasant farms, and were based on state ownership of the means of production, including land, and on the personal labor (without hired hands) of the plots' owners and their families.[16] In

---

[13] Petrikov 1995, 108; Kurtsev 1996.
[14] 'Sel'skoe khoziaistvo Rossii v 1996 godu. Ekonomicheskii obzor Goskomstata Rossii', in *APK: ekonomika, upravlenie* (1997), No. 3, 3-10, here 10.
[15] Kalugina 1991b.
[16] Kalugina 1991a.

1991, the household plots used in part-time farming were, in accordance with the Russian constitution, transferred to the ownership of the citizens. As a rule, the part-time farm is a sphere of secondary employment existing alongside primary employment in agriculture's public sector. In the process of agricultural transformation and partial disintegration of collective farming, with the protracted and complicated character of the establishment of new economic forms in the agro-industrial complex, the role of part-time farming as the most flexible, steady and self-regulating organizational-legal form of agricultural production has increased.

While in the public sector there has been a notable decline of agricultural output, on households' part-time farms, in contrast, it increased to make up in 1996 46% of total national output. At present, in a third of Russia's regions, households produce over 50% of agricultural products.[17] According to statistics from 1997, 16.4 million families in Russia have household plots, with a total area of 5.9 million hectares, or 0.36 hectares per household. In addition, 15.2 million households have land plots in collective gardens, with a total area of 1.3 million hectares, or 0.086 hectares per household. Collective kitchen gardens with a total area of 0.6 million hectares are used by 6.6 million households, amounting to 0.091 hectares per household On 1 January 1999, households had 9.9 million head of large cattle, 6.0 million dairy cows, 7.4 million pigs and 9.3 million sheep and goats combined.[18]

In 1995, however, there was stabilization or even reduction in the output of agricultural products on part-time farms. Thus, from January to August of 1995, these households produced 1.9 million tons of meat, 12.1 million tons of milk, and 7.5 billion eggs, constituting 98%, 99%, and 90% respectively of the level of production over the same period in 1994. In 1996, the number of various types of animals fell by 2-8%.[19] The trend toward a decline in household output has, in our view, several causes. One was the destruction of the production potential of collective enterprises, whose resources (fodder, seeds, agricultural equipment, transport vehicles, etc.) were given to part-time farms on easy terms. Moreover, rural families' financial opportunities have substantially diminished due to the lower standard of living, including depreciation of savings. Point three is that the labor potential of a rural family has practically been exhausted. Analysis of

---

[17] 'Sel'skoe khoziaistvo Rossii v 1996 godu. Ekonomicheskii obzor Goskomstata Rossii', in *APK: ekonomika, upravlenie* (1997), No. 3, 3-10, here 3.
[18] Goskomstat 1999a, 207, 218.
[19] Goskomstat 1995, 50; Goskomstat 1997a, 6.

the time budgets of the rural population has shown that many families are running their part-time farms at the limit of their physical power.[20]

At present, the legislative and economic prerequisites have been created for the development of part-time farms as an equal form of agricultural production and for their possible transformation into autonomous farms. First, the equality of all forms of agricultural production has been legislatively established, recognizing the full rights of part-time household farms in the agricultural sector. And labor collectives and individuals are granted the right to choose a form of production in accordance with their wishes, opportunities and needs. Second, all constraints on the number of animals held by a household have been removed. Third, according to current legislation, household land plots can be enlarged by up to one hectare from lands that are under the management of local councils. In addition, rural inhabitants who were granted land shares (agricultural workers, pensioners and some categories of workers in the social sphere) are entitled to use them for extension of their part-time farms. And, finally, according to the Russian constitution, land and other means of production can be privately owned.

Under these conditions, rural households have a choice: either to run their part-time farms in cooperation with other economic agents of the agro-industrial business and with the aid of collective enterprises, or to transform part-time farms into autonomous farms. The possibility of such a transformation is recognized by about 20% of rural respondents. Its base could thus be large. *LPKh* are an organizational form to which about a fourth of rural families are oriented. But over half of the surveyed rural families think it is impossible to transform part-time farms into autonomous farms because, they say, the former cannot do without aid from collective farms. Collective farms, even under difficult economic conditions, continue to give their workers various kinds of aid - young animals, seeds, agricultural equipment and transport vehicles - on privileged terms or free of charge.

The prospects for transforming part-time farms into autonomous farms are less favorable in the eyes of experts (professional and administrative workers in agriculture, N=566). No more than 2.9% of experts believe that part-time farms can be considered a way-station on the road to the autonomous private farm, while 61.2% believe that they can be successfully developed only in cooperation with collective enterprises.

---

[20] Artemov 1995.

In our view, the perpetuation of part-time farms of the old type is promoted by the existing order of taxation, which practically exempts household plots from income tax, because the land tax paid by part-time farms, due to its small amount, does not affect their profitability. Their profits are also substantially increased through use (free or on privileged terms) of the resources of collective enterprises. The position of part-time farms as a specific element in the non-official agricultural economy is understood by most of the rural population, and is reflected in its behavior. Rural people understand that the transition of part-time farms from the informal sector of the economy to the formal one will involve intense tax pressure and the cessation of aid from collective enterprises.

The role of part-time farms in the process of the establishment of a private sector in the agricultural economy is not unequivocal. Being developed along with, and to a substantial extent at the expense of, the resources and aid of collective enterprises, it perpetuates the old system of economic relations. But, on the other hand, it helps rural people to acquire skills of frugal and efficient management of land and develops in them social qualities required in a market economy such as a business-like character, entrepreneurship and independence. The characteristic features of part-time farmers and their families are freedom of activity, independence in economic decision-making and full economic responsibility for the results of their work. In other words, private part-time plots help shape economic agents of a new type.

Although at present most rural inhabitants do not dare to undertake operation of an autonomous farm, current realities (the decline of production in the public sector, very low wages in agriculture, irregular payments of salaries, increasing unemployment) are forcing them to expand the scale and commodity quality of their part-time farms, which, in size and functions, are approaching the autonomous farms. And the former collective and state farmers are willy-nilly becoming autonomous farmers.

These latent processes in the contemporary Russian countryside have so far remained outside of public debate, and thus need to be thoroughly researched. It is these processes, in our view, that can mold the trends and character of changes in the Russian countryside in the near and medium term. On balance, if judged by formal indicators, the planned transformations have achieved a certain purpose: the number of collective and state farms was reduced, and signs of a mixed economy and diverse forms of ownership have appeared. But what is the merit of these transformations and what is their social price? Here are some illustrations.

Socioeconomic Consequences of the Reforms (Paradoxes of Agricultural Reform)

The dynamics of the development of the three segments of the agricultural economy clearly show the first paradox of agricultural reform, which is the expansion of small commodity production. Contrary to the reformers' intentions, the leading sectors of agricultural production are now not autonomous farms or joint stock companies, but the part-time farms of rural dwellers. They have no means of mechanization, partly because of the lack of small equipment suitable for use on private plots being offered on the market, but mostly due to lack of resources for their purchase. The doubled production output and commercialization of this category of farms was due only to higher labor inputs from their owners and members of their families. But the expansion of small commodity production has many shortcomings - the economy becomes naturalized, there is a return to barter, the technological level of production declines, and environmental problems appear because requirements of agricultural technology are not met.

The second paradox in the current agricultural transformations is the inefficiency of the agricultural economy's capitalization. Policymakers themselves have had to admit that after reform, in place of an inefficient state sector of the economy, they got an inefficient private sector. In our view, the underlying cause was the formal character of the transformations. The organizational and legal status of collective and state farms was changed, but in essence, the economic relations remained the same. The position of workers in the system of relations of production remains practically unchanged. As most workers have never felt any difference between their previous state as employed workers and their present one as co-owners, no distinct change has occurred in their work motivation or pattern of behavior. In the Russian president's message to the Federal Assembly in 1997, it was noted that 'the established mutual rights and responsibilities between owners (stockholders) and managers (directors) were not observed. Directors often merely pushed the stockholders, even major ones, aside from important decisions in matters that were squarely in the area of the owners' competence'.[21] He stated that protection of stockholders' rights, the clear definition of stockholders' and managers' rights and responsibilities, and perfection of the mechanism of corporate

---

[21] The Message of the President of the Russian Federation to the Federal Assembly in *Novaia gazeta* (1997), 7 March.

management had been established as priority tasks for the government on which the course of reform in 1997 depended.

The economic mechanism by which peasants can exercise their rights of ownership to their shares of land and other assets is not yet in operation. As was found in our surveys of the Novosibirskaia oblast in 1998, over 80% of respondents had had no dividends on the shares of assets and land that they had handed over to agricultural enterprises for use. Most enterprises are in a bind, unable to pay dividends to their workers. This situation is typical of other regions of the country too.[22]

The third paradox of the reforms is that instead of developing in people a market mentality and behavior, they are in fact destroying their work motivation. The most vivid of these consequences are seen precisely in the agricultural sphere, with its gap between workers' desire for higher earnings and the diminishing ability of agricultural enterprises to reward their contribution. As things stand, the wages of agricultural workers are the lowest in the nation, less than 40% of the national average; they are below subsistence level and are systematically paid several months or more late. Moreover, the dependence of wages on work results and workers' qualifications has been destroyed. One third of rural workers said that the size of their remuneration did not depend on their enterprises' efficiency. Employment in the public sector has now ceased to be a primary source of income for rural workers. According to data from the 1997 survey (N=553) of the rural population, only 38% of respondents said that their wages were their primary source of livelihood (monetary and natural); 42% said it was their part-time farms.

Furthermore, the ability of agricultural enterprises to solve workers' social problems through their own resources and means has drastically decreased. Before reform, the distribution of many social services depended on employment. A worker could get from his enterprise free housing, a place for his children in a preschool institution, medical treatment at health resorts, and other social benefits. After reorganization, the collective and state farms were allowed to transfer responsibility for social and cultural services to the management of local governments, which, in turn, lacked sufficient financial resources and an appropriate material-technological base. This led to a substantial worsening of social service provision in the countryside.

These processes are at the core of a sharp decline in motivation for professional, high-quality and effective work, as well as of a drastic drop in

---

[22] Orlov and Uvarov 1997.

the prestige of work in the public sector, especially among rural youth. According to the 1997 survey, 31.9% of rural inhabitants would like not to work at all, if unemployment relief could provide a fairly adequate standard of living (replies of the type 'yes', 'rather yes than no'). Only three years back (in 1993, N=525), no more than 10.6% of rural respondents gave such answers to this item. In our view, this is a very alarming symptom. The destruction of the effective system of work remuneration has also been reflected in the attitudes toward work held by different social groups. Thus, over half (65.8%) of the respondents preferred a small but guaranteed income. Only 28.9% of those surveyed were not averse to high risk in exchange for high earnings. This situation makes people, on the one hand, gradually lose their self-confidence, and, on the other, get used to state paternalism. In other words, the emerging institutional space and the operating economic mechanism distort the system of individual values, decrease or destroy the instrumental value of work in the public sector of agricultural production, promote social apathy rather than developing a market mentality and behavior, strip the transformations in the agricultural sector of their social base, and hinder its modernization.

Finally, the fourth paradox is that the social result of all transformations in the agricultural sector was the impoverishment of the rural population, a degradation of rural social services due largely to their transfer from the books of the agricultural enterprises to the books of local councils. The latter have neither financial nor material and technical resources for maintaining and developing social and consumer facilities. Agricultural enterprises, being unprofitable, also are unable to finance them, so the growth rates of rural social infrastructure have greatly slowed (table 15.4).

Over the period of the reforms, the standard of living of the urban and rural population has sharply declined, including consumption of staple foods. Compared with 1985, per capita consumption of meat and meat products fell by 15%; that of dairy products and eggs, by about 20%; that of sugar and vegetables, by over 30%; that of oil, by 40%; that of fish, by about 60%. An increase was observed only in consumption of potatoes and baked products. In terms of the provision of food products, Russia receded from the 7th to the 40th position among the advanced nations of the world.

Table 15.4 Commissioning of social facilities in the Russian countryside

	1991-95, average a year	Percentage, compared to 1986-90	1996	Percentage compared to 1991-95
Housing, millions of square meters of floor space	10.3	53.6	7.8	75.7
Kindergarten places (in thousands)	29.0	25.2	6.0	20.7
High schools (places in thousands)	94.7	42.7	54.0	57.0
Clubs (places in thousands)	38.7	30.0	11.0	27.4
Hospitals (beds in thousands)	2.5	39.7	1.1	44.0
Dispensaries and out-patient institutions (visits per shift in thousands)	8.2	55.0	3.0	37.8

Source: Stroev 1997, 343.

According to *Goskomstat* data, in 1995, 54% of foods consumed by households were imported, using external loans for payment. According to this estimate, the average statistical citizen consumed in 1995, 2,300 calories per day, though, taking into account natural and climatic conditions, he needs not less than 3,200 calories. Deteriorating nutrition, among other factors, was reflected in the health of the population, the death rate and life expectancy.[23] The last indicator dropped from 68 years in 1990 to 62 in 1996.

A second consideration is that the economic decline of agricultural enterprises has led to persistent wage arrears. Thus from 1994 to August 1998, wage arrears in agriculture grew from 114% to 401%, i.e. by a factor of 3.5.[24] Moreover, in 1992-96, agricultural wages were the lowest in the nation. In 1992, they were 67% of the national average and then further declined to 48% in 1996. By the end of 1996, the purchasing power of average monthly pay in agriculture, as a percentage of the subsistence minimum, was 92% (in 1992, it had been 187%) while the national average was 190% of the subsistence minimum. Compared with a 49% total fall in

---

[23] Rutskoi and Radugin 1997.
[24] Goskomstat 1998, 311.

real wages in the national economy at large over the last five years, the real earnings of agricultural workers fell by 70%. Continued wage arrears aggravate rural poverty. According to data from monitoring the social and economic potential of families, the level of poverty in rural areas is in fact twice that in urban ones. In 1996, among the surveyed groups of the rural population, the number of families with average per capita incomes below the subsistence minimum was 50%.[25]

The situation is aggravated by the lack of prospects in the foreseeable future for improvement of material well-being. The social price that has to be paid for the reforms has led to disappointment and loss of confidence in the future. In recent sociological surveys of rural residents, over 60% of respondents said that their expectations that the reforms would lead to improvements were not met, and 20%, that they were met partially. Only a tenth said that they were met fully.

The Effect of the 17 August 1998 Financial Crisis on the Agricultural Sector

The August 1998 financial crisis affected all spheres of Russian society, including agriculture. In order to assess the effect of the financial crisis on the Russian agricultural sector, a special expert survey was conducted. The experts were participants in an exhibition, *ProdSib 98*, organized by the Siberian Fair in Novosibirsk in December 1998. The 91 surveyed experts represented different Russian regions, partner countries from the near and far abroad, and the cities of Moscow, St. Petersburg, Kaliningrad, and Novosibirsk. The experts included producers of foods, alcoholic and non-alcoholic beverages, packaging, equipment and raw materials, as well as wholesale and retail dealers, and suppliers of information services.

According to the experts, after the financial crisis, conditions in the country's food and agriculture complex deteriorated markedly. 45% noted such a decline, citing lower volumes of sales (34.9%), higher prices of raw materials (32.6%), products (18.6%) and input materials, including imported ones (14.0%), the instability of the financial situation (11.6%), the reduction of production capacities (9.3%), nonpayment (7.0%), and lower effective demand (4.7%). According to experts, effective demand by the population has a substantial influence on the prices of agricultural/food

---

[25] 'Sotsial'noe razvitie v sel'skoi mestnosti: problemy i tendentsii (ekonomicheskoe obozrenie)', in *APK: ekonomika, upravlenie* (1998), No. 2, 22-23.

products. Thus, one in two experts thinks that lower effective demand checks, in one way or other, the growth of prices, 17% hold the opposite viewpoint, and another 15% think that demand for the food of domestic producers has allowed them to raise their products' prices. About one out of five experts was uncertain about the relationship of prices to effective demand. Speaking of changes in the retail prices of products, 17% of experts thought they had not changed; one in ten was uncertain; the rest noted rises in the price of agricultural products ranging from 10% to 200%. They attributed price rises mainly to increases in the price of raw and other materials, industrial goods, energy resources and transport, to the need to reimburse financial losses, to wage increases, and to the instability of the financial situation.

An improvement in the situation of enterprises of the agro-food complex was noted by 15% of experts. The reported signs of improvement were higher sales (36.8% of respondents), greater consideration paid to domestic producers (15.8%), the appearance of new economic partners and clients (15.8%), diversification of products (5.3%), and a general improvement in the situation (5.3%). One out of four experts noted higher demand for products. As a sum total, evaluating changed demand for domestic products, the experts gave the following answers, as a percentage of the total:

No change	12.2
Sharp increase	36.7
Minor increase	21.1
Marked decrease	21.1
Uncertain	8.9

One in five experts thinks that the financial crisis of August 1998 had no perceptible effect on the agro-food complex, maintaining that the improvement was caused by seasonal sales of products.

Changes in the country's financial markets have caused a sharp drop in food imports, which, according to experts, has had both favorable (31% of answers) and negative consequences (5.7%). As benefits to agro-food markets experts noted (in diminishing order of the number of mentions): higher demand for domestic products, higher volumes of production, expanded opportunities for domestic producers, and lower competition. Half of the experts were sure that domestic producers could supply the needs of the population for food staples, while 16% thought this task beyond their power. One of four experts thought that only a few enterprises would be able to increase their output.

Already many enterprises working in the agro-food market have taken measures to increase output and diversify their goods or services. The most important measures are (in diminishing number of mentions): technological retooling, marketing development, improvement of product quality, competitive pricing, cost saving, product line diversification, manpower improvement, deepening of research, and other measures. Possible impediments include the instability of the financial market, the general situation in the country, inadequate government policies, the enterprise's poor financial standing and social disasters. One in ten experts is sure that nothing can disturb the implementation of his plan. About one in ten enterprises does nothing in this regard.

In an adverse situation, regional authorities sometimes try to regulate the agro-food market by administrative measures. But such attempts do not always succeed. The survey has shown that many experts think such measures (local taxes, fixed prices, constraints on the import and export of products to and from regions, a fixed maximum trade margin and numerous inspections and commissions) ineffective. The most effective reported measures of regulation were the creation of free economic zones, lower taxes, subsidies, organization of tenders, advertising campaigns, provision of credits and measures for the protection of home producers.

Actors in Agricultural Transformation at the Local Level[26]

All participants in economic activity can be grouped according to their degree of involvement and influence. These groups differ in their extent of integration, forms of involvement, and position in the new system of agricultural relations (table 1.5).

---

[26] Kalugina 1999a.

Table 15.5 Emerging types of economic agents (actors) in Russia's present agricultural sector

Classification basis	Type of economic agents (actors)
Degree of influence	Economic decision-makers Actors

Forms of involvement	Owners
	   Owners-proprietors
	   Owners-businessmen
	   Holders of part-time household farms
	Managers
	   Managers-shareholders
	   Hired managers
	Shareholders
	   Members of co-operatives, collective farms
	   Members of stock companies
	   Members of partnerships
	Employees
	   of enterprises of all forms of ownership

Degree of integration	Individuals Social groups Social organizations

Each of the above-mentioned groups of economic agents has a certain degree of freedom of economic activity, certain rights and duties, and a particular sphere of influence in the economy. The real status, functions and role of each group determine their economic behavior and position with respect to the ongoing reforms.

Drawing on the empirical studies we performed in 1997-99 in Novosibirskaia oblast,[27] we can draw the following conclusions: The nominal change in the status of economic agents in the agricultural sector did not lead to a radical change in rural people's economic thinking or to their adoption of market behavioral patterns. The emerging institutional environment distorts the former system of values by challenging or debasing the instrumental value of jobs in the public sector of agriculture, thus contributing more to social apathy than to market-relevant patterns of behavior, and stripping the reforms of their social base.

---

[27] Kalugina 1995; Kalugina 1996.

Although all agricultural enterprises seem to face similar conditions, they demonstrate fundamentally different strategies and ways of adaptation to the new social and economic realities. In the course of our study, we have discovered four dominant adaptation strategies used by agricultural enterprises in the changed institutional environment.[28]

The first model is that of an active market strategy, where enterprises follow a strategy of innovative adaptation of production and most families are oriented to improving or maintaining their present living standard. The second model is that of an economic strategy of conformity, comprising the adjustment of enterprises to compensate for changes in the external environment. The dominant strategy of families is one aimed at maintaining the present living level. The third model is that of mimicking the adaptation of enterprises, which is equivalent to the adjustment to a culture of deprivation, where families struggle to survive, or at the most to maintain the present living level; The last model is that of a passive economic strategy - which leads to the destruction of the enterprises and the forced orientation of families to securing their survival.

The choice and results of a particular adaptation strategy are determined to a great extent by the personality of the enterprise manager. The analysis has shown that the most successful enterprises are those in which the leader was not changed during the period of reorganization. The most successful companies are those headed by so-called 'red' directors, who do not approve of the present course of reforms from an ideological standpoint, but in practice act according to market models of economic behavior. In contrast, young leaders, while embracing and supporting the ongoing transformations, lack experience of practical work and find themselves helpless before the difficulties of the present economic environment. The role of the leader is now understood by rural people. According to 40% of people surveyed, the deterioration in the enterprises' economic situation is caused by the inadequate skills and erroneous actions of the leaders.

Conclusion

Institutional transformations in the Russian agricultural sector have had incoherent results. Positive results include expanded economic freedom, a mixed economy in agricultural production, revival of the institution of

---

[28] Kalugina 1999b.

private ownership (including land), emergence of a market in land, and the resurgence of social enterprise.

Negative results are the excessive expansion of the unofficial shadowy sector of the economy, the spread of informal, often criminal, networks, notably in the sphere of scarce budgetary resources,[29] and the local domination of unitary enterprises, monopolizing agricultural markets.

Under dramatically weakened state regulation, the role of regional and local actors in the formation and regulation of local food markets, legislation and coordination of the activity of agro-food enterprises has increased. Economic autonomy granted to agro-industrial economic agents has increased the role of managers and specialists in the formation of economic strategy and the choice of forms and ways of adaptation. But the deficiencies of the present economic mechanism impede the formation of new enterprises, and do not allow the country's agricultural sector to be modernized. Nevertheless, decentralization of agriculture encouraged new initiatives and the formation of new social networks and alliances aimed at establishing long-term ties between producers and consumers of agricultural products, and between immediate producers and processing enterprises. The August 1998 financial crisis, which drastically diminished the import of agricultural products, gave domestic producers a chance to occupy the vacated niche, but the development of the national agricultural sector is hindered by low effective demand, continued inequality in urban-rural exchange, deficiencies in the implementation of institutional changes, and other factors.

---

[29] Serova 1998, 589-602.

16 Industrial Managers' Aspirations Towards Foreign Markets: Motives, Methods and the Consequences for Companies

IGOR B. GURKOV

Since the fourfold fall of the ruble in the last quarter of 1998, Russian industries have received an unique impetus for both import substitution and export expansion. In 1999, the registered trade surplus of the Russian Federation reached US$32.2bn.[1] Russian exports of so-called 'strategic commodities' have already reshaped several important international markets.[2] The flow of Russian exports consists not only of commodities, however, but also of merchandise intended to fill the low-end niches in world markets. Most exports originate from locally-controlled Russian companies.

A number of studies suggest that most Russian industrial companies are controlled by their top management, especially by general directors (CEOs).[3] After the financial crisis of 1998, and the subsequent collapse of industrial conglomerates centered around major Moscow-based banks, Russian CEOs further strengthened their positions with respect to shareholders and other stakeholders.[4] This paper focuses precisely on this group of actors, namely, CEOs of locally-controlled Russian companies, as

---

[1] 'Emerging Markets Indicators', in *The Economist* (2000), 26 February, 138.
[2] See White 2000.
[3] Earle, Estrin and Leshchenko 1996; Blasi, Krumova and Kruse 1997; Gurkov 1998.
[4] Radygin 1999, 18.

such a group seldom becomes an object of analysis, and very rarely in terms of 'Transformation and Globalization'.

Our study is designed to serve as a link between macroeconomic and microeconomic studies on globalization and on its consequences for the Russian economy and Russian society.

In order to improve our understanding of the behavior of Russia CEOs as actors in globalization and transformation, we should address the following issues: first, what is the extent of aspirations towards international markets among CEOs of various Russian industries? Second, what are the initial (pre)conditions for such aspirations, in terms of perceived competitive positions and key competencies[5] of their companies? Third, how is expansion in international markets conjoined with other goals of top management? Fourth, how are CEOs' aspirations translated into real actions in terms of business innovations? Fifth, do export aspirations of CEOs affect their leadership styles?

We strongly believe that the study will also bring more insights on the broader questions about globalization, namely: How does globalization affect the actors? How do such actors respond to globalization?[6]

In addition, the inquiry into a 'subjective' side of globalization may also produce valuable insights into its institutional aspects. Indeed, transformations of production and management systems constitute the background for implementation of changes in business institutions. Without such transformations, any new business institutions will serve only as a facade, improving the image but possibly damaging the health of society.

We also assume that our study will be of an exploratory nature, as the empirical evidence on corporate management in Russian exporters is still rather fragmented, thus limiting broad theoretical constructions.

---

[5] We follow the distinction between key and core competences of the firm common in the resource-based theory of competitive advantage (Wernerfelt 1984; Hamel and Prahalad 1994; Grant 1991). For example, Bowman and Faulkner argue that '[k]ey competences are those required by any firm to be a serious and successful player in a particular market. Core competences are what the firm happens to be good at. Hence, key competences are derived from an understanding of the requirements to compete in a particular market arena, whereas core competences are firm-specific'. Bowman and Faulkner 1997, 35.

[6] See: Sklair 1996.

Research Design

The Sample

In the present paper, we address these issues using the results of a large-scale survey of Russian company managers. Between October and December 1998, in the direct aftermath of the financial collapse, we conducted a survey which embraced 742 CEOs and 1,402 senior and middle-level managers of Russian companies. Each respondent came from a different company. The respondents represented companies of all legal forms in the main Russian industries, situated in 78 Russian regions.

Research Instruments

The main research instrument was a questionnaire consisting of several blocks corresponding to the goals of the study.

To map the overall assessment of the company situation, we used two instruments. First, managers were asked to assess the financial situation of their firm on a five-point scale ranging from 'close to bankruptcy' to 'perfect' and to compare the present situation with the situation a year ago (again on a five-point scale ranging from 'much deteriorated' to 'much improved'). Second, managers were asked to indicate the main factors affecting day-to-day operations (e.g., 'underutilization of capacity', 'high debts', 'conflicts within the top management', 'conflicts between managers and workers').

To map the spread of aspirations towards international markets and to relate this goal to other goals of the top management, we asked managers to indicate an unspecified number of the most visible goals of the top management. We listed nine main possible goals (from production at world standards to maximizing personal benefits) and allowed managers to add to the list of goals.

To reveal the inner logic of internationalization we asked CEOs to indicate the relative position of their companies, in particular aspects of competitiveness (cost level, quality, price level and some other measures). We used here a five-point scale, ranging from one - 'much worse' to five - 'much better'. The reliability of that instrument (Cronbach's alpha[7]) is 0.8112. To depict the level of 'key competencies of the firm', CEOs were

---

[7] For a formal description of this and other statistical techniques used in the study, see the technical appendix.

asked to assess the perceived qualification level of the key staff in the main line and functional departments on a five-point scale, ranging from one - 'unacceptably low' to five - 'quite high'. The reliability of that instrument (Cronbach's alpha) is 0.8188.

To see how CEOs' aspirations are translated into real actions in terms of process and product innovations, we asked managers to report on the measures to improve business performance which had been undertaken in their companies. We offered managers a list of 16 measures with the option to add to the list. We used here the following two-pole scale: minus two = 'negative results', minus one = 'no results', zero = 'no measure', plus one = 'some positive effects', plus two = 'great positive effects'. The reliability coefficient of this instrument (Cronbach's alpha) is 0.9129. We also asked managers to indicate which type of staff members their companies needed most, which programs of management retraining had been offered to company managers in the past two years, and which type of retraining was planned now.

Finally, CEOs were asked to indicate four groups of management qualities: first, qualities that reflect their personal leadership styles; second, qualities that are perceived as missing in their personal leadership styles; third, qualities that are believed to be necessary for middle managers; fourth, qualities in which their middle managers are greatly lacking.

This group of questions was inspired by the work of Kouzes and Posner.[8] We also added questions about the main line of business, the size of the company (in terms of sales volume and number of personnel), the location, and the ownership status of the company.

Findings

Aspirations Towards Foreign Markets within the Sets of a Company's Goals

First, we selected the fractions of Russian companies in various industries whose top managers aspire towards capturing entrance onto world markets (see table 16.1).

---

[8] Kouzes and Posner 1995.

Table 16.1 Percentage of companies having expressed export orientation in various industries

Line of business (industry)	Percentage	Number of respondents
Mining	44	85
Electrical energy	19	13
Timber	42	66
Chemicals and refining	35	102
Metallurgy (ferrous and non-ferrous)	31	42
Machine-building	44	276
Electronics	37	129
Food processing	13	141
Textile and clothing	14	110
Construction and construction materials	11	201
Retail trade and catering	9	118
Wholesale trade	16	85
Information services (marketing, advertising, etc.)	13	85
Financial and insurance services	24	38
Transportation	18	125
Others	25	302
Total	25	2018

On average, 25% of Russian companies are oriented towards international markets. The greatest interest in exports was expressed by CEOs of companies in mining, the timber industry, the chemical industry and in ferrous and non-ferrous metallurgy. These industries indeed account for the lion's share of total Russian exports. We may also, however, observe a strong predilection for export activities among top managers of Russian machine-building and electronic companies. Thus, Russian middle-tech is still hoping to exploit a believed export potential.

We also found that while in most industries size does not significantly affect the export aspirations of CEOs, in machine-building and electronics there is a strong positive relationship between size and export orientation. Among the largest machine-building companies (more than 3,000 employees), export orientation was recorded for 61% of companies; among the largest electronic companies, for 65%.

It is important to note that orientation towards foreign markets does not depend on assessments of the company's current performance. In 23% of companies whose situation was assessed by their own managers as 'bankrupt', and in 30% of companies whose situation was assessed by their own managers as 'good', the top management cited exports among its main goals.

The next step in our analysis was to identify how the learning of international markets corresponds to other goals of the top management. We used here correlation analysis (see table 16.2).

Table 16.2 Correlation between the main goals of the top management

Variable	1	2	3	4	5	6	7
World standards of quality	1.000						
Maintaining the level of employment	-0.084	1.000					
Maintaining wages	0.033	0.103**	1.000				
Increasing the firm's market value	-0.049*	-0.114**	0.083*	1.000			
Supporting the company's business reputation	0.306**	0.085**	0.097*	0.074**	1.000		
Strengthening the position on domestic markets	0.098**	-0.101**	0.007	0.049*	0.045*	1.000	
Gaining acquaintance with international markets	0.112**	-0.052*	0.019	0.012	-0.010	0.092**	1.000

Note: * two-tailed significance < 0.05; ** two-tailed significance < 0.01

From table 16.2 we can clearly see that 'gaining acquaintance of international markets' is strongly correlated with two other goals of the top management: 'improving the level of quality' and 'expanding on domestic markets'. At the same time, the gaining acquaintance of international markets does not coincide with such goals as 'support of market reputation', 'increase of company's value', and 'wage increase'. Moreover, acquainting oneself with international markets is strongly opposed to the goal of 'maintaining the employment level'. All the previously mentioned correlations are significant at the 0.05 level.

What are the most important results of the correlation analysis? The close relationship between international aspirations and quality improvement signifies that Russian top managers have finally recognized the key condition for successful international competition - meeting world quality standards. This result is trivial. However, the other - and more surprising - results are the insignificant correlation between 'export orientation' and such a goal as 'maintaining the company's business reputation'; and the very significant correlation between 'business reputation' and 'improving the level of quality'. We consider this a sign of the relative maturity of the globalization process in Russia. Not all exports are viewed nowadays as respectable in and of themselves. Instead, the high quality of products and services, displayed either on domestic or international markets, serves as the main symbol of a reputable company.

In the preceding analysis, we dealt with a uniform set of respondents. We should, however, be aware of possible misinterpretations and biases in the answers of middle managers when they report on their perceptions of CEOs' behavior. Thus, in the next steps of the analysis, we will rely solely on the responses of 740 surveyed CEOs.

First, we compared the sets of goals stressed by two groups of CEOs - export-oriented and domestically oriented (see table 16.3). The data presented in table 15.3 reflect even more spectacular differences between export-oriented and domestically oriented CEOs. Almost four-fifths of export-oriented CEOs are preoccupied with constant quality improvement, while only one-third of domestically oriented Russian CEOs consider world quality standards a feasible goal.

We also see that the close attention of export-oriented CEOs to quality problems enables them to emphasize so ambitious a goal as capturing domestic markets. Two additional differences concern such goals as 'maintaining employees' compensation' and 'maximization of the company's value'. Surprisingly, export-oriented CEOs are more persistent in the pursuit of both goals than their domestically oriented colleagues.

Table 16.3 Main goals of CEOs self-assessment (in %)

	Export-oriented CEOs	Other CEOs	Two-tailed significance of mean differences
Global quality standards	80	37	0.000
Maintaining the level of employment	57	61	0.418
High wages for employees	34	26	0.082
Maximization of the company's value	18	12	0.086
Improvement of business reputation	66	65	0.788
Strengthening the position on domestic markets	73	59	0.099

Pre-conditions for Export Orientation

What are the preconditions for the top management's adoption of an export orientation? There are two plausible answers: a perception of the company's superior competitiveness, or particular problems that force Russian companies to export at 'any price'.

We examined both prepositions. First, we compared perceived competitiveness in terms of its three principal components: price, costs and quality. The comparison was performed between export-oriented and domestically oriented companies across all the surveyed industries (see table 16.4).

Table 16.4 The comparison of perceived competitiveness between export-oriented and domestically oriented companies in various industries (export-oriented/ domestically oriented)

Line of business (industry)	Cost	Price	Quality
Mining	3.25/3.40	3.50/3.10	3.50/3.20
Electrical energy	2.60/3.29	3.00/3.14	3.40/3.43
Timber	3.70/2.86	3.50/3.50	3.91/3.87
Chemistry and refining	3.50/2.81	3.33/3.29	3.50/3.81
Metallurgy (ferrous and non-ferrous)	3.67/3.10	3.33/3.10	4.00/3.89

table 16.4 cdt...

Line of business (industry)	Cost	Price	Quality
Machine-building	2.84/2.85	3.29/3.08	3.82/3.62
Electronics	3.20/2.90	3.50/3.48	3.81/3.33
Food processing	3.14/2.70	3.00/2.95	4.00/3.62
Textile and clothing	3.20/3.00	4.20/3.24	4.40/3.85
Construction and construction materials	3.25/2.96	3.08/3.37	4.08/3.62
Total	3.10/2.96	3.32/3.27	3.75/3.65

Note: The scale used was: one = much worse than competitors, three = like competitors, five = much better than competitors.

In general, Russian CEOs of both export-oriented and domestically oriented companies believe strongly in the superior quality of their goods and services. Even CEOs in the Russian textile industry, whose total output remains at 10% of its level in 1990, still perceive their goods as superior to imports. This 'systemic bias' in quality perception is clearly visible for all the surveyed industries. However, in respect to price and, especially, cost level, the answers of Russian CEOs present quite a different picture. The majority of domestically oriented companies in timber, machine-building, electronics and food-processing accept that they are forced to set competitive prices with an inadequate cost structure. This results in chronic losses and the general insolvency of companies in those industries. On the other hand, export-oriented companies in all the previously mentioned industries except electric energy and machine-building are striving to compete internationally from a much stronger position. We should remember, however, that the sharp ruble devaluation reduced the 'domestic components of costs', such as equipment depreciation, domestically procured supplies and, especially, labor costs. For most Russian industries, this was sufficient to regain cost competitiveness on the world market. The difference between export-oriented and domestically oriented companies in perceived cost level is crucial in food-processing, electronics, timber and metallurgy due to the different signals they respond to.

To test the second preposition, we compared CEOs' perceptions of the main problems confronting their businesses (e.g., high debt, conflicts between workers and the company management, conflicts within the top management). One result of our analysis is that the widespread belief that Russians 'export at any cost' is not true for the majority of Russian industries. One particular exception to this is the Russian machine-building industry, which was unable to regain cost competitiveness, but continues to strive for exports. As a result, the surveyed export-oriented Russian machine-building companies are not only more burdened with accumulated debts than their domestically oriented counterparts, but are also more deeply involved in various conflicts between workers and the management.

With all caution about the self-reported competitiveness level of Russian export-oriented companies, we may derive a general conclusion: Aspirations towards foreign markets are rooted in the perception that goods and services are sufficiently competitive in terms of price, cost and quality. Russian companies are nowadays persistently searching for competitive advantage, but such a search is bounded by the clear economic rationality of current export operations.

An additional dimension of competitiveness, besides price, costs and quality, is 'key competencies'. These may be estimated through CEOs' assessment of the skills and qualifications of the key personnel. In this respect, we compared such assessments for export-oriented and domestically oriented companies (see table 16.5).

Table 16.5 Assessment by CEOs of the qualifications of the key personnel

Department (level)	Export-oriented	Domestically oriented	Two-tailed significance
Middle level - shop managers	3.41	3.47	0.408
Foremen	3.11	3.27	0.063
Auxiliary services	3.45	3.42	0.792
R&D	3.57	3.49	0.360
Accounting and finance office	3.29	3.52	0.004
Supply	3.10	3.20	0.218
Marketing	2.97	3.01	0.641
Personnel and salary office	3.21	3.27	0.476

Note: The scale used was: one = 'unacceptably low', three = 'satisfactory', five = 'quite high'.

For most of the selected groups of personnel, there are no significant differences between export-oriented and domestically oriented companies.

However, the qualifications of two groups are rated lower in export-oriented companies - the competence of foremen and the expertise of accounting and financial officers.

The lower grades given to foremen in export-oriented companies raise doubts about the validity of CEOs' beliefs in the superior quality of their firms' goods and services. At least it marks the 'internal price' in Russian companies of keeping quality up to world standards. The lower assessment of accounting and financial officers in export-oriented companies reveals the higher requirements imposed by export operations on cost accounting and management of cash flows.

It was also proposed that export orientation changes CEOs' preferences regarding the priority of staffing for various functional departments. This preposition was tested using T-tests (see table 16.6).

Table 16.6 'List of needed specialists' (percentages of CEOs bold-faced)

Area	Export-oriented	Domestically-oriented	Two-tailed significance
Financial management	48	38	0.011
Marketing	66	48	0.000
Human resource management	24	19	0.152
Business planning	46	37	0.057
Law	43	44	0.801

Besides financial officers, who are needed in almost half of the surveyed export-oriented companies, we see a desperate search for marketers and business planners. The higher demand for business planners in export-oriented companies seems natural, as export operations prolong the time horizon of the firm. However, the very high demand for marketers (two-thirds of export-oriented companies have job postings for such positions) may indicate that export-oriented companies are indeed involved in deeper and broader marketing ventures. This proposition is tested in the next section of the paper.

Maintaining Competitiveness - Market Strategies and Business Innovations

Maintaining and strengthening competitiveness on the level of world markets usually requires constant innovations in marketing and organization.[9] Thus, we compared the surveyed companies in terms of the frequencies of measures to improve business performance (see table 16.7).

Table 16.7 Measures to improve business performance (percentage of companies implementing such measures in the past two years)

Measures	Export-oriented	Domestically oriented	Two-tailed sign. of mean differences
Quality improvement	87	82	0.276
Cost reduction	83	80	0.423
Price reduction	60	57	0.536
Modified production	77	55	0.008
New production	75	69	0.000
Improved marketing	86	76	0.009
New markets	84	63	0.000
New sale channels in existing markets	77	67	0.031
New forms of cooperation with suppliers	79	69	0.027
Cooperation with competitors	49	38	0.029
Increased advertising budgets	59	51	0.110
Advertising forms changed	55	44	0.029
Managers are retrained	62	53	0.061
Management consultants invited	40	28	0.010

In all Russian companies, there are simultaneous attempts to improve quality and to reduce costs. In this respect, export-oriented companies do not differ from domestically oriented companies. The principal difference is how they realize such attempts. Export-oriented companies are ahead of their domestically oriented counterparts in particular marketing measures: launching modified or completely new production; testing new sales

---

[9] See Denton 1999.

channels; searching for new forms of partnerships with suppliers; transforming methods of advertising. In addition, export-oriented companies are more eager to cooperate with their counterparts in similar lines of business.

We should also stress that in their pursuit of management excellence, Russian export-oriented companies rely heavily on management retraining and business consulting. In this connection, it is interesting to see the preference of export- and domestically oriented companies for different forms of management retraining (see table 16.8).

Table 16.8 Participation of company managers and key specialists in various retraining activities in the past two years (in %)

Type of program	Export-oriented	Domestically-oriented	Two-tailed difference
One-day seminars	65	63	0.530
Short programs (up to one month)	66	61	0.240
On-site training in Russian companies	10	14	0.153
On-site training in foreign companies	30	19	0.014
Long-term retraining programs (one to two years)	16	11	0.095
Russian MBA programs	15	14	0.668
Foreign MBA programs	16	7	0.005
Presidential Management Initiative	28	15	0.002
Never participated in retraining programs	10	11	0.728

First at all, the proportion of CEOs who cited the participation of managers in various forms of retraining is much higher than the share of CEOs who stressed retraining as a means to improve business performance. This shows that not all forms of retraining are perceived as contributing to business excellence. Some are viewed as merely a fashion or just another form of collective leisure. CEOs of export-oriented companies, however, are clearly ahead of their domestically oriented colleagues in organizing foreign-oriented retraining. Almost a third of export-oriented companies had used the opportunity in the past two years to send their managers abroad for on-site training. Export-oriented companies also demonstrated greater interest in the Federal Retraining Program, which includes foreign on-site training for industry managers. We should also stress that on-site training in foreign companies is perceived by all Russian CEOs as the most effective method of management retraining. Among the companies that have tested it in the past two years, more than 40% are willing to sponsor projects of that kind.

Export Aspirations and Leadership Style

The final point in our analysis was to test the proposition that export aspirations of Russian managers are rooted somehow in their leadership styles and preferences. We compared again export-oriented and domestically oriented companies in terms of the four sets of questions: First, the perceived characteristics of personal leadership style; second, opinions about the attributes of a CEO that are necessary under present Russian business conditions; third, opinions about the attributes of middle managers that are necessary under present Russian business conditions; fourth, qualities perceived to be lacking in middle managers of the firm.

Here our results were mixed. CEOs of export-oriented and domestically oriented companies significantly differ in their portrayal of 'an ideal CEO' (see table 16.9). Export-oriented CEOs have more praise for quick decision-making and team-building, and have received greater exposure to the modern Western model of the CEO as coach and facilitator. Export-oriented CEOs put greater emphasis on conflict prevention and the transfer of knowledge from a CEO to middle managers. In this respect, we see the significant departure of export-oriented CEOs from the traditional Russian model of the General Director.

Despite the differences in 'model leadership', however, export-oriented and domestically oriented CEOs do not differ in their self-description. Both groups stress such personal strengths as 'quick decision-making', 'the ability to take responsibility for one's own actions' and 'team-building skills'.[10] At the same time, all the CEOs surveyed singled out their weaknesses as insufficient knowledge of legislation and finances, and poor skills in conflict prevention and resolution. The only statistically significant difference here concerns communication skills. About 57% of export-oriented CEOs firmly believe that 'establishing relationships outside the company' is their strong point, but only 49% of domestically oriented CEOs have confidence in their interpersonal skills.

---

[10] Gurkov and Maital 1999.

Table 16.9 An ideal CEO according to Russian CEOs (in %)

Quality	Export-oriented	Domestically oriented	Two-tailed significance
In-depth knowledge of company operations	52	46	0.233
Quick assessment of the situation	65	63	0.567
Quick decision-making	75	65	0.022
Knowledge of finances	73	70	0.499
Knowledge of business legislation	41	41	0.962
Ability to establish contacts outside the company	66	58	0.065
Ability to bear responsibility	62	52	0.029
Ability to predict conflicts	35	25	0.018
Ability to resolve conflicts	19	17	0.463
Willingness to transfer his/her knowledge	17	9	0.027
Team-building skills	75	66	0.032
Ability to assess the performance of subordinates accurately	28	23	0.184
Tact	16	17	0.729

Note: Multiple answers were allowed.

As export-oriented and domestically oriented CEOs disagreed on the portrait of 'an ideal CEO' but assessed their own strengths and weaknesses in a like manner, we might expect that the two groups would differ in their description of 'an ideal middle manager', but would experience the same problems in dealing with them in real life. The data support such a proposition, but with important corrections (see table 16.10).

Indeed, in reality both export-oriented and domestically oriented CEOs complain of the same weaknesses of middle managers: their unwillingness to show initiative; their inability to accept responsibility; poor work discipline; and insufficient professional knowledge.

Table 16.10 Ideal qualities and qualities lacking in middle managers according to CEOs (in %)

	Ideal Qualities		Qualities Lacking	
Qualities (skills)	Export-oriented	Domestically oriented	Export-oriented	Domestically oriented
Professional knowledge	90	86	40	38
Willingness to show initiative	66	62	63	57
Ability for teamwork	67*	57*	28	23
Obeying orders	56	53	39*	31*
Quick assessment of the situation	41*	52*	37	34
Ability to acquire new skills	51	45	30	29
Ability to bear responsibility	42	40	46	39
Ability to establish contacts outside the company	30*	40*	27	26
Team-building skills	29	26	17*	11*
Willingness to mentor subordinates	10	12	10	6
Ability to predict conflicts	9	11	10	14
Ability to resolve conflicts	3*	6*	8	9
Willingness to teach colleagues	7	6	10	6
Tact	4	6	6	7

Note: * marks the difference at 0.10 significance between the two groups of companies.

In general, export-oriented CEOs are even more critical of their direct subordinates. Undoubtedly, export-oriented CEOs have more contacts with foreign companies and thus a higher 'reference point' for assessment of middle managers. At the same time, export-oriented CEOs, painting the portrait of 'an ideal middle manager', revealed their own highly authoritarian leadership preferences. Indeed, export-oriented CEOs accorded priority to professional knowledge, teamwork and discipline among their subordinates, but did not value independent decision making on the part of middle managers. They also attached little importance to the actions of middle managers as leaders. Fewer than a third of export-oriented CEOs value the team-building skills of middle managers, while such functions of middle managers as coaching, mentoring and conflict resolution are neglected completely.

We may conclude that export orientation makes little impression on the leadership style of Russian CEOs. On the one hand, they share very advanced ideas about the leader as a team-builder, trainer and facilitator. They are also deeply dissatisfied with the professional qualities of middle managers. On the other hand, in reality, export-oriented CEOs exhibit all the peculiarities of the traditional Russian authoritarian management style, with no support for independent decision-making by middle managers. It seems that aspirations towards foreign markets and the resulting perceived necessity to improve management efficiency leads nowadays in Russia to higher centralization of decision-making.

Conclusions

Let us first recapitulate our main findings briefly. A quarter of Russian companies are now looking towards foreign markets as outlets for their goods and services. That proportion is much higher in the energy and raw materials sectors, but also in Russian 'middle-tech' (machine-building and electronics).

Export aspirations arise in response to a 'window of opportunity' created by the perceived price competitiveness of Russian goods on foreign markets. Profitability considerations play a subordinate role, and there is a high probability that many Russian machine-building exporters practice dumping.

Nevertheless, export-oriented companies are more exposed to foreign management practices. On-site training in foreign companies is believed to be the best way to enhance management techniques, and Russian export-oriented companies place much emphasis on the transfer of technological and management know-how, either from abroad or from local management consultants.

Export aspirations are also rooted in previous experience in reconstructing marketing management and techniques. Great attention is paid to increasing cooperation along the value chain, and to exploring the potential of advertising. Export-oriented companies also tended to be far-sighted, intensively recruiting business planners.

Russian export-oriented CEOs are familiar with modern management fashions in executive leadership. But such ideas have not (yet?) been transformed into real changes in leadership patterns and preferences. Management in Russian export-oriented companies remains highly centralized and authoritarian.

So far as the overall response to globalization is concerned, we may conclude that Russian CEOs see globalization as a two-edged sword. In 1992-93, they were shocked by the massive influx of imported goods and services onto most domestic markets. Only a few sectors, such as electrical energy and basic construction materials, have had 'natural protection' against foreign competition. However, nowadays, Russian CEOs see imports as inevitable challenges and even as benchmarks for their own goods and services. The ruble depreciation improved the price competitiveness of Russian production. We cannot talk about 'revenge', but Russian oil, timber, ferrous and non-ferrous metallurgy play an important role in shaping the world commodity markets. As a result, to a great extent, Russian CEOs support globalization.

We cannot, however, derive a definitive conclusion about another question: Do Russian CEOs support the institutional changes that accompany globalization? At the micro-economic level, institutional changes should manifest themselves in new leadership patterns and preferences. Such new leadership patterns are absent in export-oriented Russian companies. In contrast, CEOs believe the efficiency of management systems may be maintained by a greater concentration of power and by centralization of decision-making authority. This doctrine is wrong, for CEOs themselves cited their incompetence in the financial and legal aspects of modern business. Moreover, export orientation does not automatically lead to superior financial performance or eliminate the usual business problems. Inasmuch as successes of export-oriented companies will be attributed mostly to unique business circumstances and/or to the dexterity of their CEOs, the superiority of new management forms and systems, occasionally borrowed or imitated from foreign partners, cannot be proved. As a result, future successes of Russian exporters will not make Russian CEOs as a group more receptive and supportive of institutional changes brought by globalization.

Technical Appendix

Correlation

It is used to estimate the strength of a linear relationship between two variables x and y. The correlation procedure calculates Pearson's pair correlation coefficient according to the formula: $r = \dfrac{\sum_{i=1}^{N}(x_i - \bar{x})(y_i - \bar{y})}{(N-1)S_x S_y}$, where N is the number of cases, $\bar{x}, \bar{y}, S_x, S_y$ - means and standard deviations of x and y.

Coefficient r rises from -1 to 1. If it is close to 0 there is no relationship between x and y. When the coefficient r is close to 1, we may speculate about the strong positive relationship between the two variables. When the coefficient r is close to -1, we may speculate about the strong negative relationship between the two variables.

Significance Level

A great number of statistical techniques, including correlations and T-tests, also include calculation of a so-called 'significance level', denoted by p, which means the probability of obtaining coefficients if there is indeed no linear relationship between variables. If $p < 0.05$, the chances are 20 to 1 that our statistical techniques have really discovered a significant relationship between variables.

T-Test

A t-test is used to test the hypothesis that the averages of some variable U in two different groups are the same. Groups are defined by choosing two different values of another variable V.

For t-testing, two statistics can be used:

- the separate variance estimate statistic, when we expect the variances in two groups to be different;

$$t - \text{value} = \dfrac{\bar{x}_1 - \bar{x}_2}{\sqrt{\dfrac{S_1^2}{N_1} + \dfrac{S_2^2}{N_2}}}, \text{ where } \bar{x}_i - \text{mean}, S_i^2 - \text{variation},$$

N_i – number of cases in group i

- the pooled variance estimate statistic – when we expect the variances in two groups to be the same;

$$t\text{-value} = \frac{\bar{x}_1 - \bar{x}_2}{\sqrt{\frac{S_p^2}{N_1} + \frac{S_p^2}{N_2}}}, \text{ where } S_p^2 = \frac{(N_1-1)S_1^2 + (N_2-1)S_2^2}{N_1 + N_2 - 2}$$

Which statistics must be chosen depends on the results of Levene's test for equality of variances, which calculates $F = \max\left(S_1^2/S_2^2, S_2^2/S_1^2\right)$ and its observed level of significance p. If p is less than 0.05, the hypothesis about equality in variances must be rejected, and we should use a separate variance estimate statistic. Otherwise, it is better to use the pooled variance estimate statistic.

For both statistics, a t-test calculates means differences and levels of significance p. If p is less than 0.05, we must reject the hypothesis that the means in two groups are the same, and therefore may suppose that they are really different.

Reliability

A Reliability test is used to estimate the reliability of a scale (the set of questions) that was chosen for measuring some characteristic. For example, we may have ten questions for which we calculate the score of the test drive ability. If for any other ten questions that can characterize this ability, we obtain with another scale the same (or close) results as for our scale, then our scale has a high reliability. Otherwise, we cannot believe that our scale measures this ability properly.

Alpha Cronbach's model is the most popular model to test reliability of a scale. In this model, reliability is measured by Cronbach's alpha coefficient, which is calculated by the formula

$$\alpha = \frac{kC/V}{1 + (k-1)C/V},$$

where k is the number of questions; C, the average covariation; and V, the average variance between questions. The alpha value is between 0 and 1. A level of Alpha above 0.70 signifies sufficient reliability.

17 Small Business in the Context of International Integration

TAT'IANA A. ALIMOVA

Globalization, understood as the active diffusion of common rules, values and technologies throughout the world, increasingly involves Russia.[1] Its influence is multilateral and touches upon political, economical, social and cultural spheres of society. Its impact on regions, sectors and social groups within countries is diverse, determined in each case by their specific characteristics. This article analyses the specificity of how small business, as one sector of the Russian economy, is influenced by global economic processes.[2] It deals on the one hand with the forms of involvement of small

---

[1] Albrow 1996, 88.
[2] According to article 3 of the federal law No. 88 'O gosudarstvennoi podderzhke malogo predprinimatel'stva v Rossiiskoi Federatsii', from 14 June 1995, small businesses are commercial organizations meeting the following requirements - the share of the Russian Federation, Russian Federation subjects (this means 'subjects' in the sense of 'administrative/ territorial entities' such as oblasts, krais, republics), public and religious organizations (associations), charity and other funds in their authorized capital should not exceed 25%; the share belonging to one or several juridical persons that are not small business subjects should not exceed 25%; the average number of personnel in the reported period cannot exceed the following levels:

in industry	100 persons;
in construction	100 persons;
in agriculture	60 persons;
in the scientific and technological sphere	60 persons;
in wholesale trade	50 persons;
in retail trade and consumer services	30 persons;
in other spheres and kinds of activity	50 persons.

The subjects of small business are also individual persons undertaking entrepreneurial activities without forming a juridical person, and farmers.
[3] At present in the statistical practice of the Russian Federation and in the analyses of Russian scholars, there is no accepted definition of the private sector of the economy. We adhere to the definition offered in Alimova and Vasilenko 1998, 27. Here, the private sector is defined as the complex of economic units characterized by the absence of direct

business in the international economy, on the other with aspects of disjuncture between them.

Globalization and Small Business: Which Actors Count?

The congruence of the main trajectories of post-Soviet transformation processes, often analyzed primarily within the national framework of the 'reforming' post-socialist states, with global transformation processes has become increasingly clear. There are two aspects to this congruence. One is situated within the national framework and consists in the move away from state property to private property and the dominance of a market orientation for economic action. The other is a transnational process consisting in the integration of national markets previously segregated from each other. These processes are not identical, but interact in complex ways. The position occupied by Russian small business with respect to them is likewise complex.

With respect to the first process - the shift to private property and market relations -, it is important to note that private property and entrepreneurship are the basic ingredients constituting small business. What is small business? A small enterprise implies not only quantitative restrictions on the scope of business, expressed by the size of the workforce; it also involves - in many countries in the European Union - maximum limits on turnover and assets. It is organized business activity initiated by one or several persons, based on private initiative and private property, that enables entrepreneurs to dispose of the results of their activity and makes them bear responsibility for decisions made. Small business is thus private and market-orientated by nature. Indeed, in 1995, 65% of the Russian private sector[3] consisted of small businesses (after the conclusion of the 'small' privatization).[4]

---

dependence on the state power bodies in making economic decisions. The degree of possible influence by the state depends on its share in the authorized capital (for private enterprises it is less than 50%), or on whether there is a golden share (the right to veto the decisions made).

[4] *Goskomstat* 1995a; *Goskomstat* 1998c.

However, this does not suffice to ascribe to small business the quality of a 'globalizing force' in itself. A second fundamental characteristic of small business is its inherent adaptability. By their nature, small enterprises accommodate and adapt to the externally imposed conditions and rules under which they operate. In the case of small business, responsiveness to global processes and phenomena takes place only to the extent that these processes constitute the dominant conditions for its operation. Thus, the degree and efficiency of small business participation in transnational relations increases as these relations grow stronger in their immediate (national) surroundings.

In this way, small business cannot be seen as an agent creating the conditions essential for its own flourishing, since individual small enterprises will speedily arrange themselves with conditions which are sub-optimal for the development of small business as a whole. Rather, it is in this respect deeply dependent on the political and economic preferences of more powerful social actors.

In particular, the role of bureaucracies is vital. Bureaucracies can secure the rules of the game necessary for small business to flourish. In fact, they have a duty to do so according to a Russian governmental order of 1993.[5] However, they can and do very easily create conditions highly detrimental to small business. Crucially, the fact that small business is underdeveloped as a Soviet legacy means that the chances of the latter happening are all the greater. This pertains especially to regional and district, rather than federal, bureaucracies. Support for small business in general can depend on the political sympathies of a particular bureaucrat, especially those of the heads of the town, district, and region.[6] Perhaps more important is, however, administrative regulation of entrepreneurship. This may include centralized fixing of prices (as in the Ul'ianovskaia oblast) and administrative bans on exporting goods from a particular territory (as in the Voronezhskaia oblast).

Russian small business is not only in a position of dependency with regard to bureaucracies, but also with regard to providers of market infrastructure, especially financial intermediaries, but also producer services such as business consultancies, information technologies, marketing services etc. The under-provision of market infrastructure -

---

[5] Order of the government of the Russian Federation 'O pervoocherednykh zadachach po razvitiiu i gosudarstvennoi podderzhke malogo predminimal'testva v Rossiikoi Federatsii' No. 446, 1993.
[6] World Bank 1998a, 45-54.

particularly striking in small and medium-sized towns - is almost as disastrous for small business as the overabundance of bureaucracy. Due to increasing efficiency from economies of scale, market infrastructure is likely to be based in a few central locations and have a fairly concentrated market structure, thus operating a few levels 'higher' than small enterprises and being actively, albeit in global terms marginally, involved in international economic processes.

Although small business is in this way dependent on more powerful actors which it cannot directly influence, considerable differentiation within small business itself exists. Such differentiation can be accounted for by (objective reasons of) origins and (subjective reasons of) entrepreneurial aptitude. The importance of enterprise origin - whether an enterprise was a privatized Soviet unit or a start-up - was especially important in the first half of the 1990s. Managers of privatized enterprises often initially focused exclusively on existing markets and economic ties irrespective of their efficiency. The main reason for this was that at the initial stage of the Russian economic reforms in some territories and some spheres of regulation administrative methods of controlling economic activity remained dominant.[7] Conversely, start-ups were necessarily aggressively market-oriented. Interestingly, the importance of origin has declined sharply since those years, with the market model of action winning out: approximately two-thirds of small businesses are primarily oriented towards markets. This might testify to learning processes at work given a much lesser degree of path-dependency on the part of small enterprises created from Soviet units than is the case with industrial giants. Small enterprises are not only organizationally more flexible than industrial enterprises, due to their size they have much less chance to win protection from market competition.

As the importance of enterprise origin has declined, the importance of entrepreneurial aptitude has risen. Thus, about one-fifth of enterprises in a given year find themselves on the brink of bankruptcy. Conversely, about one-fifth of small businesses can be said to have developed innovative entrepreneurial strategies, often with an international slant.[8]

---

[7] Alimova and Buev 1995, 27-33.
[8] Alimova and Afanas'eva 1999, 32.

The Main Vectors of Small Business' International Integration

The forms of small business' interaction with and the extent of its integration into globalization can be approached by examining it from the point of view of global processes, on one hand, and domestic factors on the other. Global processes can be subdivided into transnational producer networks and investment flows; constraints exercised by transnational competition; and the intrusion and adoption of transnational standards of business practice. Domestic factors determining the trajectory of international involvement include the shadow economy and the lobbying strength of organizations representing small business and are examined in the following section.

Integration into Transnational Flows

Networks of suppliers and producers Russian small business has, until now, by and large not integrated itself into transnational flows of resources, commodities and investment. Russian resource-extracting companies are of course integrating into international resource flows as suppliers, but this is not the case with small business. Most enterprises in the extracting industry do not of course correspond to the criteria of small enterprises valid in Russia.

Few small businesses have managed to integrate their exports into international commodity flows. Most Russian processing companies cannot compete on the international market, though there are exceptions, for example high tech goods and some innovatory products of small businesses. Ironically, in the latter case, their production is competitive on the foreign market, but sometimes cannot be sold on the domestic one due to the lack of purchasing power. Moreover, exports of such high-tech innovations and competitive consumer goods are hindered by the lack of information about would-be consumers, a well-established brand name and distribution chains. All this keeps small business exports at about 10% of sales.

Though small business has no access to the foreign market as a supplier, it participates in international integration as a consumer by switching over to imported raw materials, spare parts and equipment. Foreign deliveries amount to about half of the total purchases made by small businesses.[9]

---

[9] World Bank 1998a, 196-219.

Investment flows International integration is conducted through the flow of capital, including direct and portfolio investments, into business-friendly zones. Russia is potentially attractive for foreign investments, as it has a wealth of raw materials, cheap labor and free market space (entire economic sectors and regions of the country). But investors are cautious because of economic and political instability, bureaucracy, corruption and rampant crime. They are afraid to invest in Russian business, as the mechanisms of implementing property rights are rather weak and the threat of nationalization is not banished. A sign of integration of small business into the Russian economy would be an inflow of domestic investments into small businesses. The indicator of Russian small business participation in international integration processes would be foreign investments in domestic small business.

The potential importance of foreign investment into small business is considerably heightened by the aforementioned weakness of the financial sector as part of the market infrastructure in Russia, i.e. the absence of domestic credit opportunities for small business. The shortage of any investment resources, let alone those of foreign origin, is a thorny issue for every third small business. The key tools that help to raise financial resources are loans extended by the government and private sector support funds. About 12% of small businesses plan to obtain access to foreign loans and investments.[10] The chief obstacle that prevents a small business from obtaining a loan - whether domestic or foreign - is the lack of repayment guarantees, of an insurance system and of government guarantees. The situation is aggravated by poor business transparency and inadequately drafted business plans, the weakest point of which is the stage of access to the market and gaining a niche in it.[11]

Small businesses do not have many opportunities to raise equity financing. It is a more risky type of investment (compared to lending), requiring higher profits. Another problem is the lack of mechanisms for attracting direct and indirect investors, as many Russian small businesses are not joint-stock companies, and there are no specialized stock exchanges operating with small business shares. Such factors as poor business transparency and the inability to estimate the real value of businesses and business project efficiency take their toll. A subjective hindrance is the unwillingness of businessmen to surrender any control over their business.

---

[10] Kokorev and Simachev 1999, 40.
[11] Ibid., 44.

All these obstacles reduce the access of small business to the credit resources of foreign countries and international financial organizations. Russia's small businesses act mainly as users of market infrastructure and applicants to the selective support of small business in the framework of the government credit schemes. Investment resources of foreign countries (primarily in the form of venture capital) are quite meager in Russia. It has only about 17 foreign venture companies registered in the off-shore zones and operating on its territory. This shows that systemic risk considerably exceeds the real profits generated by investments in Russian business. Domestic venture capital is developing very slowly. There is no adequate legislative framework: To date, we have witnessed only the decision to establish the first Russian venture capital fund.[12]

Small businesses looking to compensate for the weakness of the domestic financial system and unable to participate in international capital flows are forced to resort to private business loans extended unofficially on principles of mutual trust, sometimes guaranteed by criminal groups (about 50% of small businesses do this).[13] A business loan is little dependent on business transparency, helps to compensate for the lack of guarantees provided by small business itself, and ameliorates the threat of property redistribution. It requires neither shares nor the stock market. But the partners' loan is not a good alternative to bank lending or venture capital. Its frequent use is the sign of free private capital, of the need to raise it, and of the readiness of some businessmen to act as strategic and financial investors. Business loans are an adjustment of businesses' need for external financial resources to the insufficient development of market institutions. They are an emergency mechanism of integration of small business into the Russian economy, constituting a step away from the global, since they are often virtually illegal.

The Constraints Imposed by Foreign Competition

While few small businesses can find a place in transnational flows, nearly all have to compete with foreign imports on the domestic market. Thus, most Russian small businesses are caught up in the international division of markets, fighting for the domestic consumer and competing with importers and each other.

---

[12] Bortnik 1999.
[13] Kokorev and Simachev 1999, 46.

Reform led to the liberalization of foreign trade, which resulted in a flood of imports to domestic markets. The imported goods had the required demand-supply ratio (assortment-price-quality). According to data from *Goskomstat*, the share of imported commodities on the Russian consumer market was 49% in early 1998. Due to the financial crisis, it then fell significantly, and by April 1999 made up one third of all retail trade commodity resources. Later, by the end of 1999, the share of imports on the Russian consumer market stabilized at 30% in terms of comparable prices, and 35% in terms of current prices.

No doubt the domestic producers of the first hour were less competitive than their successors, for both objective and subjective reasons. The objective ones were the weak material foundations for business, the distorted structure and level of expenses, the lack of market infrastructure, and private sector support policy and structure. The subjective ones were a lack of understanding of market laws and of practical skills of market activity, against the background of useless economic experience under the command economy. Russian producers - including small businesses - had conceded a head start to importers, as it takes much longer to start producing new goods than to distribute those already produced. The Russian goods being produced were simply not competitive. Distribution chains aimed at small business had not emerged yet, while the old ones oriented to large enterprises were dissolving. Having lost most commodity positions to importers, domestic producers have had to regain lost ground by substituting their products for imports. In other words, they have been integrating into the international division of markets by competing with foreign goods on domestic markets.

A clear understanding of the nature of market competition, what it meant for business success, of the most efficient strategies with regard to competition and strategies leading to certain failure - all these could not appear overnight. In 1994, about 6% of small business managers cited competition as the main challenge to developing their business, and the majority ranked this problem as sixth or seventh among their priorities.[14] To possible objective explanations - unsatisfied demand, the limited importance of competition and other factors related to the newness of the market environment - must be added the poor subjective understanding of the essence and forms of competition. A typical view of businessmen in those years was: 'We do not have any rivals, as all firms are experiencing difficulties and cannot sell their products'.

---

[14] Alimova and Buev 1995, 57.

A tighter competitive environment and increased professionalism among entrepreneurs led to heightened awareness of the importance and consequences of competition. In 1997, 13% of businessmen cited competition as a problem; in 1998, 15%.[15] Small businesses established on the basis of formerly state-owned companies, trading companies and microfirms had more problems with competition than new businesses, production enterprises and comparatively larger small businesses respectively.[16] The overall evaluation of competition went from low to moderate levels. Managers of small businesses with roots in the state sector thought that competition was rather strong. Most managers of trading companies were also of this opinion.[17] Small business managers have learned to identify their key rivals; Russian companies rather than foreign ones are more often treated as such. There is also a difference between small businesses that engage in production and in trading. The first group thinks that more often than not, their rivals are domestic producers, while the second considers foreign companies their most important competitors.[18] The reason for this might be that producers treat only 'visible' producers as their competitors (the number of branches and representative offices of foreign companies is very low in Russia), while traders regard imported goods as competition as well.

Competition with imports on the domestic market is part of a process which for small business enterprises additionally implies the expansion of their geographical sphere of action first of all within Russia. Since Russian small business is in its infancy, enterprises' expansion into neighboring regional markets is an important process, and a crucial ingredient in competing with imports. Since the economy has been open to the world economy in most sectors from the very beginning of the reform process, expanding access to the domestic market is, as argued, for small business one of the stages of international integration. About 80% of consumers and suppliers of small business concentrate on the domestic market.[19] In this situation, a location in a large city bestows considerable advantages in terms of easy access to a large and unified market. Until now, about one-third of small businesses have been concentrated in Moscow and St. Petersburg.[20] Small businesses are pushed to expand the geography of

---

[15] Dolgopiatova and Alimova 1998, 140.
[16] Alimova and Buev 1995, 57.
[17] Dolgopiatova and Alimova 1998, 144-145.
[18] World Bank 1998a, 207.
[19] Alimova and Afanas'eva 1999, 31.
[20] *Goskomstat* 1999b.

suppliers and consumers by growing competition on developed markets, greater information transparency regarding new markets, and a developing system of dealers. A subjective factor is also of great importance, namely a businessman's readiness to pursue an active market policy, which goes hand in hand with business diversification and the expansion of business influence.

Adoption of Global Standards and Norms of Business Activity

The Russian economy is still in the process of switching over to the market. This is especially true with regard to the behavioral habits and norms of businessmen. A high level of transparency and predictability is required for international integration. However, if they are a prerequisite of an optimal degree of integration, rather than its effect, how are they to be acquired in the first place? The answer can only lie in the 'spontaneous' development of similar standards in the domestic economy accompanied by 'trickle-down' learning effects from brushes with global flows.

Thus, small businesses must learn the theory and practice of efficient market policy - instead of a passive orientation toward their own production (the standards of the command economy), they need to actively adjust to consumer needs (market standards). An efficient market policy for entrepreneurs entails a reorientation away from old networks towards solvent consumers, the abandonment of unreliable suppliers, flexible price formation with regard to the level of demand from various groups of consumers, diversification of activity and regular renewal of the range of products, and marketing and advertising. Most businessmen have acquired all these skills, though to varying extents. About 60-70% of small businesses have adopted market mechanisms; about 15-20% follow an active market policy; and about the same number (15-20%) have proven themselves incapable of change. All these years, they have been pursuing inadequate solutions, balancing on the brink of bankruptcy, and striving only to survive.[21]

The behavioral aspect of business is historically linked to the standards of administrative regulation in the command economy, which manifests itself in slower, inconsistent reforms by the managers of small businesses established on the basis of formerly state-owned enterprises.[22] Business ethics, another aspect of business, is an important component of

---

[21] Alimova and Afanas'eva 1999, 32.
[22] Dolgopiatova and Alimova 1998, 139-148.

integration, especially at the international level. Russia has not yet developed a consistent body of contractual law, leaving in many areas a legal vacuum regarding relations between transaction partners.

Domestic Factors Affecting the Global Compatibility of the Small Business Sector

Small Business and the Shadow Economy

The shadow activity of Russian companies was not triggered by reform. Under the command economy, the entrepreneurial activity of individuals was not always recognized as legitimate, and was allowed only in restricted forms and on a limited scale (handicrafts, private small trading, household plots). The rest belonged to the shadow economy. Restructuring (*perestroika*) made private enterprise legal in the form of cooperatives. The government did not impose strict regulation of their activity in the form of taxes, price formation, or profit distribution. A business could be run openly and stay afloat. But access to resources (premises, equipment, raw materials) was rather restricted, as they were in short supply under the command economy. These problems were tackled in an informal way (e.g. bribery), which required free unrecorded money. The need to keep costs off the books provided incentives for increasing unrecorded income. No government measures and mechanisms sought to stem the tide of illegal business: the cooperatives in many cases slid into the shadow economy.

After the government had recognized the legality of private enterprise, shadow business practices were triggered by the lack of access to resources, the historical background and the weak punitive functions of the state. The initial stage of reform, which expanded the range of legal avenues for private business, resulted in two trends. The first was a universal plunge into private enterprise, primarily small business, as the public mode of production had been discredited and people were not aware of the objective difficulties entailed by market activities. They were swept up by the seeming simplicity of things and the expectation of easy success. In 1992, about 190,000 small businesses were set up, 1.4 times as many as in 1991.[23] The second trend involved increasing procedural complexities concerning entry into the market (registration, licensing, leasing) that continually

---

[23] *Goskoms at* 1993; *Goskomstat* 1998c.

complicated formal business conditions, e.g. the sudden revoking of tax privileges, the great number of different taxes.

Such were the push factors fuelling the shadow economy. The pull factors consisted in criminal groups interested in expanding business under their control, as well as poor legislation and the failure to prevent illegal activity on the part of law enforcement agencies, making avoidance of the shadow sphere impossible. What could businessmen oppose to a force that was pulling them into the shadows? They could abide by the laws, but this was not encouraged in Russia; instead, law-abidance was replaced by fear of punitive bodies. In reality, the punitive bodies - i.e. criminal groups, which punished the failure to observe the practices of the shadow economy quite efficiently – mushroomed. Thus, turnover in the shadow economy reached about 40% of the total amount of small business by 1995. New small businesses withdrew more turnover into the shadow economy than did formerly state-owned enterprises; trading companies withdrew more than producers; micro-firms withdrew more than larger small businesses.

By 1997, the shadow turnover had fallen to 25-27%.[24] In 1998 the shadow turnover of industrial small enterprises was estimated at 9%; the shadow turnover of small trading enterprises was estimated at 15%.[25] This can be accounted for by the general saturation of markets and increasing competition. The economic rationale for legalizing business is that poor transparency reduces its potential. This is of course especially pertinent regarding the possibilities of international integration. International integration of small business by raising external financing, increasing the number of partners and developing new markets requires transparency of business and the transition to international methods of accounting and reporting, thus creating incentives for formalizing activities. Of course, at the same time the tenacious grip of the shadow economy greatly restricts real levels of international integration.

Organizations Representing Interests of Small Business

The development of institutional structures representing and protecting the interests of small business could in theory be a step to pushing for a more favorable regulatory environment helping small business to formalize their activity and thus take a step towards participating in international flows.

---

[24] Dolgopiatova and Alimova 1998, 157.
[25] Dolgopiatova and Karaseva 1998, 73, 107.

Existing associations linked with small business have been established from above by the government, and from below by businessmen themselves.

Various committees, funds, ministerial sub-divisions and departments are the components of the government structure of business support that has begun to develop since 1991. Their chief objective has been to draw up and implement government policy toward the private sector. The organizations set up by the government help shape the regulatory environment. The more attention that is given to their members (small businesses) at the government level, the greater is the importance of the agencies that supervise small business activity, thus they have a certain incentive to achieve results. In their programmatic work, they arguably improve businessmen's understanding of their own interests, thus facilitating the latters' organizability.

Organizations set up by businessmen are components of public life. Their objective is to draw together businessmen on the basis of common interests and to lobby for them. The best known organizations of businessmen are the Russian Association of Small Business Development,[26] the Union of Small Businesses and the Commerce Industrial Chamber.[27] The readiness of Russian businessmen to join such organizations is, however, rather weak. In 1993-94, about one-fifth of small businesses belonged to associations and about 10% intended to join one. But the potential for growth has not been realized. In 1995-96, about one tenth of small businesses were members of associations.[28] The main reason for the decline of membership in such associations was their inefficient lobbying for interests of businessmen leading to a reduction of support for them. Pointing to the weakness of lobbies for small business is the fact that key measures of small business support mandated by federal legislation are routinely ignored. These include the reservation of a share in government orders for small businesses, and the allocation of financial resources generated by privatization to support small business. The federal and most regional budgets do not contain a separate item that provides financial resources for small business support.

---

[26] See <http://www.rasme.ru>.
[27] See <http://www.rbcnet.ru/static/ru/tppinfo/palata.htm>.
[28] Dolgopiatova and Alimova 1998, 330-332.

Conclusion

At present, the level of small business development in Russia cannot be regarded as sufficient. According to the data from *Goskomstat*, there are six small enterprises per 1,000 persons. Small business employees account for 10% of total employment. Small businesses make up 30% of all enterprises and account for an estimated 10-12% of GDP. Considering, however, the recentness of its development and the adverse circumstances it is faced with, small business can nevertheless be considered to harbor potential for the future. It is important to underline the beneficial effects a buoyant small business sector can have for the rest of the economy. It creates a competitive environment, stimulates development and implementation of innovations, and helps keep the country's entrepreneurial activity at a high level. It has the potential to help win over to the market economy away from legacies of the socialist past territories and sectors in which it gains a foothold.

However, in doing so it risks slipping into the shadow economy, and in this way losing much of its stimulating effect on market relations. The fact is, as stated earlier, that the development of small business is reliant on powerful actors which it cannot itself influence. Thus, the implementation by state actors of a package of measures is needed to strengthen the regulatory framework, create a favorable investment climate, ensure the information and legal transparency of the Russian market, and revive Russia's financial market.[29] These overall systemic measures would have to be supplemented by concrete measures in individual industries and sectors of the economy. The main problems to be addressed regarding the small business sector are ensuring equal access for small enterprises to raw material, financial and commodity resources, the elimination of administrative barriers, and lowering market entry costs.

Thus, on the one hand, the small business sector can clearly be seen to harbor a potential for strengthening market institutions and norms in Russia. A very important factor in this respect is its exposure to competition from imports, and the steep learning curve this has implied for actors. On the other hand, small business exists curiously decoupled from global production or investment networks. There is little to show that the small business sector or significant segments of it are ready to move from economic market action to strong political lobbying to improve their position. In the small business sector, we thus see the deeply contradictory

---

[29] Kuzminov and Iakovlev 2000, 20-22.

nature of globalization, accepting with one hand while rejecting with the other. We can also see the fragmentizing effects this has on Russia, with a concentration of small enterprise activity in the largest cities. A change in the trajectory of small enterprises' international involvement is in the final analysis dependent on the interaction and integration of other actors - state actors on federal and regional levels, economic actors in the financial and market infrastructure sphere - with and in the global political economy.

18 The Self-Denying Middle Class in the Global Age

HARLEY D. BALZER

A self-aware and politically active middle class constitutes a necessary, though not sufficient, condition for consolidating democratic political systems. This paper seeks to locate Russia's post-Communist middle class(es) in a rapidly evolving global context where the idea of a Russian middle class is doubly contested: Most Russians reject the suggestion that a middle class could exist in their transition-ravaged society; simultaneously, the meaning of middle class is undergoing profound change due to globalization.

The discourses of globalization contain multiple narratives, though most of these fit into the framework of existing master narratives of progressive capitalism or class struggle. Proponents of economic liberalization, free trade and integration argue that a rising tide lifts all boats, enhancing opportunities and offering unprecedented potential to improve the human condition. Without competition, economic actors do not perform at optimal levels. Critics of globalization claim that the global system sharpens the economic divide between haves and have-nots, disempowers all but the strongest actors, causes severe local dislocations, rapes the environment, exacerbates gender discrimination, invades the body and replaces historically constructed cultures with a global information pablum generated by Hollywood and McDonalds.

The middle classes are implicitly at the center of this debate, yet frequently are left out of the discussion. Proponents of globalization, put on the defensive by attacks on economic inequality, focus on 'trickle-down' to improve the lives of lower income groups rather than ways the global economy has expanded the middle classes. Critics of globalization generally ignore the middle classes as an inconvenient exception during times of economic expansion, but emphasize the harm done to these groups in economic crises. In the industrial economies of America, Europe and Japan, globalization has provoked a debate about the 'squeeze' on the middle class - is the global economy and accompanying wealth effect causing increased polarization, with the result that the middle classes are shrinking? Or is the incomprehensible wealth of 'double-digit billionaires' merely an extreme manifestation of an improvement in economic conditions shared by multiple groups? If a majority of America's five million millionaires are essentially indistinguishable from the middle class,[1] has this so raised the bar that most Americans will never achieve 'real' middle class status?

What does middle class mean in the global age? In any society, there are people economically 'in the middle'.[2] But having a portion of the population economically in the middle does not by itself create a middle class, much less the political organizations/ representation that underpin a middle class role in influencing economic policy and fostering a democratic polity. In Russia between 1995 and 1998, groups economically in the middle were the fastest-growing segment of the population.[3] Some observers suggest that the August 1998 crisis provided a new stimulus for Russian entrepreneurs,[4] while many others focus on the increase in poverty.[5] These two outcomes are not mutually exclusive. The 1998 crisis produced many losers, but also a (growing) number of winners. However, in Russia the development of a self-conscious and politically active middle class, as opposed to a more or less numerous middle stratum,[6] has been impeded by a combination of elements in the domestic political culture and contradictory currents of globalization.

To examine Russia's post-Communist middle classes in the global era, we begin by looking at how the understanding of middle class is altering in a rapidly changing environment, and noting the ways globalization complicates attempts to understand the post-communist transition. The relationship between transition and globalization provides a context for sketching the development of Russia's middle classes since the fall of Communism. The conclusion summarizes the prospects for Russian middle class agency in the complex institutional relationships generated by transition and globalization.

---

[1] Stanley and Danko 1996.
[2] Kocka 1999, 232-234.
[3] Balzer 1997; Balzer 1998a; *Srednii klass* 1999.
[4] *Srednii klass* 1999; Åslund 1999a.
[5] Silverman and Yanowitch 1997; Silverman and Yanowitch 1999; Iakovleva 1998.
[6] Drobizheva 2000.

Middle Class(es) in the Global Era

Attempts to define the middle class or bourgeoisie have never generated a consensus within industrial societies, much less across diverse economic and cultural systems. Globalization adds new complexities, as rapid economic change alters social relationships.[7] The middle class everywhere has included a range of social groups. Peter Gay, in his magisterial multi-volume study, confesses that the middle class is best thought of as a residual:

> there was no single typical bourgeois: the unscrupulous entrepreneur or ingenious engineer stood model [for Danish critic Georg Brandes] quite as much as the timid grocer or the pedantic bureaucrat. Daring was no less a bourgeois trait than caution. What nineteenth-century bourgeois had in common was the negative quality of being neither aristocrats nor laborers, and of being uneasy in their middle-class skins. But what divided them was almost as important... .[8]

Most bourgeois were in perpetual danger of falling out of the middle class. The large, financially secure middle class was a post-World War II American phenomenon that may have a limited time horizon. In postwar America, the middle class came to encompass a sizable majority of the population, and Europe and Japan have developed in similar ways: 'Searching for the American middle class is like looking for air. It is everywhere, invisible, and taken for granted'.[9] Being middle class did not always mean being rich, but it usually meant not being poor. In America, poverty was not so much a vice as a temporary condition. While many people could expect to be poor at some point during their lifetimes, a large majority could expect to enjoy a middle-class lifestyle for some portion of their lives.[10] The American experience in the latter half of the twentieth century might provide a standard many aspire to match, but it cannot serve

---

[7] Defining globalization is a separate article, if not an entire book. There are several extensive literature reviews and efforts to group research into sub-fields (e.g. Sklair 1999; Barber 1995). I tend to favor those who view globalization as something distinct from internationalization (Sklair 1999), those who view the current conjuncture as qualitatively different from earlier historical periods (Von Laue 1969; Von Laue 1987; Appadurai 1996; Waltz 1999); and those who focus on social and cultural effects, rather than debating the desirability of something that already exists.

[8] Gay 1984, 31.

[9] Baritz 1989, xi.

[10] Baritz 1989, 105.

as a model for middle classes in industrializing (or 'post-industrial') societies.

America's post-industrial middle class is different culturally and economically from earlier incarnations. Every society connected with the industrial nations is experiencing changes resulting from diminished barriers to economic interaction and the communication/ information revolution. The welfare state is in retreat, battered by increasing international economic competition and demographic pressures. This competition increasingly involves large transnational companies. Leading sectors of the global economy derive their dynamism from rapid technological change. Smokestack industries are declining in importance, replaced by information and services. The new information technologies promote both greater communication and greater disparities.

Political and economic boundaries are eroding as products, people and funds move with increasing fluidity. Multinational economic actors find it easier to move resources across borders and evade taxation. Those engaged in illegal activity are harder to trace, much less to interdict. Legal systems in many nations cannot cope with new varieties of crime: Russia lacks laws governing money-laundering; the Philippines does not have legislation covering internet abuses. Security has become a major concern in all societies, altering residential patterns (proliferation of gated communities) individual behavior (reliance on bodyguards), and landscape architecture (open vistas replace nooks and crannies).[11]

The politics of all nations now involves debates about the extent of participation in the global economy and its consequences:

> political ideas and competition are crystallizing on issues involving the legitimacy of economic outcomes in exchange among nations and linking the legitimacy of these outcomes to the nature of structures of production and distribution in the trading partner's society.[12]

The 'developing' world is part of this matrix no less than the industrial societies.[13]

Globalization, with its increased trade and competitiveness may achieve overall increased economic growth, but it comes at the expense of

---

[11] Security is one of the realms where Russians emphasize the uniqueness of their post-Communist situation rather than viewing the issue in a broader context. See Volkov 1999; Kosals 1995.
[12] Berger 1996, 24.
[13] Appadurai 1996; Escobar 1995.

local disruptions that produce far more impassioned reactions than the more diffused general gains. And the global economy is characterized by growing relative income differentials - a phenomenon sometimes referred to as the 'winner take all' economy. The middle class is coming under increased economic pressure at a time when their collective action organizations are in decline. Unions and professional guilds have lost membership and influence, as employers make use of temporary workers and other forms of itinerant labor that lower firms' overhead costs but raise the overhead costs to society.[14]

Development of a national bourgeoisie is inhibited not only by global economic conditions but by global opportunities. Rather than staying local, entrepreneurs may opt to join an international community of economic actors. This is particularly the case for professionals and 'stars' in any area of activity - medicine, law, culture, sport, cuisine. The global marketplace draws high-quality talent to locations offering the most attractive opportunities. The 'brain drain' has become a more generalized talent drain. If formerly the rich constituted the 'jet set', now there are multiple jet sets. The worlds of wealth, power and fame have merged far beyond the interpenetration described by C. Wright Mills.[15] An international business class composed of professionals, consultants, employees of international organizations and NGOs contrasts with the rich and with an increasingly mobile global underclass of low wage migrants and indigenes.[16]

Common reactions to globalization include denying its significance in particular national contexts or fostering the myth that it is a choice - something a nation/ society may participate in or not. Russians, with a cultural tradition stressing their uniqueness even among unique nations, have been particularly susceptible to this temptation.[17] Despite Russians' proclivity to regard anything that befalls them as a product of their unique history and culture, Russia's problems increasingly resemble the problems

---

[14] Three recent monographs have chronicled the demise of professionals' power and status (Brint 1995; Krause 1996; Perkin 1996). A similar literature has appeared discussing labor unions (Western 1997).
[15] Mills 1956.
[16] Appadurai 1996; Sassen 1998.
[17] Berdyaev 1947. Surprisingly, most Russians have not yet identified globalization as a target. With the exception of a few would-be social democrats (e.g. Burbach, Núñez and Kagarlitsky 1997), most of the discussion in Russia thus far reflects a belief that globalization is something about which they have a choice - to participate or to go their own (uniquely Russian) way. When Russians realize that globalization inevitably influences their lives irrespective of local decisions, opportunities for demagogues will inevitably expand.

of other nations undergoing transitions toward democratic and market societies at a time when the results of democratic capitalism are being called into question in the 'advanced' nations that provide the models. In the year 2000, Japan remains mired in a recession. In Europe, unemployment hovers at double-digit levels in many countries, while immigrants seek to fill the jobs Europeans refuse to accept.[18] In the USA, a decade of economic good times has produced vast wealth and budget surpluses but has not ended poverty or homelessness, and the middle class is once again perceived to be in crisis.

The arguments about income differentials within the industrialized world are bitter, with preconceptions about the 'world system' influencing selection and interpretation of data. Some authorities assert that the 'winner take all' economy is devastating the American middle class, and that income disparities are increasing worldwide. Others respond that the vast wealth of the super-rich and plight of the poor should not obscure the improved economic conditions for large numbers of middle- and lower-middle class individuals.[19] Is incomprehensible wealth in the hands of a few less a problem if large portions of the population are able to enjoy an unprecedented level of economic prosperity? Does proliferation of (what some would regard as obscene or excessive) wealth make enduring poverty even less acceptable? Does a growing gap between the rich and the middle class represent middle class decline? (In a status-conscious society, relative decline is a genuine problem.) In this context it helps to recall that the middle class frequently has been viewed as 'in crisis' in the past.[20]

Sassen describes the 'wealth effect' in American cities in terms that resemble discussions of the Dutch disease - wealth in the leading sector drives up prices for real estate, commodities and services, causing collateral damage to the rest of the economy.[21] Sassen's focus is on the underclass, but the implications for middle groups are clear: entry is more difficult; polarization more likely, housing segregation more pronounced, the informal economy more tempting. Cheerleaders for neoliberalism would cite evidence that far more people in Latin America, Asia and East Europe now own automobiles - a favorite definition of belonging to the middle class. The argument quickly turns both complex and emotion-laden - those

---

[18] Russia has come to look remarkably similar. There are 5 million guest workers in the country, performing jobs that Russians refuse to accept despite widespread unemployment and underemployment.
[19] Fogel 2000.
[20] Corey 1935; Grayson 1955.
[21] Sassen 1998, chapter 8; also see Bauman 1998, 21, on elites choosing isolation.

automobiles pollute the environment and permit the better-off to escape the smog-plagued urban areas for cleaner suburbs while the poor are left to inhale the fumes, adversely affecting their health and reproductive potential.

If the pie has doubled in size, and the middle classes have 3% less of the larger pie, are they better off or worse off?[22] Here again, perceptions are crucial. The pervasive belief that people are entering the middle class or maintaining their position due to their willingness to work multiple jobs strongly influences these perceptions. So does the weakness of professional organizations that provided both economic support and psychological solidarity for members of the middle classes.

If the end of the welfare state in America is largely an issue affecting the lower social strata, in Europe it is a decidedly middle-class issue. The strongest support for welfare policies in Europe comes from white collar salaried groups who are most dependent not only on redistributive allocations from the state but also on direct income from the public sector in which they or their family members are employed.[23] This is important for comparisons with Russia and other post-Communist societies, with their extensive systems of social benefits and massive state employment.

Debates over the fate of the middle class mirror cleavages within the middle strata that limit its ability to play a 'class' role in ordinary politics. The middle class is rarely a unified 'class for itself'. Olson notes that collective action becomes nearly impossible for large groups.[24] It is difficult to picture the large and diverse American or European middle class as a collective actor. Once some form of democratic governance is in place (a condition presuming the existence of a market economic system), the middle class will inevitably be politically divided. How can professionals, small and medium entrepreneurs in diverse economic sectors and regions, managers, government officials, skilled workers and service providers find common interests? They may unite when social breakdown or revolution threatens their well-being, leading them to seek the supposed security of authoritarianism. A reverse process can occur when members of this 'group' perceive the authoritarian state to be an obstacle to economic and

---

[22] Davis and Wessel 1998.
[23] Sulkunen 1992, 17. The author cites Sven Olsson (1990), *Social Policy and Welfare State in Sweden Lund*, Arkiv forlag, Stockholm, 236.
[24] Olson 2000, 87-88.

human development.[25] During times of 'normal' politics, the middle class is more likely to lack conscious class interests.

In some nations of Asia and Latin America, portions of the 'business class' have shifted from reliance on rent seeking and support for economically interventionist authoritarian states to economic openness and more democratic systems.[26] In Asian nations, entrepreneurs have found allies among the professional middle classes and intelligentsia to challenge authoritarianism. Analysis should emphasize the degree to which middle classes mobilize politically to combat authoritarianism and the inevitable rent seeking that dictatorship fosters. Middle strata in many nations have the potential to create either democratic or security-seeking systems. Outcomes depend on a combination of domestic and global economic developments, political will (agency), and leadership.

Some observers perceive a global trend of distrust in democratic politicians and dissatisfaction with market consumerism in the 'trilateral' democracies of the USA, Europe and Japan, as well as in Latin America and in many Asian newly industrialized countries.[27] In Latin America, where incomplete transitions toward markets and democracy have been a recurring feature for decades, optimistic prognoses may be seriously questioned:

> It is difficult, if not impossible, for governments to sustain popular backing for programs that may only slowly strengthen the aggregate economy and that seem to enrich a privileged few without providing a credible promise of broad prosperity. Some of the potential constituency for the reform programs has been alienated: Millions of Latin Americans who earlier thought they had entered the middle class have found their real incomes ground down by recession and austerity measures.[28]

The evolving post-Communist middle classes are joining an industrial world where the middle class enjoys unprecedented levels of material consumption, yet is less easily defined, less secure, less well-organized for collective action, less affluent in comparison to the wealthy, and less capable of making family status hereditary than was the case a generation

---

[25] In Russia the one time that the middle class (and indeed most of Russian society) came together was in 1905, between Bloody Sunday and the October Manifesto. Balzer 1996.
[26] Collier 1979; Bartell and Payne 1995; Rodan 1996.
[27] Pharr, Putnam and Dalton 2000; Crozier, Huntington and Watanyuki 1975.
[28] Lowenthal 2000, 46.

ago.[29] As we seek analogies to the Russian case, we must be aware that the models themselves are changing. The image of middle-class democracy prevalent in the industrial world in the second half of the twentieth century is likely to alter in the twenty-first century. Western assumptions that 'development' means the developing societies will eventually be 'just like us' reflects no small amount of hubris. The 'trilateral' system will not assimilate entities as large as Russia and China without itself being profoundly changed in the process.

The Russian middle class should be the social group most affected, both positively and negatively, by globalization. New Russians are wealthy enough to protect themselves, enjoy some benefits, and ignore the downsides, other than commodity price fluctuations. The poor are doubly victims, but have few chances to avail themselves of the opportunities. Yet, portions of the middle class seem to be in the forefront of Russia's anti-modern movement, believing that globalization is something about which they have a choice.

The contradictory effects of globalization on society and on the middle class are profoundly confusing in transition societies. On the one hand, international demonstration effects, geographic proximity and the potential for joining Europe have had a major positive impact on post-Communist transitions, limiting (some) conflicts and discouraging irredentist claims, while encouraging economic liberalization and democracy.[30] Yet, participation in the global economy makes development of a 'national bourgeoisie' both more difficult and less necessary.[31] If the middle class is changing in the industrial nations, its fate in transition societies is far more problematic.

---

[29] Wallulis 1998.
[30] Rupnik 2000; Whitehead 1996.
[31] Some observers have proposed a path for Russia that amounts to a new version of the 'Witte system'. Russia should adopt a national industrial policy, and protect domestic industry behind a tariff wall. (Hough 1997; Millar 1999) This is a 19th century approach to 21st century problems. Neither the Russian domestic economy nor the international environment is conducive to such a program (Strange 1996, 4). But 'savage capitalism' accentuates the desire for a stronger state role in social and economic policy.

Russia's Middle Classes

Contrary to prevailing mythology, there was a middle class in Russia before 1917.[32] There was also a middle stratum in communist societies, but class relations had a unique character. Under Communism, socio-economic status in general and consumption in particular had relatively little to do with an individual's relationship to the means of production; the crucial factor was one's relationship to the means of distribution. Party members had privileged access to various goods and services. For the rest of the population, *dostup* (access) to goods involved complicated relationships structured around informal exchange or participation in the illegal (second, gray, or shadow) economy.[33] This made efforts to describe social groups under 'actually existing socialism' somewhat farcical. In a system where bus drivers earned more than scientists, and where a saleswoman who added water to the juice in a store could earn a month's salary in one shift, 'scientific' measures of social structure tell us little. And they tell us nothing that we can use for comparative purposes.

Considering property ownership and relationship to the means of production as the defining criteria of class is becoming increasingly confusing in a global economy where knowledge and intellectual property are crucial elements. It is even more problematic in post-Communist societies, where ownership itself has become confused and contested. Researchers have generated a new vocabulary to deal with the property relations evolving in post-socialism: Katherine Verdery talks about 'fuzzy property'; David Stark has coined the term 'recombinant property'; Jean Oi focuses on 'local corporatism'; Zhiyuan Cui describes 'mobias strip property'; and Victor Nee refers to 'hybrid property'. Taken together, they indicate that something important is taking place that calls for new categories. Stark suggests that we will see 'a distinctively East European capitalism that will differ as much from West European capitalisms as do contemporary East Asian variants'.[34] Discussions of 'the new middle class' in Europe, focusing on individualism, lifestyle, and mentality as much as on salary, are particularly useful in examining social relations in post-Communism.[35]

---

[32] Balzer 1996.
[33] Ledeneva 1998. Ledeneva's excellent study on *blat* would have been even more compelling if she had also examined just how *blat*, is, or is not, similar to informal exchange in other societies. Lomnitz 1988; Appadurai 1986.
[34] Stark 1996, 993.
[35] Sulkunen 1992.

Under Communism there were several middle strata, including officials, specialists, and those operating in the 'second' economy. The 'hundred-ruble intelligentsia' even developed something of a collective identity.[36] But many of the educated specialists, government officials and skilled workers had credentials and talents that did not translate into anything of value in a transitioning-to-market economy. Those with savings saw them wiped out by rapid inflation. State employees could continue to think of themselves as middle class, but their standard of living depended on the state's ability to pay their salaries, and those unable to extract rents have generally experienced relative downward mobility. Education and intellectual capital accumulated in the Communist era were not necessarily worthless - numerous studies indicate that education in general and higher education in particular correlate strongly with both employment and income in the former Communist nations.[37] But it is not clear if this measures the value of the education or represents a correlation between smart people having received an education and now using their smarts in other ways.

In transition societies, especially post-Communist transition societies, the first challenge is to find the middle classes. In my earlier work on Russia's middle classes, I devoted much attention to consumption as a way to gauge the growth of the middle strata. If there is widespread evidence of consumption of non-luxury goods, this can reasonably be taken as evidence for the existence of an economic middle stratum. The proliferation of housewares, home renovation products, autos, cafes, mobile phone salons and service providers all attest to vibrant consumerism on the part of some non-trivial portion of the population.

Consumption is always a 'sliding scale'. It changes with economic conditions and technology. In 1998, writers in *Itogi* complained that many middle class Muscovites still drove second-hand cars and could not obtain inexpensive mortgages. In the USA in the year 2000, rising interest rates and rapidly rising prices mean many middle-class families are facing mortgage balloons that threaten their housing standards. Does this mean they are in danger of falling out of the middle class?[38] Or are they just

---

[36] The hundred ruble *intelligentsia* refers to a large group of the Soviet educated middle class who received a salary of about Rbl100, lived modestly, and emphasized cultural values. The group included teachers, doctors, and a large portion of the scientists and engineers.

[37] Balzer 1998b; Eyal, Szelenyi and Townsley 1998.

[38] The difficulties are apparent in Appadurai's comments on the consumer revolution. Russia experienced a massive consumer revolution in 1990s, as Soviet-era barriers

'repositioned' within it? Something more is needed for the relatively affluent to be a middle class: self-consciousness, a social and political agenda, other classes against which to measure themselves.

It is easier to reach consensus regarding the groups that form part of the Russian middle classes than on their numbers. Berezin, a Russian observer focusing on income level, identified five groups that form part of the middle class: (a) small and medium entrepreneurs, mainly in family businesses; (b) middle-level managers: heads of departments, shops, etc.; (c) independent professionals: lawyers, economists, accountants, teachers, journalists, programmers, drivers, tailors, masseuses, etc.; (d) skilled workers in successful enterprises, in industry and trade; and (e) those with 'some other source' of supplementary income.[39] In an article in the St. Petersburg film journal *Seans*, Moskvina opted for a lifestyle definition, suggesting that the middle class consists of those seeking to live well without risking their lives in pursuit of wealth. 'The typical representative of the contemporary middle class just barely managed to buy an apartment, and in most cases remodeling is still unfinished.'[40]

Most Russians seem to think that the definition of middle class is someone who does not need to think about money, whereas in America, the definition of middle class has generally been precisely those people who always think about money. The rich do not need to worry; the poor do not bother to worry; it is the middle class that is consumed with constant fretting about social status, how to get through the next week; how to afford a new appliance.[41] Often the entire middle class is conflated with its upper end - the haute bourgeoisie who are never more than a minority of the middle classes. Global comparisons complicate the project, encouraging comparisons across economic systems at vastly different levels of wealth.

The middle classes have been variously defined on the basis of education, economic or social status, self-ascription, and consumption. In part the diversity reflects different intellectual approaches. Weber helps us to remember that it also reflects differences in how individuals and groups define themselves in relation to other individuals and groups, and that the status could be fluid.[42] Recent survey research conducted in Russia found

---

(interdictions) dissolved, making consumption the most helpful way of identifying middle groups. But a consumer revolution points to a middle strata, not necessarily a politically self-aware middle class. Appadurai 1997, 72-75.
[39] Berezin 1997.
[40] Moskvina 1997.
[41] Andreev 2000.
[42] Weber 1976, 237-238; also, see Bourdieu 1984.

that people identify themselves as middle class on the basis of lifestyle, the prestige of their occupation, and the esteem in which they are held by others as much as on the basis of their income.[43] At the same time, one of the best recent analyses finds middle class status strongly correlated to market-oriented household strategies.[44]

The three largest middle class groups are commercial, managerial (including government officials), and professional. Soviet-era professionals have had difficulty making the transition to the new economy. Some lawyers, physicians, and others are doing well, but often on the basis of skills very different from those needed in the Soviet period. Ordinary physicians now earn low wages; whereas clinics treating the wealthy are doing quite well. Bookkeeping was a low-prestige, low-status, highly feminized profession in the USSR, but now accountants are crucial to businesses, whether they wish to pay taxes or avoid them. Banking and financial services have been a major growth area. In 1998, when I described my research to an American working as a top administrator at one of the banks in Moscow, he suggested that I visit his office: 'We have 800 people working in our Moscow offices, and 796 of them are middle-class Russians'. Other newly important professions include international and criminal law, insurance, security, advertising, marketing, and many related 'capitalist' occupations.

The psychological barriers to locating post-Communist middle classes are even more daunting than the economic statistics. The nascent Russian middle classes prefer to deny their own existence. Commentators can write unselfconsciously about the middle class in China, Thailand, Mexico or Sudan, but not in Russia. This condition is partly self-inflicted, partly a function of Communist ideology, and partly a reflection of global trends. The USSR was supposed to be a classless society, and the bourgeoisie was a defeated enemy. Anyone who lived under the Soviet regime must surmount a major psychological barrier to proclaim themselves middle class.

The difficulty is exacerbated by the crucial role played by a downwardly mobile intellectual elite (the intelligentsia). Despite a relatively low level of consumption by world standards, this group constituted a professional middle class in the Soviet Union. Their relative loss of status in the new Russian economy has caused many of them to deny that anything resembling a 'normal' middle class exists in the country.

---

[43] *Srednii klass* 1999, 250.
[44] Piirainen 1998.

Russian sociologists who study social stratification are for the most part members of this economically challenged intelligentsia, and perpetuate the view of middle class ruin. For example, Zaslavskaia suggested that 15% of the middle class live in poverty. Intelligentsia values also drive the work of Szelenyi and his colleagues in their effort to posit a: 'capitalism without capitalists'. Scholars in former communist lands have produced extensive and sometimes tortured discussions of class relationships under socialism and communism. A parallel trend is concern with the fate of the former *nomenklatura* - their ability to parlay old 'Communist capital' into new forms of economic and political power. If the guardians of truth - the intelligentsia - are sinking into the underclass and the party hacks are successful, there must be something drastically wrong.[45]

Pessimism, hardly restricted to the middle class, has been one of the major products of the neoliberal economic reforms introduced (but not fully implemented) in Russia. A serious defect of neoliberal policies almost everywhere is a worsening economic situation for state-salaried professionals, particularly teachers.[46] In the post-Soviet situation, where virtually all professionals were state employees, most physicians, scientists, engineers, professors, artists and writers share this trauma. These are precisely the groups that provided leadership for Russia's pre-Revolutionary middle class, and generate the ideas and symbols in any political system.[47]

We noted above that a global trend with particular impact on middle class cohesion is the decline of the guilds. In the 1990s, professional organizations (and labor unions) lost membership and played a diminished role in social and political life. While some attribute this to the 'world system' or the demise of community,[48] significant economic forces are at work, with profound political implications. It is clear that the professional communities that provided leadership to Russia's middle class in the Tsarist era are now far weaker economically and politically, and that they cannot look to international peer groups for models and support as they did in the past.[49]

Russia's middle classes have gone through multiple phases of development in a short period of time. If prior to the August 1998 crisis,

---

[45] Zaslavskaia 1996; Eyal, Szelenyi and Townsley 1998; Slomczynski 1998.
[46] Lomnitz and Melnick 1991.
[47] Balzer 1996; Znaniecki 1965.
[48] Sassen 1998; Putnam 2000.
[49] Balzer 1996; Jordan 1998; Lonkila 1998.

perhaps one-third of the population was economically at a middle-class level and close to half were 'psychologically' part of the middle class, in the wake of the crisis, the figures were probably one-fifth and one-third.[50] More serious than the decline in numbers, the crisis appears to have stifled rather than encouraged middle-class involvement in Russia's social and political life.[51] The institutions that would provide both evidence of and mechanisms for middle-class political participation are not visible. The middle strata continue to favor individual rather than collective action. This could change over time, but the process is likely to be protracted.

Weakness of the professional groups is one part of the explanation for the political lethargy of Russia's middle class. The mobilization of popular fronts in the late 1980s and the specialist revolt that helped topple the USSR appeared to presage genuine potential for self-organization and partnership with the government in developing institutional mechanisms to enforce norms of behavior that would make the Russian market less chaotic.[52] But, as Fish has noted, a 'movement society is not the same thing as a democracy'. Survey research conducted since August 1998 indicates that far from stimulating middle class activism, economic challenges are deterring political involvement.[53]

Some members of Russia's middle classes understand the need for political mobilization, and the time and work involved in the process. Groups in both Moscow and St. Petersburg are publishing periodicals with the name *Srednii klass*, and the Petersburg publication represents a political group that in summer 1999 was already focused on the 2004 elections (rather than the December 1999 Duma elections or the 2000 Presidential election). But the number of people involved in these promising endeavors thus far is quite small.[54] Obstacles to collective action are not limited to the diversity and economic and numerical weakness of the middle classes. Powerful and wealthy interests have little desire to see their position challenged by other social groups.

Russia's post-Elts'in leadership manifests a statist mentality. Rather than encouraging associational life and self-organization, they prefer to develop 'state plans' for fostering development of the middle class. Even

---

[50] Balzer 1998; *Srednii klass* 1999; *Srednii klass v Rossii* 2000.
[51] *Srednii klass* 1999; *Srednii klass v Rossii* 2000.
[52] Balzer 1998; Frye 1997.
[53] Fish 1995; *Srednii klass 1999*, 199-215.
[54] *Srednii klass v Rossii*, 2000.

leaders of independent middle class organizations focus their energies on writing 'state doctrines' for national programs.[55]

The August 1998 economic crisis was both the death and the birth of Russia's post-Soviet middle class. In the short term, the currency devaluation forced a turning inward, as any firm relying on imported components faced a fourfold increase in their costs. But in the longer term, firms able to produce using purely local inputs found their ability to compete with foreign products enormously enhanced. This has been particularly evident in food products and light industry, especially clothing. Thus far, the potential to utilize the cost differential to build up exports has been limited by the inferior quality of many Russian products, trade barriers and intense competition. But the experience of other nations (Malaysia, China, Mexico) suggests that these difficulties could be overcome in time.

Conclusion

The middle classes in post-communist Russia are penultimately postmodern. Unlike some other regions of the world where self-aware, cosmopolitan middle classes are embracing the opportunities offered by globalization even as they suffer from the collateral damage, Russia's nascent middle strata continue to treat globalization as a choice and their own existence as problematic. Neither rapid growth in numbers during the stabilization in 1995-98 nor the shock and opportunities created by the crisis in August 1998 have instilled the self-awareness and impetus to social and political organization that would provide a basis to argue that the Russian middle strata have become a self-conscious middle class. This may be attributed to the dislocations of the transition; failures in leadership; the vagaries of the Russian soul; and/ or the serious downward mobility experienced by groups that traditionally were leaders of the Russian middle class. But it also reflects major changes in the condition and role of the middle classes due to globalization. Globalization creates new economic challenges and fosters a transnational middle-class culture that competes with the model of a 'national bourgeoisie' that played such an important role in the development of middle classes in earlier cases of industrialization.

---

[55] Bure 2000.

Much of the discussion of globalization either accepts the cultural 'McDonaldization' of all societies as a given or posits a 'culture war' that may spur religious and national fundamentalisms.[56] Yet there are approaches that see the potential for creative adaptation within available cultural spaces, and for innovative new syntheses. New global influences will not replace, but inevitably will intermix with traditional elements. Denise Lett extends Gil Rozman's work on the Asian cultural heritage assisting 'new directions' in modernization.[57]

> Not only is awareness rising of the continued significance of a country's heritage, there is also heightened acknowledgment that elements of that heritage can contribute to unusual dynamism in development. ... Even if, for a time, the foreign impact seems to be displacing more and more of the traditional behavior, a process of interaction is at work in which some elements of tradition may be reasserted and may guide modernization in new directions.[58]

This is a variant on the 'history matters' or 'culture matters' argument that is less pessimistic than most of what derives from Robert Putnam's work on Italy or Douglass North's path dependency - that 'backward' areas are doomed to perpetual backwardness.

Russia's present trajectory is not necessarily irreversible. An excessively narrow interpretation of path dependency may divert attention from the potential for change over time. North himself is aware of the problem, and cautions against closing off options even as he warns of the institutional difficulties facing transitional societies.[59]

Critics of the lack of competition within the Russian economy may be missing the trends elsewhere, and ignoring the temporary nature of any particular configuration. Gourevitch suggests that the United States in the early phase of its capitalist development closely resembled the 'Rhinish-Alpine-Japanese mode of production: a densely networked, alliance capitalism'. This changed over time.[60] Russia's middle classes could evolve in a similar way. But there is nothing that guarantees such an evolution. Middle strata and middle classes respond to a diverse combination of stimuli, and globalization has rendered the equation even more complex.

---

[56] Beyer 1994; Barber 1996.
[57] Rozman 1991. Also see Appadurai 1997, chapter 5 on the evolution of cricket in India.
[58] Lett 1998, 19-20.
[59] North 1996, 348-354.
[60] Gourevitch 1996, 239-240.

Sklair sees four 'functional groups', all of them essentially from the middle classes, that could potentially generate 'agents of adaptation to change induced by globalization': the managers of transnational firms; globalizing bureaucrats; professionals and politicians; and consumerist elites. 'Possible' requires added emphasis here. The post-Communist middle classes encompass all four of these groups, and all of them could indeed help to facilitate Russia's development as a participant in the global economy. In Russia, these groups are notoriously loath to engage in collective action, while globalization offers them the alternative of joining the new rich in a strategy of 'exit'.

That is the danger if the middle classes join the global knowledge and service industries. But there is a greater danger that the model of independent businessmen and free professionals will not prevail in post-Communism. The Chinese middle class is overwhelmingly state-connected. The Communist Party has developed links to the new entrepreneurs, many of whom (at least for now) find it more advantageous to conduct business through strategic alliances with the political elite.[61] In Russia, the business class is increasingly criminal-connected, which is similar but not (yet) identical. Some criminal groups are merging with state agencies.[62] Volkov[63] suggests that Russia's bandits are comparable to proto-entrepreneurs in Early Modern Europe and forecasts their evolution. We might be witnessing a routinization of stationary banditry.

The growth and potential of Russia's middle classes is of more than academic interest. A struggle is underway between the 'dot Communists' and the neo-Communists, with choices about how to engage the global economy an increasingly important factor in the conflict. The 'Putin administrative elite' has stated its goal to be imposing order and control while encouraging creativity. The two goals are contradictory. The danger is that controls in the name of legality and security will stifle creative impulses. This would undermine dynamic entrepreneurship in new technologies. An alternative economic development model based on natural resources encourages an alliance between the security/ control forces and the rent seekers.

Traditional political institutions manifest 'decreasing effectiveness', yet Putin seems intent on constructing precisely those traditional institutions, rather than new, open, flexible structures. There seems to be

---

[61] Goodman 1999.
[62] Volkov 1999; Radaev 1998; Olson 2000.
[63] Volkov 1999, 752.

little understanding of the difference between a strong state and an effective state.

Russia's development trajectory is subject to an enormous struggle between the resource oligarchs and the potentially global productive middle classes. Both Russian history and examples from other natural-resource based economies suggest that the overwhelming advantage is on the side of those who would foster the country's current trajectory into some hybrid of petro- or mining states. There may be islands of alternative approaches in some regions. But if Putin has his way in imposing central control and greater uniformity, the possibility for local success stories will be far less.

As a new president searches for an economic program to extricate Russia from the 'virtual economy',[64] one of the greatest problems is that the middle strata are quiescent and uninvolved. Vladimir Putin's economic plans are being designed by a group of Moscow economists who do not represent political parties or societal interests. They are a socially disembodied intelligentsia. They may be among the best economists in the country, receive advice from leading specialists around the world, and have the benefit of a decade of practical experience. But once again their ability to sustain an economic program rests on the (admittedly sweeping) powers vested in one man. Their challenge is to alter a system that serves the needs of wealthy and powerful individuals reaping enormous rewards from natural resources. The task is daunting. Any development program that challenges the interests of the rent seekers will meet enormous resistance from 'winners'.[65] The prospects for a Chilean or Korean variant, rather than a Venezuelan or Philippine trajectory, will be immeasurably greater if Russia's leaders help to create conditions for the middle strata to overcome their political lethargy and become a genuine middle class.

---

[64] Gaddy and Ickes 1998a.
[65] Hellman 1998.

Bibliography

Albrow, Martin (1996), *The Global Age. State and Society beyond Modernity*, Polity Press, Cambridge.
Alekperov, Vagit (1996), *Vertikalno-integrirovanie neftianie kompanii Rossii*, AO RITEK, Moscow.
Aleksashenko S. et al. (1999), 'Bankovskii krizis: tuman rasseivaetcia?', in *Voprosy ekonomiki*, No. 5, 4-42.
Alimova, Tat'iana and Afanas'eva, Tat'iana (1999), 'Innovatsionnye protsessy v malom predprinimatel'stve', in *Voprosy statistiki*, No. 8, 8-42.
Alimova, Tat'iana and Buev, Vladimir (1995), 'Malyi biznes Rossii: adaptatsiia k perekhodnym usloviiam', in *Voprosy statistiki*, No. 9, 19-68.
Alimova, Tat'iana and Vasilenko, Elena (1998), 'Sovershenstvovanie metodologii statisticheskogo ucheta chastnogo sektora ekonomiki', in *Voprosy statistiki*, No. 3, 26-38.
Andreev, A. L. (1999), 'Dva srednikh klassa v rossiiskom obshchestve?', in *Srednii klass v sovremennom rossiiskom obshchestve*, Rossiiskii nezavisimyi institut sotsial'nykh i natsional'nykh problem, Moscow, 39-51.
Andrew, Jack (1999), 'The Tricks Russians Use to Funnel Cash Abroad', in *Financial Times*, 27 August.
Appadurai, Arjun (1997), *Modernity at Large. Cultural Dimensions of Globalization*, University of Minnesota Press, Minneapolis.
Appadurai, Arjun (ed.) (1986), *The Social Life of Things: Commodities in Cultural Perspective*, Cambridge University Press, Cambridge.
Artemov, V. A. (1995), 'Izmeneniai uslovii i obraza zhizni v Sibiri (1972-1993)', in *Sotsiologicheskie issledovaniia*, No. 1, 73-83.
Åslund, Anders (1995), *How Russia Became a Market Economy*, The Brookings Institute, Washington DC.
Åslund, Anders (1997), 'Observations on the Development of Small Private Enterprises in Russia', in *Post-Soviet Geography and Economics*, vol. 37, No. 4, 191-205.
Åslund, Anders (1999a), 'Russia's Collapse', in *Foreign Affairs*, vol. 78, No. 5, 64-77.
Åslund, Anders (1999b), *Why Has Russia's Economic Transformation Been So Arduous?*, paper prepared for the Annual World Bank Conference on Development Economics, Washington DC., 28-30 April, <www.worldbank.org/research>.

Aven, Petr and Shironin, Viacheslav (1987), 'Reforma khoziaistvennogo mekhanisma', in *Izvestiia SO AN SSSR: Ekonomika i prikladnaia soziologiia*, No. 3, 32-41.
Balcerowicz, L. (1994), 'Common Fallacies in the Debate on the Transition to a Market Economy', in *Economic Policy* (December Supplement), 16-50.
Balzer, Harley D. (1997), *A Shadow Middle Class for A Shadow Economy*, paper presented at XXIX Annual Convention of the AAASS (November).
Balzer, Harley D. (1998a), 'Russia's Middle Classes', in *Post-Soviet Affairs*, vol. 14, No. 2, 165-186.
Balzer, Harley D. (1998b), 'Education, Poverty and White Collar Issues in Post-communist Transitions', in *Poverty in Transition?*, United Nations Development Program, Regional Bureau for Europe and the CIS, UN, New York.
Balzer, Harley D., (ed.) (1996), *Russia's Missing Middle Class: The Professions in Russian History*, M. E. Sharpe, Armonk, NY.
Barber, Benjamin R. (1996), *Jihad vs. McWorld: How Globalism and Tribalism are Reshaping the World*, Ballantine Books, New York.
Baritz, Loren (1989), *The Good Life: The Meaning of Success for the American Middle Class*, Alfred A. Knopf, New York.
Bartell, Ernest and Payne, Leigh A (eds) (1995), *Business and Democracy in Latin America*, University of Pittsburgh Press, Pittsburgh.
Bauman, Zygmut (1998), *Globalization: The Human Consequences*, Columbia University Press, New York.
Baumgarten, L. (1996), 'Preobrazovanie otnosheniy sobstvennosti v otrasliah oboronnoi promyshlennosti', in *Voprosy ekonomiki*, No. 4, 67-71.
Beach, William, Shavey, Aaron and Isidro, Isabel (1999), 'How reliable are IMF economic forecasts?', in *The Heritage Foundation*, 27 August, 1-21.
Berdyaev, Nikolai (1992), *The Russian Idea*, translated by R. M. French, Lindisfarne Press, Hudson, NY.
Berenyi, Ivan (1998), 'Progress in Restructuring', in *Petroleum Economist*, No. 3, 22-24.
Berezin, Igor (1997), 'Rossiiane nachinaiut bogatet'', in *VEK*, No. 2, 8.
Berger, Suzanne (1996), 'Introduction', in Suzanne Berger and Ronald Dove (eds), *National Diversity and Global Capitalism*, Cornell University Press, Ithaca, 1-24.
Berger, Suzanne and Dore, Ronald (eds) (1996), *National Diversity and Global Capitalism*, Cornell University Press, Ithaca.
Beyer, Peter (1994), *Religion and Globalization*, Sage, London.
Biuro ekonomichekogo analiza (1998), *Rossiiakaia ekonomika v 1997 godu*, BEA, Moscow.
Blasi, Joseph R (1994), *Privatized Enterprises in Russia: Some Initial Observations*, Foundation for Enterprise Development, Washington DC, <http://www.fed.org/resrclib/articles/private.html>.
Blasi, Joseph R. (1995), *The Impact of Privatization on Enterprises and the Impact of Enterprises on Reform*, Report No. 3, Bonn International Center for Conversion, Bonn.

Blasi, Joseph R., Krumova, Maia and Kruse, Douglas (1997), *Kremlin Capitalism: The Privatization of the Russian Economy*, Cornell University Press, Ithaca, NY.
Bond, Andrew R. (1993), 'The Manganese Shortfall in Russia', in *Post-Soviet Geography*, vol. 34, No. 5, 293-301.
Bortnik, Ivan (1999), *Malyi biznes i innovatsii*, report at the congress 'Vtoroi vserossiiskii s"ezd predstavitelei malykh predpriiatii', Moscow, 27-28 October.
Bourdieu, Pierre (1984), *Distinction: A Social Critique of the Judgement of Taste*, translated by Richard Nice, Harvard University Press, Cambridge, Mass.
Bowman, C. and Faulkner, D. O. (1997), *Competitive and corporate strategy*, Irwin, London.
Boycko, Maxim, Schleifer, Andrei and Vishny, Robert W. (1995), *Privatizing Russia*, MIT Press, Cambridge, Mass.
Braun, Joachim von, Serova Evgeniia, Seeth, Harm tho and Melukhina, Olga (1996), *Russia's Food Economy in Transition: Current Policy Issues and the Long-Term Outlook*, IFPRI, Washington DC.
Brint, Stephen (1994), *In An Age of Experts: The Changing Role of Professionals in Politics and Public Life*, Princeton University Press, Princeton.
Bunin, I. M. (ed.) (1998), *Finansovo-industrial'nye gruppy i konglomeraty v ekonomike i politike sovremennoi Rossii*, Tsentr Politicheskih Tehnologii, Moscow.
Burbach, Roger, Núñez, Orlando and Kagarlitsky, Boris (1997), *Globalization and its Discontents*, Pluto Press, London.
Bure, Eduard G. (2000), *Gosudarstvennaia doktrina Rossiiskoi federatsii*, Petropolis, Sankt-Peterburg.
Bureau of Economic Analysis (1998), Russian Economy in 1997, Bureau of Economic Analysis, Moscow.
Carnoy, Age Martin (1998), 'The Changing World of Work in the Information Age', in *New Political Economy*, vol. 3, No. 1, 123-128.
Castells, Manuel (1996), The Information Age, vol.1: The Rise of the Network Society, Blackwell Publisher, Oxford.
Christophé, Barbara (1998), 'Von der Politisierung der Ökonomie zur Ökonomisierung der Politik. Staat, Markt und Außenpolitik in Rußland', in *Zeitschrift für internationale Beziehungen*, No. 2, 201-240.
Coase, Ronald (1937), 'The Nature Of The Firm', in *Economica*, vol. 4, No. 12, 386-405.
Collier, David (ed.) (1979), *The New Authoritarianism in Latin America*, Princeton University Press, Princeton.
Corey, Lewis (1935), *The Crisis of the Middle Class*, Covici & Friede, New York.
Crozier, Michel, Huntington, Samuel P. and Watanuki, Joji (1975), *The Crisis of Democracy*, New York University Press, New York.
Davidson, Helen (1998), 'Russian Roulette Gets Real', in *Central European. Banking and Finance in Central Europe and the CIS*, July/August, 26-30.
Davis, Bob and Wessel, David (1998), *Prosperity: The Coming Twenty-Year Boom and What It Means to You*, Times Business-Random House, New York.

Deliagin, Mikhail (2000), 'Ne vosroditsia segodnia umret savtra', in *Nezavisimaia gazeta*, 3 March.
Denton, D. K. (1999), 'Gaining Competitiveness through Innovation', in *European Journal of Innovation Management*, vol. 2, No. 2, 82-85.
Dolgopiatova, Tat'iana (1996), *The Transitional Model of the Behavior of Russian Industrial Enterprises (on the basis of regular surveys during 1991-95)*, IIASA Working Paper, WP-96-057, International Institute for Applied Systems Analysis, Laxenburg, Austria.
Dolgopiatova, Tat'iana and Alimova, Tat'iana (1998), *Malyi biznes v Rossii*, Institut strategicheskogo analiza i razvitiia predprinimatel'stva, Moscow.
Dolgopiatova, Tat'iana and Karaseva, Larisa (1998), *Neformal'nyi sektor v rossiiskoi ekonomike*, Institut strategicheskogo analiza i razvitiia predprinimatel'stva, Moscow.
Drobizheva, Leokadia M. (2000), *Multidimensional Analysis of Social Differentiation from an Ethnic Point of View and Perspectives for Integration in the Russian Federation*, paper presented at the workshop on 'Ethnicity and Social Mobility in the Republics of the Russian Federation', Georgetown University, 31 March - 1 April.
Dubrovskii, Sergei (2000), 'Smenitsia li stagnatsiia rostom?', in *Nezavisimaia gazeta*, 18 February.
Earle, J., Estrin, S. and Leshchenko, L. (1996), 'Ownership Structures, Patterns of Control, and Enterprise Behaviour in Russia,' in S. Commander, Q. Fan and M. Schaffer (eds), *Enterprise Restructuring and Economic Policy in Russia*, EDI Development Studies, World Bank, Washington DC, 205-252.
Eggertson, Thrainn (1996), 'A Note On the Economics of Institutions', in Lee Alston, Thrainn Egertsson and Douglass C. North (eds), *Empirical Studies in Institutional Change*, Cambridge University Press, Cambridge, 6-24.
Ekspert (1998), *Rossiiskaia metallurgiia. Biznes-spravochnik*, 'Ekspert-RA', Moscow.
Energy Information Administration (EIA) (2000), Russia Country Analysis Brief, <http://www.eia.doe.gov/emeu/cabs/russfull.html>, 10 May 2000.
Entov, Revol'd (1998), *Razvitie rossiiskogo finansovogo rynka i novye instrumenty privlecheniia investitsii*, IEPP, Moscow.
Escobar, Arturo (1995), *Encountering Development: The Making and Unmaking of the Third World*, Princeton University Press, Princeton.
Eyal, Gil, Szelényi, Iván and Townsley, Eleanor (1998), *Making Capitalism Without Capitalists: The New Ruling Elites in Eastern Europe*, Verso, London.
Facon, Isabelle, Huet, Jean-Paul and Ben Ouagham, Sonia (1997), 'Pouvoirs et industries de defense en Russie', in *Collection Les Cahiers du Centre de Recherche et d'etudes sur les strategies et les technologies*, 194-198.
Farrow, Paul (1998a), 'Russian Federation', in: *International Financing Review*, No. 250, 40.
Farrow, Paul (1998b), 'Going for broke', in *IMF/World Bank Report*, September, 148-150.
Farrow, Paul (1998c), 'Banks in crisis', in *IMF/World Bank Report*, September, 152.

Feigin, V. (1998), 'Gazovaia promyshlennost' Rossii: sostojanie i perspektivy', in *Voprosy ekonomiki*, No. 1, 133-147.
Fish, M. Steven (1995), *Democracy from Scratch: Opposition and Regime in the New Russian Revolution*, Princeton University Press, Princeton.
Fisher, Stanley (1998), 'Reforming World Finance. Lessons from a Crisis', in: *The Economist*, 3 October, 23-30.
Fisher, Stanley (1999a), 'What Went Wrong in Russia?', in *Financial Times*, 27 September.
Fisher, Stanley (1999b), *On the Need for an International Lender of Last Resort*, paper presented at the joint luncheon of the American Economic Association and the American Finance Association, 3 January 1999.
Fogel, Robert W. (2000), *The Fourth Great Awakening and the Future of Egalitarianism*, University of Chicago Press, Chicago.
Fortescue, Stephen (1990), *Science Policy in the Soviet Union*, Routledge, London.
Fortescue, Stephen (1997), *Policy-Making for Russian Industry*, Macmillan, Basingstoke.
Fortescue, Stephen (1999), 'The Russian Mining and Metals Sector: Integration or Disintegration?', in Vladimir Tikhomirov (ed.), *Anatomy of the 1998 Russian Crisis*, Contemporary Europe Research Centre, Melbourne.
Freinkman, Lev (1995), 'Financial-Industrial Groups in Russia: Emergence of Large Diversified Private Companies', in *Communist Economies and Economic Transformation*, vol. 7, No 1, 51-66.
Frydl, E. (1999), *The Length and Cost of Banking Crisis*, IMF Working Paper No. 99/30, IMF, Washington DC.
Frydman, Roman and Rapaczynski, Andrzej (1994), *Privatization in Eastern Europe: Is the State Withering Away?*, Central European University Press, London.
Frye, Timothy (1997), 'Governing the Russian Equities Market', in *Post-Soviet Affairs*, vol. 13, No. 4, 366-395.
Gaddy, Clifford G. (1996), *The Price of the Past*, Brookings Institution Press, Washington DC.
Gaddy, Clifford G. (1998), *Hearings on U.S.-Russian Relations. Statement to the House Committee on International Relations*, US Congress, Washington DC, 16 July.
Gaddy, Clifford G. and Ickes, Barry W. (1998a), 'Russia's Virtual Economy', in *Foreign Affairs*, vol. 77, No. 5, 53-67.
Gaddy, Clifford G. and Ickes, Barry W. (1998b), 'This Bailout Will Set the Stage for the Next Crisis', in *The Los Angeles Times*, 17 July.
Gaddy, Clifford G. and Ickes, Barry W. (1999), 'An Accounting Model of the Virtual Economy in Russia', in *Post-Soviet Geography and Economics*, No. 2, 79-97.
Gaidar, Egor (ed.) (1998), *Ekonomika perekhodnogo perioda*, IET, Moscow.
Gareev, Mykharbek (1999), 'European City in Siberia', in *Oil of Russia*, No. 1, 10-13.
Gasunie (1999), *Long-term Market Analysis 1999*, Gasunie, Groningen.

Gay, Peter (1984), *Education of the Senses: The Bourgeois Experience, Victoria to Freud*, vol. 1, Oxford University Press, New York.
Gazprom (1998): *Annual Report 1997*, Gazprom, Moscow.
Gazprom (1999): *Annual Report 1998*, Gazprom, Moscow.
Gazprom (2000), *Annual Report 1999*, Gazprom, Moscow <http://www.gazprom.ru/ eng/report99/>, 1 July 2000.
Genkel', Angelika (1997), 'Restrukturizatsiia estestvennykh monopolii', in *Neft' i biznes*, No. 3, 11-21.
Goldman, Marshall (1976), 'Autarchy or Integration - the USSR and the World Economy', in US Congress, Joint Economic Committee, *Soviet Economy in a New Perspective*, 94th Congress, 2nd session, 81-96.
Golotuk, Iurii (2000), 'Moscow-Pekin. Druzhba v kosmose', in *Izvestiia*, 20 January.
Gomery, Douglas (1998), 'Who Owns the Media', in Alison Alexander, James Owner, Rod Carveth and Rodney Carveth (eds), *Media Economics: Theory and Practice*, Lawrence Erlbaum Associates Publishers, Hillsdale, NJ, 47-70.
Goodhart, C., Hartmann, P., Llewelynn, D., Rojas-Suarez, L. and Weisbord, S. (1998), *Financial Regulation: Why, How and Where Now?*, Routledge & Bank of England, London.
Goodman, David S. G. (1999), 'The New Middle Class', in Merle Goldman and Roderick MacFarquhar (eds), *The Paradox of China's Post-Mao Reforms*, Harvard University Press, Cambridge, Mass., 241-261.
Gorbatova, Larisa (1995), 'Formation of Connections between Finance and Industry in Russia: Basic Stages and Forms', in *Communist Economies and Economic Transformation*, vol. 7, No 1, 21-34.
Goskomstat (1993), *Osnovnye pokazateli deiatel'nosti kooperativov i malykh predpriiatii v Rossiiskoi Federatsii za 1992 god*, Goskomstat, Moscow.
Goskomstat (1995a), *Maloe predprinimatel'stvo v Rossii v 1994*, Goskomstat, Moscow.
Goskomstat (1995b), *Sel'skoe khoziaistvo Rossii*, Goskomstat, Moscow.
Goskomstat (1997a), *Sel'skoe khoziaistvo Rossii*, Goskomstat, Moscow.
Goskomstat (1997b), *Rossiiskii statisticheskii ezhegodnik*, Goskomstat, Moscow.
Goskomstat (1998a), *Rossiia v tsifrakh*, Goskomstat, Moscow.
Goskomstat (1998b), *Rossiiskii statisticheskii ezhegodnik*, Goskomstat, Moscow.
Goskomstat (1999a), *Rossiia v tsifrakh*, Goskomstat, Moscow.
Goskomstat (1999b), *Rossiiskii statisticheskii ezhegodnik*, Goskomstat, Moscow.
Goskomstat (1999c), *Maloe predprinimatel'stvo v Rossii*, Goskomstat, Moscow.
Götz, Roland (1998), 'Geopolitische Rivalen oder Partner? Rußland und China in der Region des Kaspischen Meeres', in *Blätter für deutsche und internationale Politik*, No. 10, 1200-1209.
Gourevitch, Peter A. (1996), 'The Macropolitics of Microinstitutional Differences in the Analysis of Comparative Capitalism', in Suzanne Berger and Ronald Dove (eds), *National Diversity and Global Capitalism*, Cornell University Press, Ithaca, 239-259.

Grabher, Gernot and Stark, David (eds) (1997), *Restructuring Networks in Post-Socialism: Legacies, Linkages, and Localities*, Oxford University Press, Oxford.
Grande, Edgar/ Risse, Thomas (2000), 'Bridging the Gap. Konzeptionelle Anforderungen an die politikwissenschaftliche Analyse von Globalisierungsprozessen', in *Zeitschrift für Internationale Beziehungen*, vol. 7, No. 2, 235-266.
Grant, R. M. (1991), 'The Resource-based Theory of Competitive Advantage: Implications for Strategy Formulation', in *California Management Review*, vol. 33, No. 3, 114-135.
Gray, Dale F. (1998), *Evaluation of Taxes and Revenues from the Energy Sector in the Baltics, Russia, and Other Former Soviet Union Countries*, IMF Working Paper WP98/34, IMF, Washington DC.
Grayson, Henry (1955), *The Crisis of the Middle Class*, Rinehart & Co, New York.
Gurkov, Igor (1998), 'Ownership and Control in Russian Privatised Enterprises: New Evidence from a Repeated Survey', in *Communist Economies and Economic Transformations*, vol. 7, No. 4, 259-270.
Gurkov, Igor and Maital, S. (1999), *How will Future Russian CEOs Manage?*, paper presented at RABE Conference, Eilat, 1-8 October.
Gustafson, Thane (1983), *The Soviet Gas Campaign. Politics and Policy in Soviet Decision Making*, Rand Corporation R-3036-AF, Rand, Santa Monica, CA.
Habermas, Jürgen (1995), *Demokratiia, razum, nravstvennost*, Akademia, Moscow.
Hale, David (1998), 'The IMF, Now More than Ever', in *Foreign Affairs*, vol. 77, No. 6, 7-13.
Hamel, G. and Prahalad, C. K. (1994), *Competing for the Future*, Harvard Business School Press, Cambridge, Mass.
Hanson, Philip (1981), *Trade and Technology in Soviet-Western Relations*, Macmillan, London.
Harter, Stefanie (1999), *Rußland und das Internet. Ökonomische Aspekte der virtuellen Integration*, Berichte des Bundesinstitut für ostwissenschaftliche und internationale Studien No. 21, BIOst, Cologne.
Heinrich, Andreas (1998), 'Transit Pipelines', in Heiko Pleines, *Energy in Ukraine*, Financial Times Management Report, London, 141-172.
Heinrich, Andreas (1999a), *Rußlands Gazprom. Teil II: Gazprom als Akteur auf internationaler Ebene*, Berichte des Bundesinstitut für ostwissenschaftliche und internationale Studien No. 34, BIOst, Cologne.
Heinrich, Andreas (1999b), 'The European Natural Gas Market in the Next Decade: An Overview', in *Quarterly Journal of Economic Research*, No. 4, 449-465.
Heinrich, Andreas (1999c), 'Der ungeklärte rechtliche Status des Kaspischen Meeres', in *Osteuropa*, No. 7, 671-683.
Hellman, Joel (1998), 'Winners Take All: The Politics of Partial Reform in Post-communist Transitions', in *World Politics*, vol. 50, No. 2, 203-234.
Hough, Jerry F. (1997), *Democratization and Revolution in the USSR, 1985-1991*, Brookings Institution Press, Washington DC.

Hunya, Gabor (1997), *Foreign Direct Investment and its Effects in the Czech Republic, Hungary and Poland*, The Vienna Institute for Comparative Economic Studies (WIIW), Working Paper No. 186, Vienna.

Iashchenko, Anatolii (1999), 'Effekt edineniia', in *Neft' Rossii*, No. 2, 103-108.

Illarionov, Andrei (1998), 'Kak byl organizovan rossiiskii finansovyi krizis', in *Voprosy ekonomiki*, No. 11, 26-35.

IMF (1999a), *World Economic Outlook*, IMF, Washington DC.

IMF (1999b), *Russian Federation. Recent Economic Developments*, Staff Country Report No. 99/100, IMF, Washington DC.

IMF (1999c), *International Capital Markets: Developments, Prospects, and Key Policy Issues*, IMF, Washington DC.

Intriligator, Michael D. (1998), 'The Peace Dividend: Myth or Reality?', in Nils Petter Gleditsch, Olav Bjerkholt, Odne Cappelen, R. P. Smith and J. P. Dunne (eds), *The Wage of Peace*, North-Holland Publishing Co, Amsterdam, 1-13.

Ivanov, Andrei (1998), 'Gazprom khochet dotianut'sia do Shvetsii. I smozhet, esli ne promeshaet Norvegiia', in *Finansovye izvestiia*, 17 November.

Jensen, Donald (1998), *How Russia is Ruled*, RFE/RL Paper, December, posted at <http://search.rferl.org/nca/special/ruwhorules/index.html>.

Jensen, Michael (1996), 'Agency Costs of Free Cash Flow, Corporate Finance and Takeovers', in *American Economic Review*, vol. 76, No. 2, 3-9.

Jensen, Robert G., Shabad, Theodore and Wright, Arthur W. (eds) (1983), *Soviet Natural Resources in the World Economy*, University of Chicago Press, Chicago.

Johnson, Juliet (1997), 'Understanding Russia's Emerging Financial-Industrial Groups', in *Post-Soviet Affairs*, vol. 13, No. 4, 333-365.

Jordan, Pamela (1998), 'The Russian Advokatura (Bar) and the State in the 1990s', in *Europe-Asia Studies*, vol. 50, No. 5, 765-792.

Kalugina, Zemfira I. (1991a), *Lichnoe podsobnoe khoziaistvo v SSSR. Sotsial'nye reguliatory i rezul'taty razvitiia*, Nauka, Novosibirsk.

Kalugina, Zemfira I. (1991b), 'Sotsial'nye granitsy razvitiia krest'ianskikh (fermerskikh) khoziaistv', in *Izvestia SO AN SSSR. Region: Ekonomika i sotsiologiia*, No. 3, 35-42.

Kalugina, Zemfira I. (1995), 'Reformorovanie agrarnogo sektora: itogi i problemy (vzgliad sotsiologa)', in *Region: ekonomika i sotsiologiia*, No. 3, 66-84.

Kalugina, Zemfira I. (1996), 'Sel'skoe naselenie Sibiri v novom sotsial'no-ekonomicheskom prostranstve: orentatsii i povedenie', in Zemfira Kalugina (ed.), *Sibirskaia derevnia v period transformatsii sotsial'no-ekonomicheskikh otnoshenii*, IEiOPP RAN, Novosibirsk, 33-51.

Kalugina, Zemfira I. (1999a), 'Stanovlenie sub"ektov khoziaistvovaniia v reformiruemom agranom sektore Rossii', in Tat'iana Zaslavskaia and Zemfira Kalugina (eds), *Sotsial'naia traektoriia reformiruemoi Rossii*, Issledovaniia Novosibirskoi ekonomiko-sotsialogicheskoi shkoly, SO RAN, Nauka, Novosibirsk, 281-308.

Kalugina, Zemfira I. (1999b), 'Adaptatsionnye strategii sel'skokhoziaistvennykh predpriiatii v usloviiakh agrarnykh preobrazovanii', in *Region: ekonomika i sotsiologiia*, No. 3, 123-140.

Kalugina, Zemfira I. (2000), 'Survival Strategies of Enterprises and Families in the Contemporary Russian Countryside', in Alexander Norsworthy (ed.), *Russian Views of the Transition in the Rural Sector. Structures, Policy Outcomes and Adaptive Responses*, World Bank, Washington DC., 118-131.

Kalyzhnii, Viktor (2000), 'Nuzhno navodit poriadok v TEK', in *Izvestiia*, 4 March.

Keister, Lisa (1997), *Insider Lending and Economic Transition: The Structure, Function, and Performance Impact of Finance Companies in Chinese Business Groups*, William Davidson Institute, Working Paper No. 195, WDI, Ann Arbor, MI.

Khlystun, V. (1997), 'Stabilizirovat' rabotu agrapromyshlennogo kompleksa Rossii', in *APK: ekonomika, upravlenie*, No. 4, 3-16.

Klimov, Maxim (1999), *Financial-Industrial Groups: Their Emergence and Effect on Russia's Economic Growth*, B.Sc. (Econ.) dissertation (unpublished), University of Cambridge.

Kocka, Jürgen (1999), *Industrial Culture and Bourgeois Society: Business, Labor and Bureaucracy in Modern Germany*, Berghahn Books, New York.

Kokorev, Alexander and Simachev, Iurii (1999), *Finansovye tekhnologii v malom predprinimatel'stve*, Resursnyi Tsentr Malogo Predprinimatel'stva, Moscow.

Koksharov, Aleksandr (1999), 'Gazprom nuzhen vsem', in *Ekspert*, 5 April, 44.

Korotchenko, Igor (1998), 'Supernovinka 'MiG' zhdet komandu na vzlet', in *Nezavisimoe voennoe obozrenie*, 25 December 1998 – 14 January 1999.

Kosals, Leonid (1995), *Security-Seeking Society and Economic Reforms in Russia*, Occasional Papers No. 12 of the Georgetown University Russian Area Studies Program, Georgetown University Press, Washington DC.

Koshkareva, Tat'iana and Narzikulov, Rustam (1997), 'Gazprom vstupil v strategicheskii al'ians s krupnejshej b mire neftianoi kompanii Shell', in *Nezavisimaia gazeta*, 18 November.

Kouzes, J. M. and Posner, B. Z. (1995), *The Leadership Challenge*, Jossey-Bass, San Francisco.

Kozyrev, Mikhail (2000), 'Vertolyety bez politiki', in *Vedomosti*, 7 March.

Krasnov, Gregory (1997), *Robber-Barons Russian Style: An Analysis of the Oil and Gas Industries' Role in Russian Politics*, M.Phil. dissertation (unpublished), University of Cambridge.

Krasnov, Gregory (1998), *The Political Determinants of Market Value of Russian Oil Companies*, paper presented to the Second Cambridge Russian Oil Conference, Cambridge, January 1997.

Krause, Elliott A. (1996), *Death of the Guilds: Professions, States and the Advance of Capitalism, 1930 to the Present*, Yale University Press, New Haven.

Kravets, Vadim (1997), 'Regulirovanye monopolii prochodit pod zhestkim kontrolem samikh monopolii', in *Neft' i kapital*, No. 4, 20-23.

Kriukov, Valerii A. (1997), ''Estestvennoi' monopolii-estestvennye peremeny, in *Eko*, No. 6, 89 - 106.

Kriukov, Valerii A. (1998), *Institutsional'naia struktura neftegazovogo sektora. Problemy i napravleniia transformatsii*, IEiOPP SO RAN, Novosibirsk.

Krotova, Mariia (1997), 'Gazprom: pereput'e ili novye etap razvitiia?', in *Neft' Rossii*, No. 3, 28-31.

Krugman, Paul (1999), *The Return of Depression Economics*, W. W. Norton, New York.
Krugman, Paul and Venables, Anthony J. (1995), 'Globalization and the Inequality of Nations', in *Quarterly Journal of Economics*, vol. 110, No. 4, 857-909.
Kryukov, Valery (2000), Adjustment to Change: the Case of the Oil and Gas Industry, in S. Harter and G. Easter (eds.), *Shaping the economic space in Russia*, Ashgate, Aldershot, 102-126.
Kryukov, Valery and Moe, Arild (1996), *The New Russian Corporatism? A Case Study of Gazprom*, RIIA, London.
Kukushkin, Mikhail (1999), 'Ekho minuvshei voiny', in *Nesavisimoe voennoe obozrenie*, 10 December.
Kukushkin, Mikhail (2000), "Mil' i 'Kamov' letyat na Vostok', in *Vremia novostei*, No. 1, 4.
Kurtsev, I. V. (1996), *Ekonomika agrapromyshlennogo kompleksa Sibiri v period perekhoda k pynochnym otnosheniiam*, SO RASKhN, Novosibirsk.
Kuzminov, Iaroslav and Iakovlev, Andrei (2000), *Modernizatsiia ekonomiki*, GU VShE, Moscow.
Kuznetsov, Yevgeny (1998), 'Learning in Networks: Enterprise Behavior in the Former Soviet Union and Contemporary Russia', in Joan M. Nelson, Charles Tilly, and Lee Walker (eds), *Transforming Post-Communist Political Economies*, Task Force on Economies in Transition, National Research Council, National Academy Press, Washington DC, 156-176.
Kuznetsova, Olga and Kuznetsov, Andrei (1999), 'The State as Shareholder. Responsibilities and Objectives', in *Europe-Asia Studies*, No. 3, 433-445.
Kuzyk, Boris (1999), *Oboronno-promyshlennyi kompleks Rossii: proryv v XXI vek*, Russkii bibliograficheskii institut, Moscow.
Kuzyk, Boris (2000), *Nikto krome nas*, Institut ekonomicheskikh strategii, Moscow.
Lamoreaux, Naomi (1994), 'Insider Lending: Banks, Personal Connections, and Economic Development', in *Industrial New England*, vol. 3, Cambridge University Press, Cambridge.
Laue, Theodore H. von (1969), *The Global City: Freedom, Power, and Necessity in the Age of World Revolutions*, J. B. Lippincott Co, Philadelphia.
Laue, Theodore H. von (1989), *The World Revolution of Westernization: The Twentieth Century in Global Perspective*, Oxford University Press, New York.
Ledeneva, Alena V. (1998), *Russia's Economy of Favours: Blat, Networking and Informal Exchange*, Cambridge University Press, Cambridge.
Lett, Denise P. (1998), *In Pursuit of Status: The Making of South Korea's 'New' Urban Middle Class*, Harvard University Press, Cambridge, Mass.
Lloyd, John (1999), 'The Russian Devolution', in *New York Times Magazine*, 15 August.
Lomnitz, Larissa A. (1988), 'Informal Exchange Networks in Formal Systems: A Theoretical Model', in *American Anthropologist*, vol. 90, No. 1, 42-55.
Lomnitz, Larissa A. and Melnick, Ana (1991), *Chile's Middle Class: A Struggle for Survival in the Face of Neoliberalism*, translated by Jeanne Grant, Lynne Rienner Publishers, Boulder, CO.

Lonkila, Markku (1998), 'The Social Meaning of Work: Aspects of the Teaching Profession in Post-Soviet Russia', in *Europe-Asia Studies*, vol. 50, No. 4, 699-712.
Lowenthal, Abraham F. (2000), 'Latin America at the Century's Turn', in *Journal of Democracy*, vol. 11, No. 3, 41-55.
Lubin, Nancy (2000), 'Pipe Dreams. Potential Impacts of Energy Exploitation', in *Harvard International Review*, Winter/Spring, 66-69.
Lukoil (1996), *Ustav otkrytogo aktsionernogo obshchestva Neftyanaya kompaniya Lukoil*, Lukoil, Moscow.
Lukoil (1999a), *Godovoi otchet 1998*, Lukoil, Moscow.
Lukoil (1999b), *Godovoe sobranie aktsionerov (kollektsiia dokumentov)*, 29 June, Lukoil, Kogalym.
Makarevich, Lev (1999), 'Finansovo-economicheskaia situatsiia serediny 1999', in *Obshchestvo i ekonomika*, No. 7-8, 136-137.
Makienko, Konstantin (1998), 'Opasno li torgovat' oruzhiem s Kitaem?', in *Pro et Contra*, vol. 3, No. 1, 41-57.
Makienko, Konstantin (1999), 'Udachnaya vozmozhnost', in *Ekspert*, 1 November, 40-44.
Maslukov, Iurii and E. Glubokov, E. (1999), 'Planirovanie i finansirovanie voennoy promyshlennosti v SSSR', in A. Minaev (ed.), *Sovetskaia voennaia moshch ot Stalina do Gorbacheva*, Voennyi parad Publishing House, Moscow, 82-129.
Mau, Vladimir (2000), 'Russian Economic Reforms as Seen by Western Critics', in *Stanford Journal of International Relations*, vol. 1, No. 3, 4-21.
McChesney, Robert (1997), *Corporate Media and the Threat to Democracy*, The Open Pamphlet Media Series, Seven Stories Press, New York.
McQuail, Denis (1994), *Mass Communication Theory*, third edition, Sage Publications, Thousand Oaks.
Meltzer, Allan H. (1999), 'What's Wrong with the IMF? What Should Be Better?' in *Independent Review*, vol. 4, No. 2, Fall, Internet edition over UCLA library: http://128.48.120.7/mw/mwcgi.mb#LB.
Mikhailova, Victoria (2000), "'Interros' i NPK deliat sfery vliianiia', in *Vedomosti*, 22 May.
Mikheev, Vassilii (1999), 'Logika globalisatsii i interesy Rossii', in *Pro et Contra*, vol. 4, No. 3, 49-64.
Millar, James R. (1999), 'The De-development of Russia', in *Current History*, vol. 98, No. 630, 322-327.
Mills, C. Wright (1956), *The Power Elite*, Oxford University Press, New York.
Moors, Kent F. (1999), 'An OPEC for Gas? Gazprom Promotes Notion of a Gas Cartel to Offset Expanding Internal Problems', in *Russian Petroleum Investor*, November - December, 9 - 13, 28.
Moskvina, Tat'iana (1997), 'Oni khotiat zhit' mudro: Srednii klass Rossii, popitka opoznaniia', in *Seans*, No. 15, 125-128.
Naishul, Vitalii (1992), 'Liberalism i ekonomucheskie reformy', in *Mirovaia economika i mezhdunarodnie otnosheniia*, No. 8, 69-81.

Nellis, J. (1999), *Time to Rethink Privatization in Transition Economies?*, IFC Discussion Paper No. 38, World Bank, Washington DC.

Newhouse, John (1997), 'Europe's Rising Regionalism', in *Foreign Affairs*, vol. 76, No. 1, 67-84.

Norsworthy, Alexander (ed.) (2000), *Russian Views of the Transition in the Rural Sector. Structures, Policy Outcomes and Adaptive Responses*, World Bank, Washington DC.

North, Douglass C. (1996), 'Epilogue: Economic Performance Through Time', in Lee Alston, Thrainn Egertsson and Douglass C. North (eds), *Empirical Studies in Institutional Change*, Cambridge University Press, Cambridge, 342-355.

O'Sullivan, Stephen (1997), 'Raising Capital in the Global Markets, with Some Success', in *Petroleum Economist*, special issue 'Gas in the CIS and Eastern Europe', September, 44-46.

O'Sullivan, Stephen and Avdeev, Dimitry (2000), *Gazprom: One Foot in the Past?*, UFG, Moscow.

OECD (1996), *Globalization of Industry. Overview and sector reports*, OECD, Paris.

OECD (1998), *Agro-food Policy. Russian Federation*, OECD, Paris.

OECD (2000), *OECD Economic Survey. Russian Federation*, OECD, Washington.

Oganesian, M. (1998), *GAZ*, Troika Dialog Research, Moscow.

Olson, Mancur (1995), *The Devolution of Power and the Societies in Transition: Therapies for Corruption, Fragmentation, and Economic Retardation*, paper presented at the conference 'Russian reforms: Established interests and practical alternatives', Moscow, 13-15 April.

Olson, Mancur (1996), *Capitalism, Socialism, and Dictatorship, Outgrowing Communist and Capitalist Dictatorships*, mimeo, University of Maryland, College Park.

Olson, Mancur (2000), *Power and Prosperity: Outgrowing Communist and Capitalist Dictatorships*, Basic Books, New York.

Omae, K. (1990), *The Borderless World. Power and Strategy in the Interlinked Economy*, Harper, New York.

Orlov, G. M. and Uvarov, V. I. (1997), 'Selo i rossiiskie reformy', in *Sotsiologicheskie issledovaniia*, No. 5, 43-53.

Osetinskaia, Elizaveta (1998), 'Rossiyskiy rynok dal po gazam', in *Segodnia*, 22 December.

Osetinskaia, Elizaveta (1999), 'Nemtsy zaroiut den'gi blizhe k skvazhine', in *Segodnia*, 1 April.

Pappe, Iakov (1997), *Finansovo-promyshlennie gruppy i konglomeraty v economike i politike Rossii*, Tsentr politicheskikh tekhnologiy, Moscow.

Pappe, Iakov (2000), *Oligarkhi. Ekonomicheskaia khonika 1992-2000*, GU VShE, Moscow.

Parfenov, Boris (2000), 'Elektrosviaz' Rossii: deviat' mesiatsev', in *Infromkuriersviaz'*, No.1-2, 51-54.

Peregudov, Sergei (2000), 'Business Interest Groups and the State in USSR and Russia: Change of the Models', in Justin Greenwood and Henry Jacek. L. (eds),

Organized Business and the New Global Order, Advances in Political Science, St. Martins Press, New York, 128-142.
Perkin, Harold (1996), *The Third Revolution: Professional Elites in the Modern World*, Routledge, London.
Perotti, Enrico and Gelfer, Stanislav (1998), *Investment Financing in Russian Financial-Industrial Groups*, William Davidson Institute, Working Paper No. 242, WDI, Ann Arbor, MI.
Petrikov, A.V. (1995), *Spetsifika sel'skogo khoziaistva i sovremennaia agrarnaia reforma v Rossii*, Entsiklopediia Rossiiskikh dereven', Moscow.
Petukhov, Vitalii (1999), *Korporatsii v Rossiiskoi promyshlennosti. Zakonodatelstvo i praktika*, Gorodetz, Moscow.
Pharr, Susan J., Putnam, Robert D. and Dalton, Russell J. (2000), 'A Quarter-century of Declining Confidence', in *Journal of Democracy*, vol. 11, No. 3, 5-25.
Piirainen, Timo (1998), 'From Status to Class: The Emergence of a Class Society in Russia', in Markku Kivinen (ed.), *The Kalamari Union: Middle Class in East and West*, Ashgate, Aldershot, 314-341.
Pleines, Heiko (1998), *Energy in Ukraine*, Financial Times Energy Publishing, London.
Pleines, Heiko and Westphal, Kirsten (1999), *Rußlands Gazprom. Teil I: Die Rolle des Gaskonzerns in der russischen Politik und Wirtschaft*, Berichte des Bundesinstitut für ostwissenschaftliche und internationale Studien No. 33, BIOst, Cologne.
Polischuk, Leonid (1998), 'Missed Markets: Implications for Economic Behavior and Institutional Change', in Joan M. Nelson, Charles Tilly, and Lee Walker (eds), *Transforming Post-Communist Political Economies*, Task Force on Economies in Transition, National Research Council, National Academy Press, Washington DC, 80-101.
Popov, Nikolai (2000), 'Doklad itogovoi kollegii Minsviazi RF za 1999 god', in *Newsletter Operator*, No. 10, 7-8.
Poshkus, V. (1997), 'Vnutrennie rezervy APK Rossii', in *APK: ekonomika, upravlenie*, No. 3, 11-19.
Postman, Neil (1985), *Amusing Ourselves to Death: Public Discourse in the Age of Show Business*, Penguin Books, New York.
Powell, Bill and Hosenball, Mark (1999), 'The Incredible Fleecing of Russia', in *Newsweek*, 4 October.
Preuss-Neudorf, Katharina (1996), *Die Erdgaswirtschaft in Rußland*, VUB, Cologne.
Prokop, Jane (1995), 'Industrial Conglomerates, Risk Spreading and the Transition in Russia', in *Communist Economies and Economic Transformation*, vol. 7, No. 1, 35-50.
Prokopenko, Denis (2000), 'Opredepennost - problema nomer odin', in *Nezavisimaia gazeta*, 16 February.
Pryce, Vicky and Twomey, Adrian (1997), 'Prospects for the UKCS in the New Millenium', in Petroleum Economist and Ruhrgas AG (eds), *The Fundamentals of Natural Gas Industry*, second edition, Petroleum Economist, London, 65-66.

Pukhov, Ruslan (1997), 'VPK osmyslivaet svoi interesy', in *Pro et Contra*, vol. 2, No. 3, 21-32.
Pukhov, Ruslan (1999), 'Rossiysko-frantzuzskoe VTS', in *Business in Russia*, No. 90, June, 33-35.
Pukhov, Ruslan and Makienko, Konstantin (1998), "Oboronka' pered tekhnologicheskimi vyzovami XXI veka', in *Pro et Contra*, vol. 3, No. 4, 53-69.
Quinlan, Martin (1997), 'Impressive Performance, But Here Comes the Tricky Part', in Petroleum Economist and Ruhrgas AG (eds), *The Fundamentals of Natural Gas Industry*, second edition, Petroleum Economist, London, 65-66.
Radaev, Vadim (1998), *Formiranovanie novykh rossisskikh rynkov: transaktsionne izderzhki, formy kontrolia i delovaia etika*, Tsentr politicheskikh tekhnologii, Moscow.
Radygin, Aleksander (1999), *Ownership and Control in Russian Industries*, proceedings of the OECD/World Bank conference 'Corporate Governance in Russia', Moscow, 31 May - 2 June.
Raiser, Martin (1997), *Informal Institutions, Social Capital, and Economic Transition: Reflections on a Neglected Dimension*, EBRD Working Paper No. 25, EBRD, London.
Rodan, Garry (ed.) (1996), *Political Oppositions in Industrialising Asia*, Routledge, London.
Rossiiskoe Statisticheskoe Agenstvo (1999), *Sotsial'no-ekonomicheskoe polozhenie Rossii, yanvar'-sentyabr' 1999 goda*, RSA, Moscow.
Rozman, Gilbert (1991), *The East Asian Region: Confucian Heritage and its Modern Adaptation*, Princeton University Press, Princeton.
Rumer, B. Z. (1989), *Soviet Steel. The Challenge of Industrial Modernization in the USSR*, Cornell University Press, Ithaca, NY.
Rupnik, Jacques (2000), 'Eastern Europe: The International Context', in *Journal of Democracy*, vol. 11, No. 3, 114-129.
Rutskoi, A. and Radugin N. (1997), 'Agrarnyi krizis prodolzhaetsia', in *APK: ekonomika, upravlenie*, No. 1, 3-7.
Ryan, Michael (1999), 'The Barriers to Open Competition', in *Financial Times Telecoms World*, third quarter, 9-14.
Rytsareva, Elena (1999), 'Novyi poriadok rossiiskoi sviazi', in *Ekspert*, 29 November, 28-36.
Rytsareva, Elena (2000a), 'Ministr sviazi tret'ego pokoleniia', in *Ekspert*, 21 February, 48-50.
Rytsareva, Elena (2000b), 'Vladimir Petrovich zhdet kontent', in: *Ekspert*, 8 May, 44-48.
Sachs, G. (1994a), *Rynochnaia ekinomika i Rossia*, Ekonomika, Moscow.
Sachs, Jeffrey (1994b), 'Toward Glasnost in the IMF. Russia's democratization policy', in *Challenge*, vol. 37, No. 3, 4-10.
Sachs, Jeffrey (1998), 'Interlocking Economics: Unlocking the Mysteries of Globalization', in *Foreign Policy*, No. 110, Spring, 97-111.
Sagers, Matthew J. (1992), 'The Aluminum Industry in the former USSR in 1992', in *Post-Soviet Geography*, vol. 33, No. 9, 591-601.

Sagers, Matthew J. (1995), 'The Russian Natural Gas Industry in the mid-1990s', in *Post Soviet Geography*, No. 9, 521-564.
Sagers, Matthew J. (1996), 'The Iron and Steel Industry in Russia and the CIS in the mid-1990s', in *Post-Soviet Geography and Economics*, vol. 37, No. 4, 213-220.
Sagers, Matthew J., Kryukov, Valeriy A. and Shmat, Vladimir V. (1995), 'Resource Rent from the Oil and Gas Sector in the Russian Economy', in *Post Soviet Geography*, No. 7, 389 - 425.
Sassen, Saskia (1996), 'The Spatial Organization of Information Industries: Implications for the Role of the State', in James H. Mittelman (ed.), *Globalization: Critical Reflections*, Lynne Reinner, Boulder, Co., 33-52.
Sassen, Saskia (1998), *Globalization and its Discontents: Essays on the new Mobility of People and Money*, The New Press, New York.
Savchenko, E. (2000), 'Vybor prioritetov agrarnoi politiki Rossii v sovremennykh usloviakh', in *APK: ekonomika i upravlenie*, No. 3, 3-8.
Schaic, John (1999), 'The Newly-wed and the Nearly Dead', in *Euromoney*, No. 362, 254-263.
Scholte, J. A. (1997), 'Global Capitalism and the State', in *International Affairs*, vol. 73, No. 3, 427-452.
Segbers, Klaus (1999), 'Sshivaia loskutnoe odeialo', in *Pro et Contra*, vol. 4, No. 3, 65-83.
Segbers, Klaus (ed.) (2001a), *Explaining Post-Soviet Patchworks. Vol. 2: Pathways from the Past to the Global*, Ashgate, Aldershot.
Segbers, Klaus (ed.) (2001b), *Explaining Post-Soviet Patchworks. Vol. 3: The Political Economy of Regions, Regimes and Republics*, Ashgate, Aldershot.
Seligson, Mitchell A. and Passé-Smith, John T. (eds) (1998), *Development and Under-development*, second edition, Lynne Reinner, Boulder, CO.
Semenenko, Igor (2000), 'Russia Strikes a Deal to Lessen Debt Burden', in *St. Petersburg Times*, 6 February.
Sergeev, Anton and Reizhevskaia, Ksenia (2000), 'Rossii povezlo men'she, chem Peru i Chili', in *Kommersant''*, 4 May.
Sergeev, Pavel A. (1998), 'Truboprovodnyi transport Rossii i Zapadnoi Evropy', in *Mirovaia ekonomika i mezhdunarodnye otnosheniia*, No. 11, 112-119.
Serova, Evgeniia (1998), 'Institutional'nye reformy v agrapromyshlennom komplekse', in Egor Gaidar (ed.), *Ekonomika perekhodnogo perioda. Ocherki ekonomicheskoi politiki postkommunisticheskoi Rossii 1991-1997*, IEPP, Moscow, 561-648.
Serova, Evgeniia (1999), 'Agrarnaia ekonomika i gruppy interesov', in *Politekonom* vol. 12, No. 1, 36-53.
Shashenkov, M. (1996), *GAZ*, Merrill Lynch Capital Markets Research, Moscow.
Shcherbak, V. (1998), 'Po puti real'nikh preobrazovanii', in *APK: ekonomika i upravlenie*, No. 4, 3-15.
Shkuta, A. A. (1999), *Rossiiskii gaz v tsentral'noi i vostochnoi Evrope*, Delo i Servis, Moscow.

Silverman, Bertram and Yanowitch, Murray (1997), *New Rich, New Poor, New Russia: Winners and Losers on the Russian Road to Capitalism*, M. E. Sharpe, Armonk, NY.

Sklair, Leslie (1995), 'Social Movements and Global Capitalism', in *Sociology*, vol. 29, No. 3, 495-512.

Sklair, Leslie (1996), 'Who are the Globalisers? A Study of Key Globalisers in Australia', in: *Journal of Australian Political Economy*, No. 38, 1-30.

Sklair, Leslie (1999), 'Competing Conceptions of Globalization', in *Journal of World-Systems Research*, vol. 5, No. 2, 141-159.

Sklair, Leslie (2001), *The Transnational Capitalist Class*, Blackwell, Oxford.

Slay, Ben and Capelik, Vladimir (1997), 'The Struggle for Natural Monopoly Reform in Russia', in *Post-Soviet Geography and Economics*, No. 7, 396-429.

Slomczynski, Kazimierz M. (1998), 'Formation of Class Sturcture under Conditions of Radical Social Change: An East European Perspective', in Markku Kivinen (ed.), *The Kalamari Union: Middle Class in East and West*, Ashgate, Aldershot, 89-117.

Solnick, Steven L. (1999), 'Russia's "Transition": Is Democracy Delayed Democracy Denied?', in *Social Research*, vol. 66, No. 3, 789-825.

Soros, George (1998), *The Crisis of Global Capitalism: Open Society Endangered*, Little & Brown Co, London.

Srednii klass (1999), *Srednii klass v sovremennom rossiiskom obshchestve*, Rossiiskii nezavisimyi institut sotsial'nykh i natsional'nykh problem, Moscow.

Srednii klass v Rossii (2000), *Srednii klass v Rossii: proshloe, nastoiashchee, budushchee*, Sankt-Peterburgskogo filosofskogo obshchestva, St. Petersburg.

Stanley, Thomas J. and Danko, William D. (1996), *The Millionaire Next Door: The Surprising Secrets of America's Wealthy*, Simon & Schuster, New York.

Stark, David and Bruszt, Laszlo (1998), *Postsocialist Pathways*, Cambridge University Press, New York.

Starodubrovskaya, Irina (1995), 'Financial-Industrial Groups: Illusions and Reality', in *Communist Economies and Economic Transformation*, vol. 7, No. 1, 5-19.

Stern, Jonathan P. (1989), *Soviet Oil and Gas Exports to the West: Commercial Transaction or Security Threat?*, Energy Paper No. 21, Gower, Aldershot.

Stern, Jonathan P. (1997), 'Will Gazprom Need Yamal Before 2010?', in *Petroleum Economist*, No. 5, 110-114.

Stiglitz, Joseph E. (1999), *Whither Reform? Ten Years of Transition*, paper prepared for the Annual World Bank Conference on Development Economics, Washington D.C., 28-30 April, 1999, <http://www.worldbank.org/research/abcde/pdfs/stiglitz.pdf>.

Strange, Susan (1996), *The Retreat of the State: The Diffusion of Power in the World Economy*, Cambridge University Press, Cambridge.

Stroev, E. S. (ed.) (1997), *Kontseptsiia agrarnoi politiki Rossii v 1997-2000 godakh*, Vershina-Klub, Moscow.

Sulkunen, Pekka (1992), *The European New Middle Class: Individuality and Tribalism in Mass Society*, Avebury, Aldershot.

Svetlova, Elena (1999), 'Nikto ne khochet Sviazinvesta', in *Delovye liudi*, No. 5, May, 6-8.
Thackery, Fred (1998), 'Supply Surplus Looms Over Europe's Gas Market', in *Petroleum Economist*, No. 10, 16-19.
Thornton, Judith (1998). Restructuring Production Without Market Infrastructure, in Joan M. Nelson, Charles Tilly, and Lee Walker (eds), *Transforming Post-Communist Political Economies*, Task Force on Economies in Transition, National Research Council, National Academy Press, Washington DC, 133-155.
Timoshenko, Liudmila: Doklad itogovoi kollegii Minsviazi RF za 1999 god, in: Newsletter Operator, No. 10, 2000, 7-8.
Tordjman, Helene (1998), *Some General Questions About Markets*, IIASA Interim Report IR-98-025/May, International Institute for Applied Systems Analysis, Laxenburg Austria.
Troika Dialog Research (1999), *Corporate Governance in Russia*, Troika Dialog, Moscow.
Troika Dialog Research (2000), *Gazprom: Kak nam reorganizobat' Gazprom?*, Analiticheskoe upravlenie, Troika Dialog, Moscow.
Troschke, Manuela (1998), *Die Energiewirtschaft Rußlands im Transformationsprozeß*, LDV, Munich.
Trudy Chetvertogo Kongressa Staleplavil'shchikov (1997), Chermetinformatsiia, Moscow.
Turbanov, Aleksandr (1999), 'O roli i meste ARKO v restrukturizatsii bankovskoi sisteme', in *Den'gi i kredit*, No. 6, 4-6.
Vlasov, Petr (1998), 'Novye plany Gazproma', in *Ekspert*, 12 October.
Vneshekonombank (1999), *Annual Report*, Vneshekonombank, Moscow.
Volkov, Vadim (1999), 'Violent Entrepreneurship in Post-Communist Russia', in *Europe-Asia Studies*, vol. 51, No. 5, 741-754.
Wallulis, Jerald (1998), *The New Insecurity: The End of the Standard Job and Family*, State University of New York Press, Albany.
Waltz, Kenneth N. (1999), 'Globalization and Governance', in *Political Science and Politics*, vol. 32, No. 4, 693-700.
Weber, Eugen (1976), *Peasants into Frenchmen: The Modernization of Rural France, 1870-1914*, Stanford University Press, Stanford.
Wedel, Janine R. (1998), *Collision and Collusion. The Strange Case of Western Aid to Eastern Europe 1989-1998*, St. Martin's Press, New York.
Wedel, Janine R. (1999), *U.S. Assistance for Market Reforms: Foreign Aid Failures in Russia and the Former Soviet Bloc*, Policy Analysis No. 338, Cato Institute, Washington DC., 3-15.
Wehrheim, Peter, Serova, Evgeniia and Frohberg, Klaus (eds) (2000), *Russia's Agro-Food Sector: Towards Truly Functioning Markets*, Kluwer Academic Publisher, The Hague.
Weir, Fred (1999), 'Why Russians Keep Dollars Under Beds', in *Christian Science Monitor*, 27 August.
Wernerfelt, B. (1984), 'A Resource-based View of the Firm', in *Strategic Management Journal*, No. 5, 171-180.

Western, Bruce (1997), *Between Class and Market: Postwar Unionization in the Capitalist Democracies*, Princeton University Press, Princeton.

Westin, Peter (1999), 'One Year After the Crisis', in *Russian Economic Trends, Monthly update*, September, 3-9.

Westlake, Melvyn (1998), 'Banks Set to Boom or Bust', in *Emerging Markets Investor*, vol. 4, No. 8, 20-27.

White, G. L. (2000), 'Car Makers Swerve as Palladium Goes through the Roof. Russian Moves Lift Price of Exhaust-cleaning Metal', in *The Wall Street Journal Europe*, 6 March.

Whitehead, Laurence (ed.) (1996), *The International Dimensions of Democratization: Europe and the Americas*, Oxford University Press, Oxford.

Winters, L. Alan, Rubin, Marc and Bond, Andrew R. (1998), 'Anti-dumping action on American imports from Russia', in *Post-Soviet Geography and Economics*, vol. 39, No. 4, 183-224.

Woodruff, David (1998), 'Why Market Liberalism and the Ruble's Value are Sinking Together', in *East European Constitutional Review*, vol. 7, No. 4, 73-76.

Woodruff, David M. (1999), 'It's Value that's Virtual. Bartles, Rubles and the Place of Gazprom in the Russian Economy', in *Post-Soviet Affairs*, No. 2, 130-148.

World Bank (1996), *Fiscal Management in Russia*, World Bank, Washington DC.

World Bank (1998a), *Program Regional'nye issledovaniia po formirovaniu chastnogo sektora. The Intermediate Report on the Investigation of the Environment and Policy Directly Influencing Private Sector Development*, stage IV, Mezhvedomstvennyi analiticheskii tsentr, Moscow.

World Bank (1998b), *World Debt Table*, World Bank, Washington DC.

World Bank (1999), *Global Development Finance 1999*, World Bank, Washington DC.

Zaslavskaia, T. I. (1996), 'Transformatsiia sotsial'noi struktury rossiiskogo obshchestva', in T. I. Zaslavskaia (ed.), *Kuda idet Rossiia? Sotsial'naia transformatsiia postsovetskogo prostranstva*, Aspekt Press, Moscow, 21-33.

Zatsepilov, Sergei (2000), *Investionno-bankovskaia gruppa NIKoil - strategiia ustoichivogo rosta - 'God planety'*, Republika, Moscow.

Znaniecki, Florian (1965), *The Social Role of the Man of Knowledge*, Octagon Books, New York.

Index

References from notes indicated by 'n' after page preference

Abramovich, Roman 146
Agency for the Restructuring of Credit Organizations (*ARKO*) 92-3, 174
Agip oil company 123
Agrarian party (*APR*) 299-301
agricultural sector 13, 17, 310-3, 319, 323, 325, 328-30
Alekperov, Vagit 125, 127, 131n
Alfa group 146, 167, 172, 195, 199, 209, 213, 302-3
Arco oil company 123, 126
Asian crisis 40, 57, 62, 64, 77, 214

balance of payments 37, 42-4, 46, 49-50, 53, 56, 73, 81, 84
bandits, roving or stationary 98, 133-4, 197, 383
Bank of Moscow 167, 224
banking sector 16, 86, 89, 91-3, 164, 167, 173-6
bargaining 3, 6
barter 88, 103, 105, 321
BASF natural gas company 110-1
Berezovskii, Boris 146, 210, 212-5, 217, 219, 220-5
BP-Amoco oil company 123n

capital flight 42-3, 53, 67, 92, 153, 192
Central Bank of Russia (CBR) 11, 21, 38, 40-1, 43, 47, 49, 50, 57, 72, 80, 83-5, 91-2, 165-7, 170, 174, 176
CEOs 331-5, 337-41, 343-8
Conco oil company 123
corporate governance 168

defense sector 16, 140-1, 291
Deripaska, Oleg 141, 146, 153, 156, 158

directors 17, 46, 85, 102, 125-6, 157, 185, 188, 252, 268-80, 283-91, 299, 305, 321, 329, 331
Duma 11, 13, 127, 130, 155n, 218, 220, 298-9, 305, 380

Elektrosviaz' telecommunications company 231, 235-6
elites
  owners, managers 17, 33, 120n, 126n, 127, 129, 131-3, 153-4, 157-9, 162, 168, 171, 179-1, 185, 188, 192-3, 199, 203-4, 211, 235, 252-3, 269-78, 280-1, 288, 290, 299-300, 310-1, 316-7, 321, 328-30, 333-5, 337, 340, 343-76 358, 359, 360, 372, 377, 383
  regional 22, 154, 156
Eni natural gas company 110-1
Eurobonds 38, 58, 67, 166, 172
European Bank for Reconstruction and Development (EBRD) 12, 174
exports 13n, 42, 44, 45n, 56, 64, 67, 99, 104-7, , 111, 113-4, 138, 139n, 140-2, 143n, 147, 149, 151, 153-4, 160, 162, 233, 245n, 246, 253, 257n, 265n, 287, 289, 293, 297, 304, 307, 331, 335-7, 340, 355, 381

financial crisis (August 1998) 15, 36, 40, 55, 66, 69, 72-3, 77-8, 80, 87, 91, 102, 107, 167, 169, 250-2, 293, 304, 311, 325-6, 330-1, 357
financial-industrial groups (FIGs) 16, 100, 120, 121, 168-9, 177-91, 193-7, 199-200, 249-50
foreign debt 38, 47, 56, 65, 69, 70, 190

foreign investment, foreign direct investment 40-1, 43, 59, 92, 136, 154, 160, 175-6, 184, 224-5, 227, 308, 356

Gazprom 15, 21, 23, 59, 97-115, 126-7, 133, 191-2, 194, 195, 198, 213, 223-4, 238-40, 286-7
GKOs (treasury bills) 57-9, 62-3, 66, 88, 166, 168
global financial markets 14, 55, 61
globalization 1-2, 4, 6, 8, 10, 14-5, 17-8, 22-3, 31, 33, 35-6, 55, 71-2, 75-6, 97, 114-6, 132-7, 142, 144, 147-51, 152n, 154-7, 159-62, 183, 190, 209, 214, 226, 228, 240, 243, 246, 248, 267, 291, 308, 332, 337, 348, 354, 364, 366-8, 370, 374, 381-3
Gusinskii, Vladimir 212, 214, 221-4

human capital 200

imports 17, 34-5, 43-4, 45n, 106n, 112, 137-9, 142-5, 150-2, 154, 256, 293, 298, 302-4, 306-7, 310-1, 326-7, 330-1, 364
inflation 38, 40, 47, 49, 60, 65, 74, 83, 90, 160, 205, 376
Inkombank 167-8, 171-2, 197, 199, 250-2
institutional development 181, 199
International Monetary Fund (IMF) 12, 14, 32, 36, 38-9, 41, 43-50, 52-3, 55, 58-9, 66, 68-70, 74, 79, 85, 93, 95, 102, 160
internet 18, 214n, 216, 222, 230, 234, 242
Interros group 188-9, 251
Iukos oil company 130, 133, 168, 170, 192-5

Krasnoiarsk Aluminum Plant 150, 158

laws 49, 177n, 207, 215, 226, 248n, 293, 297-8, 303, 358, 362, 369
lobbying 15, 118, 127, 132, 156, 169, 197, 241, 250, 292, 298, 301, 303-4, 351n, 355, 363-4
London Club 12, 51-2, 65-8, 90
LukArco oil company 123, 132

Lukoil oil company 15, 98, 116, 122-34, 191, 213, 225

mafia 197
managers, see also directors, CEOs 17, 33, 120n, 126n, 127, 129, 131, 154, 157, 158, 159, 162, 179-80, 185, 188, 192-3, 199, 253, 269-75, 281, 288, 290, 300, 310-1, 321, 328-30, 333-5, 337, 340, 343-7, 358-60, 372, 377, 383
media
  print media 210, 224
  radio 12, 189, 203, 205, 210, 214, 218, 222, 225, 242
  regional media 206
  television 12, 203, 205-8, 210-1, 218-22, 224-6, 231, 242
middle classes 18, 366-84
mining and metals (M&M) 15, 136-40, 142, 145-6, 148, 151-6, 160, 162
Ministry of Agriculture 295, 304
Ministry of Anti-Monopoly Policy and the Support of Private Enterprise (MAP) 236
Ministry of Defense 11, 245-8, 253-5, 258, 287, 289
Ministry of Finance (MinFin) 11, 66, 69, 72, 80, 83, 85, 166, 287, 289, 295
Ministry of Internal Affairs 11, 253, 287, 289
Ministry of Railways (MPS) 11, 101, 238-9, 286-8
Ministry of Telecommunications 11, 230, 235-6, 241
Ministry of Trade 154, 159
money-laundering 48-9
Mosbiznessbank 171
Moscow Aviation Production Organization (MAPO) 248-51, 254-5
Most group 167, 207, 210, 214, 219, 221, 223-4, 242

natural monopolies 21, 169, 286-8
networks 3, 6, 13, 113, 196, 201, 209, 212, 217, 223, 226, 229-32, 235-6, 238, 241-2, 268, 330, 355, 360, 364
nomenklatura 125, 272, 284, 288, 299, 379

oil sector 35
oligarchs 22, 25, 33, 126-7, 130, 196, 209, 212, 250, 384
Oneksim bank 167-8, 170, 172, 212-3, 224, 250n, 251

Paris Club 12, 51-2, 65, 67-70, 86, 91
part-time farming (*LPKh*) 317, 319
payment arrears 112
perestroika 11, 118, 120, 202, 216, 301, 361
president, president's administration 9, 11, 21, 48, 115, 126, 161-2, 215-9, 223, 249, 287, 289, 306, 312, 321, 384
private ownership 230, 240, 268, 276, 301, 312, 330
privatization 51, 53, 60, 118-9, 121-3, 125-6, 143n, 145, 153, 157-8, 160, 177, 184-5, 191-3, 195, 200, 202, 208-9, 218n, 226, 237, 250, 268-9, 271, 275n, 277n, 279-80, 282, 284, 288, 290, 297, 303, 310, 312, 352, 363
Promstroibank 169-70

rent-seeking 14, 115, 181
Rosprom group 170, 192-6
Rossiiskii Kredit 167, 170-1, 190
Rostelekom telecommunications company 230-1, 233, 235, 237-40
Ruhrgas natural gas company 100, 110-1

Saiansk Aluminum Plant 146-7, 153
Sberbank 11, 85, 166-8
SBS-*Agro* 167, 170, 172, 302
shadow economy 284, 288, 355, 361-2, 364
shareholder, stakeholder 100, 101-2, 125, 126, 128, 133, 168, 171, 186, 188, 194, 199, 221, 223, 328, 331
Shell group 110
Sibneft' oil company 130, 146-7, 221
Sidanko oil company 130, 168, 188, 195
small business 351-2, 354, 361, 363

special interest groups 76
state-owned enterprises 280, 283, 360, 362
Sukhoi 248-51, 258
Surgutneftegaz oil company 130, 133
Sviaz'invest telecommunications holding 16, 230-2, 235-8

taxation
 tax 37, 44, 49-50, 52, 56, 59, 69, 81, 83, 85-6, 91, 101-2, 125, 131, 152-3, 155-6, 170, 176, 190, 254, 276, 284, 288, 295, 304, 316, 320, 327, 361, 369, 378
 tax arrears, tax debts 86, 89
 tax collection 54, 56, 71, 88-9
 tax evasion 209, 282
 taxpayer 32, 52, 95, 101, 170, 217
 tax police 72, 103
telecommunications 12, 16, 33, 190, 228-38, 240-3
Tokobank 171, 173
Transneft' oil pipeline company 12, 101, 125
TransWorld Group (TWG) 146, 152, 157, 158, 162
treasury bills (*GKO-OFZs*) 82-4, 88, 90, 168

United Energy System (*EES*) 12, 21, 23, 109, 126, 238-40, 286n, 287

virtual economy (VE) 98, 103-4, 384
Vneshekonombank 65-7, 69-70, 167
Vneshtorgbank 11, 167, 171
Vympelkom telecommunication company 232-4

Wintershall natural gas company 110-1
World Bank 12, 37-8, 41-2, 44-5, 48, 57-9, 61, 63, 66, 78, 86, 88, 174, 353, 355, 359
World Trade Organization (WTO) 151, 292, 306-8

Explaining Post-Soviet Patchworks

Volume 2
Pathways from the Past to the Global

Klaus Segbers
Institutional Change in Russia: A Research Design

Gerald M. Easter
Networks, Bureaucracies, and the Russian State

Alena V. Ledeneva
Networks in Russia: Global and Local Implications

Andrei N. Nesterenko
Markets between Soviet Legacy and Globalization: Neoinstitutionalist Perspectives on Transformation

Georgii B. Kleiner
Person, Position, Power and Property: The General Director in the 'Economy of Individuals'

Nina Iu. Oding
Profit or Production? Enterprise Behavior after Privatization

Valerii A. Kriukov
Ownership Rights, Hierarchical Bargaining and
Globalization in the Oil Sector

Aleksandr D. Radygin
The Corporate Securities Market: Bridgehead or Barrier
for Globalization?

Leonid I. Kosals, Rozalina V. Ryvkina
The Institutionalization of the Shadow Economy: Rules
and Roles

Vladimir I. Tikhomirov
Capital Flight: Causes, Consequences and Counter-
Measures

Andrei E. Shastitko, Vitalii L. Tambovtsev
Institutionalization and Property Rights: The
Reincarnation of Managerial 'Economic Authority' over
State Property

Andrei E. Shastitko, Vitalii L. Tambovtsev
Institutionalization and Property Rights: Trademark
Usage, Specification and Enforcement

Simon G. Kordonskii
Everyday Life as Flight from the State: 'Housing
Portfolios' and the 'Diversified Way of Life'

Vadim V. Radaev
Urban Households in the Informal Economy

Anton N. Oleinik
Changes in the Organization of Everyday Life in the
Wake of Financial Crisis

Aleksandr I. Kurylev
Value Change and Learning Effects at the Global-Local
Nexus